Freedom Press

MACHINE GUNS - CREW SERVED 5.56MM & 7.62MM

The Following are Military Manuals without Copyright released to the General Public.

They are provided for informational purposes only.

ISBN-13: 978-1511505840
ISBN-10: 1511505842

FAIR USE ASSERTION

Any materials used in this book to illustrate and assist in comprehension, have been used under the Fair Use Copyright assertion of Section 107

Section 107 contains a list of the various purposes for which the reproduction of a particular work may be considered fair, such as criticism, comment, news reporting, teaching, scholarship, and research. Section 107 also sets out four factors to be considered in determining whether or not a particular use is fair:

- The purpose and character of the use, including whether such use is of commercial nature or is for nonprofit educational purposes
- The nature of the copyrighted work
- The amount and substantiality of the portion used in relation to the copyrighted work as a whole
- The effect of the use upon the potential market for, or value of, the copyrighted work

The distinction between fair use and infringement may be unclear and not easily defined. There is no specific number of words, lines, or notes that may safely be taken without permission. Acknowledging the source of the copyrighted material does not substitute for obtaining permission.

The 1961 Report of the Register of Copyrights on the General Revision of the U.S. Copyright Law cites examples of activities that courts have regarded as fair use: "quotation of excerpts in a review or criticism for purposes of illustration or comment; quotation of short passages in a scholarly or technical work, for illustration or clarification of the author's observations; use in a parody of some of the content of the work parodied; summary of an address or article, with brief quotations, in a news report; reproduction by a library of a portion of a work to replace part of a damaged copy; reproduction by a teacher or student of a small part of a work to illustrate a lesson; reproduction of a work in legislative or judicial proceedings or reports; incidental and fortuitous reproduction, in a newsreel or broadcast, of a work located in the scene of an event being reported." Copyright protects the particular way authors have expressed themselves. It does not extend to any ideas, systems, or factual information conveyed in a work.

CREW-SERVED MACHINE GUNS, 5.56-mm AND 7.62-mm

M249, 5.56-MM MACHINE GUN

M60, 7.62-MM MACHINE GUN

M240B, 7.62-MM MACHINE GUN

JANUARY 2003

FIELD MANUAL
No. 3-22.68

HEADQUARTERS
DEPARTMENT OF THE ARMY
Washington, DC, 31 January 2003

CREW-SERVED MACHINE GUNS, 5.56-mm AND 7.62-mm

CONTENTS

Page

DISTRIBUTION RESTRICTION: Approved for public release; distribution is unlimited.

*This publication supersedes FM 23-67, 29 February 1984.

PREFACE

This manual provides technical information, training techniques, and guidance on the crew-served machine guns, 5.56-mm and 7.62-mm (M249/M60/M240B). The purpose of this manual is, to provide a **one-source document for all three weapons.** This prohibits having several sources to rely on. Unit leaders, trainers, and the designated gunners will find this information invaluable in their efforts to successfully integrate these automatic weapons into their combat operations.

Trainers must ensure that safety procedures are observed at all times. Leaders, trainers, and soldiers must remember that safety is everyone's responsibility. All training should be conducted as though the weapon is fully loaded. At no time while using this manual does speed or accuracy override the safety procedures.

Unless this publication states otherwise, masculine nouns and pronouns do not refer exclusively to men.

The proponent of this publication is the United States Army Infantry School. Send comments and recommendations on DA Form 2028 directly to Commandant, U.S. Army Infantry School, ATTN: ATSH-IN-S3, Fort Benning, GA 31905-5596, or send email to doctrine@benning.army.mil.

CHAPTER 1
M249 MACHINE GUN

The 5.56-mm M249 machine gun supports the soldier in both the offense and defense. The M249 provides a medium volume of close and continuous fire the soldier needs to accomplish the mission. With it, units can engage the enemy along with the capability of individual weapons with controlled and accurate fire. The medium-range, close defensive, and final protective fires delivered by the M249 MG form an integral part of a unit's defensive fires. Although the M249 MG is described here as a machine gun, it also plays the role of the automatic rifleman. This FM or chapter supersedes FM 23-14, which describes the M249 MG in the automatic rifle role. This chapter also describes the weapon and the types of ammunition in detail and provides a table of general data.

Section I. DESCRIPTION AND COMPONENTS

This section describes the M249 machine gun and its components and purposes. It also discusses the different types of ammunition that is fired from the M249 machine gun. This section describes how to install the blank firing adapter for the M249 machine gun and how to take care of the machine gun while using the blank firing adapter.

1-1. DESCRIPTION

The M249 machine gun is a gas-operated, air-cooled, belt or magazine-fed, automatic weapon that fires from the open-bolt position (Figure 1-1). It has a maximum rate of fire of 850 rounds per minute. Primarily, ammunition is fed into the weapon from a 200-round ammunition box containing a disintegrating metallic split-link belt. As an *emergency* means of feeding, the M249 machine gun can use a 20- or 30-round M16 rifle magazine but increases the chance of stoppages. This gun can be fired from the shoulder, hip, or underarm position; from the bipod-steadied position; or from the tripod-mounted position. See Table 1-1, on page 1-2, for general data.

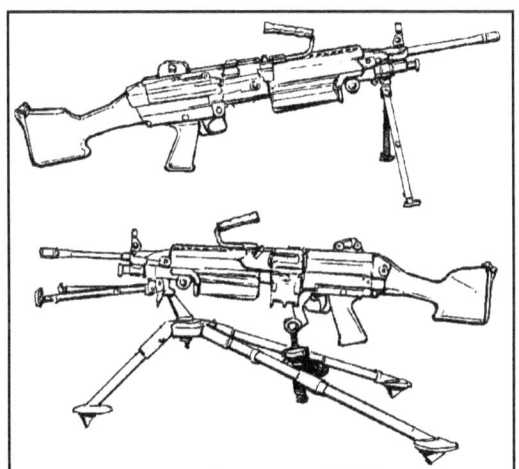

Figure 1-1. M249 machine gun, bipod and tripod mounted.

Ammunition .... 5.56-mm ball and tracer (4:1 mix) ammunition is packaged in 200-round drums, each weighing 6.92 pounds; other types of ammunition available are ball, tracer, blank, and dummy.

Tracer burnout .... 900 meters (+)

Length of M249 .... 40.87 inches

Weight of M249 .... 16.41 pounds

Weight of tripod mount M122
   with traversing and elevating
   mechanism and pintle .... 16 pounds

Maximum range .... 3,600 meters

Maximum effective range .... 1,000 meters with the tripod and T&E

Area:
   Tripod .... 1,000 meters
   Bipod .... 800 meters

Point:
   Tripod .... 800 meters
   Bipod .... 600 meters

Suppression .... 1,000 meters

Maximum extent of grazing
   fire obtainable over uniformly
   sloping terrain .... 600 meters

Height of M249 on tripod
   mount M122A1 ....…… 16 inches

Rates of Fire:
   Sustained .... 100 rounds per minute
                             Fired in 6- to 9-round bursts with 4 to 5 seconds between bursts (change barrel every 10 minutes)
   Rapid .... 200 rounds per minute
                             Fired in 6- to 9-round bursts
                             2 to 3 seconds between bursts (change barrel every 2 minutes)
   Cyclic .... 650 to 850 rounds per minute
                             Continuous burst (change barrel every minute)

Basic load, ammunition .... 1,000 rounds (in 200-round drums)

Elevation, tripod controlled .... +200 mils

Elevation, tripod free .... +445 mils

Depression, tripod controlled .... -200 mils

Depression, tripod free .... -445 mils

Traverse, controlled by traversing
   and elevating mechanism .... 100 mils

Normal sector of fire (with
   tripod) ....…………….......... 875 mils

Table 1-1. General data.

1-2. COMPONENTS

The components of the M249 machine gun and their purposes are described in Table 1-2 and shown Figure 1-2. The item numbers in Table 1-2 correspond to the callout numbers in Figure 1-2. The sights and safety button are shown in Figures 1-3 and 1-4. (See Table 1-1 for general data.)

COMPONENTS		PURPOSES
(1)	Barrel assembly	Houses cartridges for firing, directs projectile, and supports the gas regulator.
(2)	Heat shield assembly	Provides protection for the gunner's hand from a hot barrel.
(3)	Rear sight assembly	Adjusts for both windage and elevation.
(4)	Cover and feed mechanism assembly	Feeds linked belt ammunition, and positions and holds cartridges in position for stripping, feeding, and chambering.
(5)	Feed tray assembly	Positions belted ammunition for firing.
(6)	Cocking handle assembly	Pulls the moving parts rearward. Moves in a guide rail fixed to the right side of the receiver.
(7)	Buttstock and buffer assembly	Contains a folding buttplate. Serves as a shoulder support for aiming and firing M249. Contains a folding shoulder rest and a hydraulic buffer to absorb the recoil.
(8)	Bolt assembly	Provides feeding, stripping, chambering, firing, and extraction, using the projectile gases for power.
(9)	Slide assembly	Houses firing pin and roller assembly.
(10)	Return rod and transfer mechanism assembly	Absorbs recoil for bolt and operating rod assembly at the end of recoil movement.
(11)	Receiver assembly	Serves as a support for all major components and houses action of weapon. Through a series of cam ways, controls functioning of weapon.
(12)	Trigger mechanism	Controls the firing of the weapon. Provides storage area for lubricant in grip portion.
(13)	Handguard assembly	Provides thermal insulation to protect the gunner's hand from heat or extreme cold and houses the cleaning equipment.
(14)	Sling and snap hook assembly	Provides a means of carrying the weapon.
(15)	Bipod	Supports the M249 machine gun in the prone position. The telescopic legs can be individually adjusted to three different lengths.

Table 1-2. Components and purposes.

COMPONENTS		PURPOSES
(16)	Gas cylinder assembly	Locks bipod in place and provides passageway for gases.
(17)	Piston assembly	Holds the bolt and slide assemblies and houses the return spring.
(18)	Return spring	Returns bolt, slide, and piston assemblies to locked position during counterrecoil cycle.
(19)	Tripod (M122) (Not shown)	The tripod and T&E mechanism, with pintle, provides a stable mount and permits a higher degree of accuracy and control.
(20)	M145 straight telescope (Not shown)	Machine gun optic (MGO) provides target acquisition and identification at greater ranges.

Table 1-2. Components and purposes (continued).

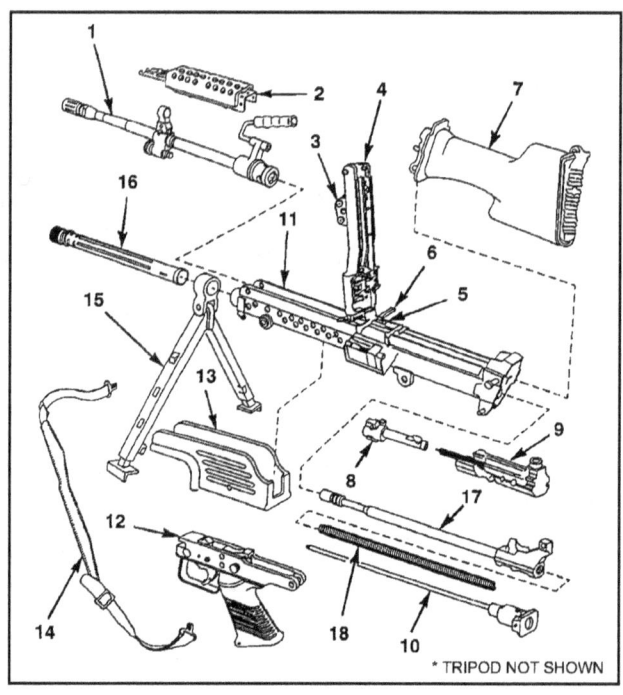

Figure 1-2. M249 machine gun components.

a. **Sights**. The M249 machine gun has a hooded and semifixed front sight (Figure 1-3). The rear sight assembly mounts on the top of the cover and feed mechanism assembly. The elevation knob drum has range settings from 300 meters to 1,000 meters. Range changes are made on the M249 machine gun sight by rotating the elevation knob to the desired range setting. Rotation of the rear sight aperture (peep sight) is used for fine changes in elevation or range adjustments, such as during zeroing. Each click of the peep sight. One click moves the sight 180 degrees, or one-half turn. This equals a one-half-mil change in elevation, which is .5 cm at 10 meters. The sight adjusts for windage by rotating the windage knob. Each click of windage adjustment also equals a one-half-mil change, which is .5 cm at 10 meters. There is also a windage sliding scale marked with index lines for centering the rear sight aperture.

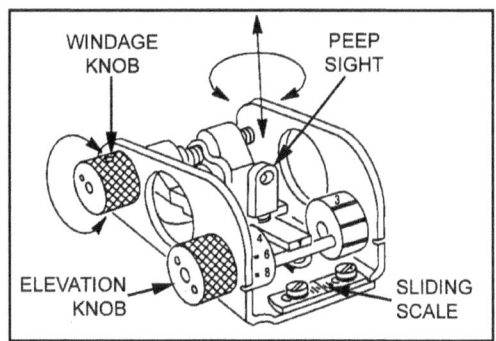

Figure 1-3. Sights.

b. **Safety.** The safety (Figure 1-4) is in the trigger housing. The safety is pushed from left to right (red ring not visible) to render the weapon safe, and the bolt cannot be released to go forward. The safety is pushed from right to left (red ring visible) to render the weapon ready to fire. The cocking handle on the right side of the weapon is used to pull the bolt to the rear.

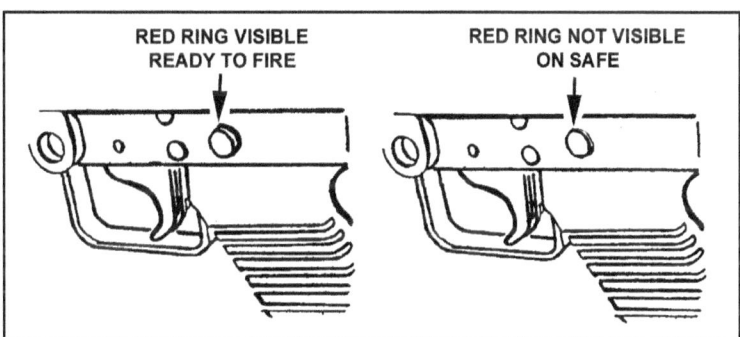

Figure 1-4. M249 machine gun safety.

1-3. AMMUNITION

The M249 machine gun uses several different types of 5.56-mm standard military ammunition. Soldiers should use only authorized ammunition that is manufactured to US and NATO specifications. The 5.56-mm NATO cartridge is identified by its appearance, the painted projectile tips, the stamped manufacturer's initials and year of manufacture on the base of the cartridge case, and the markings on the packing containers. When removed from the original packing container, the cartridge can be identified by its physical characteristics. The M193 and M196 cartridge for the M16 can be fired with the M249, but accuracy is degraded; therefore, it should only be used in emergency situations when M855 or M856 ammunition is not available.

a. **Type and Characteristics**. The specific types of ammunition (Figure 1-5) and its characteristics are as follows.

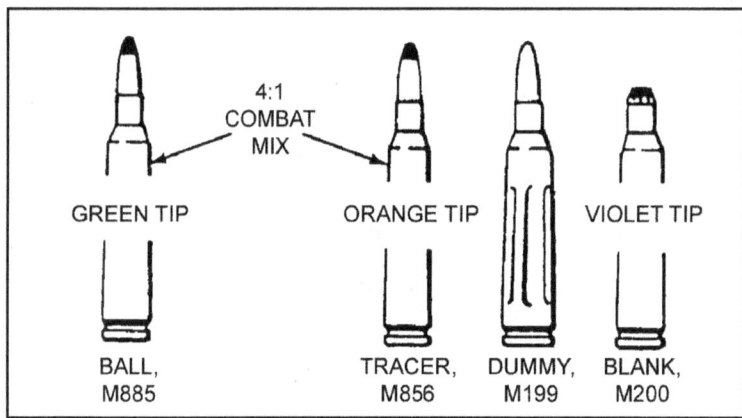

Figure 1-5. Cartridges for the M249.

(1) *Cartridge, 5.56-mm ball M855 (A059).* The M855 cartridge has a gilding, metal-jacketed, lead alloy core bullet with a steel penetrator. The primer and case are waterproof. This ammunition is linked by a disintegrating metallic split-linked belt so that the ammunition can feed from the ammunition box (Figure 1-6). In an emergency, the M855 round can also be fired from the M16A2, A3, or A4 when loaded in a 20- or 30-round magazine. It is identified by a green tip, has a projectile weight of 62 grains, and is 2.3 cm long. This is the NATO standard round. It is effective against personnel and light materials, not vehicles.

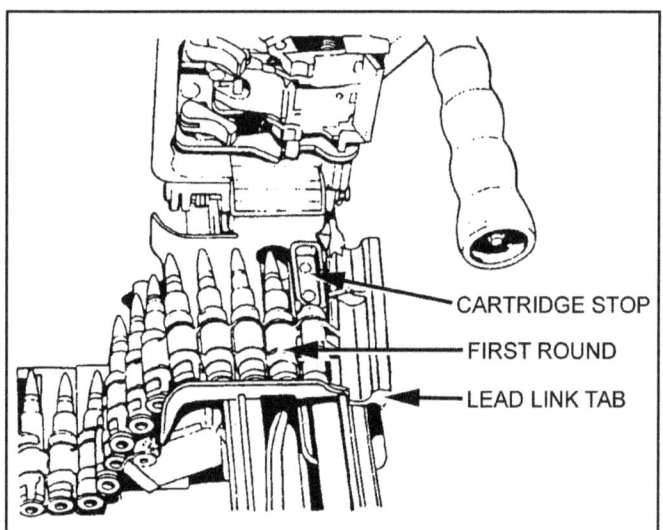

Figure 1-6. M855 cartridges in metallic belt.

(2) *Cartridge, 5.56-mm tracer, M856 (A064).* This cartridge has a projectile weight of 63.7 grains and lacks a steel penetrator. It is identified by an orange tip. The tracer is used for adjustments after observation, incendiary effects, and signaling. When tracer rounds

are fired, they are mixed with ball ammunition in a ratio of four ball rounds to one tracer round. The DODAC for ball and tracer mix is A064.

(3) *Cartridge, 5.56-mm dummy M199 (A060).* This cartridge can be identified by the six grooves along the side of the case beginning about one-half inch from its head. It contains no propellant or primer. The primer well is open to prevent damage to the firing pin. The dummy round is used during mechanical training, dry-fire exercises, and function checks.

NOTE: The 5.56-mm NATO cartridge may be identified by its appearance, the painting of projectile tips, the stamping of the manufacturer's initials and year of manufacture on the base of the cartridge case, and the markings on the packing containers. When removed from the original packing container, the cartridge can be identified by its physical characteristics. The M193 and M196 cartridge for the M16 can be fired with the M249, but accuracy is degraded; therefore, it should only be used in emergency situations when M855 or M856 ammunition is not available.

(4) *Cartridge, 5.56-mm blank M200 (M2 link, A075).* The blank cartridge has no projectile. The case mouth is closed with a seven-petal rosette crimp and has a violet tip. The original M200 blank cartridge had a white tip. Field use of this cartridge resulted in residue buildup, which caused malfunctions. Only the violet-tipped M200 cartridge should be used. The blank round is used during training when simulated live fire is desired. The M249 blank-firing attachment (NSN 1005-21-912-8997) must be used to fire this ammunition. (See paragraph 1-4.)

DANGER

DO NOT FIRE BLANK AMMUNITION AT ANY PERSON WITHIN 20 FEET BECAUSE FRAGMENTS OF A CLOSURE WAD OR PARTICLES OF UNBURNED PROPELLANT CAN CAUSE INJURY OR DEATH.

---

b. **Storage.** Ammunition is stored under cover. If ammunition is in the open, it must be kept at least 6 inches above the ground and covered with a double thickness of tarpaulin. The cover must be placed so that it protects the ammunition yet allows ventilation. Trenches are dug to divert water from flowing under the ammunition.

c. **Care, Handling, and Preservation.** Ammunition should not be removed from the airtight containers until ready for use. Ammunition removed from the airtight containers, particularly in damp climates, may corrode.

(1) Ammunition must be protected from mud, dirt, and moisture. If it gets wet or dirty, the ammunition must be wiped off before use. Lightly corroded cartridges are wiped off as soon as the corrosion is discovered. Heavily corroded, dented, or loose projectiles should not be fired.

(2) Ammunition must be protected from the direct rays of the sun. Excessive pressure from the heat may cause premature detonation.

(3) Oil should never be used on ammunition. Oil collects dust and other abrasives that may possibly damage the operating parts of the weapon.

d. **Packaging**. The ammunition can contains two plastic ammunition drums. Each drum contains 200 rounds and weighs 6.92 pounds. Dummy ammunition (M199) is packed in boxes of 20 rounds each.

1-4.   BLANK FIRING ATTACHMENT

The M249 BFA is the only BFA (NSN 1005-21-912-8997) authorized for use with the M249 MG.

a. **Installation**. The BFA is attached to the M249 machine gun by using the three steps shown in (Figure 1-7).

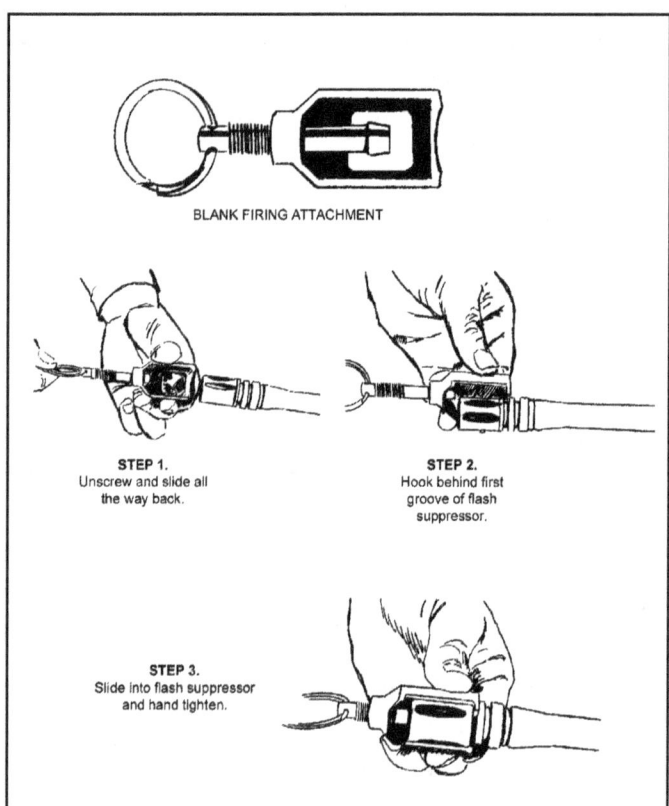

Figure 1-7. M249 blank firing attachment.

b. **Care of the M249 While Using the BFA**. A buildup of carbon inside the weapon causes friction between the moving parts. Carbon deposits build rapidly when blanks are fired. When these deposits become excessive, stoppages occur. Therefore, keeping the weapon—especially the gas system and chamber—clean, during blank firing is very important. To get the best performance with the BFA, the automatic rifleman performs the following:

(1) Inspects the weapon for damaged parts, excessive wear, cleanliness, and proper lubrication before firing.

(2) When feasible, test fires the weapon using ball ammunition before attaching the BFA.

(3) Adjusts the BFA to fit the weapon.

(4) Applies immediate action when stoppages occur.

(5) Cleans the gas system after firing 500 rounds.

(6) Cleans and lubricates the entire weapon after firing 1,000 rounds.

Section II. MAINTENANCE

Proper maintenance contributes to weapon effectiveness as well as to unit readiness. This section discusses the maintenance aspects of the M249 machine gun to include inspection; cleaning and lubrication; maintenance before, during, and after firing, and during NBC conditions. Associated tasks essential to maintenance (clearing, general assembly and disassembly, and function checks) are provided in detail.

1-5. CLEARING PROCEDURES

The first step in maintenance is to clear the weapon (Figure 1-8). This applies in all situations, not just after firing. The gunner must always assume the M249 machine gun is loaded. To clear the M249, the gunner performs the following procedures:

a. Moves the safety to the fire "F" position by pushing it to the left until the red ring is visible.

b. With his right hand, palm up, pulls the cocking handle to the rear, locking the bolt in place.

c. While holding the resistance on the cocking handle, moves the safety to the SAFE position by pushing it to the right until the red ring is not visible. (The weapon cannot be placed on safe unless the bolt is locked to the rear.)

d. Returns and locks the cocking handle in the forward position.

DANGER

WHEN OPENING THE FEED COVER ON A HOT GUN, MAKE SURE THE WEAPON IS ON THE GROUND AWAY FROM YOUR FACE. WITH THE WEAPON ON YOUR SHOULDER, POSSIBLE DEATH OR INJURY COULD OCCUR IF A ROUND GOES OFF WHEN THE COVER IS RAISED.

---

e. Raises the cover and feed mechanism assembly, and conducts the *five-point safety check* for brass, links, or ammunition:

(1) Checks the feed pawl assembly under the feed cover.

(2) Checks the feed tray assembly.

(3) Lifts the feed tray assembly and inspects the chamber.

(4) Checks the space between the bolt assembly and the chamber.

(5) Inserts two fingers of his left hand in the magazine well to extract any ammunition or brass.

f. Closes the cover and feed mechanism assembly and moves the safety to the "F" position. With his right hand, palm up, returns the cocking handle to the rear position. Presses the trigger and at the same time eases the bolt forward by manually riding the cocking handle forward.

CAUTION
The cocking handle must be manually returned to the forward and locked position each time the bolt is manually pulled to the rear.

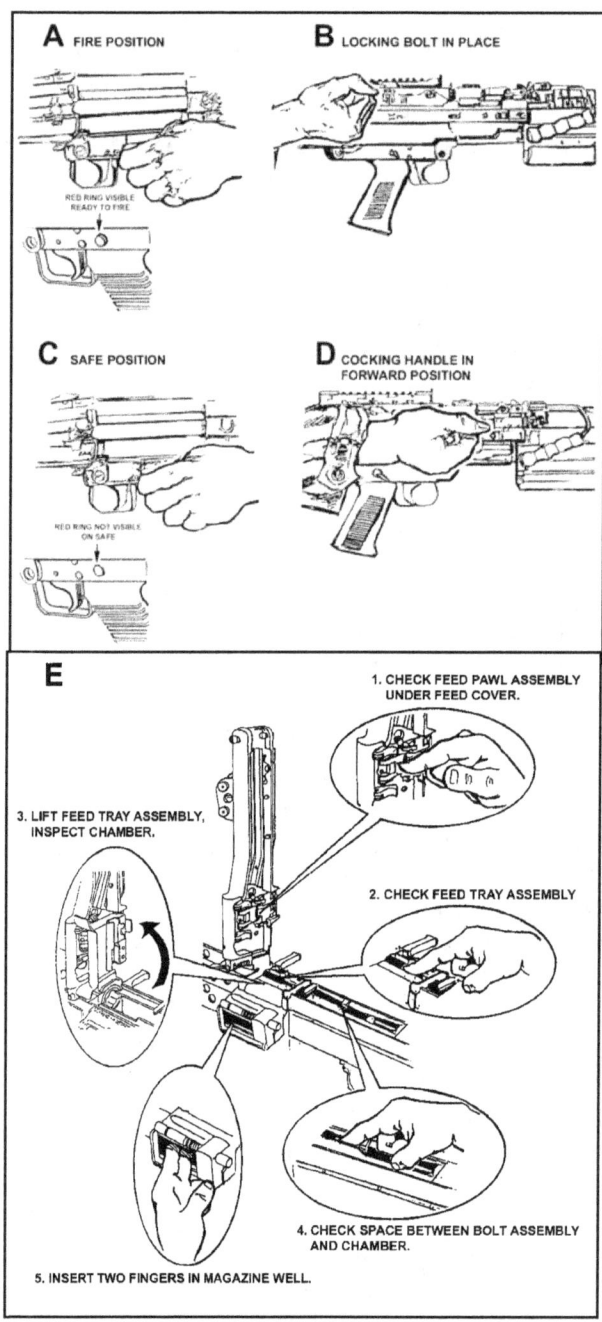

Figure 1-8. Clearing procedures.

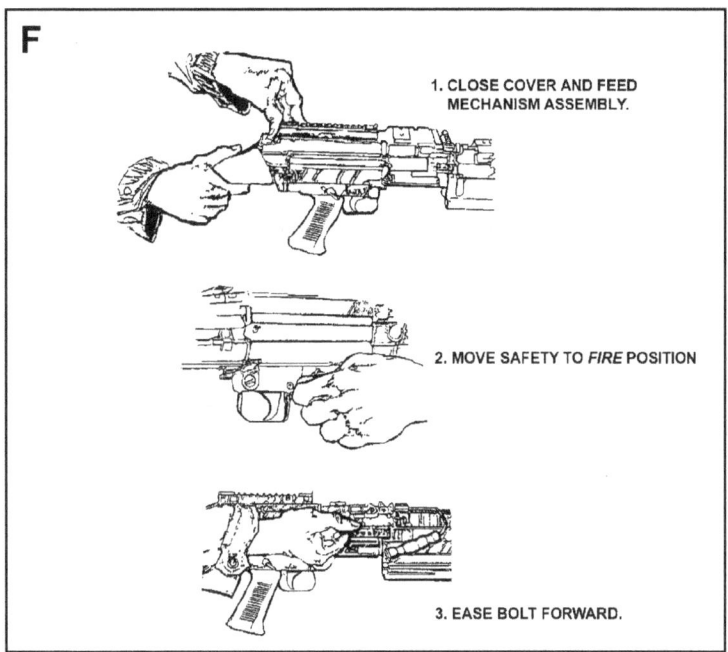

Figure 1-8. Clearing procedures (continued).

1-6. GENERAL DISASSEMBLY

General disassembly is removing and replacing the eight major groups (Figure 1-9, page 1-12). The unit armorer performs detailed disassembly. Disassembly beyond what is explained in this manual is prohibited, except by ordnance personnel. During general disassembly, each part is placed on a clean flat surface such as a table or mat. This aids in assembly in reverse order and avoids the loss of parts. Before disassembly, the bipod legs must be released from under the receiver and placed into the bipod mode position.

DANGER

BE SURE THE BOLT IS IN THE FORWARD POSITION BEFORE DISASSEMBLY. THE GUIDE ROD CAN CAUSE DEATH OR INJURY IF THE GUIDE SPRING IS RETRACTED WITH THE BOLT PULLED TO THE REAR.

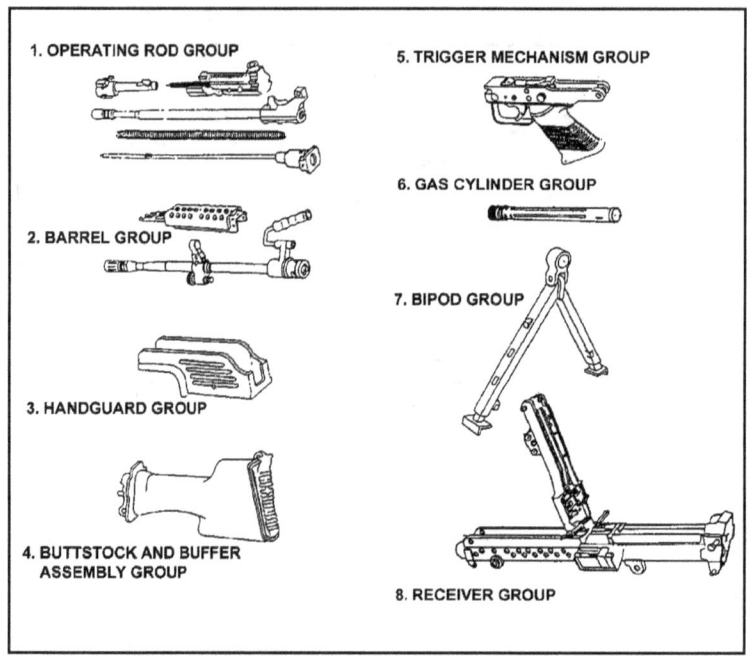

Figure 1-9. Eight major groups.

a. **Removing the Operating Rod Group.** The operating rod group (Figure 1-10), operating rod spring, slide assembly, piston assembly, and bolt assembly consists of the spring guide rod.

(1) To remove the operating rod, pull the upper retaining pin at the rear of the receiver to the left. Allow the buttstock to pivot downward and place it on a surface to support the weapon for disassembly.

(2) To release the operating rod assembly from the positioning grooves inside the receiver, hold the weapon with one hand on the buttstock assembly. Use the thumb of the other hand to push in and upward on the rear of the operating rod assembly.

(3) Pull the operating rod and spring from the receiver group and separate the parts.

(4) Hold the buttstock assembly with your left hand to stabilize the weapon. With your right hand, pull the cocking handle to the rear to lock the bolt. Return the cocking handle to the forward position. Place a finger on the face of the bolt and push until your finger makes contact with the bridge at the end of the receiver. This leaves the piston, slide, and bolt assemblies exposed.

(5) Hold the slide assembly while pulling the moving parts out the rear of the receiver. This leaves the piston, slide, and bolt assemblies exposed.

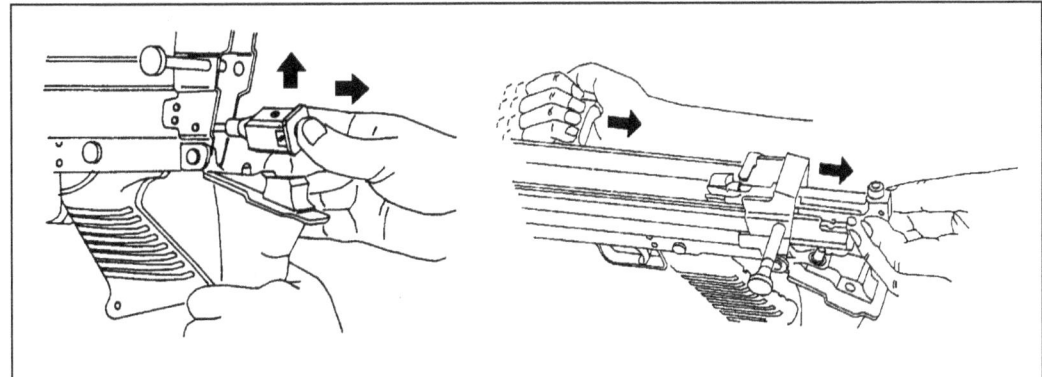

Figure 1-10. Removal of the operating rod group.

(6) To separate the operating rod group (Figure 1-11), hold the piston assembly in one hand, place your other hand on the bolt assembly, and rotate the bolt to disengage it bolt from the slide assembly. Remove the firing pin spring from the firing pin, but be careful not to break the spring. If the spring sticks, rotate it clockwise to free it. The weapon will function without the spring, but this weakens the firing pin action. To separate the slide assembly from the piston, press the retaining pin at the rear of the slide assembly to the left and lift the slide assembly.

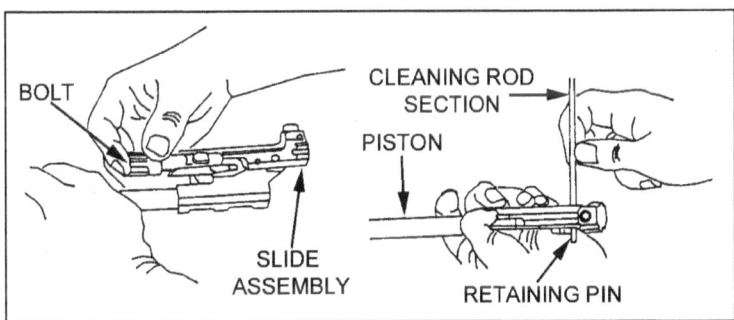

Figure 1-11. Separation of the operating rod group.

b. **Removing the Barrel Group.** The barrel group consists of barrel, heat shield, flash suppressor, front sight, gas regulator, and gas regulator collar. The following steps correspond to the callouts in Figure 1-12, page 1-14.

CAUTION
Barrels must not be interchanged with those from other M249s unless the headspace has been certified for that weapon by direct support personnel.

---

(1) To remove the barrel from the receiver, close the cover and feed mechanism assembly. Depress the barrel locking lever with your left hand, then lift the carrying handle using your right hand and push the barrel forward. To remove the heat shield, place the barrel with the muzzle end on a hard, flat surface, with the heat shield facing

away from your body. Place the index fingers of each hand inside the chamber. Use your thumbs to push up on the top clip.

Figure 1-12. Removal of the barrel.

(2) Raise the feed cover.

(3) To remove the gas regulator and collar, rotate the gas collar pin out of the notch. Place the tip of the scraper with the concave side facing the pin of the collar inside the notch. (Be careful not to use too much pressure, so as not to break the tip of the scraper.) Rotate the collar counterclockwise over the concave portion of the tip, which is on the scraper, and past the notch until the collar slides off (Figure 1-13). Deficiencies that are not correctable by the operator must be reported to the squad leader or NCOIC.

NOTE: The newest style barrel has an internal gas system, which cannot be disassembled.

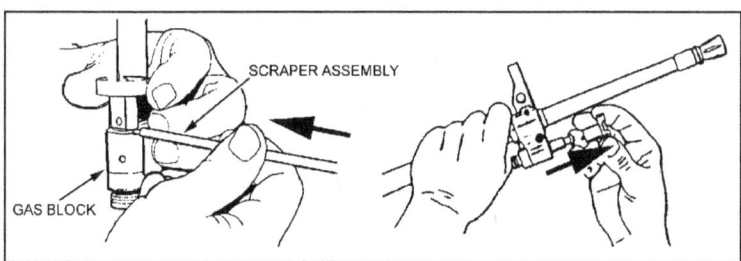

Figure 1-13. Removal of the collar.

(5) To remove the gas regulator (Figure 1-14), separate it from the gas block.

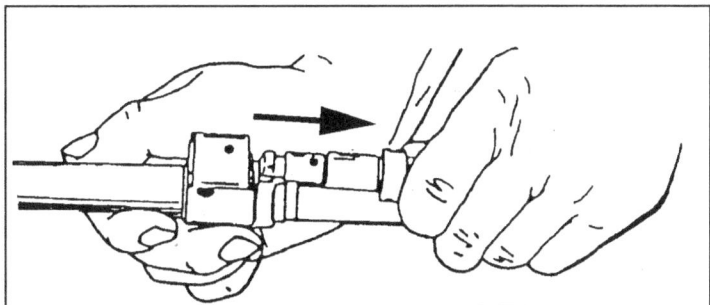

Figure 1-14. Removal of the gas regulator.

c. **Removing the Handguard Group.** The handguard group (Figure 1-15) consists of the handguard, handguard retaining pin, and cleaning equipment retaining clip. Push the handguard retaining pin to the left using a cartridge or the spring guide rod; then pull the handguard down.

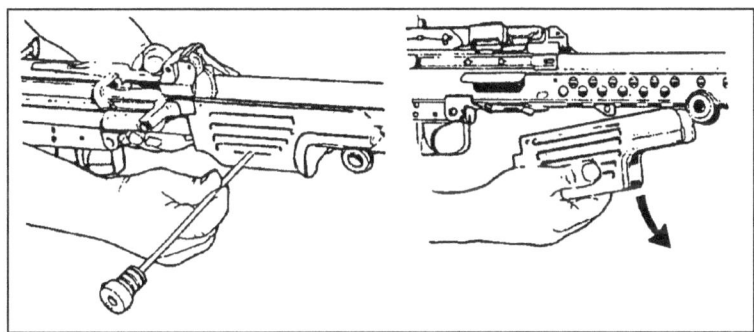

Figure 1-15. Removal of the handguard.

CAUTION

Do not attempt to remove the handguard retaining pin completely. It is a captured pin.

---

d. **Removing the Buttstock and Buffer Assembly Group.** To remove the buttstock and buffer assembly (Figure 1-16, page 1-15), use a cartridge or the spring guide rod to push the lowermost retaining pin on the rear of the receiver to the left. It is a captured pin; it is not removable. Remove the buttstock and shoulder assembly by pulling them rearward, while supporting the trigger mechanism.

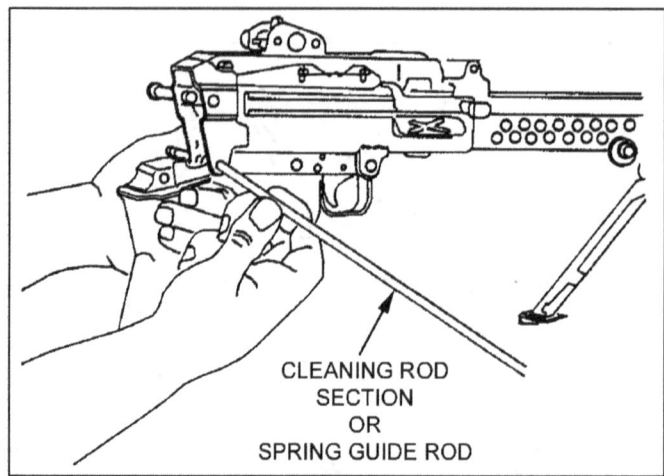

Figure 1-16. Removal of the buttstock and buffer assembly.

e. **Removing the Trigger Mechanism Group.** After the release of the support, the trigger mechanism will automatically be removed because the lowermost retaining pin holds it on.

f. **Removing the Gas Cylinder Group.** To remove the gas cylinder from the receiver (Figure 1-17), grasp the gas cylinder at the top of the bipod legs, turn it to the left or right to release the locking spring, and then pull it away from receiver.

CAUTION
Do not attempt to remove the upper and lower retaining pins completely. They are captured pins.

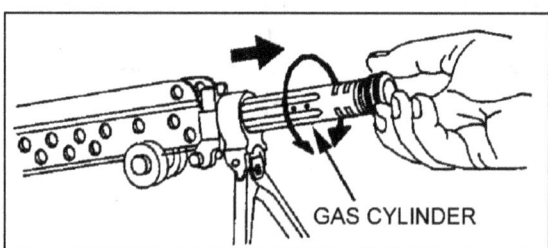

Figure 1-17. Removal of the gas cylinder group.

g. **Removing the Bipod Group**. Once the gas cylinder group is removed, remove the bipod group (Figure 1-18) by pulling it away from the receiver.

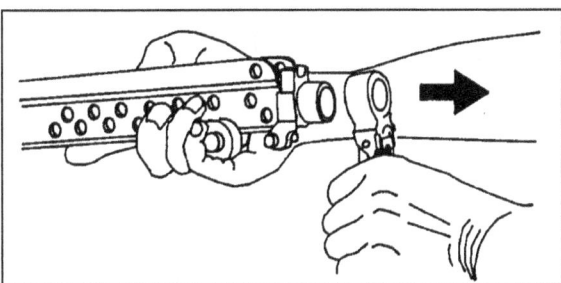

Figure 1-18. Removal of the bipod group.

h. **Removing the Receiver Group**. Once the bipod group is removed, the part remaining is the receiver group, and disassembly is complete.

1-7. INSPECTION

Inspection begins with the weapon disassembled in its major groups. Shiny surfaces do not mean the parts are unserviceable. The parts of the weapon and related equipment are inspected. Any broken or missing parts are repaired or replaced IAW TM 9-1005-201-10. The gunner performs preventive maintenance checks and services (PMCS) every 90 days. If the weapon has not been used in 90 days, PMCS is performed as stated in the operator's manual. If rust is seen on the weapon, perform PMCS immediately:

a. **Operating Rod Group**. The operating rod should not be bent, broken, or cracked. The buffer spring should not have breaks. Lug pins should protrude equally on both sides of the buffer spacer. The operating rod spring should not have kinks or separated strands or broken strands. It can have a maximum of one break on any one strand.

(1) Check the bolt assembly for visible damage. The cartridge extractor should not be cracked or chipped.

(2) Check the slide assembly for visible damage. Check the feed roller for spring tension when compressed and to ensure that the pivot slide is locked onto the slide assembly.

(3) Check the firing pin for straightness and cracks. Ensure the tip is completely rounded.

(4) Ensure the firing pin spring is not crushed or bent. Ensure the beveled end is not stretched.

(5) Check the sear notch on the piston assembly for signs of excessive wear or burring. Slight rotation of the piston on its housing is normal and is not cause for rejection.

b. **Barrel Group**. The flash suppressor should not be cracked, and it should be fastened securely. The front sight post and front sight base must not be bent, cracked, or broken. Weapons already zeroed should not be adjusted. The heat shield assembly is inspected for damage, cracks, or broken retaining clamps. The gas regulator and collar are checked for cracks or burrs. The barrel is checked for bulges, cracks, bends, obstructions, or pits in the chamber or bore. The gas plug is checked for obstructions, cracks, and bulges. The carrying handle is checked to ensure it is not cracked, broken, or missing; that it can be folded under spring pressure to the right and left; and that it remains locked in an upright position.

c. **Handguard Group**. The handguard should not be cracked or broken. The retaining clip must be attached to the handguard retaining pin.

d. **Buttstock and Buffer Assembly Group**. The buttstock is checked for cracks, bends, or breaks; and for missing components. It is checked for linkage and tension on the buffer rod. The shoulder rest is checked to ensure it is not bent or broken and that it locks in both positions.

e. **Trigger Mechanism Group**. The shoulder of the sear should not show excessive wear. The safety should function properly. That is, the sear should move only slightly when the safety is on "S" and freely when the safety is on "F". The sear pin should not protrude from the trigger mechanism, because, if it does protrude, the trigger mechanism will not go back in place.

f. **Gas Cylinder Group**. The gas cylinder should not be cracked, bent, or broken.

g. **Bipod Group**. The bipod group should not be cracked, bent, or broken. The bipod legs should extend and collapse easily.

h. **Receiver Group**. The cover latch should work properly. All parts inside the cover assembly should move under spring tension. All spotwelds are checked for cracks. The cover assembly should remain open without support. The belt-holding pawl must be under spring tension. The receiver should not be bent or cracked. The cocking handle should slide freely within its guide and lock in its forward position. The windage and elevation knobs on the rear sight should be movable and legible. The windage scale screws should not be worn or burred.

1-8. CLEANING, LUBRICATION, AND PREVENTIVE MAINTENANCE

The M249 machine gun should be cleaned immediately after firing. It should be disassembled into its major groups before cleaning. After it has been cleaned and wiped dry, a thin coat of CLP is applied by rubbing with a cloth. This lubricates and preserves the exposed metal parts during all normal temperature ranges. When not in use, the M249 should be inspected weekly and cleaned and lubricated when necessary.

a. **Cleaning**. All metal components and surfaces that have been exposed to powder fouling should be cleaned using CLP on a bore-cleaning patch. The same procedure is used to clean the receiver.

> **CAUTION**
> When using CLP, no other type cleaner can be used. Never mix CLP with RBC or LSA.

(1) Clear and disassemble the weapon.

(2) Clean the bore and chamber using CLP and fresh swabs.

(3) Clean the gas regulator with the special tool (scraper). Remove all carbon dust. *Do not use CLP on the collar, gas block, or body.*

(a) Clean the gas-vent hole (Figure 1-19).

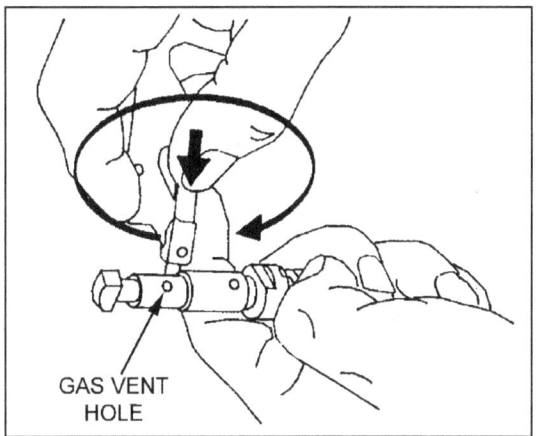

Figure 1-19. Cleaning of the gas vent hole.

(b) Clean the central hole with the appropriate part of the scraper by turning it clockwise and pushing it inward toward the bottom of the housing (Figure 1-20).

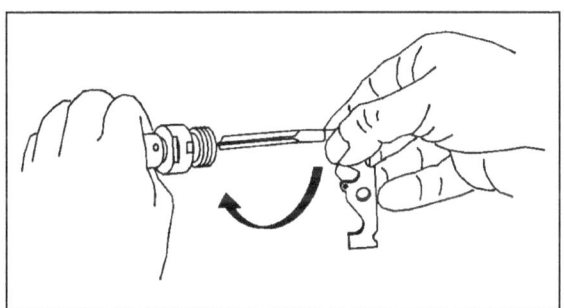

Figure 1-20. Cleaning of the central hole.

(c) Use the protruding tips of the scraper to clean the two grooves of the body (Figure 1-21).

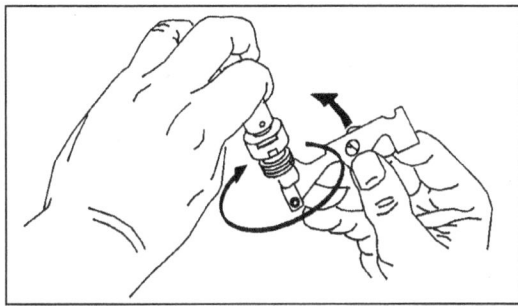

Figure 1-21. Cleaning of the grooves of the body.

(4) Clean the gas cylinder and piston with the special tool (scraper). Do not use CLP on the gas cylinder or piston.

(a) Clean the front interior of the gas cylinder (repositioned in receiver with bipod in place) by inserting and turning the flat side of the scraper in a 360-degree circular motion (Figure 1-22).

(b) Clean the internal grooves of the front side of the gas cylinder the same as, except insert the scraper farther into the gas cylinder (Figure 1-22).

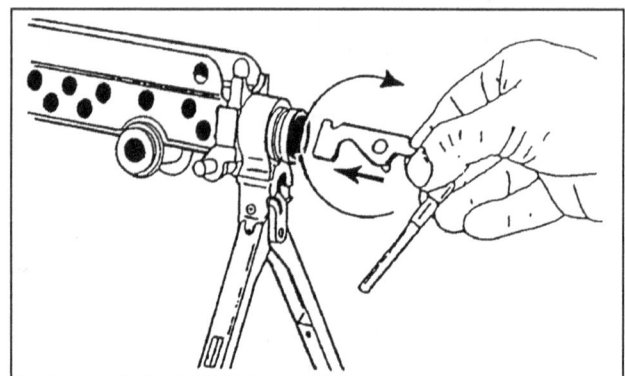

Figure 1-22. Cleaning of the front interior and internal grooves of the gas cylinder.

(c) Clean the three grooves of the piston using a 360-degree circular motion (Figure 1-23). Remove all carbon dust from the piston, inside and out.

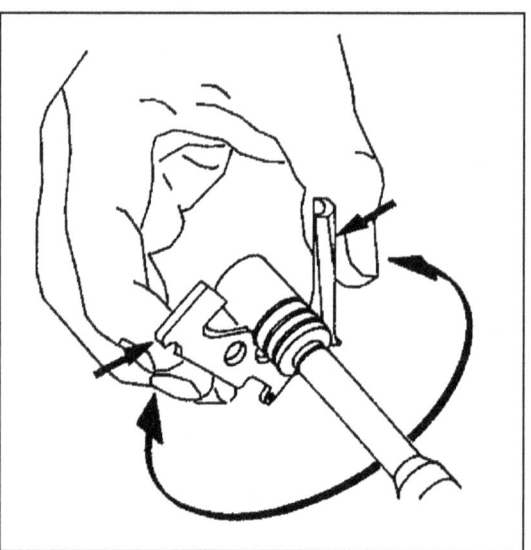

Figure 1-23. Cleaning of the grooves of the piston.

(d) Clean the hole in the front of the piston by inserting and turning the flat side of the scraper in a 360-degree circular motion (Figure 1-24).

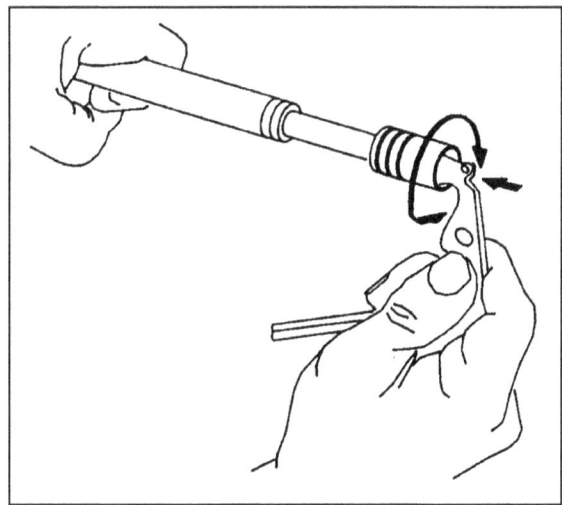

Figure 1-24. Cleaning of the hole in the front of the piston.

(5) Clean carbon and dirt from all other parts of the weapon.

(6) A cloth saturated in CLP is used on exterior surfaces to prevent corrosion.

b. **Lubrication.** After the M249 machine gun is cleaned and wiped dry, a thin coat of CLP is applied by rubbing it on with a cloth. This lubricates and preserves the exposed metal parts during all normal temperature ranges. The moving parts are also lubricated with CLP. After lubricating, the components are rubbed by hand to spread the CLP.

(1) *Operating rod group.* Use CLP on the operating rod and spring, the slide assembly, the feed roller, and the bolt-locking lug.

(2) *Barrel group.* Use CLP on the cam surfaces of the bolt-locking lugs, the heat shield, and along the outer surfaces of the barrel clamp.

(3) *Receiver group.* Use CLP on all moving parts on the cover assembly and the receiver rails.

c. **Preventive Maintenance.** Weapons that are seldom fired or stored for prolonged periods should have a light film of CLP applied to the interior of the gas plug, the gas regulator, and the piston immediately after cleaning or inspecting. Preventive maintenance is performed every 90 days, unless inspection reveals more frequent servicing is necessary. The use of the lubricant does not eliminate the need for cleaning and inspecting to ensure that corrosion has not formed. The gas regulator, gas plug, and piston must be clean and free of oil and lubricants before using the weapon. If it is not clean and oil free, stoppages will occur. CLP is the only lubricant to use on the M249 machine gun. The following procedures apply to cleaning and lubricating the M249 machine gun during unusual conditions:

(1) Extremely hot—use CLP, grade 2.

(2) Damp or salty air—use CLP, grade 2. Clean and apply frequently.

(3) Sandy or dusty areas—use CLP, grade 2. Clean and apply frequently. Remove excess with a rag after each application.

(4) Below -18 degrees Celsius (0 degrees Fahrenheit)—use CLP, grade 2, generously. Lubricate heavily enough so that the lubricant can be spread with finger. Although CLP provides required lubrication at temperatures between 0 degrees Fahrenheit and -35

degrees Fahrenheit, it will not flow from a 1/2-ounce bottle at temperatures below 0 degrees Fahrenheit.

1-9. GENERAL ASSEMBLY
The M249 machine gun is assembled in reverse order of the disassembly.

a. **Replacing the Receiver Group and Bipod Group.** Place the bipod group on the receiver group with the bipod legs open and pointed downward. (See Figure 1-18.)

b. **Replacing the Gas Cylinder Group.** Push the gas cylinder through the bipod yoke into the receiver. Push the cylinder to the rear while countering the pressure of the locking spring and guiding the end of the cylinder into the receiver with the other hand applying downward pressure. Position the recess in the cylinder near the spring. Turn the cylinder until the spring clicks into the recess at the rear of the gas cylinder (Figure 1-25).

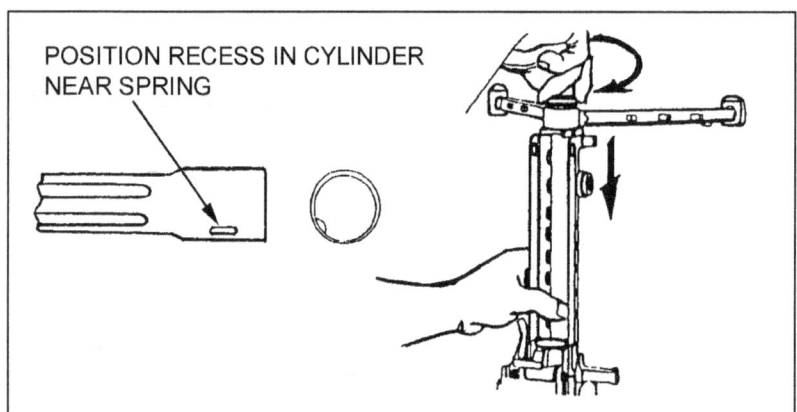

Figure 1-25. Replacement of gas cylinder group.

c. **Replacing the Trigger Mechanism Group.** Align the trigger mechanism (Figure 1-26) with the slot on the bottom of the receiver. Hold the trigger mechanism in position to accomplish the next step.

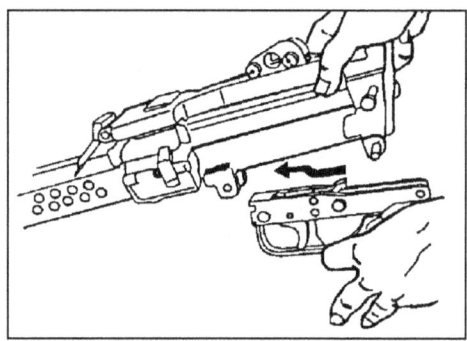

Figure 1-26. Replacement of the trigger mechanism group.

d. **Replacing the Buttstock and Buffer Assembly Group.** Align the lower hole in the buttstock and buffer assembly with the rear hole in the trigger mechanism; then push the lower retaining pin to the right (Figure 1-27).

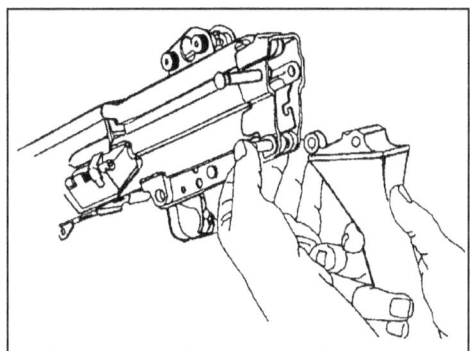

Figure 1-27. Replacement of the buttstock and buffer assembly group.

e. **Replacing the Handguard Group**. To replace the handguard (Figure 1-15), place it on the receiver from the bottom and push it to the rear until it stops. Using the guide rod, push the handguard retaining pin to the right, which locks the handguard into position. Push the handguard down to make sure it is locked.

f. **Replacing the Barrel Group**. Insert the gas regulator into the gas block and align the notch on the gas regulator with the notch of the gas block. With the gas regulator already installed and supported on a firm surface, place the gas regulator collar onto the protruding end of the body and align the spring with the stud. Push the gas regulator collar downward firmly and rotate it until it slips into place. Then, press it in and rotate it to lock it in place. Depress the barrel locking lever to the rear with your left hand, while holding the carrying handle with your right hand. Pull the barrel rearward and push downward; align the gas regulator with the gas cylinder and lock it by releasing the barrel locking lever. Check the barrel to ensure it is locked into the receiver by pulling or lifting on the carrying handle. Replace the heat shield by placing the hook end of the heat shield under the front sight post and press down until the clamps lock on the barrel. (Figure 1-28).

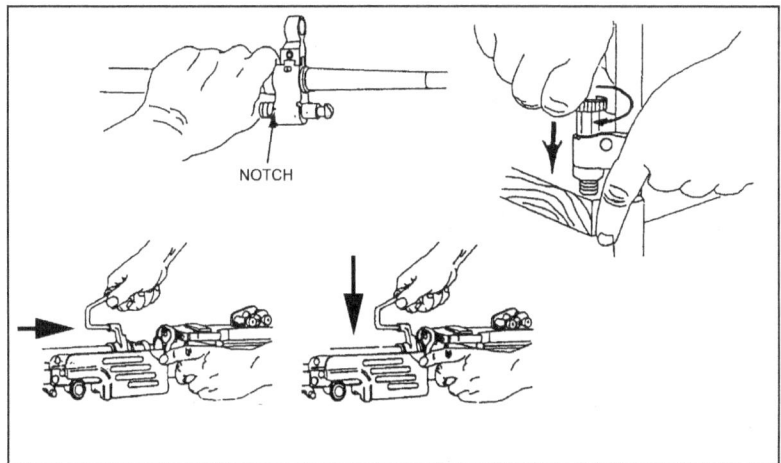

Figure 1-28. Replacement of the barrel group.

g. **Replacing the Operating Rod Group**. Hold the piston in one hand with the face of the piston facing outward and the sear notches downward. With the other hand, place the slide assembly onto the rear of the piston with the firing pin toward the front of the piston. (Check the slide assembly retaining pin to make sure it is out.) (Figure 1-29).

(1) Push the slide assembly retaining pin to the right. This locks together the piston assembly and the slide assembly.

(2) Put the firing pin spring on the firing pin of the slide assembly. Place the bolt on the slide assembly, aligning the driving lug of the bolt with the slot of the slide assembly. Apply pressure to the face of the bolt to compress the firing pin spring. Then, rotate the bolt to hook the driving lug into the slide assembly. Open the cover assembly on the receiver. Insert the face of the piston into the receiver, aligning the bolt lugs onto the receiver rails. Pull the trigger and push the moving parts forward until the bolt is seated into the chamber.

(3) Place the operating rod tip into the operating rod spring. Then, insert the free end of the operating rod and spring into the rear of the piston. Depress the rear of the operating rod assembly until the two lugs on the buffer are positioned in the receiver grooves.

(4) Pivot the buttstock upward into position and push the upper retaining pin to the right, locking the buttstock to the receiver.

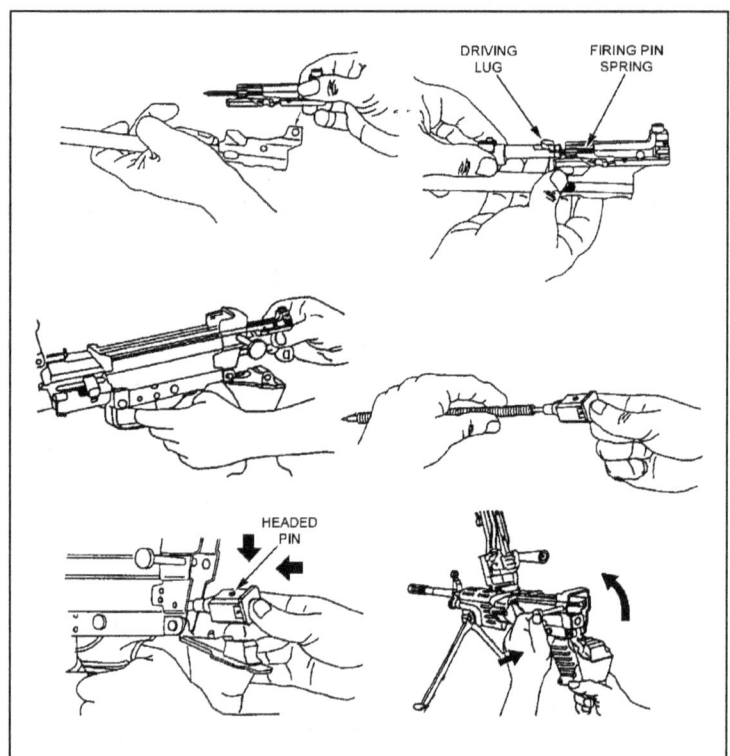

Figure 1-29. Replacement of the operating rod group.

1-10. FUNCTION CHECK

A function check must be performed to ensure that the M249 machine gun has been assembled correctly. The procedures, in order, are as follows:

a. Grasp the cocking handle with the right hand, palm up, and pull the bolt to the rear, locking it in place.

b. While continuing to hold the resistance on the cocking handle, use the left hand to move the safety to the SAFE position.

c. Push the cocking handle forward into the forward lock position.

d. Pull the trigger (The weapon should not fire).

e. Grasp the cocking handle with the right hand, palm up, and pull and hold it to the rear.

f. Move the safety to the FIRE position.

g. While continuing to hold resistance on the cocking handle, use the left hand to pull the trigger and ease the bolt forward to prevent it from slamming into the chamber area and damaging the face of the bolt.

h. If the weapon fails the function check, check for missing parts or repeat the reassembly procedures. Before disassembling the weapon, make sure it is positioned where the guide rod and spring cannot cause bodily harm if the bolt is locked to the rear. The cover and feed mechanism assembly can be closed with the bolt in either the forward or the rearward position.

CAUTION

Ease the bolt forward to prevent damage to the hardened surfaces on the bolt, barrel, and so forth.

1-11. MAINTENANCE PROCEDURES

There are certain actions that must be taken before, during, and after firing to properly maintain the M249 machine gun.

    a. Before firing—

        (1) Wipe the bore dry.

        (2) Inspect the weapon as outlined in the operator's TM.

        (3) Lubricate the weapon.

    b. During firing—

        (1) Inspect the weapon periodically to ensure that it remains lubricated.

        (2) When malfunctions or stoppages occur, follow the procedures in Section IV.

    c. After firing—

        (1) Immediately clear and clean the weapon.

        (2) Every 90 days during inactivity, clean and lubricate the weapon, unless inspection reveals more frequent servicing is necessary.

1-12. MAINTENANCE DURING NUCLEAR, BIOLOGICAL, CHEMICAL CONDITIONS

If the M249 machine gun is contaminated by chemical, biological, or radiological agents, the appropriate action must be taken to reduce exposure and penetration.

    a. **Chemical.** Use towelettes from the M258A1 kit to wipe off the weapon. If these are not available, wash the weapon with hot, soapy water, and rinse.

    b. **Biological.** Use towelettes or hot, soapy water and rinse the weapon as above.

c. **Radiological**. Brush or wipe the weapon, or wash with water, and rinse. For more details, see FM 3-5.

Section III. OPERATION AND FUNCTION

This section discusses the operation and function of the M249 machine gun. They include loading, firing, unloading, cycle of functioning, adjusting the sight, and using the bipod.

1-13. OPERATION

The M249 machine gun operations are loading, firing, unloading, and using belted ammunition or, in an emergency, a 20- or 30-round M16 magazine. The firing operation works on gas pressure created as a fired round passes through the barrel. The M249 is loaded, fired, unloaded, and cleared from the open-bolt position. The safety must be in the FIRE position before the bolt can be pulled to the rear. Before using belted ammunition, it must be checked to ensure it is properly linked with the double link or the link tab at the open end of the box. It must be free of dirt and corrosion. When using a magazine of ammunition, it must be loaded into the magazine well and be free of dirt and corrosion.

1-14. LOADING

To load the M249, the weapon must be cleared as described. (With the feed cover raised, the gunner makes sure his face is not exposed to the open chamber area while loading.) (Figure 1-30).

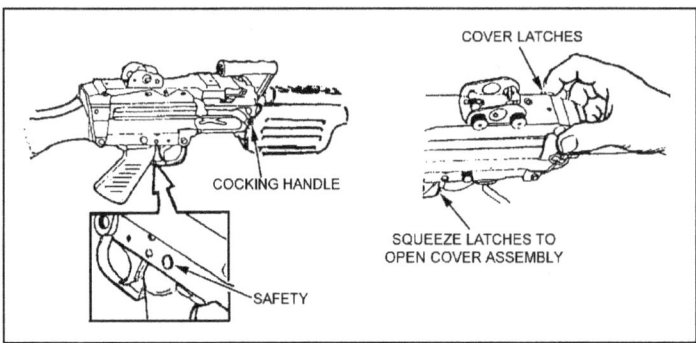

Figure 1-30. Loading.

a. **Belt**. When loading belted ammunition (Figure 1-31), always cant the weapon to the right. Make sure the open side of the links is facing down, and place the lead link tab or first round of the belt in the tray groove against the cartridge stop. The rounds should be placed flat across the feed tray. With your left hand, count five to six rounds down to hold ammunition in place on the feed tray, while at the same time closing the feed cover with your right hand. When closing the feed cover, always place your hand in front of the rear sight to prevent accidentally changing the sight adjustment.

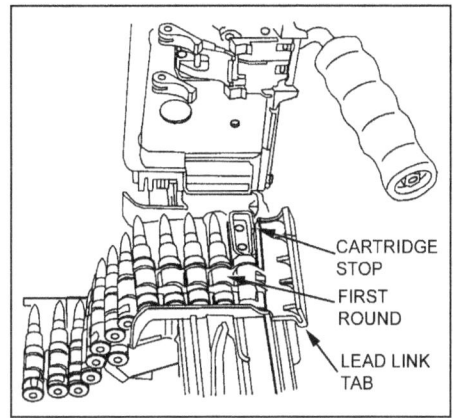

Figure 1-31. Belt-fed ammunition.

NOTE: Use the 20- or 30-round magazine for emergency use only when linked ammunition is not available.

b. **Magazine.** Load the 20- or 30-round magazine by inserting it into the magazine well on the left side of the receiver. Push the magazine firmly into the well until it seats and the release tab clicks into the recess on the magazine (Figure 1-32).

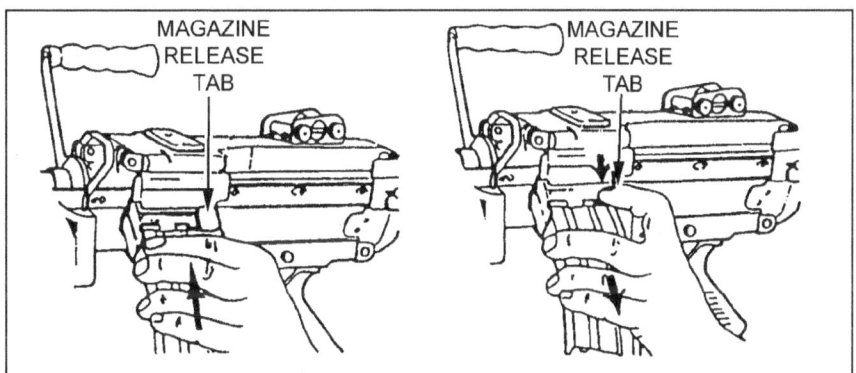

Figure 1-32. Loading of a magazine.

1-15. UNLOADING

To unload the weapon, pull the bolt and, if it is not already locked lock it in the rear position, it is locked there at this time. The safety is placed on "S". Depending on whether belt-fed or magazine-fed ammunition is used, the following procedures are used:

<table>
<tr><td>

WARNING

With a hot gun, **before you raise the feed cover, move the weapon away from your face so that you are not exposed to the open chamber.**

</td></tr>
</table>

a. **Belt.** Raise the feed cover and remove any ammunition or links from the feed tray. Perform the five-point safety check.

b. **Magazine**. Push the magazine release tab down and pull the magazine from the magazine well. Raise the feed cover and perform the five-point safety check.

1-16. CYCLE OF FUNCTIONING

The gunners can recognize and correct stoppages when they know how the M249 machine gun functions. The weapon functions automatically as long as ammunition is fed into it, and the trigger is held to the rear. Each time a round is fired the parts of the weapon function in a cycle or sequence. Many of the actions occur at the same time. These actions are separated in this manual only for instructional purposes.

a. The cycle is started by putting the first round of the belt in the tray groove or by inserting the magazine into the magazine well. Then the trigger is pulled, releasing the sear from the sear notch. When the trigger is pulled to the rear, the rear of the sear is lowered and disengaged from the sear notch. This procedure allows the piston and bolt to be driven forward by the expansion of the operating rod spring. The cycle stops when the trigger is released and the sear again engages the sear notch on the piston.

b. The sequence of functioning is as follows:

(1) *Feeding*. As the bolt starts its forward movement, the feed lever is forced to the right, causing the feed-pawl assembly to turn in the opposite direction. This forces the feed-pawl assembly over the next round in the belt, and the feed-pawl assembly is ready to place the next round into the tray groove when the rearward action occurs again. As the bolt moves to the rear after firing, the feed roller forces the feed lever to the left. The feed lever is forced to turn, moving the feed pawl to the right. This places a round in the tray groove.

(2) *Chambering*. As the bolt travels forward, the upper stripping (belt-fed or magazine-fed) lug engages the rim of the round. The pressure of the front and rear cartridge guides holds the round so that a positive contact is made with the upper stripping lug of the bolt. The front cartridge guide prevents forward movement of the link as the round is stripped from the belt. The upper locking lug carries the round forward. The chambering ramp causes the nose of the round to be cammed downward into the chamber. When the round is fully seated in the chamber, the extractor snaps over the rim of the round, and the ejector on the rail inside the receiver is depressed.

(3) *Locking*. As the round is chambered, the bolt enters the barrel socket. The upper and lower locking lugs contact the bolt camming surfaces inside the barrel and start the bolt turning clockwise. The action of the bolt into the slide assembly, as the piston continues forward, turns the bolt to complete its 90-degree (one-quarter turn) clockwise rotation. Locking is now complete.

(4) *Firing*. After the bolt is fully forward and locked, the piston continues to go forward independently of the bolt for a short distance. The piston assembly carries the firing pin through the face of the bolt. The firing pin strikes the primer of the round, and the primer fires the round.

(5) *Unlocking*. After the round is fired and the bullet passes the gas port, part of the expanding gases go into one block (new style) or into the gas regulator through the gas plug. The rapidly expanding gases enter into the gas cylinder from the gas regulator, forcing the piston to the rear. As the piston continues to the rear, the slide assembly's simultaneous movement to the rear causes the bolt to begin its counterclockwise rotation. The upper and lower locking lugs of the bolt contact the bolt camming surfaces inside the

barrel socket and, as the bolt continues toward the rear, it completes a one-quarter turn counterclockwise. The rotation and movement to the rear unlocks the bolt from the barrel socket.

(6) *Extracting.* Extracting begins during the unlocking cycle. The rotation of the bolt loosens the cartridge case in the chamber. As the piston and bolt move to the rear, the extractor pulls the cartridge case from the chamber.

(7) *Ejecting.* As the cartridge case is pulled from the chamber, the bolt passes by the ejector. This procedure causes the ejector clip to expand, forcing the ejector to push the expended cartridge. The extractor grips the right side of the cartridge and causes it to spin from the weapon as it reaches the ejection port. The empty belt links are forced out of the link ejection port as the rearward movement of the bolt causes the next round to be positioned in the tray groove.

(8) *Cocking.* The piston assembly acts against the firing pin, pulling the firing pin from the primer of the spent cartridge case. The action of the piston assembly, continuing to the rear with the firing pin, releases the compression of the firing pin spring. As long as the trigger is held to the rear, the M249 will continue to complete the eight steps of functioning automatically. When the trigger is released and the sear again engages the sear notch, the cycle of functioning is stopped and the weapon is cocked. To prevent undue wear to the sear and sear notch, the automatic rifleman must hold the trigger firmly to the rear during firing.

1-17. SIGHTS

This paragraph provides information on how to set the sights for elevation and windage for the M249 machine gun. It also includes information on how to make corrections if the initial setting on the windage knob or peep sight is not accurate. On a 10-meter target, each paster is 1 cm. Therefore, two clicks on the windage knob in either direction moves the strike of the round left or right 1 cm, and two turns on the peep sight moves the strike of the round up or down 1 cm. For example, if the shot group was 2 cm above and 1 cm to the right of the paster, sight corrections are made first by correcting the windage. In this case, the windage knob is rotated two clicks toward the buttstock (clockwise). The elevation knob is rotated four turns toward the buttstock (clockwise) to lower the strike of the round. (See Figure 1-33, below and Table 1-3, on page 1-31.)

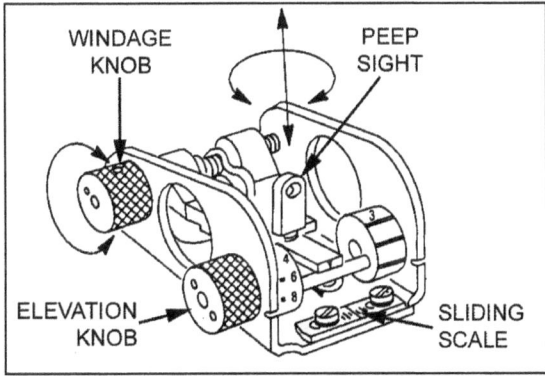

Figure 1-33. Sliding scale on sight.

a. **Elevation.** Adjustments for elevation (range) require the automatic rifleman to turn the elevation knob (closest to the buttstock) on the rear sight to the desired range setting. Range settings are graduated increments from 300 to 1,000 meters. Even-numbered settings are on the left side of the scale wheel and are numbered 4, 6, 8, 10, which represent 400, 600, 800, and 1,000 meters, respectively. Odd-numbered settings are on the right side of the scale wheel and marked with the number 3 and three index lines, which represent 300, 500, 700, and 900 meters, respectively. Rotation of the elevation knob toward the muzzle (counterclockwise) increases the range, while rotation toward the buttstock (clockwise) decreases the range. Fine adjustments, like zeroing, are made by adjusting the peep sight. Each 180-degree turn equals a half-mil change in elevation, which equals a half-cm change in impact at a range of 10 meters. Clockwise (to the right) rotations decrease elevation, while counterclockwise (to the left) rotations increase elevation. The peep sight can be turned nine 180-degree turns from top to bottom. To make the peep sight easier to grasp, the elevation knob is turned to its highest point (1,000 meters). The appropriate adjustment is made for the peep sight, and then the sight is returned to the desired range. Whenever readjusting the range, the point of aim is never changed. The point of aim is the center base of the target.

b. **Windage.** Adjustments for windage are made by traversing the rear sight right and left along the sliding scale. The sliding scale is marked or graduated with index lines. Each index line is equal to a half-mil change in direction or a half-cm change of impact at 10 meters. Rotation of the windage knob (closest to the muzzle end) toward the muzzle (counterclockwise) moves the rear sight aperture right, which moves the strike of the rounds right. Rotation toward the buttstock (clockwise) moves the aperture left, which moves the strike of the rounds left.

c. **10-Meter Zero, Setting of the Sights (Mechanical Zero).** The gunner indexes or places the elevation knob on a range of 700 meters. He centers the rear peep sight by rotating it clockwise (right) as far as it will go, then rotating counterclockwise (left) five clicks or half-turns. He rotates the windage knob toward the muzzle until the peep sight is *completely* to the right, then rotates the windage knob toward the buttstock twelve clicks to the left. This places the peep sight in the approximate center of the sight. Each sight may vary as to how many clicks are needed. To check the sight, the gunner starts with the sight all the way to the right and, while counting the clicks, rotates the windage knob until it stops on the left side. He divides the clicks by two. If the click is an uneven number, he rounds it up. To center the sight, he rotates the windage knob toward the center (right) while counting the appropriate number of clicks. He adjusts the sliding scale at the rear of the sight to center the large index line under the zeroed windage mark on the sight. Two threads should be showing on the front sight post. If more or less are showing, the gunner turns in the weapon for maintenance.

100 meters—one click moves the strike 5 cm (2 inches).

200 meters—one click moves the strike 10 cm (4 inches).

300 meters—one click moves the strike 15 cm (6 inches).

400 meters—one click moves the strike 20 cm (8 inches).

500 meters—one click moves the strike 25 cm (10 inches).

600 meters—one click moves the strike 30 cm (12 inches).

700 meters—one click moves the strike 35 cm (14 inches).

800 meters—one click moves the strike 40 cm (16 inches).

900 meters—one click moves the strike 45 cm (18 inches).

Table 1-3. Windage and elevation (peep sight) correction chart.

NOTE: The primary and spare barrels are zeroed by making adjustments on the front sight.

1-18. M122 TRIPOD

The M122 tripod provides a stable mount for the M249, and it permits a higher degree of accuracy and control. The tripod is recommended for all marksmanship training and defensive employment.

a. **Mounting the M122 Tripod.** The tripod assembly provides a stable and relatively lightweight base that is far superior to the bipod. The tripod may be extended and collapsed without difficulty. It consists of a tripod head, one front leg and two rear legs, and traversing bar. The traversing bar connects the two rear legs. The traversing bar is hinged on one side with a sleeve and sleeve latch on the other. This procedure allows the tripod to collapse to a closed position for carrying or storage, or to lock in an open, extended position for use. The traversing bar also supports the T&E mechanism. Engraved on the bar is a scale, which measures direction in mils. It is graduated in 5-mil increments. It is numbered every 100 mils to 425 mils right of center, and it is numbered every 100 mils to 450 mils left of center.

(1) The T&E mechanism provides controlled manipulation and the ability to engage predetermined targets.

(a) The traversing portion of the mechanism consists of the traversing handwheel and traversing slide-lock lever. As the traversing handwheel is turned, the muzzle of the weapon will turn to the left or right, depending on the direction it is turned. Each click of the traversing handwheel indicates a 1 mil change in direction of the muzzle: 1 click equals 1 mil. There is a total of 100 mils traverse (50 mils right and 50 mils left of center).

(b) The elevating portion of the mechanism consists only of the elevating handwheel. The elevating handwheel has a mil-click device built into it (1 click equals 1 mil). Engraved into the handwheel is a scale divided into 5-mil divisions and 1-mil subdivisions, for a total of 50 mils increments. There are 200 mils above and 200 mils below the zero mark ,for a total of 400 mils in elevation change. Elevation readings are taken in two parts. First, the major reading is taken from the elevation screw plate. The second, minor reading is from the handwheel. The two readings are separated by a slash ("/") when they are recorded.

(c) The traversing slide-lock lever allows rapid lateral adjustments along the traversing bar. Direction readings are taken from the scale on the traversing bar, using the left side of the traversing slide as an index. The direction of the reading comes from the position of the muzzle, not the position of the slide.

(2) To set up the tripod, unfold the front leg and spread the rear legs until the leg lock engages. Insert the pintle assembly and rotate the pintle lock-release cam to lock. Ensure that the locking lever of the pintle is facing forward toward the front leg (Figure 1-34).

(3) Attach the traversing and elevating mechanism (which requires a special adapter). Ensure that the adapter pin is to the right and the opening between it is to the rear. Center the elevating and traversing handwheels. To do this, he rotates the elevation handwheel until about 1-1/2 inches (two fingers) are visible on the upper elevating screw; he rotates the traversing slide until about two fingers are visible on the lower elevating screw. He rotates the traversing handwheel towards his body as far as it will go, then turns it away two complete revolutions. He checks the traversing handwheel scale to ensure the "0" on the scale is aligned with the "0" index line before and after the two revolutions. The T&E is now roughly centered. At night, he positions the traversing mechanism by turning the traversing handwheel toward his body as far as it will go, and then turning it away 50 clicks (two revolutions) (Figure 1-34).

(4) With the T&E roughly centered, he lowers the traversing slide on to the traversing bar with the locking lever to the rear, and the traversing handwheel to the left, and secures it by turning the locking lever clockwise (Figure 1-34).

(5) The weapon attaches to the M122 tripod. First, he extends the bipod legs forward. Then, he engages the mounting pins (Located between the front of the handguard and the bipod legs) of the M249 into the pintle of the tripod by squeezing the locking lever of the pintle. He lowers the rear of the weapon so that the hole above the trigger guard can be engaged with the locking pin of the T&E adapter. He aligns the hole with the pin of the adapter and pushes the pin from right to left to secure the M249 to the M122 tripod (Figure 1-34).

(6) After the M249 is attached and secured to the tripod, the gunner must attach a special ammunition adapter to the M249. He inserts the adapter into the magazine well, as if inserting a magazine. This procedure allows the gunner to use the 200-round drum of ammunition (Figure 1-34).

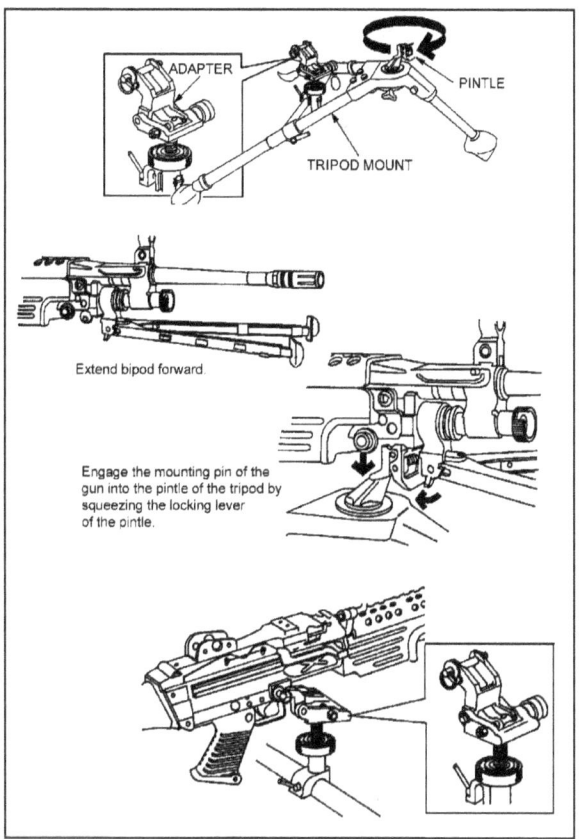

Figure 1-34. Tripod mount.

b. **Dismounting The M249 From The M122 Tripod**. The gunner dismounts the M249 from the tripod by first removing the traversing and elevation mechanism from the weapon. He pulls the locking pin of the adapter to release the T&E from the trigger guard. He grasps the carrying handle with his left hand and squeezes the pintle-locking lever with his right hand. He lifts the weapon from the pintle assembly and the tripod.

1-19. BIPOD OPERATIONS

The bipod group is used to fire from the prone position. The shoulder rest on the buttstock provides support for the gunner when fired in the bipod mode. The gas cylinder group holds the bipod group in place. Once the gas cylinder is removed, the bipod group can also be removed from the receiver.

a. To lower the bipod legs, hold the legs together and pull down and away from the handguard. Release the legs so that they lock in the vertical position. To extend the bipod legs, grasp the foot of each leg and pull down (Figure 1-35, page 1-34).

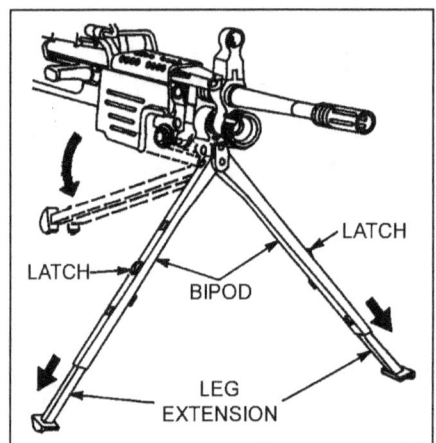

Figure 1-35. Lowering of the bipod.

    b. To retract the bipod legs, push in the latches and push in the legs.

    c. Before transporting the weapon, the gunner folds the bipod legs. To place the legs in the closed position, the gunner holds them together; he pulls the them back under the handguard; he then releases them so that the hooks on the legs grip the handguard. The bipod can be folded only when the legs are in the closed position (Figure 1-36).

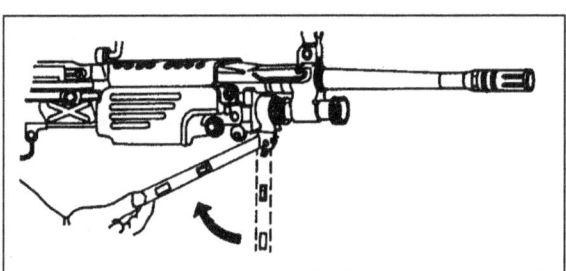

Figure 1-36. Folding of bipod under the handguard.

1-20. VEHICULAR MOUNT

The standard vehicular mount for the M249 machine gun is the M6 pedestal mount used on the (HMMWV). One component of the pedestal mount is the M197 machine gun mount (travel lock). This mount also adapts to other vehicles (Figure 1-37).

    a. To mount the weapon, the gunner ensures that the release lever of the pintle is facing forward. To extend the bipod legs forward, he places the front mounting pins of the M249 into the pedestal by squeezing the locking lever of the pintle. He ensures that the M60 machine gun adapter assembly is pivoted away from the M249 fork (clevis). He lowers the rear of the weapon so that the locking pin of the machine gun mount can engage the hole above the trigger guard. The gunner engages this part of the weapon into the fork of the mount and pushes in the locking pin.

    b. To dismount the weapon, the gunner pulls the locking pin of the mount. He raises the rear of the weapon slightly and squeezes the locking lever of the pintle. Once the front mounting pins are released, the gunner lifts the weapon from the mount.

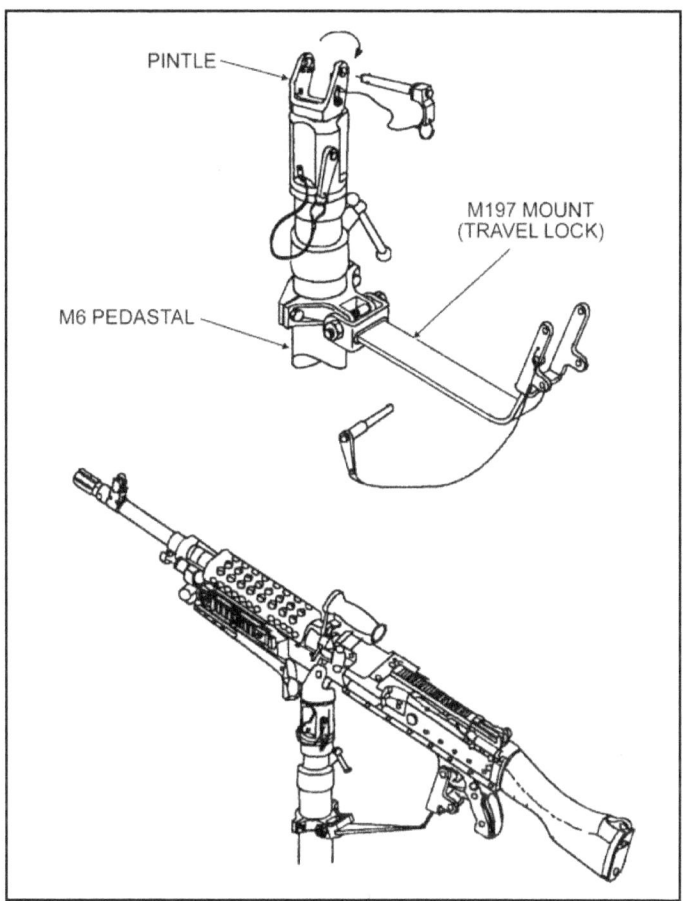

Figure 1-37. Vehicular mount.

1-21. TRIPOD POSITIONING

The M122 tripod provides a stable mount for the M249, and it permits a high degree of accuracy and control. The gunner unfolds the front leg and positions it toward the target and spreads the rear legs until the leg lock engages.

Section IV. PERFORMANCE PROBLEMS AND DESTRUCTION

This section identifies some of the problems that cause the M249 to perform improperly. It also explains how to identify unserviceable parts and how to destroy the M249 when authorized to do so.

1-22. MALFUNCTIONS

A malfunction occurs when a mechanical failure causes the M249 to fire improperly. Defective ammunition or improper operation by the automatic rifleman is not considered a malfunction. If cleaning and or lubricating the weapon does not fix the problem, then it is turned in to the unit armorer. Table 1-4 shows malfunctions, their probable causes, and the corrective actions.

MALFUNCTION	PROBABLE CAUSES	CORRECTIVE ACTIONS
Sluggish operation.	Lack of lubricant. Carbon buildup in the gas system. Burred parts.	Lubricate. Clean the gas regulator, piston, and cylinder. Notify unit maintenance.
Failure to cock or a runaway weapon.	Broken, worn, or burred sear. Piston assembly sear notch worn. Sear stuck in trigger housing. Short recoil. Carbon buildup in the gas system.	Notify unit maintenance. Notify unit maintenance. Notify unit maintenance. Clean and lubricate the bolt and slide assembly. Clean the gas regulator, piston, and cylinder.

Table 1-4. Malfunctions.

1-23. STOPPAGES

A stoppage is any interruption in the cycle of functioning caused by faulty action of the weapon or faulty ammunition.

a. Stoppages are classified by their relationship to the cycle of functioning. Table 1-5 shows types of interruptions or stoppages, their probable causes, and the corrective actions.

STOPPAGE	PROBABLE CAUSE	CORRECTIVE ACTION
Failure to feed.	Insufficient lubrication. Defective ammunition link. Obstruction in receiver. Insufficient gas pressure. Unlatched cover. Long or short rounds. Inverted link belt. Damaged, weak, or worn operating parts.	Lubricate as required. Remove and replace ammunition. Remove obstruction. Clean the gas regulator, piston, and cylinder. Latch cover. Align rounds in the link belt. Reinstall link belt with the open end of the link facing down. Notify the unit maintenance.

Table 1-5. Stoppages.

STOPPAGE	PROBABLE CAUSE	CORRECTIVE ACTION
Failure to fire.	Safety on.	Push safety to the left, exposing red ring.
	Link belt improperly loaded.	Remove and reinstall link belt properly.
	Defective ammunition.	Eject round.
	Faulty ammunition.	Replace ammunition.
	Broken or damaged firing pin.	Notify unit maintenance.
	Broken or weak driving spring.	Notify unit maintenance.
Failure to extract.	Dirty chamber or bolt and slide assembly.	Clean chamber or bolt slide assembly. If problem continues, notify unit maintenance.
	Carbon buildup in the gas system.	Clean the gas regulator, cylinder, and piston.
	Damaged extractor or spring.	Notify unit maintenance.
Failure to chamber.	Dirty ammunition.	Clean the ammunition.
	Carbon buildup in the gas cylinder.	Clean the gas cylinder.
	Carbon buildup in the receiver.	Clean the receiver.
	Damaged round.	Remove the round and recock the weapon.
	Damaged or weak driving spring.	Notify unit maintenance.
	Dirty chamber.	Clean the chamber.
	Damaged gas regulator.	Notify unit maintenance.
Failure to eject.	Short recoil.	Clean and lubricate the eject bolt and slide assembly. If problem still exists, notify unit maintenance.
	Damaged ejector or spring.	Notify unit maintenance.
	Carbon buildup in the gas system.	Clean the gas regulator, piston, and cylinder.

Table 1-5. Stoppages (continued).

```
┌─────────────────────────────────────────────────────┐
│                      DANGER                          │
│ IF NOTHING IS EJECTED AND THE WEAPON IS HOT (200 OR  │
│ MORE ROUNDS FIRED IN LESS THAN 2 MINUTES), DO NOT    │
│ OPEN THE COVER. PUSH THE SAFETY TO THE RIGHT (RED    │
│ RING NOT VISIBLE), WHICH PLACES THE WEAPON ON SAFE.  │
│ KEEP THE WEAPON POINTED DOWNRANGE FOR 15 MINUTES,    │
│ THEN CLEAR THE WEAPON. BE CAREFUL CLEARING THE       │
│ WEAPON WHEN THE BARREL IS HOT; A ROUND MAY FIRE      │
│ (COOK OFF) DUE TO THE BARREL'S HEAT INSTEAD OF THE   │
│ FIRING MECHANISM. DURING TRAINING OR ON A FIRING     │
│ RANGE, AFTER THE WEAPON HAS FIRED 200 ROUNDS, THE    │
│ BARREL IS CONSIDERED "HOT."                          │
│    •  DURING COMBAT, WAIT 5 SECONDS (BECAUSE OF THE  │
│       POSSIBILITY OF A HANGFIRE) BEFORE APPLYING     │
│       IMMEDIATE ACTION OR REMEDIAL ACTION.           │
│    •  DURING TRAINING, WAIT 15 MINUTES BEFORE        │
│       CLEARING A HOT WEAPON AND APPLYING IMMEDIATE   │
│       OR REMEDIAL ACTION.                            │
└─────────────────────────────────────────────────────┘
```

b. If a round is in the chamber (this means any part of the round, ranging from the tip of the bullet to the rim) when applying immediate or remedial action on a cold or hot gun. The gunner removes the ammunition from the feed tray only, then closes the cover and attempts to fire. If the weapon fires, he reloads and continues firing. If it does not fire, he clears the weapon (removes the round using a clearing rod, with the cover closed). He does not use anything other than a cleaning rod. Then, he inspects weapon and ammunition.

1-24. IMMEDIATE ACTION
Immediate action is action taken to *reduce a stoppage without looking for the cause.* Immediate action should be taken in the event of a misfire or a cook off. A misfire is the failure of a chambered round to fire. Such failure can be due to an ammunition defect or faulty firing mechanism. A cook off is the firing of a round due to the heat of a hot barrel and not to the firing mechanism. Cook offs can be avoided by applying immediate action within 10 seconds of a failure to fire. The gunner keeps the M249 on his shoulder while performing immediate action procedures. If the M249 stops firing, he takes the following immediate actions. An effective memory aid is POPP, which stands for Pull, Observe, Push, and Press:

a. Pull and lock the cocking handle to the rear while observing the ejection port to see if a cartridge case, belt link, or round is ejected. Ensure that the bolt remains to the rear to prevent double feeding if a round or cartridge case is not ejected.

b. If a cartridge case, belt link, or round is ejected, push the cocking handle to its forward position, take aim on the target, and press the trigger. If the weapon does not fire, take remedial action. If a cartridge case, belt link, or round is not ejected, take remedial action.

1-25. REMEDIAL ACTION

Remedial action is any action taken to determine the cause of a stoppage and to restore the weapon to an operational condition. This action is taken only after immediate action does not remedy the problem.

a. **Cold Weapon Procedures.** When a stoppage occurs with a cold weapon, and if immediate action has failed, use the following procedures:

(1) While the weapon is on your shoulder, grasp the cocking handle with the right hand, palm up; pull the cocking handle to the rear, locking the bolt. While holding the resistance on the cocking handle, move the safety to SAFE and return the cocking handle.

(2) Place the weapon on the ground or away from your face. Open the feed cover and perform the five-point safety check. Reload and continue to fire.

(3) If the weapon does not fire, clear the weapon and inspect it and the ammunition.

b. **Hot Weapon Procedures.** If the stoppage occurs with a hot weapon (200 or more rounds in less than 2 minutes, or as noted previously for training), move the safety to SAFE, wait 5 seconds (during training, let the weapon cool for 15 minutes), and use the same procedures as outlined for cold weapon procedures.

c. **Jammed Cocking Handle.** If a stoppage occurs, and if the cocking handle cannot be pulled to the rear by hand (the bolt may be fully forward and locked or only partially forward), the gunner takes the following steps:

(1) Tries once again to pull the cocking handle *by hand*.

CAUTION

Do not try to force the cocking handle to the rear with your foot or a heavy object. This could damage the weapon.

---

(2) If the weapon is hot enough to cause a cook off, moves all Soldiers a safe distance from the weapon and keeps them away for 15 minutes.

(3) After the gun has cooled, opens the cover and disassembles the gun. Ensures rearward pressure is kept on the cocking handle until the buffer is removed. (The assistant gunner helps the gunner do this.)

(4) Removes the round or fired cartridge. Uses cleaning rod or ruptured cartridge extractor if necessary.

(a) In a training situation, after completing the remedial action procedures does not fire the gun until an ordnance specialist has conducted an inspection.

(b) In a combat situation, after the stoppage has been corrected, the gunner changes the barrel and tries to fire. If the weapon fails to function properly, he sends it to the unit armorer.

1-26. DESTRUCTION PROCEDURES

Destruction of any military weapon is only authorized as a last resort to prevent enemy capture or use. This paragraph discusses the field-expedient means of this destruction; it does not replace published policies. In combat situations, the commander has the authority to destroy weapons, but he must report this destruction through channels.

a. Disassemble the weapon as completely as time permits. Use the barrel to destroy the bolt, operating rod group, bipod, sights (rear and front), and receiver.

b. Bury the disassembled weapon or dump the parts into a stream, a sump, or a latrine.

c. Burn the weapon by placing an incendiary grenade on the receiver group over the bolt (with the cover feed mechanism assembly resting on the grenade) and detonating the grenade.

CHAPTER 2
M60 MACHINE GUN

The 7.62-mm M60 machine gun supports the rifleman in offense and defense. It provides the heavy volume of close and continuous fire the rifleman needs to accomplish his mission. The M60 is used to engage targets beyond the range of individual weapons, with controlled and accurate fire. The long-range, close defensive, and final protective fires delivered by the M60 form an integral part of a unit's defensive fires. This chapter describes the weapon and the types of ammunition it uses in detail and provides a table of general data.

Section I. DESCRIPTION AND COMPONENTS

This section describes the M60 machine gun and its components and purposes, ammunition, and blank firing adapters, and how to install them. The primary use of the M60 is to support the rifleman in both offense and defense. It provides the heavy volume of close and continuous fire he needs to accomplish the mission. It can engage targets beyond the capability of individual weapons with controlled, accurate bursts.

2-1. DESCRIPTION

The M60 is a gas-operated, air-cooled, belt-fed, automatic machine gun that fires from the open-bolt position (Figure 2-1). It has a maximum rate of fire of 550 rounds per minute. Ammunition is fed into the weapon from a 100-round bandoleer containing a disintegrating metallic split-link belt. It can be fired from the shoulder, hip, or underarm position; from the bipod-steadied position; or from the tripod-mounted position. (See Table 2-1, on page 2-2, for general data.)

```
┌────────────────────────────────────────────────────────┐
│                        DANGER                           │
│  DO NOT INTERCHANGE THE BARREL ASSEMBLY OR THE          │
│  BOLT ASSEMBLY FROM ONE WEAPON TO ANOTHER. IF           │
│  YOU DO SO, IT MAY RESULT IN DEATH OR INJURY.           │
└────────────────────────────────────────────────────────┘
```

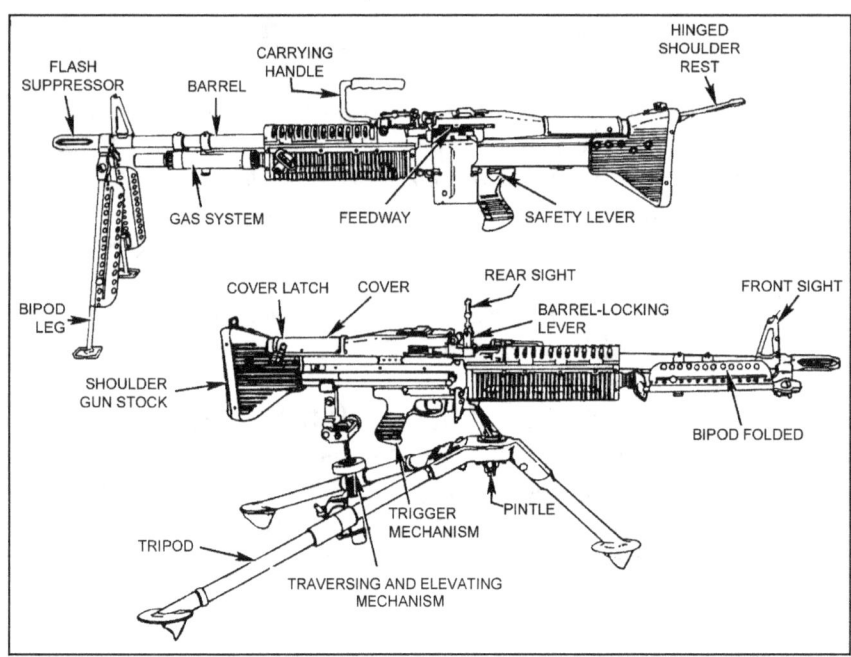

Figure 2-1. M60 machine gun, bipod- and tripod-mounted.

Ammunition .... 7.62-mm ball, tracer, armor-piercing, blank, dummy. Armor-piercing is not authorized for training.

Tracer burnout .... 900 meters

Length of the M60 .... 43.5 inches

Weight of the M60 .... 23 pounds

Weight of tripod mount M122
   with traversing and elevating
   mechanism and pintle .... 16 pounds

Maximum range .... 3,725 meters

Maximum effective range .... 1,100 meters with tripod and T&E

Area:
   Tripod .... 1,100 meters
   Bipod .... 800 meters

Point:
   Tripod .... 800 meters
   Bipod .... 600 meters

Maximum extent of grazing
   fire obtainable over level or
   uniformly sloping terrain .... 600 meters

Height of the M60 on
tripod mount M122 .... 16.5 inches

Table 2-1. General data.

Rates of fire:
    Sustained .... 100 rounds per minute.
                                        6- to 9-round bursts.
                                        4 to 5 seconds between bursts.
                                        Barrel changed every 10 minutes.
    Rapid .... 200 rounds per minute.
                                          10- to 13-round bursts.
                                          2 to 3 seconds between bursts.
                                          Barrel changed every 2 minutes.
    Cyclic .... 550 rounds per minute.
                                          Fire continuous burst.
                                          Barrel changed every minute.
Basic load of ammunition
    for a three-man crew .... 600 to 900 rounds.
Elevation, tripod controlled .... +200 mils
Elevation, tripod free .... +445 mils
Depression, tripod controlled........ -200 mils
Depression, tripod free................. -445 mils
Traverse, controlled by
    traversing and elevating
    mechanism............................... 100 mils
Normal sector of fire
    (with tripod) .... 875 mils

Table 2-1. General data (continued).

2-2. COMPONENTS

The major components of the M60 and their purposes are shown in Table 2-2 and Figures 2-2 and 2-3. The sights and safety lever are discussed in paragraphs a and b and shown in Figures 2-4 and 2-5.

COMPONENTS	PURPOSES
(1) Stock assembly	Provides a shoulder support for aiming and firing the M60 machine gun. The stock assembly has a shoulder rest.
(2) Buffer assembly	Absorbs recoil from the bolt and operating rod assembly at the end of the recoil movement.
(3) Bolt assembly	Feeds, chambers, fires, and extracts, using the propellant gases and recoil spring for power. It houses the firing pin.
(4) Operating rod assembly	Transfers power from propelling gases to the bolt and slide assemblies.

Table 2-2. Components and purposes.

COMPONENTS	PURPOSES
(5) Cover, hanger, and feed assembly	Feeds linked-belt ammunition. Holds the cartridges in position for stripping, feeding, and chambering.
(6) Barrel assembly	Houses cartridges for firing, directs projectiles, supports fixed front sight, and provides passageway for operating gases. The bipod supports the M60 in the prone position. The telescopic legs can be adjusted to three different lengths.
(7) Trigger assembly	Controls the firing of the weapon.
(8) Forearm assembly	Provides thermal insulation to protect the gunner's hands from heat. Has a slotted top to allow air to circulate around the barrel for cooling purposes.
(9) Receiver assembly	Supports all assembly major components and houses the action of the weapon.
(10) Rear sight assembly	Adjustable for both windage and elevation allowing the gunner to make changes rapidly.
(11) Cocking handle assembly	Pulls the moving parts rearward. Moves in a guide rail fixed to the right side of the receiver.
(12) Tripod (M122) assembly	Together with the tripod, T&E mechanism, and pintle, provides a stable mount and permits a higher degree of accuracy and control.

Table 2-2. Components and purposes (continued).

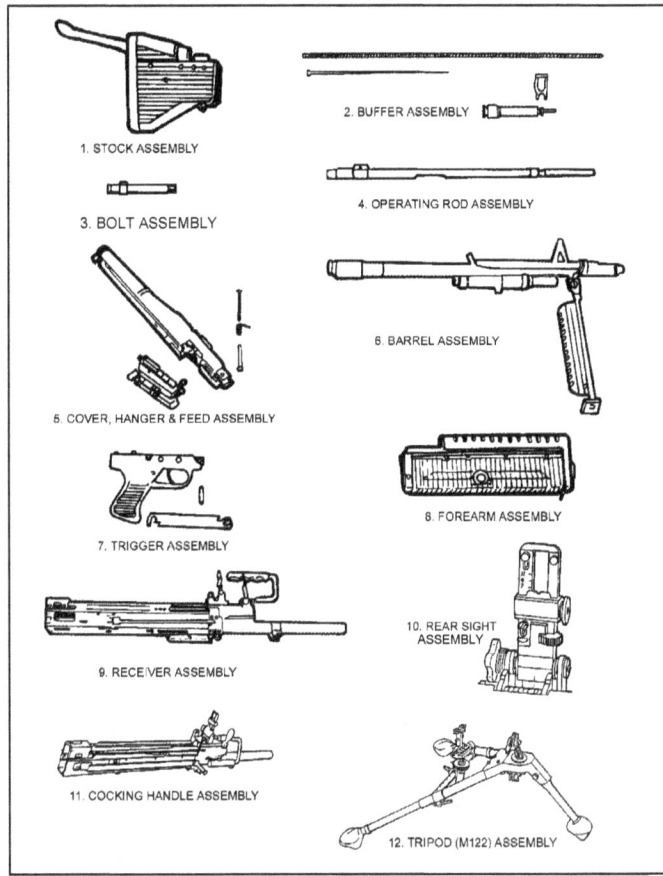

Figure 2-2. M60 components and tripod.

a. **Sights.** The front sight is attached to the barrel. The rear sight is mounted on a spring-type dovetail base, and it can be folded down when the gun is moved (See Figure 2-1).

b. **Safety Lever.** The safety lever is on the left side of the trigger group (Figure 2-1). It has an "S" and an "F" position. On the "S" position, the bolt cannot be pulled to the rear or released to go forward.

WARNING
Manually return the cocking handle to its forward position each time the bolt is pulled to the rear to prevent damage to the cocking and injury to the gunner.

2-3. AMMUNITION

The M60 machine gun uses several different types of 7.62-mm standard military ammunition. The specific type ammunition and its characteristics are shown in Figure 2-3. Soldiers must use only authorized ammunition that is manufactured to US and NATO specifications. The ammunition is issued in a disintegrating, metallic, split-linked belt (Figure 2-4).

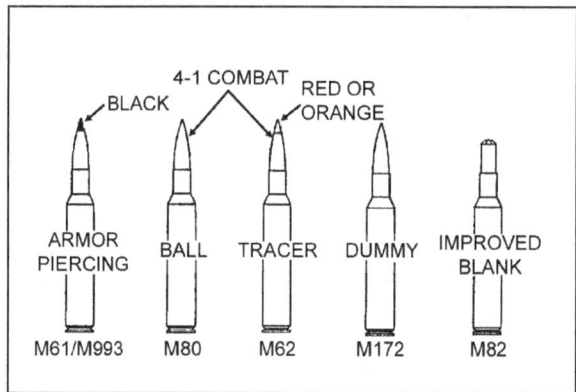

Figure 2-3. 7.62-mm cartridges for the M60 machine gun.

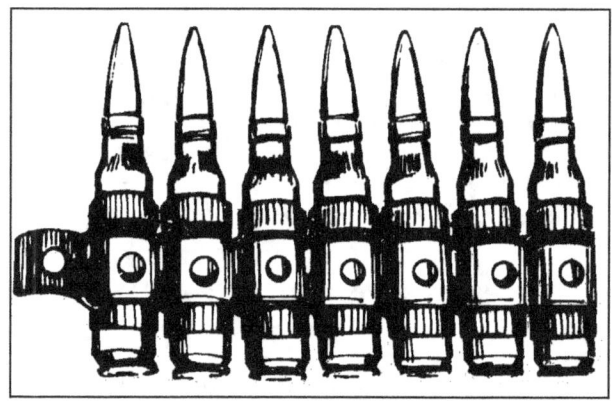

Figure 2-4. 7.62-mm cartridges in metallic belt.

a. **Classification.** The M60 machine gun ammunition is classified as follows:

(1) *Cartridge, 7.62-mm Ball M80.* This cartridge is used against light materials and personnel, and for range training.

(2) *Cartridge, 7.62-mm Armor-Piercing M61.* This cartridge is used against lightly armored targets.

(3) *Cartridge, 7.62-mm Tracer M62.* This cartridge is used for observation of fire, incendiary effects, signaling, and for training. When tracer rounds are fired, they are mixed with ball ammunition for a mix of four ball rounds to one tracer round.

(4) *Cartridge, 7.62-mm Dummy M63.* This cartridge is used during mechanical training.

(5) *Cartridge, 7.62-mm Blank M82.* This cartridge is used during training when simulated live fire is desired. A blank firing attachment is used to fire this ammunition.

b. **Storage**. The ammunition is stored under cover. If ammunition is in the open, it must be kept at least 6 inches above the ground and covered with a double thickness of tarpaulin. The cover must be placed so that it protects the ammunition yet allows ventilation. Trenches are dug to divert water from flowing under the ammunition.

c. **Care, Handling, and Preservation.** Ammunition should not be removed from the airtight containers until ready for use. Ammunition removed from the airtight containers, especially in damp climates, may corrode.

(1) Ammunition must be protected from mud, dirt, and moisture. If ammunition gets wet or dirty, it must be wiped off before use. Lightly corroded cartridges are wiped off as soon as the corrosion is discovered. Heavily corroded, dented, or loose projectiles should not be fired.

(2) Ammunition must be protected from the direct rays of the sun. Excessive pressure from the heat may cause premature detonation.

(3) Oil should never be used on ammunition. Oil collects dust and other abrasives that may possibly damage the operating parts of the weapon.

d. **Packaging.** The ammunition box contains two cartons. Each carton has a bandoleer for carrying purposes. Each carton contains 100 rounds and weighs about 7 pounds. Ammunition in the bandoleers may be linked together, attached to the hanger assembly, and fired from the container; or, the bandoleers may be removed for firing.

2-4. BLANK FIRING ATTACHMENTS, M13 AND M13A1

The M13 BFA is used on the M60 machine gun when blank cartridges are fired to simulate live firing during training where live firing is not practical. An M13A1 BFA is also available for the M60 machine gun. The difference between the M13 and the M13A1 is that, on the M13A1, the restrictor tube can be tightened (using a flat tip screwdriver) for a more secure fit, to prevent gas leakage.

DANGER
DO NOT FIRE BLANK AMMUNITION AT ANY PERSON WITHIN 20 FEET. FRAGMENTS OF A CLOSURE WAD OR PARTICLES OF UNBURNED PROPELLANT CAN CAUSE DEATH OR INJURY.

---

a. **Installation of the M13**. The BFA must be adjusted to fit the machine gun barrel. The orifice tube fits inside the flash suppressor, flush against the muzzle and flush with the forward end of the flash suppressor. The BFA is clamped tightly to the front sight (Figure 2-5, page 2-8). When properly adjusted, it will fit snugly against the muzzle, thus preventing the escape of gas during firing. When the BFA is manufactured, the distance the orifice tube screws into the restrictor bushing is fixed and fitted by *staking* the restrictor bushing. This fixed distance, set in the restrictor bushing, does not provide the correct adjustment for every machine gun, because the distance from the muzzle to the forward end of the flash suppressor varies from weapon to weapon. In some instances, the *stake* mark must be broken, the orifice tube adjusted to fit the barrel, and "restaked."

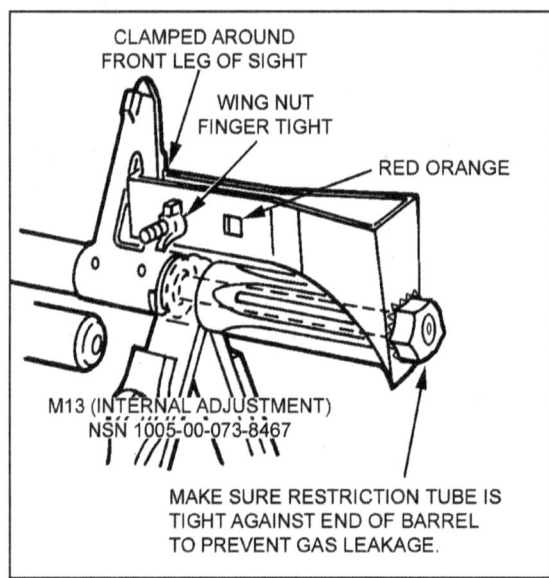

Figure 2-5. M13 blank firing attachment.

b. **Installation of the M13A1.** The M13A1 is installed by (Figure 2-6) loosening the lock nut, turning the restrictor tube out a few turns, and loosening the wing nut a few turns. The restrictor tube is inserted in the flash suppressor as far as possible and is clamped around the front sight. The wing nut is tightened finger tight. The restrictor tube is screwed in until it seats tightly against the muzzle end of the barrel to prevent gas leakage, and then the lock nut is tightened.

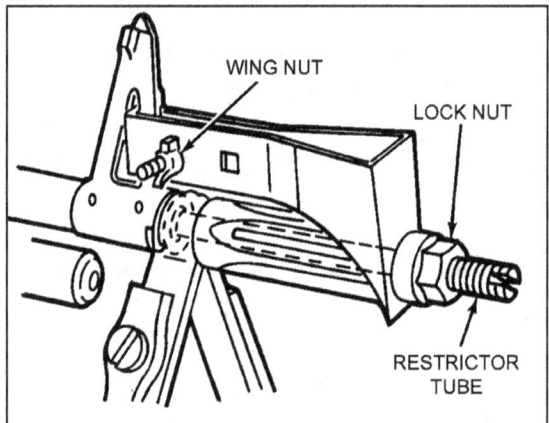

Figure 2-6. M13A1 blank firing attachment.

c. **Care of the M60 While Using the BFA.** A buildup of carbon inside the weapon causes friction between the moving parts. Carbon deposits build rapidly when blanks are fired. Stoppages occur when these deposits become excessive. Therefore, the weapon must be kept clean, especially the gas system and chamber, during blank firing. To obtain the best performance when using the BFA, the gunner performs the following:

(1) Inspects the weapon before firing for damaged parts, excessive wear, cleanliness, and proper lubrication.

(2) Test fires the weapon using ball ammunition when feasible before attaching the BFA.

(3) Adjusts the BFA to fit the weapon.

(4) Applies immediate action when stoppages occur.

(5) Cleans the weapon including barrel assembly, gas cylinder, gas piston, gas port, chamber bore, and BFA.

(6) Cleans and lubricates the entire weapon after 1,000 rounds.

DANGER
NEVER LOAD ANY AMMUNITION OTHER THAN BLANKS WHEN THE BFA IS IN PLACE. NEVER FIRE THE BFA-FITTED MACHINE GUN AT PERSONNEL WHO ARE WITHIN 20 FEET OF THE WEAPON. IT COULD CAUSE DEATH OR INJURY.

Section II. MAINTENANCE

Proper maintenance contributes to weapon effectiveness as well as unit readiness. Maintenance aspects of the M60 include inspection; cleaning and lubrication; and maintenance before, during, and after firing, and during NBC conditions. Associated tasks essential to maintenance (clearing, general assembly and disassembly, and function checks) are discussed in detail.

2-5. CLEARING PROCEDURES

The first step in maintenance is to clear the weapon. This applies in all situations, not just after firing. The gunner must always assume the M60 is loaded. To clear the M60, the gunner performs the following procedures. (Subparagraph letters are keyed to the lettered callouts in Figure 2-7, page 2-10.)

a. Moves the safety lever to the "F" position.

b. With his right hand, palm up, pulls the cocking handle in the rear. Moves the safety lever to the "S" position. Returns and locks the cocking handle in the forward position.

c. Raises the cover and conducts the *four-point safety check* for brass, links, or ammunition.

(1) Checks the feed pawl assembly under the cover.

(2) Checks the feed tray.

(3) Lifts the feed tray and hanger assembly and inspects the chamber.

(4) Checks the space between the face of the bolt and the chamber.

d. Closes the cover and moves the safety lever to the "F" position. Pulls the cocking handle to the rear position. Pulls the trigger and at the same time eases the bolt forward by manually riding the cocking handle forward.

e. Places the safety lever on "S" and raises the cover. (If not disassembling the gun, keep the cover down.)

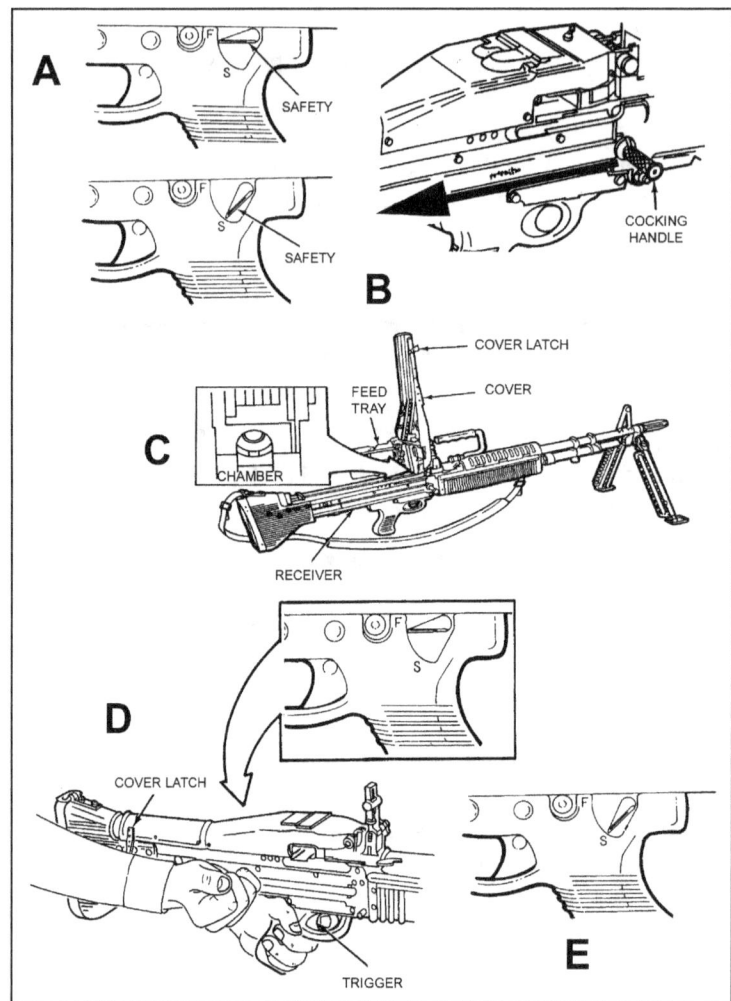

Figure 2-7. Clearing procedures.

> **CAUTION**
> Manually return the cocking handle to the forward and locked position each time the bolt is manually pulled to the rear, or it could cause damage to the weapon.

2-6. GENERAL DISASSEMBLY

The gunner performs general disassembly, which is removing and replacing the eight major groups (Figure 2-8). (The unit armorer performs the detailed disassembly. Disassembly beyond this point is prohibited except by ordnance personnel.) During general disassembly, the gunner clears the weapon and places each part on a clean flat surface such as a table or mat. This aids in assembly in reverse order and avoids the loss of parts.

DANGER
BE SURE THE BOLT IS IN THE FORWARD POSITION BEFORE DISASSEMBLY. THE SPRING GUIDE CAN CAUSE DEATH OR INJURY IF THE OPERATING ROD SPRING IS RETRACTED WITH THE BOLT PULLED TO THE REAR.

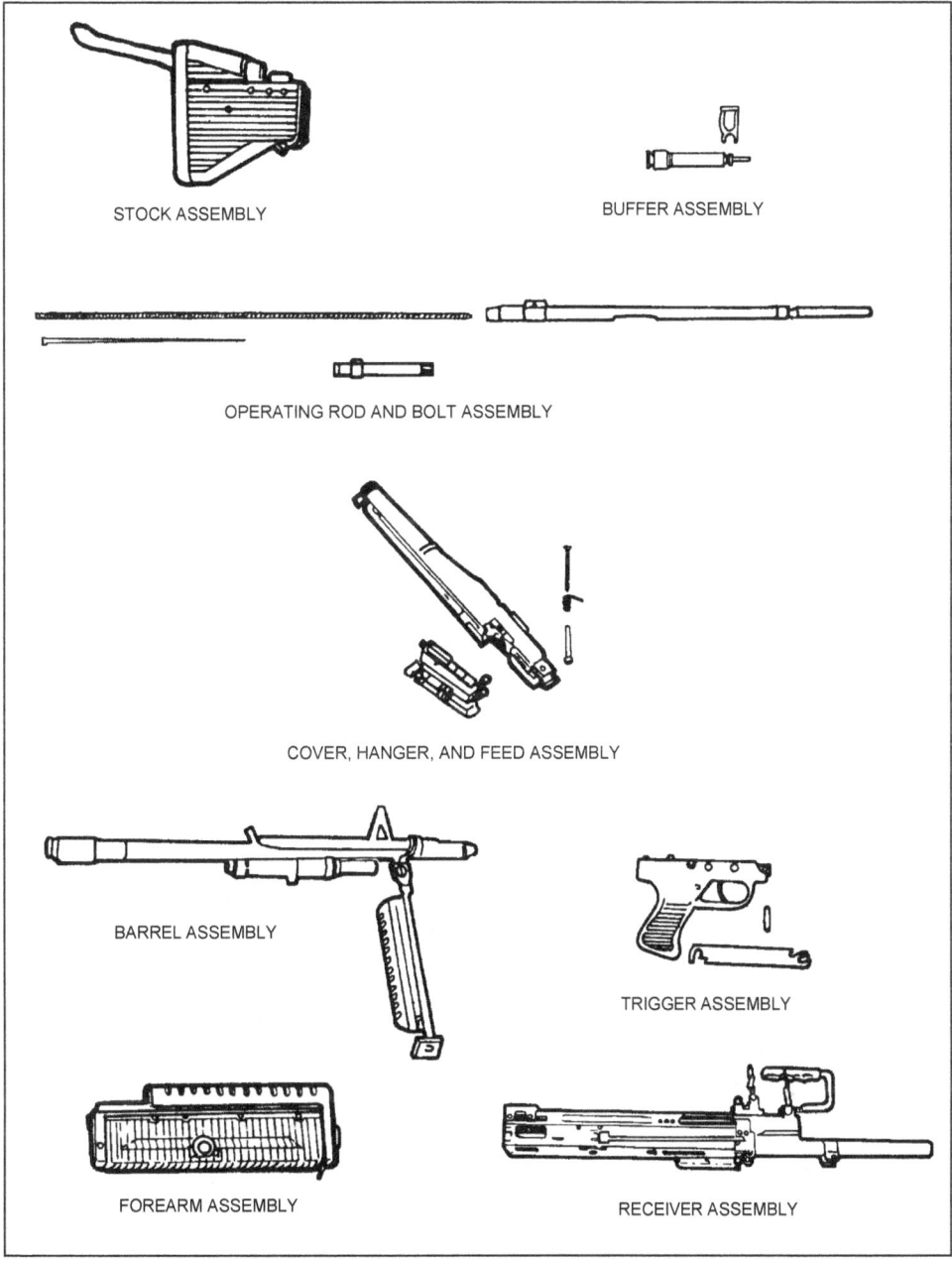

STOCK ASSEMBLY

BUFFER ASSEMBLY

OPERATING ROD AND BOLT ASSEMBLY

COVER, HANGER, AND FEED ASSEMBLY

BARREL ASSEMBLY

TRIGGER ASSEMBLY

FOREARM ASSEMBLY

RECEIVER ASSEMBLY

Figure 2-8. Eight major assemblies.

a. **Removing the Stock Assembly**. First, the gunner makes sure the bolt is in the forward position. To remove the stock, he raises the shoulder rest, inserts a cleaning rod into the hole to release the latch. He pulls the shoulder stock from the receiver, turns the latch lever, and opens the cover (Figure 2-9).

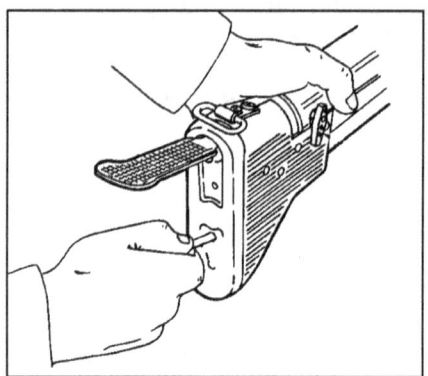

Figure 2-9. Removal of the stock.

b. **Removing the Buffer, Operating Rod, and Bolt Assemblies.**

(1) To remove the buffer assembly, the gunner applies slight palm pressure to the rear of the hydraulic buffer assembly. He reaches inside the receiver and pulls up and out on the yoke to remove it from the receiver. He reaches in the back of the receiver and pulls the guide rod and drive spring out the rear of the receiver. (Figure 2-10).

```
                    WARNING
The  bolt  assembly  is  under  spring
tension;  it  can  twist  and  injure  your
hand.
```

(2) The gunner removes the operating rod assembly and bolt assembly as a unit. He reaches in the top of the receiver, places a finger on the face of the bolt, and pushes rearward until the bolt and operating rod assemblies extend past the rear of the receiver. Then, he pulls them out as a unit. To separate the bolt from the operating rod, he places the operating rod in his left hand and, with his right hand, pulls the bolt down and away.

```
                    CAUTION
Do not use the tip of the driving spring guide
assembly as a tool because it could damage
the weapon.
```

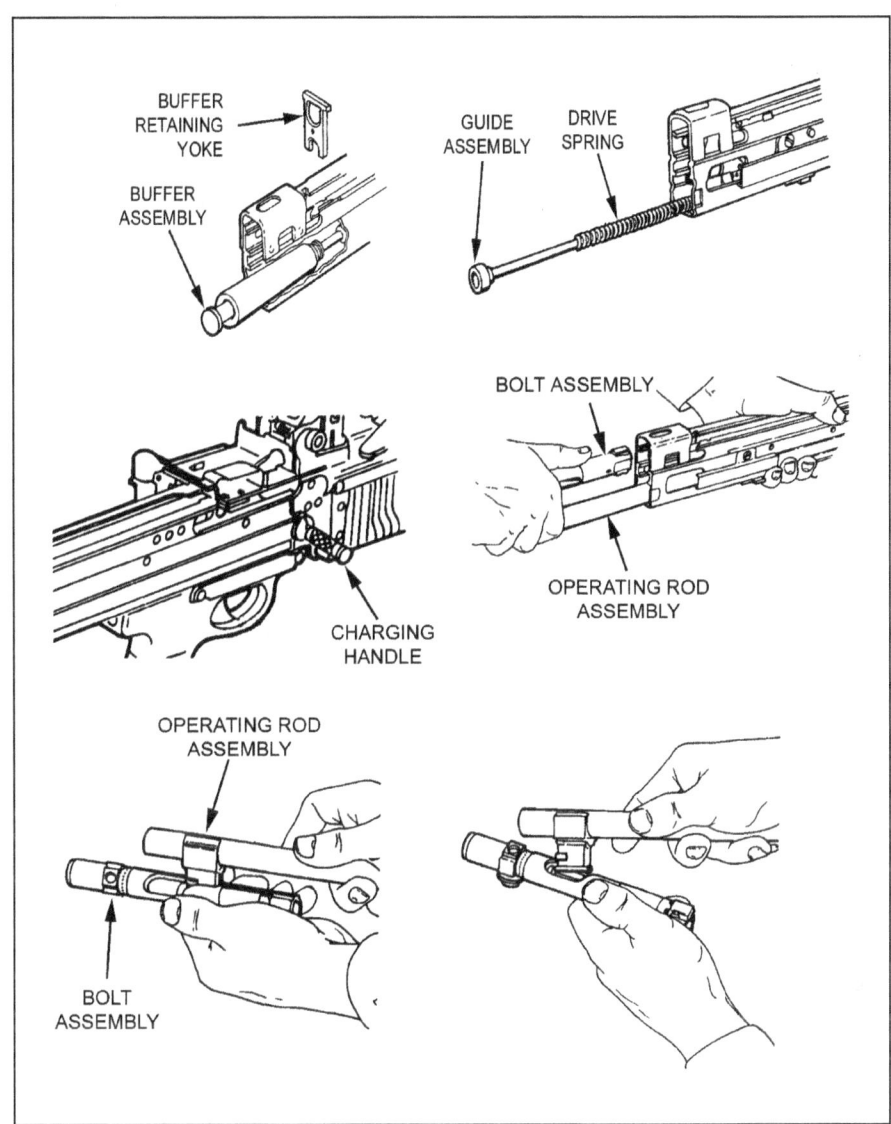

Figure 2-10. Removal of the buffer, operating rod, and bolt assemblies.

c. **Removing the Cover, Hanger and Cartridge Feed Tray Assemblies**. The gunner uses a cleaning rod to unlatch the hook of the hinge pin latch. He removes the hinge pin latch and cover hinge pin. He removes the cover assembly, torsion spring, and hanger and cartridge feed tray assembly (Figure 2-11).

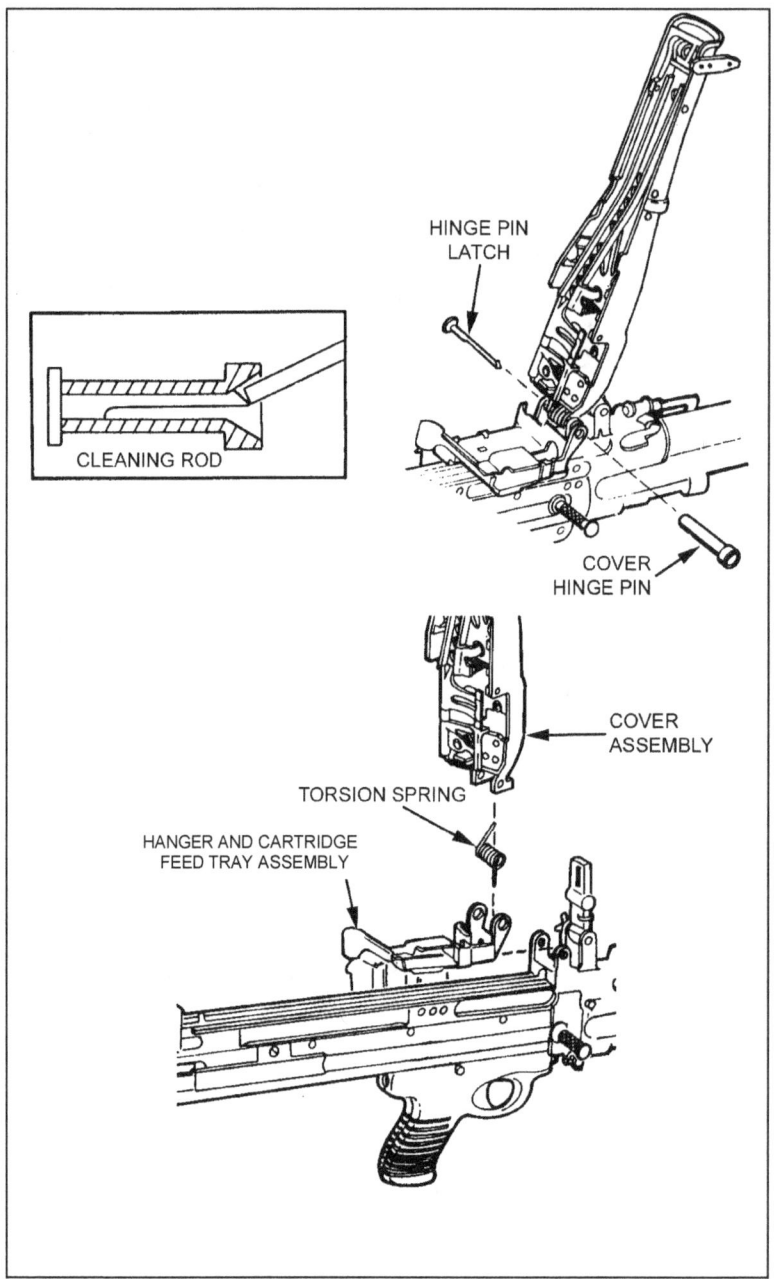

Figure 2-11. Removal of the cover, hanger and cartridge feed tray assemblies.

d. **Removing the Barrel Assembly**. The gunner pushes in the spring detent, raises the barrel lock, and removes the barrel assembly (Figure 2-12).

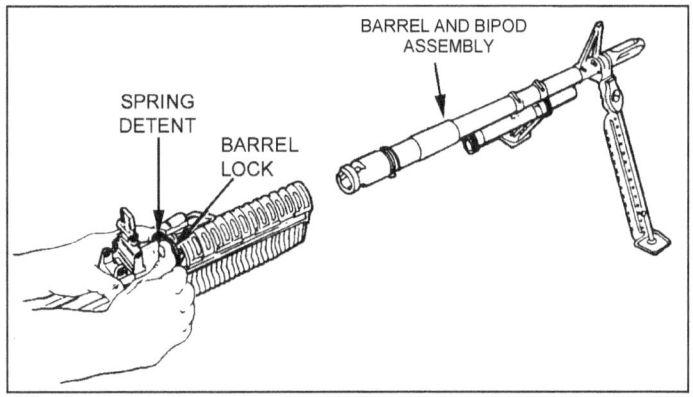

Figure 2-12. Removal of the barrel assembly.

e. **Removing the Trigger Mechanism Grip Assembly**. The gunner pushes in and removes the flat leaf spring. He pushes out the *front pin* and slides the trigger mechanism grip assembly slightly forward, then pulls it out to remove it (Figure 2-13).

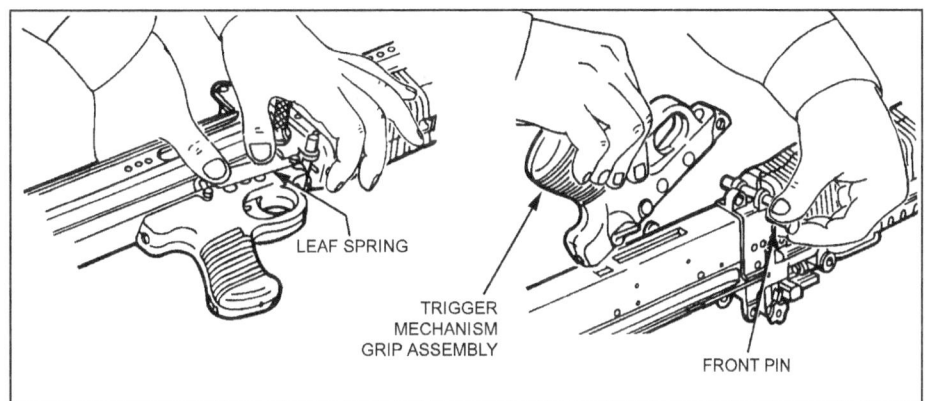

Figure 2-13. Removal of the trigger mechanism grip assembly.

f. **Removing the Forearm Assembly**. The gunner inserts a cleaning rod or the reamer portion of a combination wrench through the round opening in the forearm assembly, and then he pushes down on the spring. He lifts and gently slides the forearm assembly from the receiver (Figure 2-14, page 2-16).

> **CAUTION**
> Be careful not to damage the internal ribs of the forearm assembly. It can cause damage to the weapon.

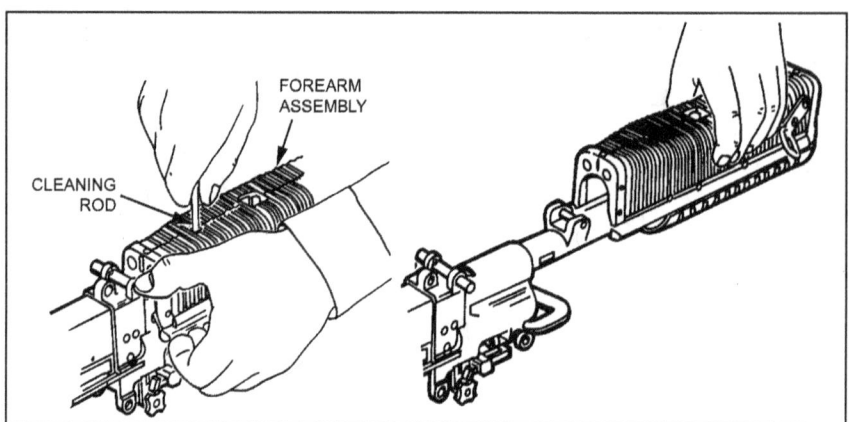

Figure 2-14. Removal of the forearm assembly.

g. **Removing the Receiver Assembly**. Once the forearm assembly is removed, the part remaining is the receiver assembly, and general disassembly is complete.

2-7. INSPECTION

Inspection begins with the weapon disassembled in its major groups. Shiny surfaces do not mean the parts are unserviceable. The gunner inspects each area of the weapon and related equipment for the conditions indicated. Any broken or missing parts should be repaired or replaced IAW TM 9-1005-224-10. The gunner should perform Preventive maintenance checks and services (PMCS) every 90 days. If the weapon has not been used in 90 days, the PMCS in the operator's manual should be performed regardless. If he sees rust on a weapon, he should perform PMCS immediately.

a. **Stock Assembly**. The stock assembly should not be cracked and must fit securely on the receiver assembly. The shoulder rest and latch lever should function correctly.

b. **Buffer Assembly**. The buffer yoke and recess should not be burred, cracked, or bent. The buffer plunger must fit easily into the recess in the spring guide.

c. **Operating Rod Assembly**. The operating rod, yoke, sear notch, and pins should not have burrs, cracks, or chips. The roller should operate freely. The driving spring should have tension and should not have kinks, breaks, or wear. The guide assembly stop should be tight. If it is loose, the gunner notifies unit maintenance.

d. **Bolt Assembly**. The bolt assembly is checked for burrs or cracks, especially in the locking lug area.

(1) The roller should operate freely and not be cracked.

(2) The spring should not be kinked.

(3) The threads on the bolt plug assembly and in the breech bolt should not be damaged.

e. **Cover Assembly**. The cover assembly is checked for burrs, cracks, looseness, or missing parts. The spring action of the front and rear cartridge guides, feed pawls (beneath the cartridge guides), and feed cam assembly are checked. The feed cam assembly should be secure and operate freely.

f. **Hanger and Cartridge Feed Tray Assembly**. The hanger and cartridge feed tray assembly is checked for burrs, cracks, and missing or loose parts. The feed tray is checked to make sure it fits on the receiver and that the cartridge-retaining pawl works properly. The hanger is checked for obstructions.

g. **Barrel Assembly**. The barrel assembly is checked for burrs, cracks, and wear, especially in the barrel socket area. The sight and flash suppressor are checked to make sure they are tight. The bipod should work properly, the legs should be straight, and connections should be tight. The bipod plungers should operate smoothly.

h. **Trigger Mechanism Grip Assembly**. The sear is checked for chips, cracks, or signs of wear. The sear plunger and spring are checked for wear.

i. **Forearm Assembly**. The forearm assembly is checked for damage.

j. **Receiver Assembly**. The receiver rails are checked for burrs and wear. The cocking handle should move freely.

k. **M122 Mount**. The T&E mechanism should not bind. The numbers on the scales and dials must be legible.

(1) Distinct clicks must be heard when the handwheels are turned. Index lines should be calibrated with the indicator pointer.

(2) The pintle should fit snugly in the pintle bushing, and the pintle lock should hold the pintle securely.

(3) The sleeve latch should function properly, and the traversing bar should be tight when the tripod legs are extended and latched.

l. **Carrying Case**. Maintenance tools and equipment should be complete and serviceable. The case should be serviceable. Frequent washing of the case should be avoided. Such washing may destroy the waterproofing and shrink the case.

2-8. CLEANING, LUBRICATION, AND PREVENTIVE MAINTENANCE

The M60 machine gun should be cleaned immediately after firing. The gunner disassembles the M60 into its major groups for cleaning. All metal components and surfaces that have been exposed to powder fouling should be cleaned using CLP on a bore-cleaning patch. The CLP is used on the bristles of the receiver brush to clean the receiver. After the M60 is cleaned and wiped dry, a thin coat of CLP is rubbed on with a cloth. This lubricates and preserves the exposed metal parts during all normal temperature ranges.

```
                          CAUTION
Do not get CLP in the gas cylinder when cleaning the
barrel. Turn the barrel upside down so that the gas
cylinder is above the barrel during cleaning.
```

a. The gas cylinder components are removed and cleaned only when inspection shows that the piston will not move within the cylinder when the barrel is tilted end-for-end. Unit maintenance personnel must supervise disassembly of the gas system. The receiver brush and swab-holding section of the cleaning rod may be used to clean the interior of the gas cylinder. When CLP is used, the gas cylinder and gas piston must be wiped dry before assembly. After assembly, the piston is checked for free movement. The unit armorer replaces safety wire. The gunner cleans the rest of the weapon as follows:

(1) Cleans the bore using CLP and a bore brush attached to a cleaning rod. Does not reverse the direction of the bore brush while in the bore.

(a) Runs the brush through the bore several times until most of the powder fouling and other foreign matter have been removed.

(b) Swabs the bore several times using a cleaning rod and a swab wet with CLP.

(c) Swabs the bore several times using a cleaning rod and dry swab.

(2) Cleans the chamber using CLP and a chamber brush attached to a cleaning rod.

(a) Runs the brush through the chamber several times until most of the powder fouling and other foreign matter have been removed.

(b) Swabs the chamber several times using a cleaning rod and a swab wet with CLP.

(c) Swabs the chamber several times using a cleaning rod and dry swab.

(3) Cleans the receiver using a receiver brush and CLP.

(a) Brushes the receiver until most of the powder fouling and other foreign matter have been removed.

(b) Swabs the receiver several times using a cleaning rod section and a swab wet with CLP.

(c) Swabs the receiver several times using a cleaning rod section and dry swab.

(4) Wipes all the parts of the weapon except those that are rubber coated, using a rag wet with CLP.

(5) Dries completely all parts cleaned with CLP.

(6) Lubricates the following moving parts with CLP as instructed:

(a) Barrel Assembly. Lubricates on the camming surfaces of the bolt-locking lugs.

(b) Operating Rod Assembly. Lubricates on the rollers and those surfaces immediately below the yoke that ride within the receiver rails.

(c) Cover assembly. Lubricates inside the feed cam assembly.

(d) Bolt assembly. Lubricates on the bolt locking lugs and cam actuator roller, and in the camming recess (for the operating rod).

b. After lubricating, the components are cycled by hand to spread the CLP. Weapons fired infrequently or stored for prolonged periods should have a light film of CLP applied to the interior of the gas cylinder and the gas piston immediately after cleaning or inspection. Preventive maintenance is performed every 90 days, unless inspection reveals more frequent servicing is necessary. The use of the lubricant does not eliminate the requirement for cleaning and inspecting to ensure that corrosion has not formed. Before the weapon is used, the gas system and components must be clean and free of oil and lubricants.

c. All exposed surfaces of the M122 tripod, pintle assembly, and T&E mechanism are wiped down with a clean rag. For stubborn areas with hard-to-remove dirt, a steel brush or bore brush is used to loosen the particles. Then a clean rag is used to wipe them down and CLP is used to lubricate them.

d. The following procedures apply to cleaning and lubricating the M60 during unusual conditions:

(1) Below 0 degrees Fahrenheit—use lubricating oil, arctic weather (LAW). Oil lightly to avoid freeze-up.

(2) Extreme heat—use a light coat of CLP.

(3) Damp or salty air—use CLP. Clean and apply frequently.

(4) Sandy or dusty areas—use CLP. Clean and apply frequently. Wipe with a rag after each application to remove excess.

2-9. GENERAL ASSEMBLY

After cleaning, lubricating, and inspecting the weapon, the gunner reassembles it in the reverse order of disassembly.

```
                    CAUTION
Be careful not to damage the internal ribs when
installing the forearm assembly.
```

a. **Replacing Receiver Assembly and Forearm Assembly.** To replace the forearm assembly, the gunner slides it onto the receiver. He presses in on the bottom of forearm assembly to latch. He shakes the forearm assembly up and down to ensure it is seated.

b. **Replacing the Trigger Mechanism Grip Assembly.** To replace the trigger mechanism grip assembly, the gunner positions it on the bottom of the receiver, aligns it with the T-slot, and installs the front pin from the left side. He slides the slotted end of the flat leaf spring on the front pin. (The hooked end of the flat leaf spring should bend outward.) He pushes down and slides the hooked end of the flat leaf spring onto the grooved pin (Figure 2-15).

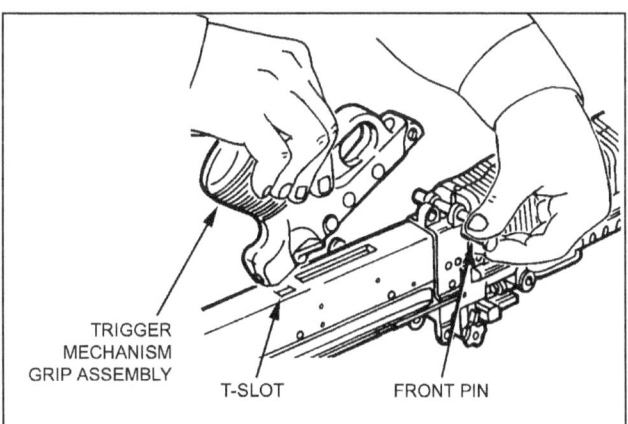

TRIGGER
MECHANISM
GRIP ASSEMBLY

T-SLOT

FRONT PIN

Figure 2-15. Replacing the trigger mechanism grip assembly.

c. **Replacing the Barrel Assembly.** To replace the barrel assembly, the gunner ensures that the barrel lock is up (unlocked) before inserting the barrel in the forearm assembly. He pushes the barrel lock down to lock it. Then, he lifts it up by the bipod and shakes it to ensure it is seated.

d. **Replacing the Cover, Hanger and Cartridge Feed Tray Assembly**. The gunner positions the hanger and cartridge feed tray assembly on the receiver. He installs the torsion spring and cover assembly and makes sure the ends of the torsion spring stick in the holes of the cover and receiver. (The hinge pin is inserted from right to left.) The gunner applies slight pressure to line up the torsion spring and inserts the cover hinge pin. He installs the hinge pin latch through the hinge pin until it locks. He keeps the cover assembly open until the machine gun is assembled.

e. **Replacing the Bolt Assembly, Operating Rod Assembly, and Buffer Assembly**. The gunner places the yoke of the operating rod assembly against the spool of the firing pin in the slot of the bolt assembly (Figure 2-16). Then, he pushes the spool forward. He seats the yoke between the spools of the firing pin and lets the yoke slide back in the bolt assembly.

(1) Slides the operating rod assembly with the bolt assembly into the weapon. Turns the bolt assembly so that the stripping lugs line up with the upper rails. Pushes in until the stripping lugs engage the rails.

(2) Turns the roller straight up and pushes the bolt assembly and operating rod assembly as a unit into the weapon.

(3) Pulls and holds the trigger while pushing the bolt assembly into the receiver until it locks in place.

(4) Installs the drive spring and guide assembly in the rear of the receiver.

(5) Inserts the buffer assembly against the end of the guide assembly and pushes until the groove on the buffer assembly lines up with the slot for buffer retaining yoke. Inserts the buffer retaining yoke.

f. **Replacing the Stock**. The gunner positions the stock on the rear of the receiver and pushes until it snaps in place. He pulls the cocking handle to the rear to lock the bolt assembly to the rear, and then he places the safety on "S." He closes the cover. While holding the charging handle, he pulls the trigger and eases the charging handle forward.

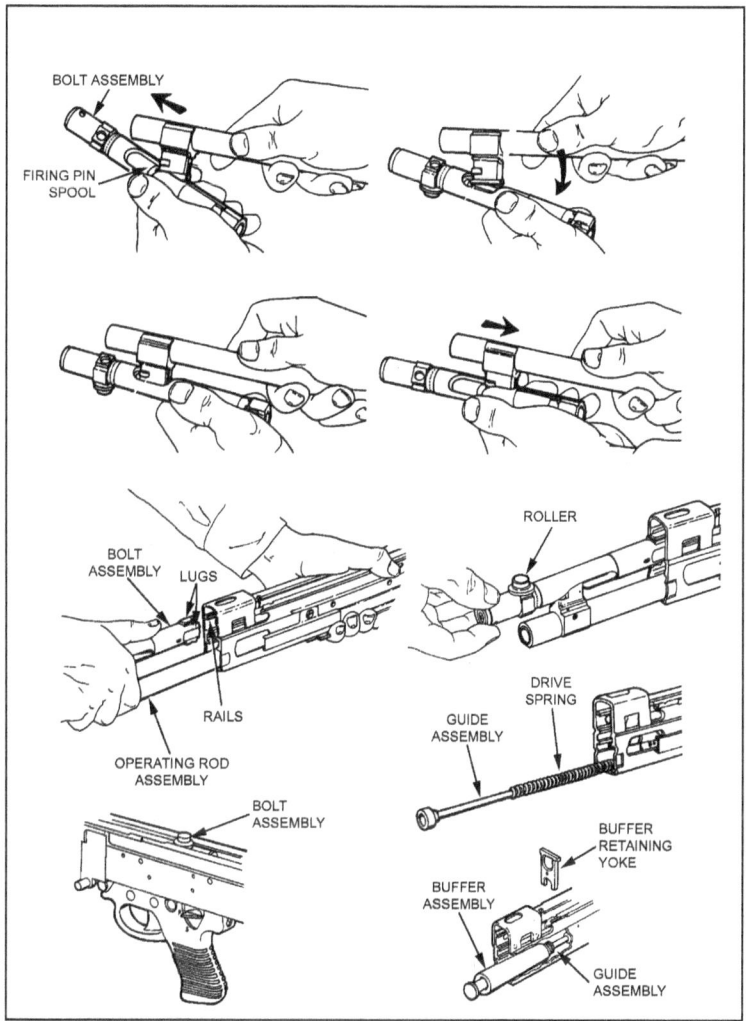

Figure 2-16. Replacing the bolt assembly, operating rod assembly, and buffer assembly.

2-10. FUNCTION CHECK

The gunner must perform a function check to ensure that the M60 is correctly assembled. The procedures, in order, are:

- Open the cover and pull the cocking handle to the rear.
- Place the safety on "S" position.
- Return the cocking handle to the forward position.
- Close the feed tray cover.
- Place the safety on "F" position.
- Grasp the cocking handle with the right hand, pull the trigger with the left hand, and ease the bolt forward.

2-11. MAINTENANCE PROCEDURES

Maintenance of the M60 requires certain actions to be taken before, during, and after firing.

a. **Before firing—**
- Wipe the bore dry.
- Inspect the weapon as outlined in operator's TM.
- Inspect the spare barrel.
- Lubricate the weapon.

b. **During firing—**
- Change the barrels. Barrel changing will prolong the life of both barrels.
- Periodically inspect the weapon to ensure that it is properly lubricated.
- When malfunctions or stoppages occur, follow the procedures in Section IV.

c. **After firing—**
- Clear and clean the weapon immediately.
- Every 90 days during inactivity, clean and lubricate the weapon unless inspection reveals more frequent servicing is necessary (TM 9-1005-224-10).

2-12. MAINTENANCE DURING NUCLEAR, BIOLOGICAL, CHEMICAL CONDITIONS

If the M60 machine gun is contaminated by chemical, biological, or radiological agents, the gunner takes the appropriate action to reduce the exposure and minimize the penetration.

a. **Chemical.** The gunner uses towelettes from the M258A1 kit to wipe off the weapon. If these are not available, he washes the weapon with soap and water.

b. **Biological.** The gunner uses towelettes or soap and water as above.

c. **Radiological.** The gunner wipes the weapon with warm soapy water if it is available. If not, he uses towelettes or rags. (For more details, see FM 3-5.)

Section III. OPERATION AND FUNCTION

This section discusses the operation of the M60 machine gun. This includes loading, firing, unloading, cycle of functioning, adjustment of the sight, using both the bipod and tripod, and use of the M60 on a vehicular mount.

2-13. OPERATION

The M60 machine gun is loaded, fired, unloaded, and cleared from the open-bolt position. The safety lever must be in the "F" position before the bolt can be pulled to the rear. Before use belted ammunition must be linked with the double link at the open end of the bandoleer. It must be free of dirt and corrosion.

2-14. LOADING

The gunner makes sure the weapon is cleared as previously described. He places the safety lever on "F". With his palm up, he pulls the cocking handle to the rear, then pushes it forward until it locks. With the bolt held to the rear, he places the safety lever on "S" and manually returns the cocking handle to the forward position. He turns the latch lever and opens the cover. He raises the cartridge feed tray and places the bandoleer on the bandoleer hanger. He places the first round of the belt in the feed groove with the double link first and the open side of the links down. He ensures that the round remains in the feed groove and holds the belt up (about six rounds from the loading end) while closing the cover (Figure 2-17).

Figure 2-17. Loading.

2-15. UNLOADING

The gunner unloads the M60 by pulling and locking the bolt to the rear position. He places the safety lever on "S", raises the cover and tray, and removes any ammunition or links from the tray. He performs the *four-point safety check* (see Section II).

2-16. CYCLE OF FUNCTIONING

The M60 gunners can recognize and correct stoppages when they know how the weapon functions. The weapon functions automatically as long as ammunition is fed into it and the trigger is held to the rear. Each time a round is fired, the parts of the weapon function in a cycle or sequence. Many of the actions occur at the same time. These actions are separated in this manual only for instructional purposes.

a. The first round of the belt is placed in the tray groove to start the cycle. Then, the trigger is pulled, releasing the sear from the sear notch. The rear of the sear is lowered and disengaged from the sear notch when the trigger is pulled to the rear. This procedure allows the operating rod and bolt to be driven forward by the expansion of the operating rod spring. The cycle stops when the trigger is released and the sear again engages the sear notch on the operating rod.

b. The sequence of functioning is as follows:

(1) *Feeding*. As the bolt starts its forward movement, the feed cam is forced to the right causing the feed cam lever to turn in the opposite direction and forcing the belt feed pawl over the next round in the bolt. The next round is then ready to be placed into the tray groove when the rearward action occurs again. As the bolt moves to the rear after firing, the cam roller forces the feed cam to the left. The feed cam lever is forced to turn, which moves the feed pawl to the right and places a round in the tray groove.

(2) *Chambering*. As the bolt travels forward, the upper locking lug engages the rim of the round. The pressure of the front and rear cartridge guides holds the round so that positive contact is made with the upper locking lug of the bolt. The front cartridge guide prevents forward movement of the link as the round is stripped from the belt. The upper

locking lug carries the round forward. The chambering ramp causes the nose of the round to be cammed downward into the chamber. When the round is fully seated in the chamber, the extractor snaps over the rim of the round, and the ejector on the rail inside the receiver is depressed.

(3) *Locking*. As the round is chambered, the bolt enters the barrel socket. The upper and lower locking lugs contact the bolt camming surfaces inside the barrel and start turning the bolt clockwise. The action of the operating rod yoke against the bolt camming slot as the operating rod continues forward turns the bolt, completing its 90-degree (one-quarter turn) clockwise rotation. Locking is now complete.

(4) *Firing*. After the bolt is fully forward and locked, the operating rod continues to go forward, independent of the bolt, for a short distance. The yoke, engaged between the firing pin spools, carries the firing pin through the face of the bolt. The firing pin strikes the primer of the round and the primer fires the round.

(5) *Unlocking*. After the round is fired and the bullet passes the gas port, part of the expanding gases go into the gas regulator through the gas plug. The rapidly expanding gases enter the hollow gas piston, forcing the piston to the rear. As the operating rod continues to the rear, the operating rod yoke acts against the bolt camming slot. This causes the bolt to begin its counterclockwise rotation. The upper and lower locking lugs of the bolt contact the bolt camming surfaces inside the barrel socket and, as the bolt continues toward the rear, it completes a one-quarter turn counterclockwise. The rotation and movement to the rear unlocks the bolt from the barrel socket. Unlocking begins as the yoke of the operating rod contacts the curve of the bolt camming slot and ends as the bolt clears the end of the barrel socket.

(6) *Extracting*. Extracting begins during the unlocking cycle. The rotation of the bolt loosens the cartridge case in the chamber. As the piston and bolt move to the rear, the extractor pulls the cartridge case from the chamber.

(7) *Ejecting*. As the cartridge case is pulled from the chamber, the bolt passes by the ejector. This procedure causes the ejector clip to expand, forcing the ejector to push the expended cartridge. The extractor grips the right side of the cartridge and causes it to spin from the weapon as it reaches the ejection port. The empty belt links are forced out the link ejection port as the rearward movement of the bolt causes the next round to be positioned in the tray groove.

(8) *Cocking*. As the expanding gases force the gas piston to the rear, the operating rod first moves independently of the bolt. The yoke of the operating rod acts against the rear firing pin spool, pulling the firing pin from the primer of the spent cartridge case. The action of the piston assembly, continuing to the rear with the firing pin, releases the compression of the firing pin spring. As long as the trigger is held to the rear, the M60 continues to complete the eight steps of functioning automatically. When the trigger is released and the sear engages the sear notch, the cycle of functioning is stopped and the weapon is cocked. To prevent undue wear to the sear and sear notch, the gunner must hold the trigger firmly to the rear during firing.

2-17. SIGHTS

The range scale on the rear sight is marked for each 100 meters from 300 to 1,100 meters. It can be adjusted for zeroing. Range changes are made by using either the scale retaining/adjusting screw or elevation knob. The scale retaining/adjusting screw is used to make major adjustments in elevation. The elevation knob is used to make minor adjustments, such as during zeroing (Figure 2-18, page 2-26). Four clicks on the elevation knob are equal to a 1-cm change in elevation or point of aim 1 cm. From the rear of the weapon, the elevation knob is turned clockwise to raise the rear sight and lower the strike of the round. It is turned counterclockwise to lower the sight and raise the strike of the round. The rear sight is adjustable for windage, 5 mils right or left of the zero index line. The windage knob is on the left side of the rear sight. One click on the windage knob equals a 1-cm change in deflection or point of aim 1 cm. The windage knob is turned toward the muzzle of the weapon to move the sight and the strike of the round to the right. It is turned toward the rear to move the sight and the strike of the round to the left.

a. **Elevation.** Before making elevation adjustments, the range knob must be at its highest setting. If the center of the shot group is above or below the aiming point, the gunner rotates the elevation knob by moving the rear sight slide in the direction of the desired change. One 180-degree turn in either direction moves the strike of the round 1/4 cm at 10 meters, or four clicks equals 1-cm change.

b. **Windage.** If the center of the group is to the left or right of the black aiming paster, the gunner must correct for windage. To correct windage, he rotates the windage knob to move in the direction of the desired change. For example, he rotates the windage knob toward the muzzle (counterclockwise) to move the strike of the round to the right; he rotates the windage knob toward the buttstock [clockwise] to move the strike of the round to the left. One click in either direction moves the strike of the round 1/2 cm at 10 meters.

c. **10-Meter Zeroing, Set the Sights (Mechanical Zero).** The gunner indexes or places the range scale on a range of 500 meters. He aligns the windage by placing zero windage on the index line. He assumes a prone position and sights on the target.

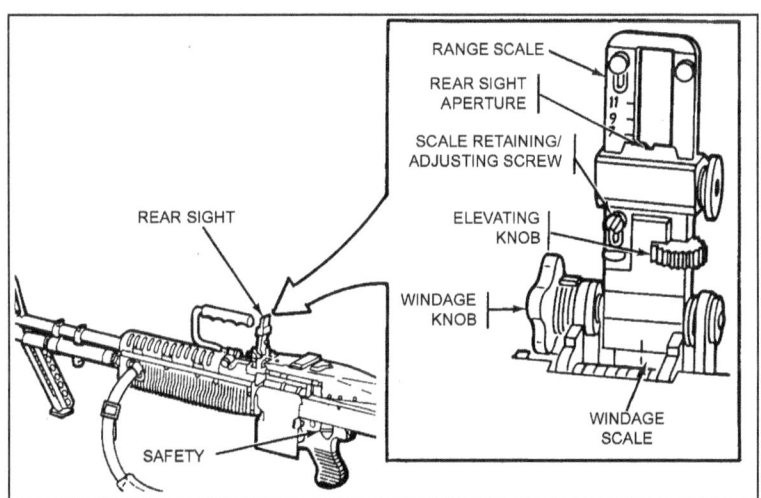

Figure 2-18. Sight settings.

2-18. M122 TRIPOD

The M122 tripod provides a stable mount for the M60, and it permits a high degree of accuracy and control. The tripod is recommended for marksmanship training and defensive employment.

a. **Mounting M60 on the Tripod.** The tripod assembly provides a stable and relatively lightweight base that is far superior to the bipod. The tripod may be extended and collapsed without difficulty. It consists of a tripod head, one front leg and two rear legs, and traversing bar. The traversing bar connects the two rear legs. It is hinged on one side with a sleeve and sleeve latch on the other, which allows the tripod to collapse to a closed position for carrying or storage or to lock in an open extended position for use. The traversing bar also supports the T&E mechanism. Engraved on the bar is a scale that measures direction in mils. It is graduated in 5-mil increments. It is numbered every 100 to 425 mils right of center and numbered every 100 to 450 mils left of center.

(1) The T&E mechanism is to provide controlled manipulation and the ability to engage predetermined targets.

(a) The traversing portion of the mechanism consists of the traversing handwheel and traversing slide-lock lever. As the traversing handwheel is turned, the muzzle of the weapon turns to the left or right, depending on the direction it is turned. Each click of the traversing handwheel indicates a 1-mil change in direction of the muzzle: 1 click equals 1 mil. The total of 100 mils traverse includes 50 mils right and 50 mils left of center.

(b) The elevating portion of the mechanism consists only of the elevating handwheel. The elevating handwheel has a mil-click device built into it (1 click = 1 mil). Engraved into the handwheel is a scale divided into 5-mil divisions and 1-mil subdivisions, for a total of 50-mil increments. There are 200 mils above and 200 mils below the zero mark, for a total of 400 mils in elevation change. Elevation readings are taken in two parts. First, the major reading is taken from the elevation screw plate. The second, minor reading is taken from the handwheel. The two readings are separated by a slash (/) when they are recorded.

(c) The traversing slide-lock lever allows rapid lateral adjustments along the traversing bar. Direction readings are taken from the scale on the traversing bar, using the left side of the traversing slide as an index. The direction of the reading comes from the position of the muzzle, not the position of the slide.

(2) To set up the tripod, the gunner unfolds the front leg and spreads the rear legs until the leg lock engages. He inserts the pintle assembly and rotates the pintle lock release cam to lock (Figure 2-19).

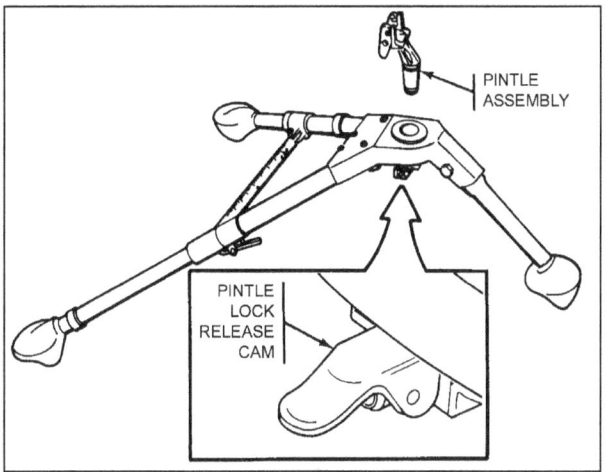

Figure 2-19. M122 tripod.

(3) To mount the M60, the gunner places the ends of the M60's front mounting pin on top of the pintle assembly. He presses the bottom of the latch to open the pintle assembly. The ends of the M60 mounting pin should lock in place on the pintle assembly (Figure 2-20).

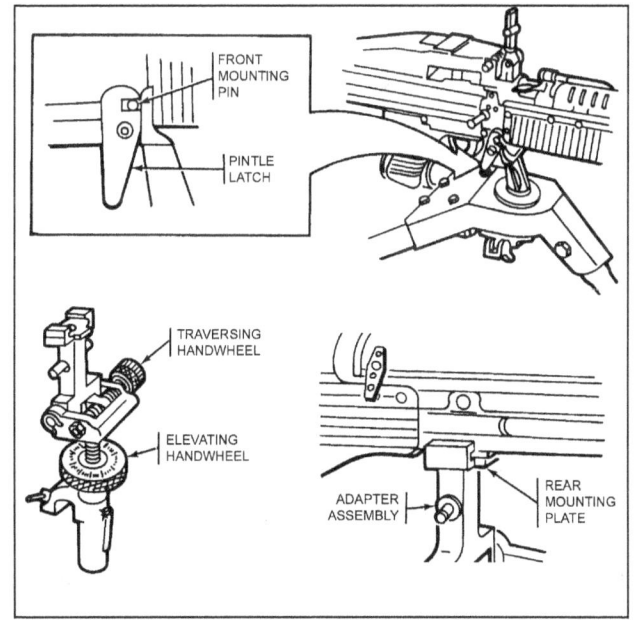

Figure 2-20. Mounting of the M60 on the tripod.

(4) To attach the T&E mechanism to the weapon mounted on the tripod (Figure 2-21), the gunner centers the elevating and traversing handwheels. To do this, he turns the traversing handwheel toward his body as far as it will go, then turns it away two complete revolutions. He checks the traversing handwheel scale to ensure the "0" on the scale is aligned with the "0" index line before and after the two revolutions. At night, the

gunner positions the traversing mechanism by turning the traversing handwheel toward his body as far as it will go, turns it away 50 clicks (two revolutions), and then allows the weapon to go forward.

(a) With the slide lock lever to the rear and the traversing handwheel to the left, the gunner places the mounting plate recess on the rear of the mounting plate. He pulls down the locating pin release and pushes the adapter assembly forward. (The locating pin automatically locks into position in the bottom of the mounting plate.)

(b) The gunner lowers the rear of the weapon, places the traversing slide on the traversing bar with the locking lever to the rear, and locks it into position. He indexes the left edge of the slide lock at zero.

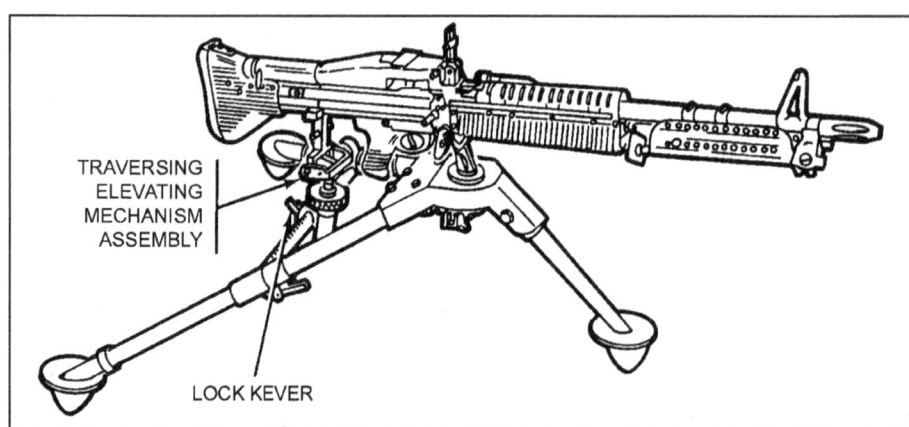

Figure 2-21. Attachment of the T&E mechanism.

b. **Dismounting M60 From the M122 Tripod**. The gunner dismounts the M60 from the tripod by first removing the T&E mechanism. He releases the lock lever and raises the rear of the weapon. He grasps the carrying handle with his left hand and depresses the pintle latch with his right hand. He lifts the weapon from the pintle assembly.

2-19. BIPOD OPERATIONS

The bipod assembly is used to fire from the prone position. The shoulder rest on the buttstock provides support for the weapon when fired in the bipod mode. The bipod group is held in place between the front sight and flash suppressor.

a. To lower a bipod leg, the gunner pulls it to the rear (compressing the lock spring) and rotates it downward (Figure 2-22). The leg automatically locks when in the down position. To return the legs up, the gunner pulls down on the legs and rotates upward.

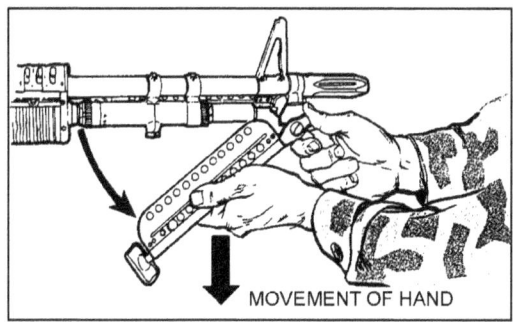

Figure 2-22. Lowering of the bipod.

b.   To extend a bipod leg, the gunner pulls down on the foot. The bipod leg plunger engages a notch in the bipod leg extension and holds it in the desired position. To shorten the bipod leg, the gunner depresses the bipod leg plunger and pushes up on the bipod foot (Figure 2-23).

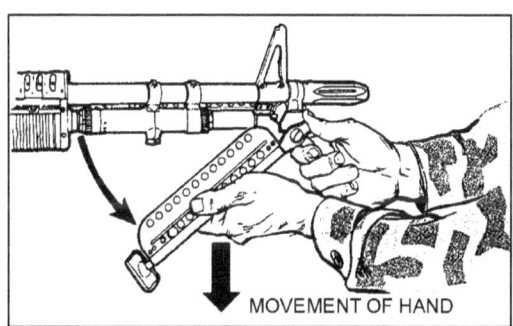

Figure 2-23. Adjustment of the bipod leg extension.

2-20.   VEHICULAR MOUNT

The standard vehicular mount for the M60 machine gun is the M4 pedestal mount used on the HMMWV. One component of the pedestal mount, the M142 machine-gun mount, (which serves as a cradle for the weapon), is also adaptable to other vehicles (Figure 2-24).

a.   To mount the weapon, the gunner locks the platform in the horizontal position by inserting the travel-lock pin into the travel lock. He places the front mounting pin (in the forearm assembly) into the front mounting lug. He lowers the receiver so that the rear locating pin snaps into the platform latch.

b.   To dismount the weapon, the gunner ensures that the travel lock is engaged (holding the platform in a horizontal position). He grasps the carrying handle with one hand and depresses the platform latch with the other. He raises the rear of the weapon slightly and lifts it from the mount.

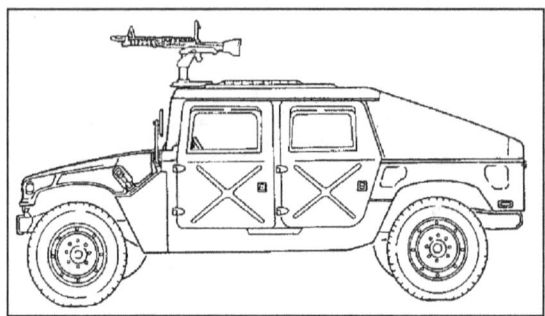

Figure 2-24. M60 mounted on a HMMWV.

2-21. TRIPOD POSITIONING

The M122 tripod provides a stable mount for the M60, and it permits a high degree of accuracy and control. The gunner unfolds the front leg, positions it toward the target, then spreads the rear legs until the leg lock engages.

Section IV. PERFORMANCE PROBLEMS AND DESTRUCTION

This section identifies some of the problems that cause the weapon to perform improperly. It also explains how to identify unserviceable parts, and how to destroy the M60 when authorized to do so.

2-22. MALFUNCTIONS

A malfunction occurs when a *mechanical failure* causes the *weapon to fire improperly*. Neither defective ammunition nor improper operation by the gunner is considered a malfunction. If cleaning and lubricating the weapon does not fix the problem, then the gunner turns it in to the unit armorer. Table 2-3 shows malfunctions, their probable causes, and the corrective actions.

MALFUNCTION	PROBABLE CAUSE	CORRECTIVE ACTION
Sluggish operation.	Carbon buildup in the gas system.	Clean gas regulator, piston, and cylinder.
	Lack of lubricant.	Lubricate.
	Burred parts.	Notify unit maintenance.
Uncontrolled fire (runaway weapon).	Worn or broken sear.	Send to DS maintenance.
	Worn or broken operating rod sear notch.	Send to DS maintenance.
	Sear installed backwards.	Install correctly.
		Install correctly.
		NOTE: Always install the rod yoke between the two firing pin spools.
	Carbon buildup in gas port.	Clean gas port.

Table 2-3. Malfunctions.

2-23. STOPPAGES

A stoppage is any *interruption* in the cycle of functioning caused by *faulty action* of the weapon or *faulty ammunition*. Stoppages are classified by their relationship to the cycle of functioning. Table 2-4 shows types of interruptions or stoppages, their probable causes, and the corrective actions.

STOPPAGE	PROBABLE CAUSE	CORRECTIVE ACTION
Failure to chamber.	Ruptured cartridge case.	Remove cartridge IAW TM 9-1005-224-10.
	Carbon buildup in gas cylinder.	Remove carbon.
	Carbon buildup in receiver.	Remove carbon.
	Damaged round.	Remove round and reload gun.
	Dirty chamber.	Clear barrel and clean and lubricate as required.
	Weak or short operating rod.	Replace.
Failure to lock.	Weak or short operating rod spring.	Replace.
	Foreign matter in chamber of receiver.	Clean and lubricate as required.
Failure to fire.	Faulty ammunition.	Replace.
	Broken or damaged firing pin or firing pin spring.	Replace.
	Defective trigger.	Send to DS maintenance.
	Broken or deformed sear plunger or spring.	Send to DS maintenance.
	Failure to lock.	See "Failure to Lock."
Failure to extract.	Gas piston installed backwards.	Install properly IAW TM 9-1005-224-10.
	Broken extractor spring.	Replace.
	Chipped or broken extractor.	Replace.
	Defective extractor plunger.	Replace.
	Short recoil.	Clean gas port and operating rod tube, and lubricate as required. Replace operating rod spring.

Table 2-4. Stoppages.

STOPPAGE	PROBABLE CAUSE	CORRECTIVE ACTION
Failure to cock.	Broken sear.	Send to DS maintenance.
	Worn operating rod sear notch.	Send to DS maintenance.
	Broken, defective, or missing sear plunger or spring.	Send to DS maintenance.
	Short recoil.	Clean gas port and operating rod tube, and lubricate as required. Replace operating rod spring.

Table 2-4. Stoppages (continued).

DANGERS

1. IF NOTHING IS EJECTED AND THE WEAPON IS HOT (200 OR MORE ROUNDS FIRED IN LESS THAN 2 MINUTES), DO NOT OPEN THE COVER. MOVE THE SAFETY TO "S", WHICH PLACES THE WEAPON ON "S". KEEP THE WEAPON POINTED DOWNRANGE AND KEEP AWAY FROM THE WEAPON FOR 15 MINUTES, THEN CLEAR THE WEAPON.
2. BE CAREFUL IN CLEARING THE WEAPON WHEN THE BARREL IS HOT, A ROUND MAY FIRE (COOK OFF) DUE TO THE BARREL'S HEAT INSTEAD OF DUE TO THE FIRING MECHANISM. DURING TRAINING OR ON A FIRING RANGE, AFTER THE WEAPON HAS FIRED 200 ROUNDS, ITS BARREL IS CONSIDERED A HOT BARREL.
3. DURING COMBAT, WAIT 5 SECONDS, BECAUSE OF THE POSSIBILITY OF A "HANGFIRE," BEFORE APPLYING IMMEDIATE AND REMEDIAL ACTION. DURING TRAINING, WAIT 15 MINUTES BEFORE CLEARING A HOT WEAPON AND APPLYING IMMEDIATE OR REMEDIAL ACTION.

NOTE: When applying immediate or remedial action on a cold or hot gun, if any part of the round (ranging from the tip of the bullet to the rim) is in the chamber, the gunner removes the ammunition from the feed tray only, then closes the cover and attempts to fire. If the weapon fires, he reloads and continues firing. If it does not fire, he clears the weapon (removes the round using a clearing rod with the cover closed, not using anything other than a clearing rod), then he inspects the weapon and ammunition.

2-24. IMMEDIATE ACTION

Immediate action is action taken to *reduce a stoppage without looking for the cause.* Immediate action should be taken in the event of either a misfire or a cookoff. A *misfire* is the failure of a chambered round to fire. Such failure can be due to an ammunition defect or faulty firing mechanism. A *cookoff* is the firing of a round caused by the heat of a hot barrel and not by the firing mechanism. A cookoff can be avoided by applying immediate action within 10 seconds after a failure to fire. If the M60 stops firing, the gunner performs the following immediate actions. An effective memory aid is POPP, which stands for Pull, Observe, Push, and Press:

a. Pulls and locks the cocking handle to the rear while observing the ejection port to see if a cartridge case, belt link, or round is ejected. Ensures that the bolt remains to the rear to prevent double feeding if a round or cartridge case is not ejected.

b. If a cartridge case, belt link, or a round is ejected, returns the cocking handle to the forward position, aims on the target, and presses the trigger. If the weapon still does not fire, takes remedial action. If a cartridge case, belt link, or round is not ejected, takes remedial action.

2-25. REMEDIAL ACTION
Remedial action is any action taken to determine the cause of a stoppage and to restore the weapon to an operational condition. This action is taken only after immediate action fails to remedy the problem.

a. **Cold Weapon Procedures**. When a stoppage occurs with a cold weapon and immediate action has failed, the gunner uses the following procedures:

(1) Pulls the cocking handle to the rear, locking the bolt. Moves the safety to "S" and returns the cocking handle.

(2) Places the weapon on the ground or away from his face, opens the cover, and performs the four-point safety check. Reloads and continues to fire.

(3) If the weapon does not fire, clears the weapon and inspects it and the ammunition.

b. **Hot Weapon Procedures**. If the stoppage occurs with a hot weapon (200 rounds or more fired in 2 minutes or noted as previously for training), the gunner moves the safety to "S", waits 5 seconds (during training, lets the weapon cool for 15 minutes), then uses the same procedures as outlined for cold weapon procedures.

c. **Jammed Cocking Handle**. If a stoppage occurs and the cocking handle cannot be pulled to the rear by hand (the bolt may be fully forward and locked or only partially forward), the gunner takes the following steps:

(1) Tries once again to pull the cocking handle *by hand*.

CAUTION
Do not try to force the cocking handle to the rear with your foot or a heavy object. This could damage the weapon.

---

(2) If the weapon is hot enough to cause a cookoff, moves all soldiers a safe distance from the weapon and keeps them away for 15 minutes.

(3) After the gun has cooled, opens the cover and disassembles the gun. Ensures rearward pressure is kept on the cocking handle until the buffer is removed. (The assistant gunner helps the gunner do this.)

(4) Removes the round or fired cartridge. Uses cleaning rod or ruptured cartridge extractor if necessary.

(a) In a training situation, after completing the remedial action procedures, the gunner does not fire the weapon until it has been inspected by an ordnance specialist.

(b) In a combat situation, after the stoppage has been corrected, the gunner changes the barrel and tries to fire. If the weapon fails to function properly, the gunner sends it to the unit armorer.

2-26. DESTRUCTION PROCEDURES
Destruction of any military weapon is only authorized as a last resort to prevent enemy capture or use. This paragraph discusses the field-expedient means of this destruction; it does not replace published policies. In combat situations, the commander has the authority to destroy weapons, but he must report this destruction through channels.

a. Disassemble the weapon as completely as time permits. Use the barrel or tripod mount to destroy the bolt, buffer, and operating rod group, barrels, rear and front sights, and mounts.

b. Bury the disassembled weapon or dump the parts into a stream, a sump, or a latrine.

c. Burn the weapon by placing an incendiary grenade on the receiver group over the bolt (with the cover resting on the grenade) and detonating the grenade.

d. Smash the T&E mechanism and pintle assembly. Bend the tripod legs.

CHAPTER 3
M240B MACHINE GUN

The M240B machine gun supports the rifleman in both offensive and defensive operations. The M240B provides the heavy volume of close and continuous fire needed to accomplish the mission. The M240B is used to engage targets beyond the range of individual weapons, with controlled and accurate fire. The long-range, close defensive, and final protective fires delivered by the M240B form an integral part of a unit's defensive fires. This chapter describes the weapon and the types of ammunition in detail and provides a table of general data.

Section I. DESCRIPTION AND COMPONENTS

This section describes the M240B machine gun and its components and purposes. It also discusses the different types of ammunition that are fired from the M240B machine gun. This section also discusses the ammunition adapter and the blank firing adapter for the M240B machine gun.

3-1. DESCRIPTION

The M240B is a general-purpose machine gun. (Figure 3-1) It can be mounted on a bipod, tripod, aircraft, or vehicle. The M240B is a belt-fed, air-cooled, gas-operated, fully automatic machine gun that fires from the open bolt position. Ammunition is fed into the weapon from a 100-round bandoleer containing a disintegrating metallic split-link belt. The gas from firing one round provides the energy for firing the next round. Thus, the gun functions automatically as long as it is supplied with ammunition and the trigger is held to the rear. As the gun is fired, the belt links separate and are ejected from the side. Empty cases are ejected from the bottom of the gun. A spare barrel is issued with each M240B, and barrels can be changed quickly as the weapon has a fixed head space. However, barrels from different weapons should not be interchanged. The bore of the barrel is chromium plated, reducing barrel wear to a minimum.

> ## DANGER
> DO NOT INTERCHANGE THE BARREL ASSEMBLY OR THE BOLT ASSEMBLY FROM ONE WEAPON TO ANOTHER. IF YOU DO SO, IT MAY RESULT IN DEATH OR INJURY.

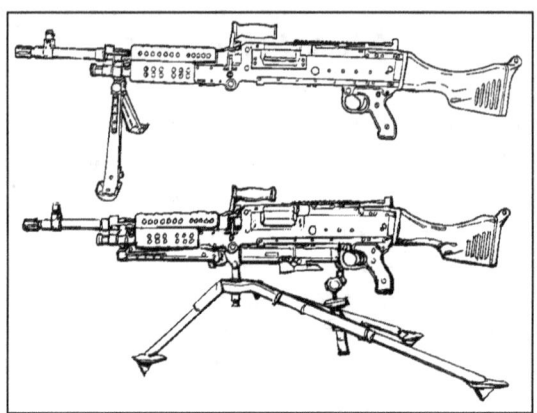

Figure 3-1. M240B machine gun, bipod and tripod mounted.

Ammunition	7.62-mm ball, tracer, armor-piercing, blank, dummy. Armor-piercing round is not authorized for training.
Tracer burnout	900 meters
Length of the M240B	49 inches
Weight of the M240B	27.6 pounds
Weight of tripod-mount M122A1 tripod with/flex-mount, complete	20 pounds
Maximum range	3,725 meters
Maximum effective range	1,100 meters with tripod and T&E
Area:	
Tripod	1,100 meters
Bipod	800 meters
Point:	
Tripod	800 meters
Bipod	600 meters
Suppression	1,800 meters
Maximum extent of grazing fire obtainable over level or uniformly sloping terrain	600 meters
Height of the M240B on the tripod mount M122A1	17.5 inches
Rates of fire:	
Sustained	100 rounds per minute fired in 6- to 9-round bursts and 4 to 5 seconds between bursts (barrel change every 10 minutes).
Rapid	200 rounds per minute fired in 10- to 13-round bursts and 2 to 3 seconds between bursts (barrel change every 2 minutes).

Table 3-1. General data.

Cyclic ....650 to 950 rounds per minute in continuous
                                          bursts (barrel change every minute).
Basic load of ammunition
    (three-man crew) ....900 to 1200 rounds.
Elevation, tripod controlled ....+247 mils
Elevation, tripod free ....+300 mils
Depression, tripod controlled....................-200 mils
Traverse, controlled by T&E
    mechanism...100 mils
Normal sector of fire
    (with tripod) ....875 mils
Free gun ....6,400 mils

Table 3-1. General data (continued).

3-2. COMPONENTS

The components of the M240B machine gun and their purpose are shown in Table 3-2 and Figure 3-2, page 3-4.

COMPONENTS		PURPOSES
(1)	Barrel assembly.	Consists of the barrel, flash suppressor, carrying handle, heat shield, front sight assembly, and gas-regulator plug. Houses the cartridge for firing and directs the projectile.
(2)	Heat shield assembly.	Protects the gunner's hand from a hot barrel.
(3)	Buttstock/buffer assembly and buffer and spade grip assembly/buttstock and buffer assembly.	Composite buttstock: buffer housing that contains spring washers to absorb recoil from bolt and operating rod assembly at the end of recoil movement.
(4)	Receiver assembly.	Consists of receiver, handguard, bipod, and rear sight assembly. Serves as support for all major components. Houses action of the weapon and, through a series of cam ways, controls function of weapon.
(5)	Handguard assembly (not shown).	Provides thermal insulation to protect the gunner's hands from heat or extreme cold.
(6)	Cocking handle assembly.	Pulls the moving parts rearward. Moves in a guide rail fixed to the right side of the receiver.
(7)	Trigger housing assembly.	Controls the firing of the machine gun. Contains trigger and safety components
(8)	Sling and snap hook assembly.	Provides a means of carrying the weapon.
(9)	Bipod.	Supports M240B machine gun in prone position.

Table 3-2. Components and purposes.

COMPONENTS		PURPOSES
(10)	Drive spring rod assembly.	Provides energy for returning bolt and operating rod assembly to firing position.
(11)	Bolt/operating rod assembly.	Provides feeding stripping, chambering, firing, extracting, and ejecting of cartridges using propellant gases for power.
(12)	Cover assembly.	Feeds linked belt, positions and holds cartridges in position for stripping, feeding, and chambering. Top rail configuration allows mounting of optical and electronic sights.
(13)	Feed tray.	Serves as guide for positioning cartridge to assist in chambering. Has a slotted top to allow air to circulate around barrel for cooling purposes.
(14)	Tripod assembly (not shown).	The tripod T&E mount assembly is flexible, provides a stable mount, absorbs recoil, and improves accuracy.
(15)	Ejection port.	Provides guide for ejection of spent cartridges.

Table 3-2. Components and purposes (continued).

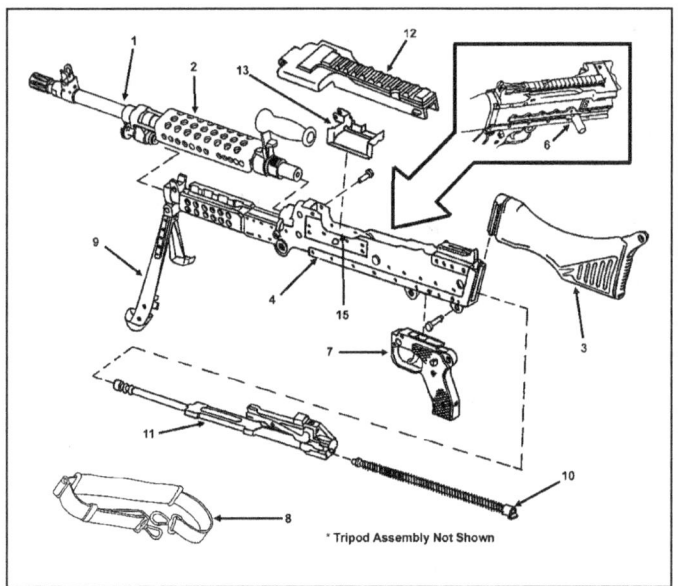

Figure 3-2. Major components of the M240B.

a. **Sights**. The front sight is attached to the barrel and can be adjusted for elevation and windage to allow the gunner to zero his weapon. Since the sight on the barrel is adjusted to zero the machine gun, both barrels must be zeroed before combat and training. The rear sight is attached to the rear of the receiver and is marked for each 100 meters of range, from 200 to 800 meters on the upper surface of the leaf, and on the reverse side of the leaf from 800 to 1,800 meters. (Figure 3-1)

b. **Safety Mechanism**. The safety mechanism is located on the pistol grip just behind the trigger well. When the safety is pushed to the right, the letter "S" is visible indicating the weapon is on safe. When pushed to the left, the letter "F" is visible on the safety indicating the weapon is on fire. The safety can only be engaged when the bolt is in the rear position. On the "S" position, the bolt cannot be released to go forward (Figure 3-1).

3-3. AMMUNITION

The M240B machine guns use several different types of 7.62-mm standard military ammunition. The specific type ammunition and its characteristics are as shown in (Figure 3-3). Soldiers use only authorized ammunition that is manufactured to US and NATO specifications. The ammunition is issued in a disintegrating, metallic, split-linked belt (Figure 3-4).

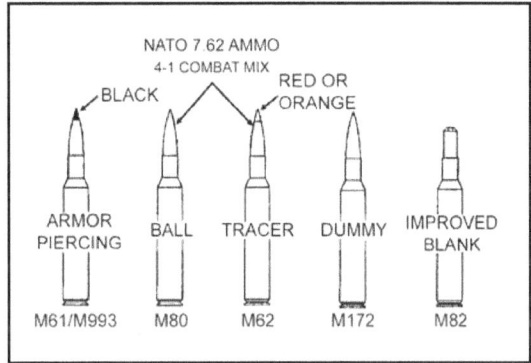

Figure 3-3. 7.62-mm cartridges for the M240B machine gun.

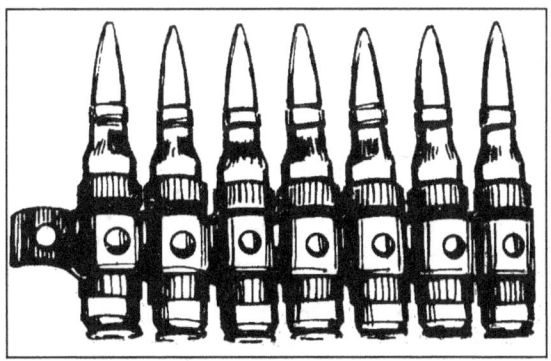

Figure 3-4. 7.62-mm cartridge in metallic belt.

a. **Classification**. The M240B machine guns ammunition are classified as follows:

(1) *Cartridge, 7.62-mm Ball M80*—for use against light materials and personnel, and for range training.

(2) *Cartridge, 7.62-mm Armor-Piercing M61*—for use against lightly armored targets.

(3) *Cartridge, 7.62-mm Tracer M62*—for observation of fire, incendiary effects, signaling, and for training. When tracer rounds are fired, they are mixed with ball ammunition in a ratio of four ball rounds to one tracer round.

(4) *Cartridge, 7.62-mm Dummy M63*—for use during mechanical training.

(5) *Cartridge, 7.62-mm Blank M82*—for use during training when simulated live fire is desired. A BFA should be used to fire this ammunition.

b. **Storage**. Ammunition is stored under cover. If ammunition is in the open, it must be kept at least 6 inches above the ground and covered with a double thickness of tarpaulin. The cover must be placed so that it protects the ammunition yet allows ventilation. Trenches are dug to divert water from flowing under the ammunition.

c. **Care, Handling, and Preservation**. Ammunition should not be removed from the airtight containers until ready for use. Ammunition removed from the airtight containers, particularly in damp climates, may corrode.

(1) Ammunition must be protected from mud, dirt, and moisture. If it gets wet or dirty, the ammunition must be wiped off before using. Lightly corroded cartridges are wiped off as soon as the corrosion is discovered. Heavily corroded, dented, or loose projectiles should not be fired.

(2) Ammunition must be protected from the direct rays of the sun. Excessive pressure from the heat may cause premature detonation.

(3) Oil should never be used on ammunition. Oil collects dust and other abrasives that may possibly damage the operating parts of the weapon.

d. **Packaging.** The ammunition box contains two cartons. Each carton has a bandoleer for carrying purposes. Each carton contains 100 rounds and weighs about 7 pounds. Ammunition in the bandoleers may be linked together, attached to the hanger assembly, and fired from the container or the bandoleers may be removed for firing.

3-4. AMMUNITION ADAPTER

The ammunition adapter is used on the M240B machine gun when firing. This adapter allows the gunner to use the 100-round carton and bandoleer. (Figure 3-5)

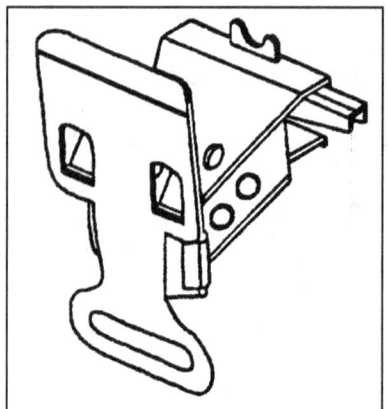

Figure 3-5. Ammunition adapter.

a. **Attaching the Ammunition Adapter**. The ammunition adapter is fitted to the left side and under the feed tray of the receiver. When looking at the left side of the receiver, you will see a slot and a button under the feed tray (Figure 3-5). The gunner first attaches the bandoleer holder to the base of the adapter by inserting the tapered end (green plastic) of the holder into the adapter. Then the gunner opens the cover assembly, and raises the feed tray. He inserts the curved lip of the adapter assembly into the slot located in the rail on the left of the receiver, below the feed tray, depressing the lever on the adapter assembly, and pushing the assembly towards the receiver, until it is against the receiver. Releasing the lever to allow the adapter assembly to secure itself onto the button on the receiver (Figure 3-5).

b. **Care of the Ammunition Adapter**. Over a prolonged period, the moving parts, to include plastic, will start to wear out and break.

(1) Inspect the adapter for damaged parts, excessive wear, and cleanliness when every the weapon is taken out of the arms room.

(2) When feasible, test-fit the adapter.

(3) After using the adapter, inspect to ensure it is still operational.

3-5. BLANK FIRING ATTACHMENT

The BFA is used on the M240B machine gun when blank cartridges are fired to simulate live firing during training where live firing is not practical (Figure 3-6).

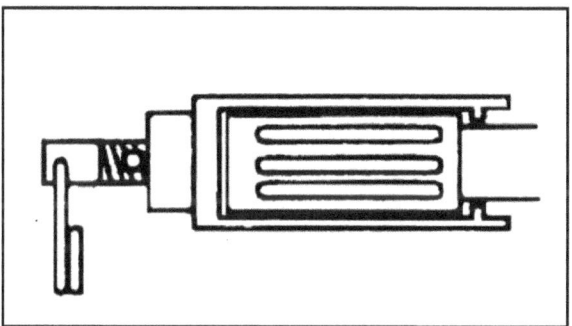

Figure 3-6. Blank firing attachment.

> # DANGER
> DO NOT FIRE BLANK AMMUNITION AT ANY PERSON WITHIN 20 FEET BECAUSE FRAGMENTS OF A CLOSURE WAD OR PARTICLES OF UNBURNED PROPELLANT CAN CAUSE DEATH.

a. **Install the BFA on the M240B Machine Gun**. The BFA is used on the M240B machine gun when blank cartridges are fired to support MILES force-on-force operations to simulate live-fire exercises. The BFA fits any M240B barrel. The tube fits inside the flash suppressor with the remaining portion fitting over the outside of the flash suppressor, flush against the gun muzzle and flush with the forward end of the flash suppressor. The BFA is secured by using the following procedures:

(1) *Attach the BFA* (Figure 3-7). Unscrew the shaft (1) until it slides all the way to the rear. Install the chamber device (2) over the flash suppressor (3). Slide the shaft (1)

into the throat of the flash suppressor. Engage the threads on shaft into the body of the chamber device (2); turn clockwise until it is hand tight.

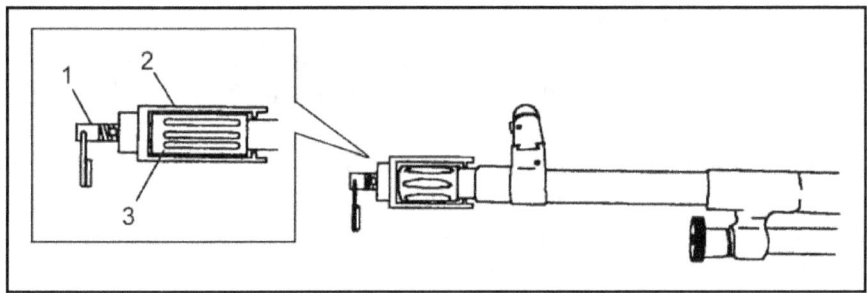

Figure 3-7. Attach the blank firing attachment.

(2) *Remove the BFA* (Figure 3-8). Hold the barrel and rotate the chamber of the body (2) about 180 degrees counterclockwise to break any carbon sealed between the shaft (1) and the suppressor (3). Unscrew the shaft (1) until the threads disengage. Remove the chamber device from the suppressor (3).

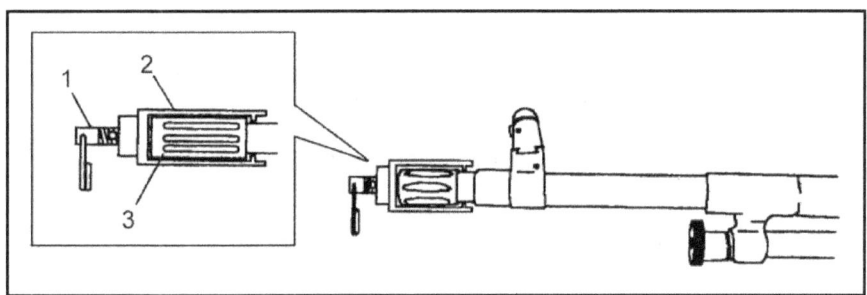

Figure 3-8. Remove the blank firing attachment.

b. **Care of the M240B While Using the BFA.** A buildup of carbon inside the weapon causes friction between the movi00ng parts. Carbon deposits build up rapidly when blanks are fired. When these deposits become excessive, stoppages occur. Therefore, the weapon must be kept clean, especially the gas system and chamber, during blank firing. To get the best performance with the BFA, the gunner performs the following:

(1) Inspects the weapon for damaged parts, excessive wear, cleanliness, and proper lubrication before firing.

(2) When feasible, test fires the weapon using ball ammunition before attaching the BFA.

(3) Adjusts the BFA to fit the weapon.

(4) Applies immediate action when stoppages occur.

(5) Cleans the weapon including barrel assembly, gas cylinder, gas piston, gas port, chamber bore, and BFA.

(6) Cleans and lubricates the entire weapon after firing 400 blank rounds.

DANGER
1. NEVER LOAD ANY AMMUNITION OTHER THAN BLANKS WHEN THE BLANK FIRING ATTACHMENT IS IN PLACE.
2. NEVER FIRE THE BFA-FITTED MACHINE GUN AT PERSONNEL WHO ARE WITHIN 20 FEET OF THE WEAPON. DEATH OR INJURY COULD OCCUR.

Section II. MAINTENANCE

Proper maintenance contributes to weapon effectiveness as well as unit readiness. Maintenance aspects of the M240B include inspection; cleaning and lubrication; and maintenance before, during, and after firing, and during NBC conditions. Associated tasks essential to maintenance (clearing, general disassembly and assembly, and function checks) are provided in detail.

3-6. CLEARING PROCEDURES

The first step in maintenance is to clear the M240B (Figure 3-9). This applies in all situations, not just after firing. The gunner must always assume the M240B is loaded. To clear the M240B, the gunner performs the following procedures:

    a. Move the safety to the fire "F" position.

    b. With his right hand, (palm up) pulls the cocking handle to the rear, ensuring the bolt is locked to the rear (bipod mode).

    c. Return the cocking handle to its forward position.

    d. Place the safety on safe "S."

    e. Raise the cover assembly and conduct the four-point safety check for brass, links, or ammunition.

    (1) Check the feed pawl assembly under the cover.

    (2) Check the feed tray.

    (3) Lift the feed tray and inspects the chamber.

    (4) Check the space between the face of the bolt and chamber to include the space under the bolt and operating rod assembly.

    f. Close the feed tray and cover assembly and place the safety to the fire "F" position. Pull cocking handle to the rear, and pull the trigger while manually riding the bolt forward. Close the ejection port cover.

CAUTION
MANUALLY RETURN THE COCKING HANDLE TO THE FORWARD AND LOCKED POSITION EACH TIME THE BOLT IS MANUALLY PULLED TO THE REAR.

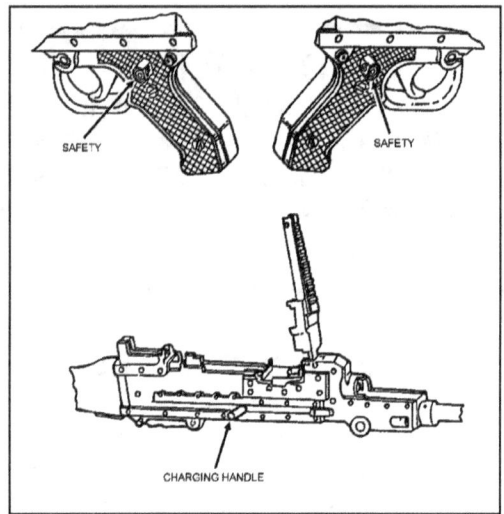

Figure 3-9. Clearing procedures.

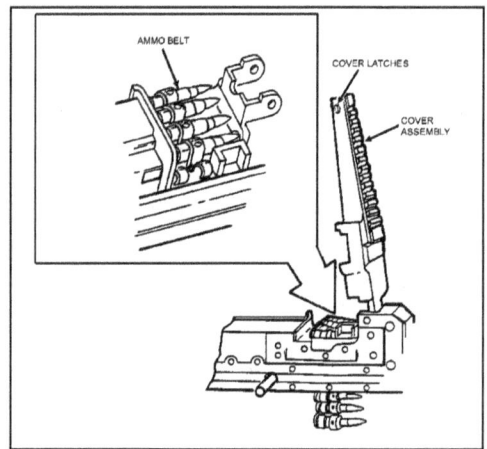

Figure 3-9. Clearing procedures (continued).

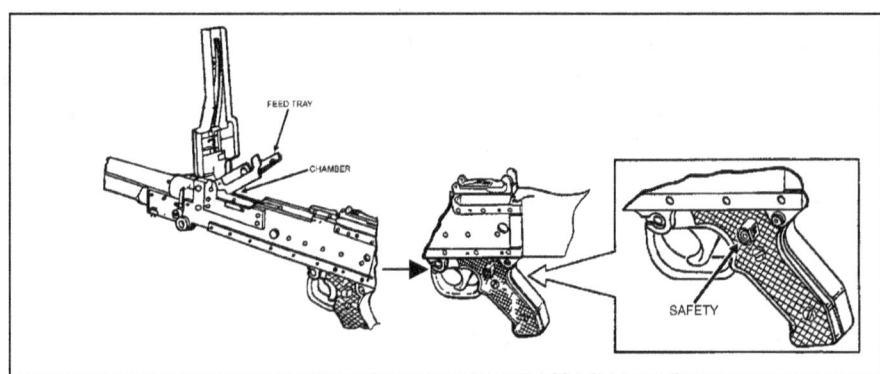

Figure 3-9. Clearing procedures (continued).

3-7. GENERAL DISASSEMBLY

The gunner performs general disassembly, which is removing and replacing the eight major groups (Figure 3-10). (The unit armorer performs detailed disassembly. Disassembly beyond what is explained in this manual is prohibited, except by ordnance personnel.) During general disassembly, the gunner clears the weapon. He ensures the bolt is forward before disassembly, and he places each part on a clean, flat surface such as a table or mat. This aids in assembly in reverse order and avoids the loss of parts.

DANGER

BE SURE THE BOLT IS IN THE FORWARD POSITION BEFORE DISASSEMBLY. THE SPRING GUIDE CAN CAUSE DEATH OR INJURY IF THE OPERATING ROD SPRING IS RETRACTED WITH THE BOLT PULLED TO THE REAR.

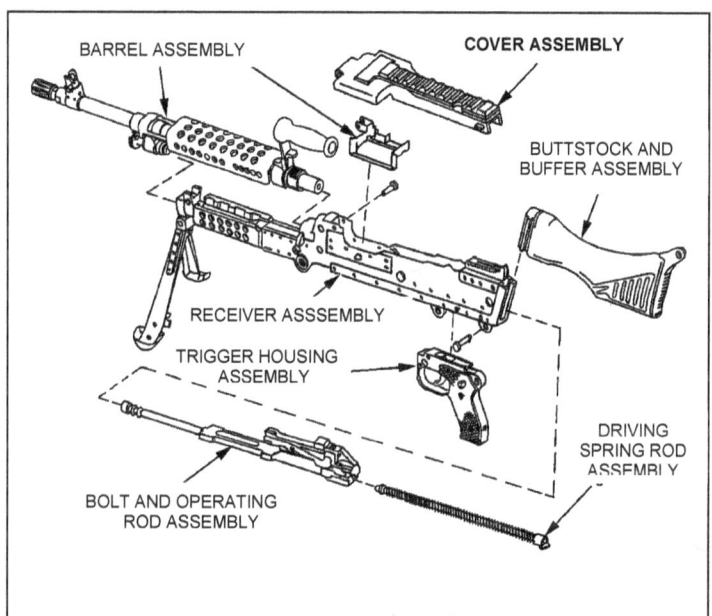

Figure 3-10. Eight major assemblies.

a. **Remove the Buttstock and Buffer Assembly**. Depress the back plate latch located on the underside of the butt stock where it joins the receiver. Slide the butt stock upward (straight up) and remove it from the receiver (Figure 3-11, page 3-12).

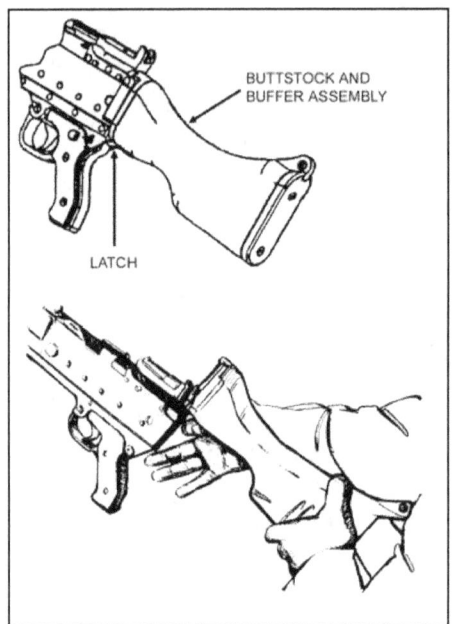

Figure 3-11. Removal of buttstock.

b. **Remove the Driving Spring Rod Assembly**. Push the driving spring rod assembly forward and up to disengage its retaining stud from inside the receiver (Figure 3-12). Pull rearward on the drive spring rod assembly, removing it from the receiver (Figure 3-13).

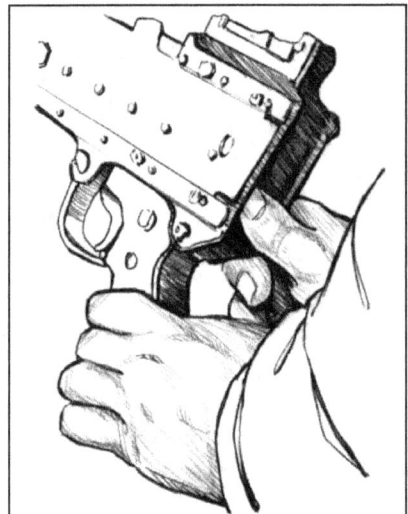

Figure 3-12. Removal of driving spring rod assembly.

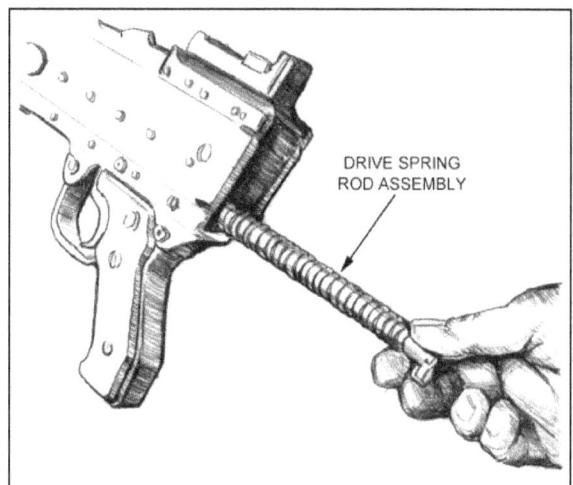

Figure 3-13. Driving spring rod assembly.

WARNING

To avoid injury, keep face away from rear of receiver. Hold rod assembly securely as it is under tension.

---

c. **Remove the Bolt and Operating Rod Assembly.** Pull the cocking handle to the rear to start the rearward movement of the bolt and operating rod assembly inside of the receiver. With the index finger, reach inside the top of the receiver and push rearward on the face of the bolt until the bolt and operating rod assembly are exposed at the rear of the receiver. Grasp the bolt and operating rod and remove them from the rear of the receiver. Return the cocking handle to the forward position (Figure. 3-14).

NOTE: Pulling the trigger maybe necessary to lower the sear and allow the bolt to release.

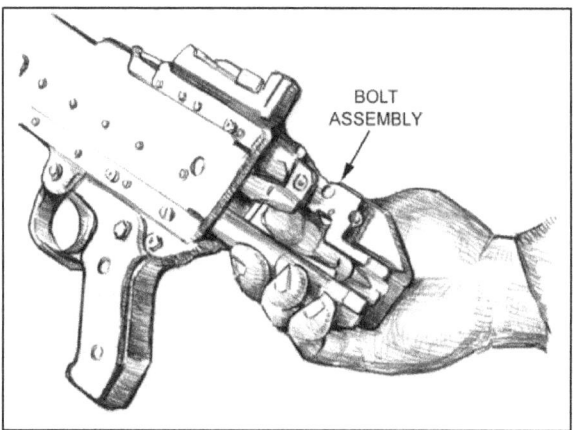

Figure 3-14. Bolt assembly.

WARNING

When buttstock is off, do not pull the cocking handle to the rear without first removing the drive spring assembly.

---

d. **Remove the Trigger Housing Assembly**. Depress spring pin and remove. You may need to use the back of the back plate of the buttstock to tap on the spring pin, then remove pin with fingers. All pins go from right to left (Figure 3-15, page 3-14). Rotate the rear of the trigger-housing group assembly down, disengage the holding notch at the front of the assembly from its recess on the bottom of the receiver, and remove the assembly from the receiver (Figure 3-16, page 3-14).

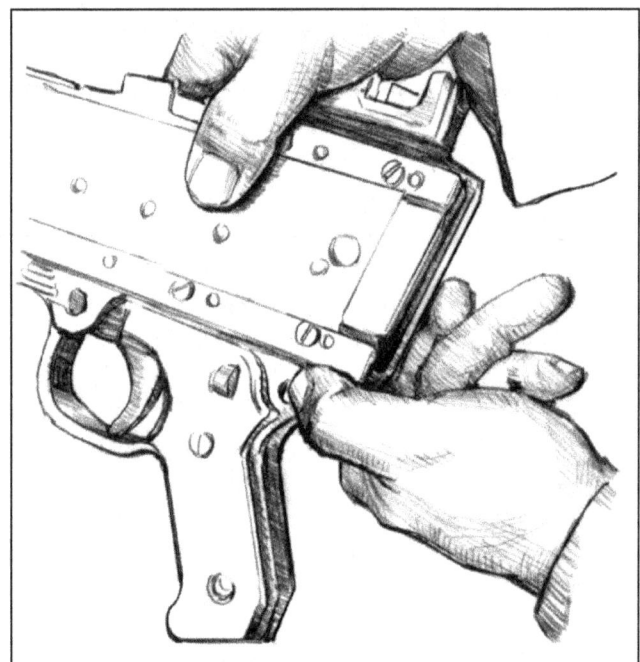

Figure 3-15. Trigger spring pin.

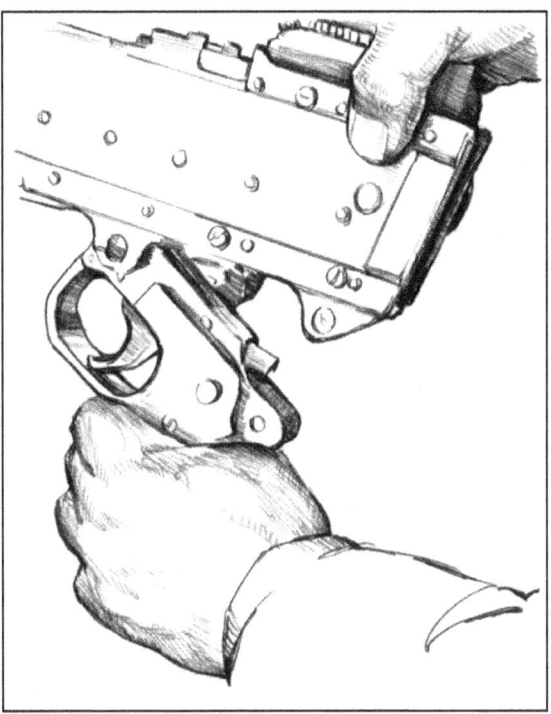

Figure 3-16. Removal of trigger housing.

   e. **Remove the Cover Assembly**. (A) Close cover. Depress spring pin and remove. You may need to use the back of the back plate of the buttstock to tap on the spring pin. (B) Then remove pin with fingers. All pins go from right to left. (C) Depress cover latches, lift upwards and remove cover assembly. (D) Remove feed tray (Figure 3-17, page 3-16).

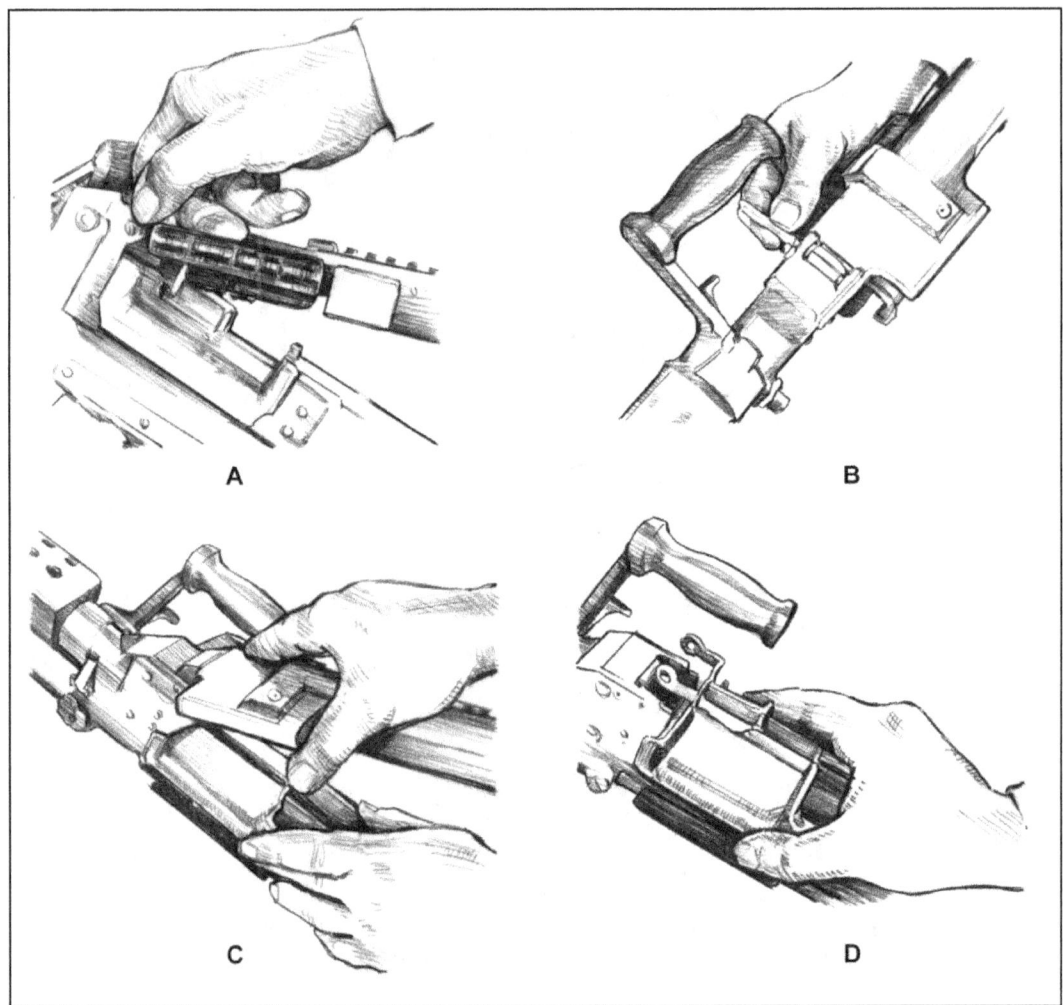

Figure 3-17. Removal of cover, feed tray, and spring pin.

f. **Remove the Barrel Assembly**. (A) Make sure that the barrel-carrying handle is to the right side. Depress the barrel-locking latch located on the left side of the receiver where the barrel joins the receiver and hold. (B) Grasp the barrel carrying handle and rotate the carrying handle to the upright position (without pulling up on the barrel release). (C) Then push forward and pull up, separating the barrel from the receiver (Figure 3-18).

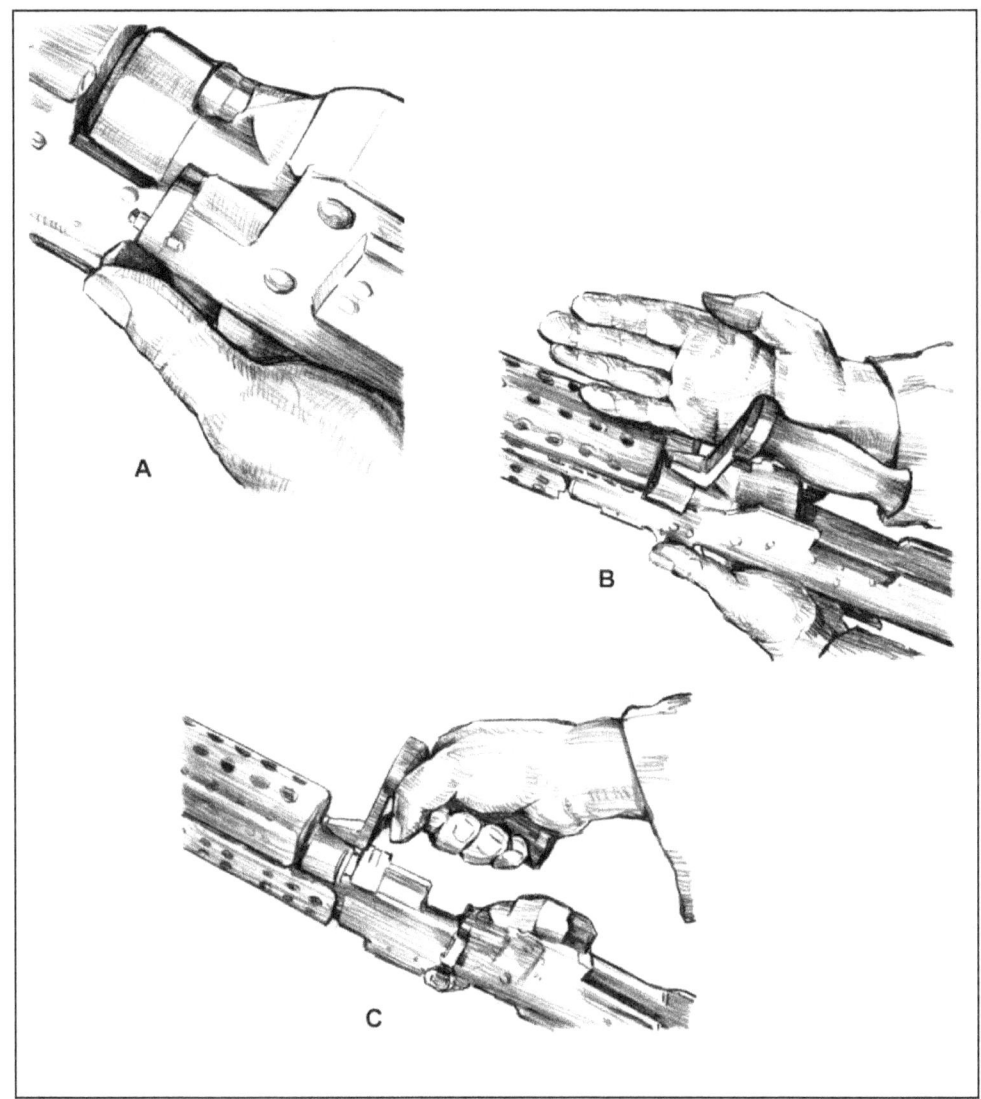

Figure 3-18. Removal of barrel.

g. **Disassemble the Barrel Assembly.** (A) Hold the barrel at the point where the gas system attaches to it. (B) Grasp and rotate the gas collar clockwise until it releases from the gas plug. Remove the collar from the gas plug. (C) Slide the gas regulator plug from front to rear, removing it from the gas hole bushing. (D) Remove heat shield. Lift the rear of heat shield assembly off the barrel, then pry one of the front metal tabs out of hole on gas hole bushing, rotate the heat shield towards the other metal tab, and remove heat shield from the barrel. This completes the general disassembly (Figure 3-19, page 3-18).

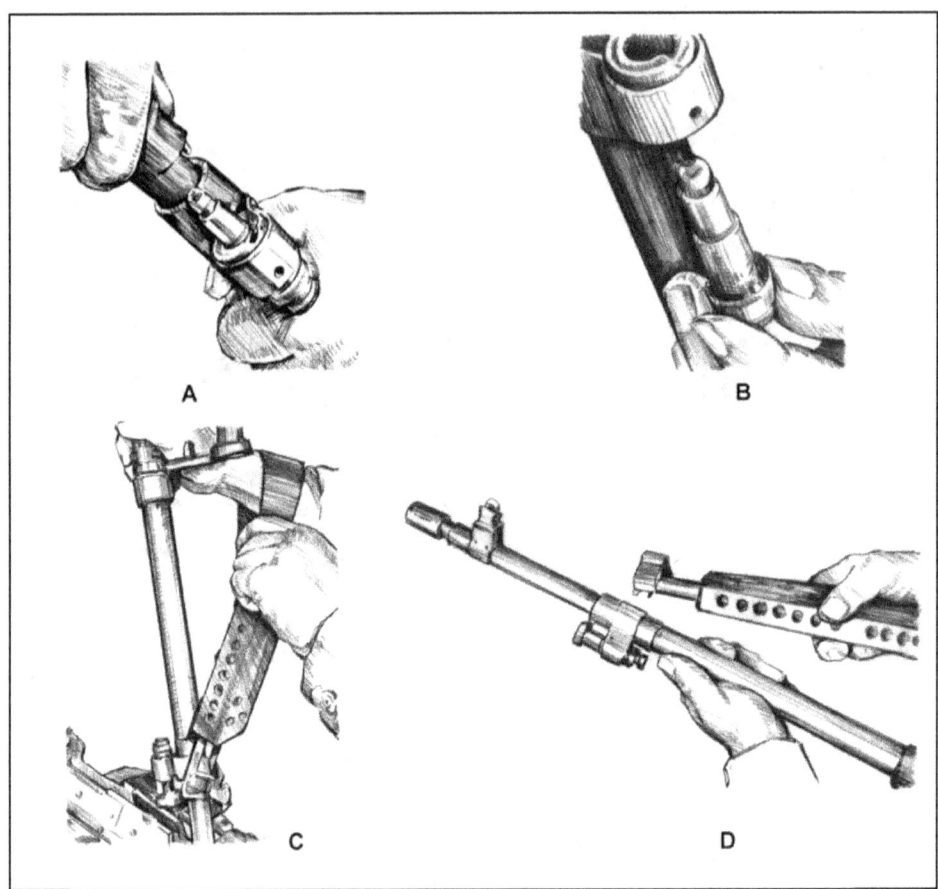

Figure 3-19. Gas regulator and collar.

3-8. INSPECTION

Inspection begins with the weapon disassembled into its eight major assemblies. Note that a shiny surface on a part does not mean the parts are unserviceable. The gunner inspects each area of the weapon and related equipment for the conditions indicated. Any broken or missing parts should be repaired or replaced IAW TM 9-1005-313-10. The gunner should perform PMCS every 90 days. If the weapon has not been used in 90 days, the PMCS in the operator's manual should be performed regardless. If you see rust on a weapon, the PMCS should be done immediately. Inspect all of the components for broken or missing parts. Inspect parts for cracks, dents, burrs excessive wear, rust, or corrosion. Inspect external surfaces for adequate finish.

a. **Barrel Assembly.** Check barrel for bulges, bends, burrs, obstructions and obstructions or pits in the chamber or bore. Disassemble, inspect, and clean the gas collar and plug. Ensure the flash suppressor is fastened securely. Inspect the front sight for damage or looseness. Inspect carrying handle assembly for bent, broken, or missing parts. Assure the heat shield is present, on the barrel assembly, and is not bent or broken, and does not have any missing parts.

NOTE: Some heat distortion or charring may be observed on the outer nonmetallic portion of the heat shield and is not cause for replacement. Do not apply lubricants to composite or rubber components.

b. **Buttstock and Buffer Assembly.** Check for burrs and rough edges on mating grooves and flanges. Check to be sure the back plate latch locks the buffer assembly securely to the receiver assembly when installed. Make sure the buffer plug sticks out through the back plate and is flush or higher than the protrusion below it. Make sure there is no rattling sound when the buffer is shaken and that the plug cannot rotated by finger pressure. Inspect the butt stock for cracks. Check to make sure the back plate locks the butt stock securely to the receiver assembly when installed.

c. **Driving Spring Rod Assembly.** Check the spring for broken strands. Ensure the rod assembly is not bent.

d. **Bolt And Operating Rod Assembly.** Inspect entire area of the bolt and operating rod assembly for missing parts, broken or cracked areas, burrs, bends, or pits on the surface. Looking at the bolt, you can see if the firing pin is broken. The extractor should not move. The operating rod piston should have a slight movement from left to right (about 1/8-inch turn). When the bolt and operating rod are pulled to the rear, the piston should move freely without binding.

NOTE: Always turn both barrels in with the weapon if damage is found on the bolt assembly.

e. **Trigger Mechanism/Housing Assembly.** Inspect the tripping lever and sear for burrs on edges. Push the tripping lever back to raise the sear, put the safety on "S," and pull the trigger. The sear should not drop down far enough to lock in the downward position. Place the safety on "F," and pull the trigger. The sear should drop down and lock in the downward position. Check the sear spring, ensuring the leg of the spring is behind the trigger pin and not between the trigger and the pin. Check grip assembly for loose or missing grip screws. Check trigger guard for bends or cracks. Check trigger spring pin for bends, and or broken or missing spring.

f. **Cover Assembly.** Pivot the feed lever back and forth to ensure it operates smoothly without binding. Push in on the cover latches to make sure the retaining clip is not weak or missing and that they do not bind in the housing. Push down on the cartridge guides and feed pawls to make sure the springs are not weak or missing. Inspect accessory mounting rail for nicks or burrs.

g. **Feed Tray.** Check for cracks, deformation, broken welds, or loose rivets.

h. **Handguard.** Check handguard for cracks, broken or missing parts.

i. **Receiver Assembly.** Check that the rear sight assembly is securely mounted to the receiver and operates properly. Check that the cocking handle operates the slide properly. Pull the cocking handle to the rear and allow it to slowly return forward, making sure that the slide does not bind in the receiver. Check for damaged or missing ejection port cover, spring, and pin. Lower and raise the bipod legs, ensuring they move freely without binding. Check bipod legs for cracks, or twisted or incomplete assembly. Check the exterior surface of the M240B for the exterior protective finish.

j. **Machine Gun**. Assemble the weapon. Be sure parts are installed correctly and are in good working condition. When installing the barrel, move the barrel release slowly to the right and count the number of clicks. Fewer than two and more than seven clicks indicate defective parts. Check both barrels. Check weapon functioning with belted dummy ammunition by performing a function check. If weapon does not function properly and the cause cannot be determined using troubling shooting procedures, notify direct-support maintenance.

k. **M122A1 Mount**. The traversing and elevating mechanism should not bind. The numbers on the scales and dials must be legible.

(1) Distinct clicks must be heard when the handwheels are turned. Index lines should be calibrated with the indicator pointer.

(2) The pintle should fit snugly in the pintle bushing, and the pintle lock should hold the pintle securely.

(3) The sleeve latch should function properly, and the traversing bar should be tight when the tripod legs are extended and latched.

l. **Carrying Case**. Maintenance tools and equipment should be complete and serviceable. The case should be serviceable. Frequent washing of the case should be avoided. Such washing may destroy the waterproofing and shrink the case.

3-9. CLEANING, LUBRICATION, AND PREVENTIVE MAINTENANCE

The M240B machine gun should be cleaned immediately after firing. At a minimum, the M240B should be cleaned after firing a basic load of 900 to 1,200 rounds. The gunner disassembles the M240B into its major groups for cleaning. All metal components and surfaces that have been exposed to powder fouling should be cleaned using CLP on a bore-cleaning patch. CLP is used on the bristles of the receiver brush to clean the receiver. After the M240B is cleaned and wiped dry, a thin coat of CLP is rubbed on using a cloth. This lubricates and preserves the exposed metal parts during all normal temperature ranges.

CAUTION
When using CLP, do not use other cleaners. Never mix CLP with RBC or LSA. When cleaning the barrel, avoid getting CLP or RBC in the gas regulator. Damage could occur to the weapon.

---

a. When cleaning the weapon, any of the previously mentioned cleaning lubricating agents can be used. As soon as possible after firing the M240B, the gunner disassembles the weapon into its eight major assemblies and cleans them as follows. Before the weapon is disassembled, ensure it is clear:

(1) Clean the bore using CLP or RBC and a bore brush with a cleaning rod. Do not reverse direction of the bore brush while it is in the bore.

(a) Run the brush through the bore several times until most of the powder fouling and other foreign matter has been removed.

(b) Swab out the bore several times using a cleaning rod and a swab wet with CLP.

(c) Swab out the bore several times using a cleaning rod and a dry swab.

(2) Clean the chamber using CLP and a chamber brush attached to a cleaning rod.

(a) Run the brush through the chamber several times until most of the powder fouling and other foreign matter has been removed.

(b) Swab out the chamber several times using a cleaning rod and a swab wet with CLP.

(c) Swab out the chamber several times using a cleaning rod and a dry swab.

(3) Clean the receiver using a receiver brush and CLP.

(a) Brush the receiver until most of the powder fouling and other foreign matter is removed.

(b) Swab out the receiver several times using a cleaning rod section and a swab wet with CLP.

(c) Swab out the receiver several times using a cleaning rod section and a dry swab.

(4) Clean the gas regulator plug with special tools (cleaning reamers and combination regulator scraper). Remove *all* carbon dust. Do not use CLP on the collar, gas block, or body.

(a) Clean each gas inlet hole of the gas regulator plug. Insert the small reamer into each hole and twist back and forth to remove the carbon (apply hand pressure only) (Figure 3-20).

(b) Clean the central hole of the gas plug by inserting the scraper tool down to the bottom of the hole and twisting firmly (Figure 3-21).

(c) Clean the two grooves by inserting the scraper tool into the grooves and applying pressure as firmly as possible (Figure 3-21).

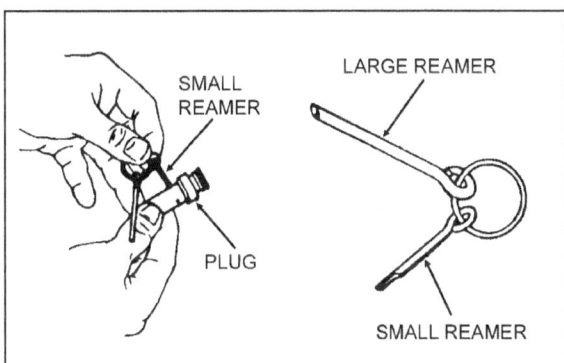

Figure 3-20. Tools for cleaning the gas regulator plug inlet holes.

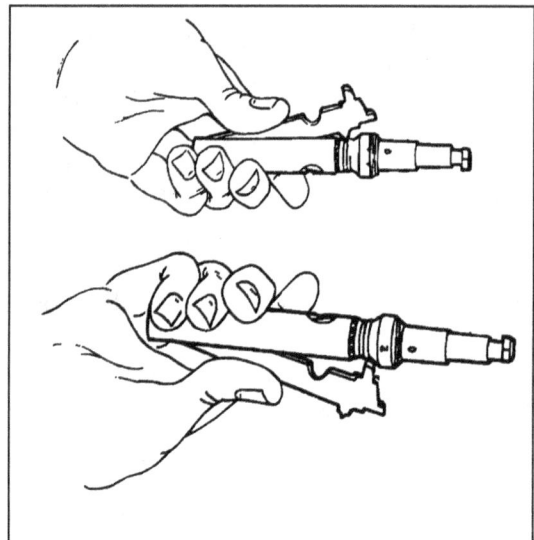

Figure 3-21. Cleaning of the gas regulator plug grooves.

(5) Clean the gas cylinder with the special tool scraper-extraction combination tool.

(a) Clean the front interior of the gas cylinder by carefully inserting the combination tool, with the handle upward. Be sure the tool is fully inserted and seated against the gas cylinder. Apply slight pressure to the handles and turn clockwise to remove carbon (Figure 3-22).

(b) Clean gas cylinder bore with gas cylinder cleaning brush dampened with CLP.

(c) Brush the gas cylinder until most of the powder fouling and other foreign matter are removed.

> **CAUTION**
> When inserting the scraper-extractor combination tool into the gas cylinder, ensure before scraping that it is fully seated against the fore-end face of the cylinder. Damage to the fore-end of the gas cylinder could cause gas leakage and subsequent weapon stoppage.

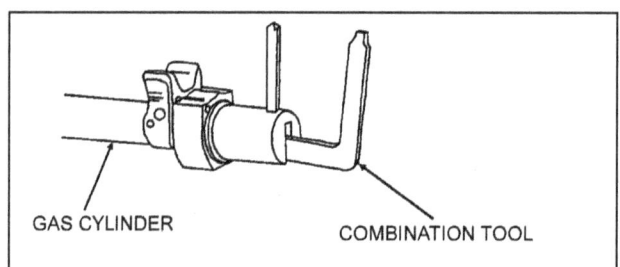

Figure 3-22. Cleaning tool for the gas cylinder.

(6) Clean the bolt and operating rod with the special scraper-extraction combination tool.

(a) Clean the piston head cavity by inserting the combination tool into the piston bottom of the operating rod. Squeeze handles firmly and twist the tool to remove carbon (Figure 3-23).

(b) Insert the screwdriver end of the tool into the piston to remove carbon residue on the bottom.

(c) Clean the bolt and operating rod with rag and CLP.

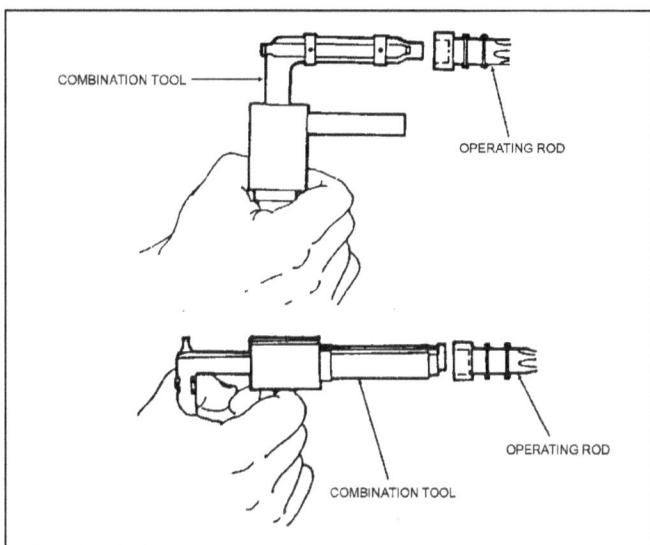

Figure 3-23. Cleaning tool of the piston head cavity.

(7) Remember the following important points during cleaning:
- Do not use gasoline, kerosene, benzene, shaving cream, high-pressure water, steam, or air for cleaning.
- Keep the gas hole bushing free of CLP or RBC. It must remain dry.
- During sustained firing, especially when using blank ammunition, the extractor assembly must be stripped and cleaned periodically.
- Improper cleaning of the gas cylinder and gas regulator plug will result in the two temporarily welding themselves together during firing.

(8) Lubricate the following parts with CLP as instructed:
- Driving spring rod assembly.
- Bolt.
- Receiver inner walls.
- Cover assembly (springs, and feed pawls).
- Trigger housing (inside only).

b. After lubricating, the components are cycled by hand to spread the CLP. Weapons fired infrequently or stored for prolonged periods should have a light film of CLP. This should be applied to the interior of the gas cylinder and the gas piston immediately after cleaning or after inspection. Preventive maintenance is performed every 90 days, unless inspection reveals more frequent servicing is necessary. The use of the lubricant does not eliminate the requirement for cleaning and inspecting to ensure that corrosion has not formed. Before the weapon is used, the gas system and components must be cleaned and free of oil and lubricants.

c.   All exposed surfaces of the M122A1 tripod, flex-mount assembly, complete pintle and T&E mechanism are cleaned by wiping them down with a clean rag. For T&E and pintles that have stubborn areas with hard-to-remove dirt, a steel brush or bore brush is used to loosen the dirt (do not use on the flex-mount itself). A clean rag is then used to wipe them down and CLP is used to lubricate them.

d.   The following procedures apply to cleaning and lubricating the M240B during unusual conditions:

(1) Below 0 degrees Fahrenheit—use lubricating oil, arctic weather (LAW). Oil lightly to avoid freeze-up.

(2) Extreme heat—use light coat of CLP.

(3) Damp or salty air—use CLP. Clean and apply frequently.

(4) Sandy or dusty areas—use CLP. Clean and apply frequently. Wipe with rag after each application to remove excess.

3-10.   GENERAL ASSEMBLY

After cleaning, lubricating, and inspecting the weapon, the gunner assembles the weapon and performs a function check.

a.   **Replacing the Barrel Assembly**. Insert the gas regulator plug into the gas hole bushing so that it is on the number one setting. (number 1 gas setting on the regulator faces towards the barrel). Place the gas collar over the front end of the gas regulator plug, while pushing against the spring, rotate counterclockwise until it stops. Insert one of the metal tabs of the heat shield in to the hole located of the sides of the gas hole bushing, than rotate it so that the other tab locks in place. Then push down on the heat shield so that it snaps onto the barrel. With gas regulator downward and carrying handle in the vertical position, place barrel on the barrel support (located on the gas cylinder). Keeping the gun upright, pull the barrel to the rear ensuring the gas regulator is guided into the gas cylinder. Pull the barrel fully into the receiver and rotate the carrying handle completely to the right, ensuring to count the number of clicks. If the number of clicks fall between 2 to 7, the headspace is set correctly. If the number falls outside 2 to 7, turn it in to the unit armor (make sure that the threads on the barrel are located on top and bottom and on the inside of the receiver make sure that the threads are located on the left and right) (Figure 3-24).

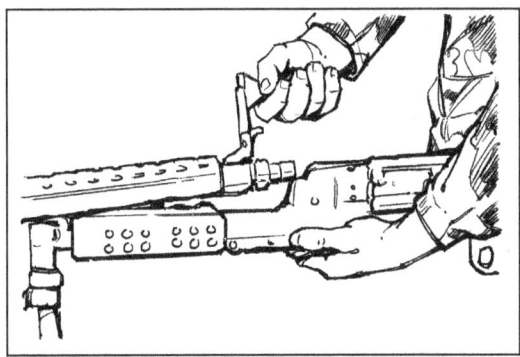

Figure 3-24. Replacement of the barrel assembly.

b. **Replacing the Cover Assembly and Feed Tray**. Position the feed tray on the receiver so that the feed tray guides are aligned with the receiver brackets. Place the cover assembly onto the receiver aligning its mounting holes with the mounting brackets on the receiver, close the cover assembly. Then, insert the spring pin into the holes to affix the cover and feed tray to the receiver (insert the spring of the spring pin into the hole than push in from right to left).

c. **Replacing the Trigger Housing Assembly**. Insert the holding notch on the front of the trigger housing into the forward recess on the bottom of the receiver. Rotate the rear of the trigger housing upwards and align the holes of the trigger housing with the mounting bracket on the receiver. Hold the trigger housing assembly and insert the spring pin into the hole, securing the assembly to the receiver. (insert the spring of the spring pin into the hole than push in from right to left) (Figure 3-25).

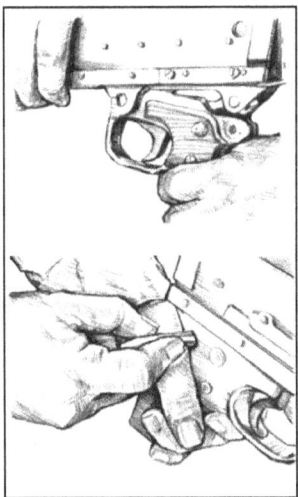

Figure 3-25. Replacement of the trigger housing assembly.

d. **Replacing the Bolt and Operating Rod Assembly**. Make sure the bolt and operating rod are fully extended (unlocked position). Insert the bolt and operating rod into the rear of the receiver (bolt upward, operating rod beneath bolt) ensuring the bolt is on top of the rails located on the left and right inner walls of the receiver. Push the entire bolt and operating rod assembly into the receiver as far forward as possible. Pull the trigger to allow the sear to drop and the group to slide all the way into the receiver (Figure 3-26).

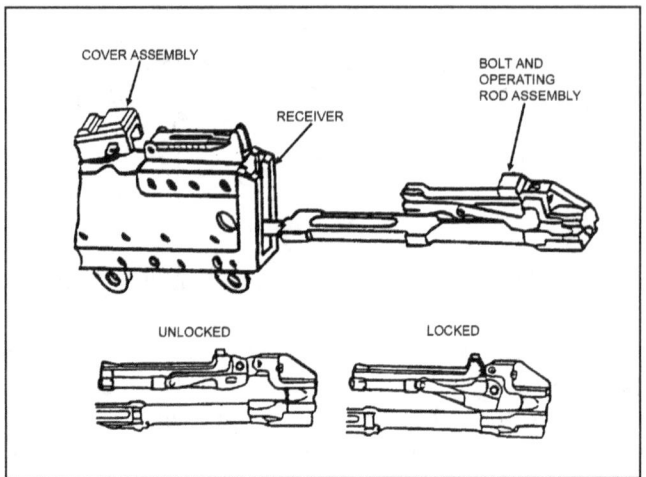

Figure 3-26. Replacement of the bolt and operating rod assembly.

e. **Replacing the Driving Spring Rod Assembly**. Insert the driving spring rod assembly into the receiver, sliding it all the way forward against the recess in the rear of the operating rod. Push in and lower the driving spring rod assembly to engage the retaining stud into the hole located on the bottom of the receiver (Figure 3-27).

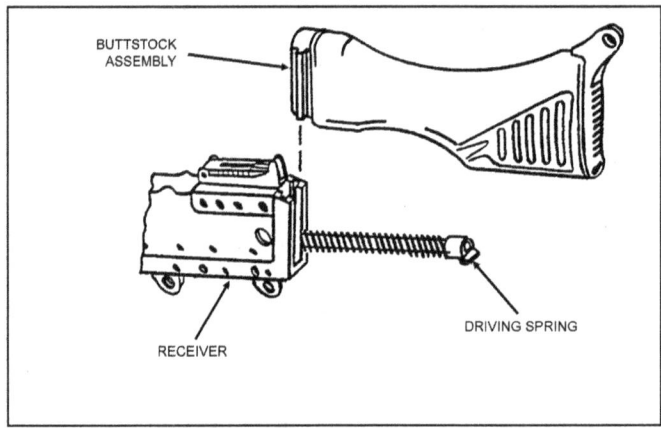

Figure 3-27. Replacement of the driving spring rod assembly.

f. **Replacing the Butt stock and Buffer Assembly**. Position the bottom recess grooves of the butt stock onto the top of the receiver recess grooves. Slide the butt stock down until it locks in place on the receiver. Ensure the butt stock is secure.

g. **Replacing the Handguard**. Line the handguard on the bottom of the gas cylinder and push upwards. The handguard snaps in place.

3-11. FUNCTION CHECK

The gunner must perform a function check to ensure that the M240B is correctly assembled. The procedures, in order, are—

    a. Places the safety on "F."

    b. Pulls the cocking handle to the rear, locking the bolt to the rear of the receiver.

    c. Returns the cocking handle to the forward position.

    d. Places the safety on "S," and closes the cover.

    e. Pulls the trigger. (Bolt should not go forward).

    f. Places the safety on "F."

    g. Pulls the cocking handle to the rear, pulls the trigger, and rides the bolt forward.

    h. Closes the ejection port cover.

3-12. MAINTENANCE PROCEDURES

Maintenance of the M240B requires certain actions to be taken before, during, and after firing.

    a. Before firing—

    (1) Wipe the bore dry.

    (2) Inspect the weapon as outlined in operator's TM.

    (3) Inspect the spare barrel.

    (4) Lubricate the weapon.

    b. During firing—

    (1) Change the barrels. Changing the barrel prolongs the life of both barrels.

    (2) Periodically inspect the weapon to ensure that it is properly lubricated.

    (3) When malfunctions or stoppages occur, follow the procedures in Section IV.

    c. After firing—

    (1) Clear and clean the weapon immediately.

    (2) Every 90 days during inactivity, clean and lubricate the weapon unless inspection reveals more frequent servicing is necessary (TM 9-1005-313-10).

3-13. MAINTENANCE DURING NUCLEAR, BIOLOGICAL, CHEMICAL CONDITIONS

If the M240B is contaminated by chemical, biological, or radiological agents, the gunner takes appropriate action to reduce exposure and minimize penetration.

    a. **Chemical.** The gunner uses towelettes from the M258A1 kit to wipe off the weapon. If these are not available, he washes the weapon with soap and water.

    b. **Biological.** The gunner uses towelettes or soap and water as previously described.

    c. **Radiological.** The gunner wipes the weapon with warm soapy water if it is available. If not, he uses towelettes or rags. (For more details, see FM 3-5.)

Section III. OPERATION AND FUNCTION

This section discusses the operation of the M240B machine gun. This includes loading, unloading, cycle of functioning, adjustment of the sights, and use of both the bipod and tripod.

3-14. OPERATION

The M240B machine gun is loaded from the closed bolt position. The M240B is fired, unloaded, and cleared from the open bolt position. The safety must be placed on "F" before the bolt can be pulled to the rear. Before belted ammunition can be used, it must be linked with the double link at the open end of the bandoleer. It must be free of dirt and corrosion. In almost all cases, the M240B machine gun can be best used when fired from a tripod; the M240B's potential for continuous, accurate fire and control manipulation is maximized. However, in some circumstances, the gunner may use the bipod mount.

3-15. LOADING

The gunner makes sure the weapon is cleared. He place the safety on "F." With his palm facing up, he pulls the cocking handle to the rear. This puts the bolt assembly in the rear position. When the bolt is held to the rear by the sear, he manually returns the cocking handle to the forward position, places the safety on "S." He raises the cover assembly and ensures the feed tray, receiver assembly, and chamber are clear. He lowers the feed tray, places the safety on "F," and pulls the cocking handle to the rear. While maintaining rearward pressure, he pulls the trigger and eases the bolt assembly forward. He places the first round of the belt in the feed tray groove, double link leading, with open side of links face down. He holds the belt about six rounds from the loading end, while closing the cover assembly. *Ensure that the round remains in the feed tray groove, and close the cover assembly* (Figure 3-28).

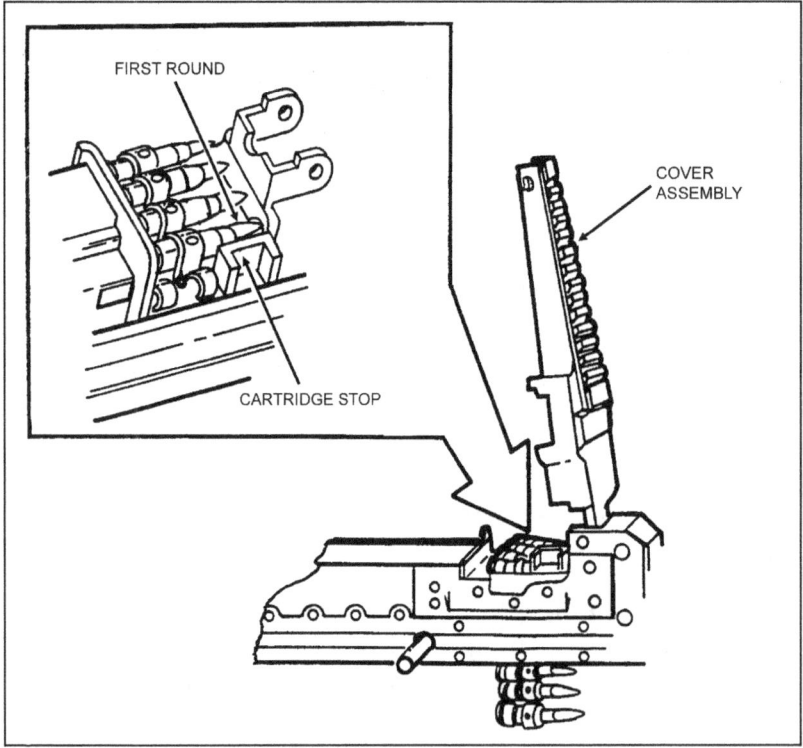

Figure 3-28. Loading.

WARNING

The M240B is carried loaded with the bolt locked to the *rear* in all *tactical situations* where noise discipline is critical to the success of the mission. Trained gun crews are the only personnel authorized to load the M240B and only when command directs the crew to do so. During *normal training exercises*, the M240B is loaded and carried with the bolt in the *forward position*.

3-16. UNLOADING

The gunner unloads the M240B by pulling and locking the bolt to the rear position, if it is not already there. He manually returns the cocking handle to its forward position. He places the safety on "S." He raises the cover assembly and removes any ammunition or links from the feed tray. He performs the four-point safety check (see Section III).

3-17. CYCLE OF FUNCTIONING

Crew members can recognize and correct stoppages when they know how the weapon functions. The weapon functions automatically as long as ammunition is fed into it and the trigger is held to the rear. Each time a round is fired, the parts of the weapon function in a cycle or sequence. Many of the actions occur at the same time and are separated only for teaching purposes. The sequence of functioning is known as the "cycle of functioning."

a. The cycle starts when the first round of the belt is placed in the tray groove. Then the trigger is pulled, releasing the sear from the sear notch. When the trigger is pulled to the rear, the rear of the sear lowers and disengages from the sear notch. This allows the bolt and operating rod assembly to be driven forward by the expansion of the driving spring rod assembly. The cycle stops when the trigger is released and the sear again engages the sear notch on the bolt and operating rod assembly.

b. The details of the cycle of functioning follows:

(1) *Feeding*. The actuating roller moves the feed lever side to side, which in turn moves the feed pawls. The forward movement of the bolt forces the outer pawls to the right, fully feeding the round. The inner pawl rides over the round and settles behind it. The rearward movement forces the inner pawl to the right, fully feeding the round. The action of fully feeding a round pushes the link of a fired round out of the side of the gun. The last link in a belt cannot be pushed out and is cleared during the unloading.

(2) *Chambering*. The first round is positioned in line with the chamber and is held in position by the cartridge stop and cartridge guide pawl. On trigger squeeze, the nose of the sear is depressed thus freeing the piston rod extension. The driving spring rod assembly pushes the working parts forward. The feed horn strikes the base of the round. The bolt strips the round from the belt link. The chambering ramp angles downward and, along with the spring tension of the cartridge guide pawl, forces the round toward the chamber. The cartridge guide pawl also holds back the belt link. When the round is fully seated in the chamber, the extractor snaps over the extractor rim of the cartridge, and the ejector is depressed.

(3) *Locking.* During chambering, as soon as the piston begins to move, the firing pin is withdrawn into the bolt block. The breech remains locked during the primary movement. The bolt enters the barrel breech as the operating rod is driven forward by the drive spring, and as the locking lever, which the bolt is riding on, swings forward, pushing the bolt forward and locking it to the barrel breech. Although the term "locking" is used here, in the M240B, the bolt and barrel do not physically interlock. This way, the barrel can be removed when the bolt is forward.

(4) *Firing.* As the working parts come forward and the round is fed into the chamber, the locking lever is forced down by the locking cams. This slows down the forward movement of the bolt assembly. The piston rod extension, still moving forward, causes the locking lever link to rotate downward and back. This forces the arms down to their fullest extent in front of the locking shoulder. The extractor rises over the base of the round and the ejector is compressed. The round is now fully home with the breech locked. The final forward movement of the piston extension drives the firing pin through the bolt assembly onto the cartridge primer and fires the round. The working parts are now fully forward.

(5) *Unlocking.* When the round is fired, some of the gases pass through the gas plug regulator into the gas cylinder. The rapidly expanding gases enter the hollow end cap of the gas piston and force the operating assembly to the rear. This powers the last four steps in the cycle of functioning. During the primary movement of the operating rod assembly, it moves independently of the bolt for a short distance. At this point, the locking lever begins to swing toward the rear, carrying the bolt with it into its unlocked position, and clearing the barrel breech. When the bolt assembly has been jerked back, slightly enough to unlock the breech, the primary effort is extraction of the empty case.

(6) *Extraction.* When the breech is fully unlocked and the bolt assembly starts its rearward movement, the extractor withdraws the empty case from the chamber.

(7) *Ejecting.* As the cartridge case is withdrawn from the chamber, the ejector pushes from the top, and the extractor pulls from the bottom. The casing falls down from the face of the bolt as soon as it reaches the cartridge-ejection port. The empty belt links are forced out the link ejection port as the rearward movement of the bolt causes the next round to be positioned in the tray groove.

(8) *Cocking.* As the working parts continue toward the rear, the return spring is compressed; the trigger is kept squeezed; sufficient is gas made available by the gas-regulator adjustment, which causes the working parts to rebound off the buffer; and the action of feeding and firing continues. In releasing the trigger, the sear remains down, but the tripping lever rises. As the working parts come to the rear, the end of the piston rod extension hits the tripping lever, which, in turn, allows the sear to rise and engage the sear notch, which holds the working parts to the rear.

3-18. SIGHTS

This paragraph provides information on how to make corrections if the initial setting is not accurate. At a 10-meter target, each paster is 1 cm. Therefore, ten clicks on the adjusting screw (windage) of the front sight assembly in either direction moves the strike of the round left or right 1 cm. One complete turn on the front sight blade moves the strike of the round up or down 1 cm.

a. **Elevation Correction**. If the shot group is above or below the point of aim, the front sight posts must be adjusted using the front sight-adjusting tool. Unlock the front-sight retaining strap and rotate it up. If the shot group is above the point of aim, rotate the sight post counterclockwise. If the shot group is below the point of aim, rotate the sight post clockwise. Rotating the front sight post counterclockwise brings the point of impact *down* on the target. Rotating the front sight post clockwise brings the point of impact *up* on the target. At a range of 10 meters, one-half turn of the front sight post blade will move the point of impact by 5 mm or .5 cm. One full turn of the front sight post blade moves the point of impact by 1 cm. After rotating the front sight post blade the desired amount, lower the retaining strap, but *do not* lock it down until elevation is confirmed. If the front sight post blade must be rotated counterclockwise to a point where its base is past flush (Number 2 blade), it should be replaced with a Number 1 front sight blade, which is smaller than a Number 2 blade. If the front sight post blade must be rotated counterclockwise to a point where its base is more than one full turn past flush (Number 1 blade), it should be replaced with a Number 2 front sight blade which is taller than a Number 1 blade (Table 3-3, page 3-32).

b. **Windage Correction.** If the shot group is to the left of the point aim, move the front sight assembly to the right to shift the point of impact to the left (towards the point of aim). Using the front sight adjusting tool, loosen (turn counterclockwise) the adjusting screw on the front sight assembly the desired amount. Then tighten (turn clockwise) the opposite side screw on the left *exactly* the same number of clicks. At a range of 10 meters, one complete rotation of the adjusting screws will move the point of impact 8 mm or .8 cm. As the adjusting screws are turned, noticeable clicks (eight per revolution) should be detected. Each click is 1 mm or .1 cm. If this is not the case, have your armorer repair it. The front sight windage adjusting procedure is the combination of creating slack on one side, and then taking up that slack from the opposite side. The front sight protector assembly should always be clamped between the heads of the two opposing screws. *Remember, each time one screw is loosened or backed off, the opposite screw must be turned exactly the same amount.* Check for play in the front sight assembly by lightly clamping it between finger and thumb and attempting to move the sight assembly laterally. If you feel no play, the windage adjustment is completed. If evident, *carefully* check both screws for looseness (Table 3-4, page 3-32).

c. **10-Meter Zeroing (Mechanical Zero).** Ten-meter zero (mechanical zero) is the standardized starting point for all weapons in the United States Army. The gunner places the range scale on a range of 500 meters on the rear sight. He gets the front sight post blade approximately centered for both elevation and windage. The gunner identifies what number blade is on the weapon for elevation.

(1) *Number 1 blade (low 9.8mm).* Unlock the retaining strap and unscrew (counterclockwise) until the base of the blade is flush with the front sight protector surface, then make one full turn (counterclockwise). This should put the base of the blade past the base of the protector. Screw in (clockwise), counting the number of turns it takes until it stops, making sure the blade is on line with the barrel. If needed, back off until the blade is on line. Unscrew (counterclockwise) half the number of turns. This brings the blade to about the center.

(2) *Number 2 blade (high 11.8mm).* Unlock the retaining strap and unscrew (counterclockwise) until the base of the blade is flush with the front sight protector

surface. Screw in (clockwise), counting the number of turns it takes until it stops, making sure the blade is on line with the barrel, if needed back off until the blade is on line. Unscrew (counterclockwise) half the number of turns. This procedure brings the blade to about the center. Assume the prone position and sight on the target. Ensure windage is accomplished by making sure the front sight protector is centered left and right on its base.

100 meters—one full turn moves strike 10.8 cm (4.25 inches)
200 meters—one full turn moves strike 21.6 cm (8.5 inches)
300 meters—one full turn moves strike 32.4 cm (12.75 inches)
400 meters—one full turn moves strike 43.2 cm (17 inches)
500 meters—one full turn moves strike 54 cm (21.25 inches)
600 meters—one full turn moves strike 64.8 cm (25.5 inches)
700 meters—one full turn moves strike 75.6 cm (29.75 inches)
800 meters—one full turn moves strike 86.4 cm (34 inches)
900 meters—one full turn moves strike 97.2 cm (38.25 inches)

Table 3-3. Elevation correction chart.

100 meters—one full turn moves strike 8 cm (3.15 inches).
200 meters—one full turn moves strike 16 cm (6.3 inches).
300 meters—one full turn moves strike 24 cm (9.45 inches).
400 meters—one full turn moves strike 32 cm (12.6 inches).
500 meters—one full turn moves strike 40 cm (15.75 inches).
600 meters—one full turn moves strike 48 cm (18.9 inches).
700 meters—one full turn moves strike 56 cm (22 inches).
800 meters—one full turn moves strike 64 cm (25.2 inches).
900 meters—one full turn moves strike 72 cm (28.35 inches).

Table 3-4. Windage correction chart.

3-19. M122A1 TRIPOD

The M122A1 tripod provides a stable mount for the M240B, and it permits a higher degree of accuracy and control. The tripod is recommended for marksmanship training and defensive employment. The M122A1 tripod consists of the tripod, and flex-mount with T&E mechanism.

a. **Mounting the M240B on the Tripod.** The tripod assembly provides a stable and relatively lightweight base that is far superior to the bipod. The tripod may be extended and collapsed without difficulty. It consists of a tripod head, one front leg and two rear legs, and traversing bar. The traversing bar connects the two rear legs. It is hinged on one side, and has a sleeve and sleeve latch on the other that allows the tripod to collapse to a closed position for carrying or storage, or to lock in an open, extended position for use. The traversing bar also supports the T&E mechanism. The increments are numbered every 100 mils to 425 mils right of center. On the bar, there is a scale that measures direction in mils. It is graduated in 5-mil increments and numbered every 100 mils to 450 mils left of the center.

(1) The T&E mechanism provides controlled manipulation and the ability to engage predetermined targets.

(a) The traversing portion of the mechanism consists of the traversing handwheel and traversing slide-lock-lever. As the traversing handwheel is turned, the muzzle of the weapon turns to the left or right depending on the direction it is turned. Each click of the traversing handwheel indicates a 1-mil change in direction of the muzzle: 1 click equals 1 mil. There is a total of 100-mils traverse (50 mils right and 50 mils left of center).

(b) The elevating portion of the mechanism consists of the elevating handwheel. The elevating handwheel has a mil-click device built into it (1 click equals 1 mil). Engraved into the handwheel is a scale divided into 5-mil divisions and 1-mil subdivisions for a total of 50-mil increments. There are 200 mils above and 200 mils below the zero mark for a total of 400 mils in elevation change. Elevation readings are taken in two parts. First, the major reading is taken from the elevation screw plate. The second, minor reading is from the handwheel. The two readings are separated by a slash (/) when they are recorded.

(c) The traversing slide-lock-lever allows rapid lateral adjustments along the traversing bar. Direction readings are taken from the scale on the traversing bar, using the left side of the traversing slide as an index. The direction of the reading comes from the position of the muzzle, not the position of the slide.

(2) The flex-mount consists of the mount itself and the traversing and elevating mechanism. It joins the weapon and the T&E mechanism to the tripod. The flex-mount enhances the stability of the tripod platform and dampens the recoil of the weapon.

(3) To setup the tripod, the gunner unfolds the front leg and spreads the rear legs until the leg lock engages (Figure 3-29, page 3-34).

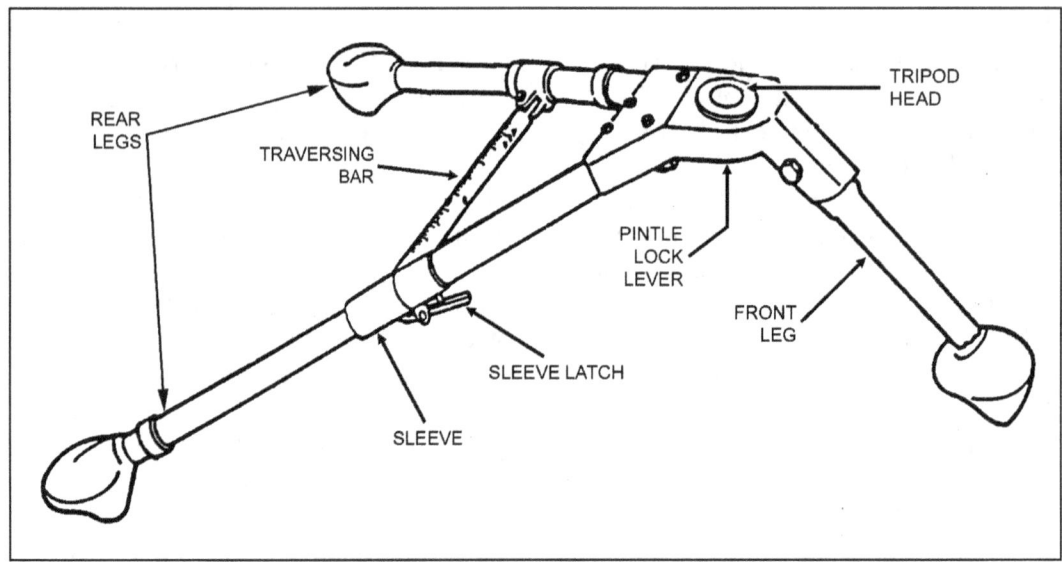

Figure 3-29. M122A1 tripod extended.

(4) Prepare the T&E mechanism for mounting. First center the elevating and traversing handwheel. To do this, he rotate the elevation handwheel until about 1 1/2 inches (two fingers) are visible on the upper elevating screw; rotating the traversing slide until approximately two fingers are visible on the lower elevating screw. The gunner rotates the traversing handwheel towards his body as far as it will go, then he turns it away two complete revolutions. He checks the traversing handwheel scale to ensure the "0" on the scale is aligned with the "0" index line before and after the two revolutions. The T&E should be centered now (Figure 3-30).

(5) Mount the T&E mechanism, pintle assembly, and fork assembly to the M122A1 tripod. With the T&E roughly centered, place the pintle assembly (1) into the sleeve bushing on the tripod leg assembly (2). Release the pintle lock (3) on the tripod leg assembly to secure the pintle assemblly to the tripod (Figure 3-30).

NOTE: The deflector on the fork assembly should deflect to the right.

(6) Align the holes in the fork assembly (4) with the holes in the T&E (5). Insert the pin (6) through the fork assembly and the T&E and secure with "C" clamps (7) (Figure 3-30).

(7) Mount the weapon on the M122A1 tripod assembly (Figure 3-30). Tilt the muzzle down slightly and insert the weapon's front receiver bushing (1) into the slots in the pintle assembly (2). Insert the quick-release pin (3) through the pintle (2) and front receiver bushing (1). Place the T&E assembly (5) (with fork assembly attached) onto the traverse bar (8) of the tripod leg assembly (2). Lock the T&E mechanism into place by turning the lock lever (9) clockwise. Lower the rear of the weapon into the fork assembly (4). Align the mounting holes (5) in the trigger housing with the hole in the fork assembly (4). Insert the spring pin (6) through the holes in the trigger assembly and fork but make sure the weapon is securely attached.

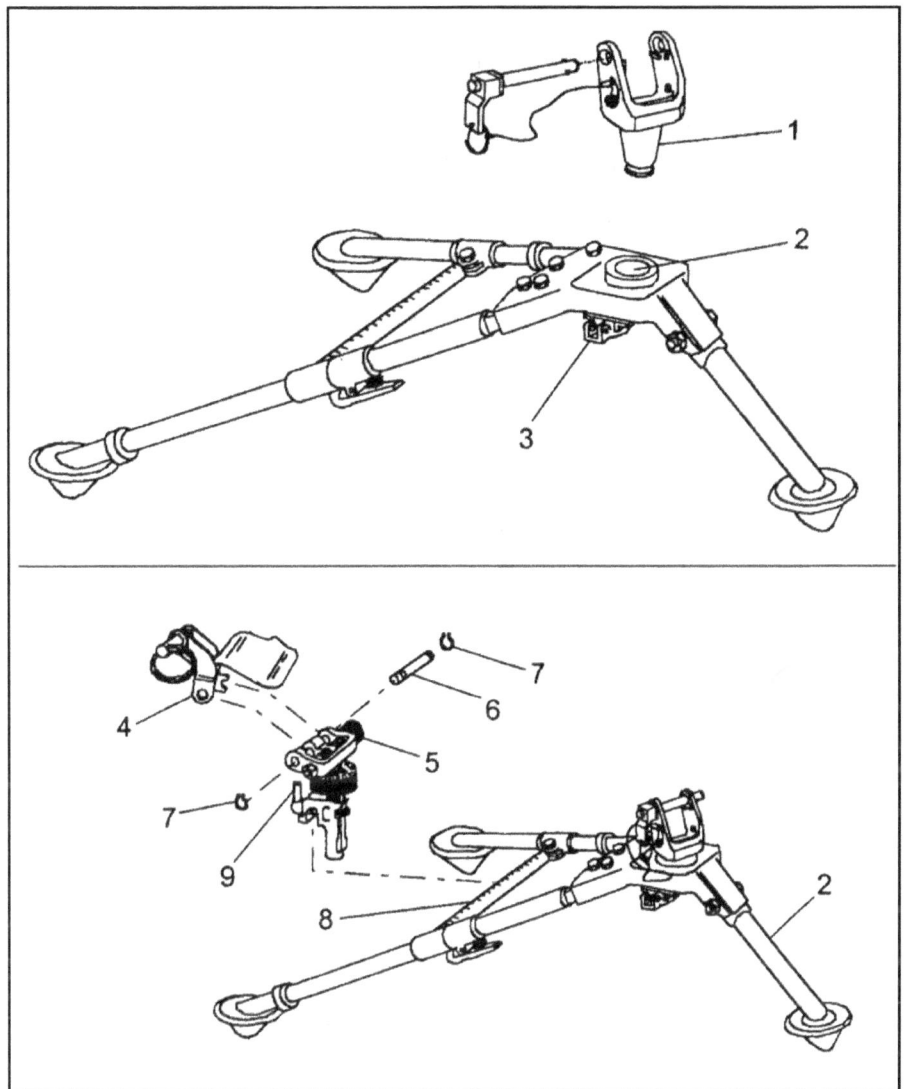

Figure 3-30. Mounting the M240B on the M122A1.

b. **Dismounting the M240B From the M122A1 Tripod.** The gunner dismounts the M240B from the M122A1 tripod by first removing the spring pin from the fork assembly, then he disengages the quick-release pin from the pintle and the front receiver bushing. Now, he raises the weapon up and off the tripod assembly.

3-20. BIPOD OPERATIONS

The bipod assembly is used to fire from the prone position. The buttstock in conjunction with the gunners nonfiring hand provides support for the weapon when firing in the bipod mode. The gas cylinder holds the bipod in place.

a. To lower the bipod legs, the gunner depresses the bipod retaining latch, while holding the bipod legs together to disengage from slots in the receiver. Then rotate the bipod legs down and release them so they lock in the vertical position. The bipod legs of the M240B do not extend (Figure 3-31).

b.   To return the bipod to the locked upright position, the gunner holds the bipod legs together to disengage them from the locked vertical position. Then he rotates the bipod legs rearward, depressing the bipod retaining latch, and engage the bipod leg hooks into the slots of the receiver. The bipod retaining latch will return to its original position, locking the bipod legs into position.

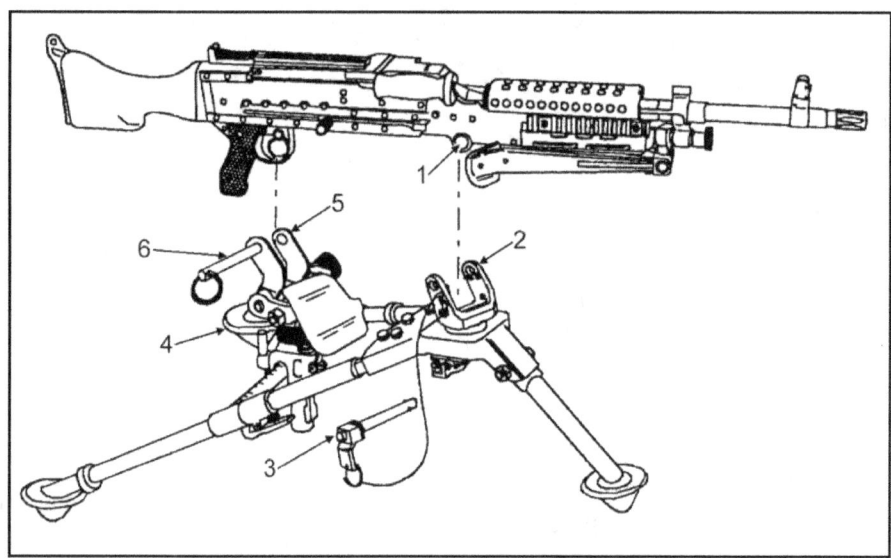

Figure 3-31. Lowering the bipod.

3-21.   TRIPOD OPERATIONS

The M122A1 tripod provides a stable mount for the M240B, and it permits a high degree of accuracy and control. The gunner unfolds the front leg and positions it toward the target and spreads the rear legs until the leg lock engages.

Section IV. PERFORMANCE PROBLEMS AND DESTRUCTION

This section identifies some of the problems that cause the weapon to perform improperly. It also explains how to identify unserviceable parts, and how to destroy the M240B when authorized to do so.

3-22.   MALFUNCTIONS

A malfunction occurs when a *mechanical failure* causes the *weapon to fire improperly*. Defective ammunition or improper operation by the gunner is not considered a malfunction. Sluggish operation and uncontrolled fire are the most common malfunction. If cleaning and or lubricating the weapon does not fix the problem, then the gunner turns it in to the unit armorer. Table 3-5 shows malfunctions, their probable causes, and the corrective actions.

MALFUNCTIONS	PROBABLE CAUSES	CORRECTIVE ACTIONS
Sluggish operation on gas regulator.	Carbon build-up.	Clean gas regulator.
Uncontrolled fire (runaway gun).	Broken or stuck Trigger.	
	Stuck sear.	Replace trigger.
	Broken of damaged sear spring	Replace sear spring

Table 3-5. Malfunctions.

a. **Uncontrolled Fire (Runaway Gun).** Uncontrolled fire (the weapon continues to fire after the trigger is released). This is usually caused by, the gunner not pulling and holding the trigger all the way to the rear. The following are immediate actions for uncontrolled fire:

(1) The gunner holds the weapon on target and fires the remaining ammunition.

(2) The assistant gunner stops the weapon from firing by breaking the belt of ammunition.

(3) The gunner as a last resort pulls the cocking handle to the rear thus, locking the bolt to the rear of the receiver.

b. **Sluggish Operation**. Sluggish operation is due to excessive friction caused by carbon build-up, improper lubrication, or burred parts. Corrective action includes cleaning, lubricating inspecting, and replacing worn parts. The gunner may adjust the gas regulator to maintain the rate of fire until he has a chance to clean the machine gun.

3-23. STOPPAGES

A stoppage is any *interruption* in the cycle of functioning caused by *faulty action* of the weapon or *faulty ammunition*. Stoppages are classified by their relationship to the cycle of functioning. Table 3-6 shows types of interruptions or stoppages, their probable causes, and the corrective actions.

STOPPAGE	PROBABLE CAUSE	CORRECTIVE ACTION
Failure to feed.	Insufficient gas pressure.	Clean gas port, inserts, and gas plug.
	Improper lubrication.	Lubricate as required.
	Defective links or ammunition.	Insert new link or ammunition.
	Ammunition belt installed wrong.	Reverse belt with open side of link down.
	Damaged or weak feed pawls and springs or feed lever.	Replace.
	Obstruction in receiver.	Remove obstruction; clean and lubricate as required.
	Damaged or weak feed pawls	Send to DS maintenance.
	Defective links or ammunition.	Insert new link or ammunition.
	Ammunition belt installed wrong.	Reverse belt with open side of link down.
Failure to chamber.	Ruptured cartridge case.	Remove IAW TM 9-1005-313-10.
	Damaged driving spring rod assembly.	Replace driving spring rod assembly.
	Damaged gas plug/collar (cracks/burrs).	Replace gas plug/collar.
	Built-up carbon on gas plug/collar, gas cylinder, piston or dirty chamber.	Remove carbon and clean IAW TM 9-1005-313-10.
Failure to extract.	Broken extractor or spring. Chipped or broken extractor. Defective extractor plunger. Insufficient gas pressure.	Replace. Replace. Replace. Clean and lubricate as required.
Failure to lock.	Dirty Chamber.	Clean IAW TM 9-1005-313-10.
	Dirty receiver or lack of lubrication.	Clean and lubricate IAW TM 9-1005-313-10.
	Insufficient gas pressure.	Clean gas regulator.

Table 3-6. Stoppages.

STOPPAGE	PROBABLE CAUSE	CORRECTIVE ACTION
Failure to fire.	Faulty ammunition. Broken or damaged firing pin or defective trigger. Insufficient gas pressure.	Replace. Replace or send to DS maintenance. Clean gas port, inserts, and gas plug.
Failure to cock.	Broken sear. Worn operating rod sear notch. Broken, defective, or missing sear plunger and or spring.	Send to DS maintenance. Send to DS maintenance. Send to DS maintenance.
Short to recoil.		Clean gas port and operating rod tube. Lubricate as required. Replace operating rod spring. See runaway gun (Malfunctions).

Table 3-6. Stoppages, (continued).

DANGER

1. IF NOTHING IS EJECTED AND THE WEAPON IS HOT (200 OR MORE ROUNDS FIRED IN LESS THAN 2 MINUTES), DO NOT OPEN THE COVER. MOVE THE SAFETY TO "S," WHICH PLACES THE WEAPON ON "S." KEEP THE WEAPON POINTED DOWNRANGE AND KEEP AWAY FROM THE WEAPON FOR 15 MINUTES, THEN CLEAR THE WEAPON.

2. BE CAREFUL IN CLEARING THE WEAPON WHEN THE BARREL IS HOT, A ROUND MAY FIRE (COOK OFF) DUE TO THE BARREL'S HEAT INSTEAD OF DUE TO THE FIRING MECHANISM. DURING TRAINING OR ON A FIRING RANGE, AFTER THE WEAPON HAS FIRED 200 ROUNDS, ITS BARREL IS CONSIDERED A HOT BARREL.

3. DURING COMBAT, WAIT 5 SECONDS, BECAUSE OF THE POSSIBILITY OF A "HANGFIRE" BEFORE APPLYING IMMEDIATE OR REMEDIAL ACTION. DURING TRAINING, WAIT 15 MINUTES BEFORE CLEARING A HOT WEAPON AND APPLYING IMMEDIATE OR REMEDIAL ACTION.

NOTE: When applying immediate or remedial action on a cold or hot gun, the gunner checks to see if any part of the round (ranging from the tip of the bullet to the rim) is in the chamber. The gunner removes the ammunition from the feed tray only, then closes the cover and attempts to fire. If the weapon fires, he reloads and continues firing. If it does not fire, he clears the weapon, and he inspects the weapon and ammunition.

3-24. IMMEDIATE ACTION

Immediate action is action taken to *reduce a stoppage without looking for the cause.* Immediate action should be taken in the event of either a misfire or a cook off. A *misfire* is the failure of a chambered round to fire. Such failure can be due to an ammunition defect or faulty firing mechanism. A *cook off* is the firing of a round by the heat of a hot barrel and not by the firing mechanism. Cookoffs can be avoided by applying immediate action within 10 seconds after a failure to fire. If the M240B stops firing, the gunner performs the following immediate actions are taken. (An effective memory aid is POPP, which stands for pull, observe, push, and press.)

a. Pulls and locks the cocking handle to the rear while observing the ejection port to see if a cartridge case, belt link, or round is ejected. Ensures that the bolt remains to the rear to prevent double feeding if a round or cartridge case is not ejected.

b. If a cartridge case, belt link, or a round is ejected, returns cocking handle to forward position, aim on the target, and presses the trigger. If the weapon still does not fire, takes remedial action. If a cartridge case, belt link, or round is not ejected, takes remedial action.

3-25. REMEDIAL ACTION

Remedial action is any action taken to determine the cause of a stoppage and to restore the weapon to an operational condition. This action is taken only after immediate action did not remedy the problem.

a. **Cold Weapon Procedures**. When a stoppage occurs with a cold weapon and immediate action has failed, the gunner uses the following procedures.

(1) Pulls the cocking handle to the rear, locking the bolt. Returns the cocking handle and places the safety to SAFE.

(2) Places the weapon on the ground or away from his face and opens the cover, performs the four-point safety check. Reloads and continues to fire.

(3) If the weapon does not fire, clears the weapon and inspects it and the ammunition.

b. **Hot Weapon Procedures**. If the stoppage occurs with a hot weapon (200 rounds or more in 2 minutes or as noted above for training), the gunner moves the safety to SAFE, waits 5 seconds (during training, lets the weapon cool for 15 minutes), uses the same procedures as outlined for cold weapon procedures.

c. **Jammed Cocking Handle**. If a stoppage occurs and the cocking handle cannot be pulled to the rear by hand (the bolt may be fully forward and locked or only partially forward), the gunner takes the following steps.

(1) Tries once again to pull the cocking handle *by hand.*

WARNING
Do not try to force the cocking handle to the rear with your foot or a heavy object. This could damage the weapon.

---

(2) If the weapon is hot enough to cause a cook off, moves all soldiers a safe distance from the weapon and keeps them away for 15 minutes.

(3) After the gun has cooled, the gunner will pull the cocking handle to the rear. Ensures rearward pressure is kept on the cocking handle until the driving spring rod

assembly is removed. Opens the cover and disassembles the gun. (The assistant gunner helps the gunner do this.)

(4) Removes the round or fired cartridge. Uses cleaning rod or ruptured cartridge extractor if necessary.

(a) In a training situation, after completing the remedial action procedures, the gun should not be fired until an inspection by an ordnance specialist has been made.

(b) In a combat situation, after the stoppage has been corrected, the gunner changes the barrel and tries to fire. If the weapon fails to function properly, the gunner sends it to the unit armorer.

3-26. STUCK BARREL

Stuck barrel is the result of the machine gun crew not properly cleaning the gas cylinder and gas regulator plug. During training or range firing the M240B should be cleared, disassemble and cleaned immediately. In combat, the M240B should be cleaned as soon as possible. The gun crew performs the following actions, only if the weapon can not be properly cleaned at that time.

a. Pulls the cocking handle to the rear, locking the bolt. Returns the cocking handle and places the safety to SAFE.

b. Places the weapon on the ground or away from his face and opens the cover, performs the four-point safety check.

c. The gunner ensures that the barrel is still locked to the receiver with the carrying handle to the right.

d. The assistant gunner places the heat protective mitten on his right hand. With the mitten on he will remove the gas regulator collar from the barrel that is secured to the receiver.

e. With the gas regulator collar removed, the gunner and assistant gunner remove the barrel as outlined in Section II.

f. After removal of the barrel, the assistant gunner will remove the gas regulator collar and gas regulator plug from the spare barrel.

g With these removed the gunner and assistant gunner inserts the barrel into the socket of the receiver ensuring that the gas regulator plug is going into the gas hole bushing. Once the barrel is secured to the receiver the assistant gunner secures the gas regulator collar on the gas regulator plug.

h. The gunner, after ensuring the barrel is secured to the receiver (2 to 7 clicks) and the collar is secure, will reload and continue firing.

3-27. DESTRUCTION PROCEDURES

Destruction of any military weapon is only authorized as a last resort to prevent enemy capture or use. This paragraph discusses the field-expedient means of this destruction; it does not replace published policies. In combat situations, the commander has the authority to destroy weapons, but he must report this destruction through channels.

a. Disassemble the weapon as completely as time permits. Use the barrel or tripod mount to destroy the bolt and operating rod assembly, barrels, rear and front sights, and mounts.

b. Bury the disassembled weapon or dump the parts into a stream, a sump, or a latrine.

c. Burn the weapon by placing an incendiary grenade on the receiver group over the bolt (with the cover resting on the grenade) and detonating the grenade.

d. Smash the traversing and elevating mechanism and pintle assembly. Bend the tripod legs.

CHAPTER 4

MACHINE GUN MARKSMANSHIP TRAINING

This chapter aids trainers in preparing and conducting machine gun marksmanship training for the machine gun. Machine gun marksmanship training is conducted in three phases: preliminary gunnery, basic gunnery, and advanced gunnery in Chapter 5.

Section I. INTRODUCTION

Marksmanship begins with nonfiring individual skill proficiency and concludes with collective proficiency firing under demanding conditions.

4-1. OBJECTIVES

The objectives of machine gun marksmanship training are to produce gunners that are thoroughly capable of the following:

a. **Accurate Initial Burst.** Obtaining an accurate initial burst of fire on the target is essential to good marksmanship. This requires the gunner to estimate range to the target, set the sights, and apply the fundamentals of marksmanship while engaging targets.

b. **Adjustment of Fire.** The gunner must observe the strike of the rounds when the initial burst is fired. If not on target, he manipulates the T&E mechanism until the rounds do strike the target. The assistant gunner must be proficient in observing the strike of rounds and in observing and using tracers so the gunner can rapidly relay the machine gun on the target for engagement.

c. **Speed.** Speed is also essential to good marksmanship; it is attained by practice in both dry-fire and live-fire exercises. It is an acquired skill gained through extensive training that combines other skills when delivering fire. Speed should not be stressed to the detriment of accuracy.

4-2. TRAINING PHASES

Marksmanship training for the machine gun is progressive in nature. It begins with nonfiring individual skill proficiency and concludes with collective proficiency firing under demanding conditions. Gunners and leaders must master the fundamentals before attempting individual and collective firings. More effective and efficient marksmanship occurs if live firing is preceded with good preliminary marksmanship training. Likewise, proficient individual firing will achieve more proficient collective firing.

a. **Preliminary Gunnery.** In this phase, the gunner learns and demonstrates proficiency on individual skills that prepare him to fire live ammunition. This includes mastering mechanical training, the four fundamentals of marksmanship, T&E manipulation, sight adjustments, crew drill, and fire commands.

b. **Basic Gunnery.** In this phase, the gunner applies the fundamentals in live-fire exercises during day and night conditions. This includes zeroing, 10-meter firing with crew drill, field zeroing, and transition firing with crew drill.

c. **Advanced Gunnery.** In this phase, gunners are trained on combat techniques of fire, techniques of employment, and live-fire exercise during NBC conditions.

4-3. TRAINING STRATEGY

Training strategy involves the overall concept for integrating resources into a program that trains individual and collective skills needed to perform a wartime mission. The goal of a marksmanship program is to produce well-trained gunners who can win and survive on the battlefield.

a. Leaders implement training strategies for machine gun marksmanship in TRADOC institutions (IET, NCOES, IOBC, and IOAC) and in units. The overall training strategy is multifaceted and is inclusive of the specific strategies used in institution and unit programs. Also included are the supporting strategies that use resources such as publications, ranges, ammunition, training aids, devices, simulators, and simulations. These strategies focus on developing critical soldier skills and leader skills that are required for the intended outcome.

b. The training strategies contain two components: initial training and sustainment training. Both may include individual and collective skills. Initial training is critical because a task that is taught correctly and learned well is retained longer. When an interim of nonuse occurs, well-trained skills are more quickly regained and sustained. The more difficult and complex the task, the harder it is to sustain the skill. Personnel turnover plays a major factor in the decay of collective skills, since the loss of critical team members requires retraining to regain proficiency. Retraining becomes necessary when a long period elapses between initial and sustainment training sessions or when the training doctrine is altered.

c. The training strategy for machine gun marksmanship begins in the institutions and continues in the unit. Figure 4-1, illustrates an example of this overall process, which provides a concept of the flow of unit sustainment training. Combat arms IET provides field units with soldiers who are familiar with standards in basic marksmanship tasks. The soldiers graduating from these courses have been trained to maintain their machine guns and to hit a variety of targets. They have learned range determination, target detection, application of marksmanship fundamentals, and other skills needed to engage a target.

d. Additional skills trained in the institution include techniques for employment, classes of fire, and fire commands. These skills must then be reinforced in the unit. Related soldier skills of camouflage, cover and concealment, maneuver, and preparation and selection of a fighting position are addressed in STP 21-24-SMCT, which must be integrated into tactical training.

e. Training continues in units on the basic skills taught in combat arms IET. Additional skills, such as suppressive fire and supporting fire, are trained and then integrated into collective training exercises, which include squad and platoon live-fire exercises. (A unit machine gun marksmanship training program is explained in Appendix B.) The strategy for sustaining the basic marksmanship skills that is taught in combat arms IET involves periodic preliminary gunnery, followed by 10-meter, transition firing, and qualification range firing. However, a unit must establish a year-round program to sustain skills. Key elements include training the trainers and refresher training of nonfiring skills.

f. In the unit, individual proficiency and leader proficiency of marksmanship tasks are integrated into collective training that includes squad, section, and platoon drills and STXs. The collective tasks in these exercises, and how they are planned and conducted, are in ARTEP 7-8-MTP and ARTEP 7-8-DRILL. Collective tasks are evaluated to standard and discussed during leader and trainer after-action reviews. Objective evaluations of both individual and unit proficiency provide readiness indicators and future training requirements.

g. A critical step in the Army's overall marksmanship training strategy is to train the trainers and leaders first. Leader courses include limited machine gun training, but unit publications will help develop officer and NCO proficiency necessary to plan and conduct gunnery training and to evaluate the effectiveness of their programs. Proponent schools provide training support materials to include field manuals, training aids, devices, simulators, and programs that are doctrinal foundations and guidance for training the force.

h. Once the soldier understands the weapon, knows how to zero, and has demonstrated proficiency at 10-meter and transition ranges, he should be exposed to more difficult ranges and scenarios.

i. IET culminates in the soldier's proficiency assessment, which is conducted on the 10-meter and transition and record fire ranges. Unit training culminates in a collective, live-fire, tactical exercise that provides an overview of unit proficiency and training effectiveness.

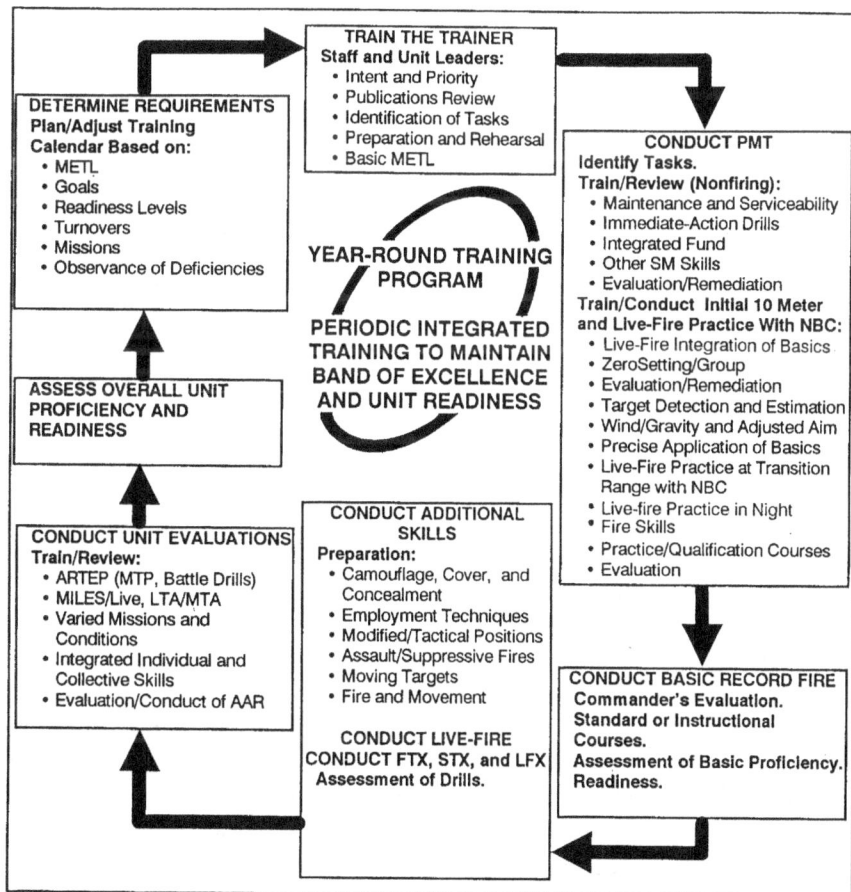

Figure 4-1. Unit marksmanship sustainment strategy.

4-4. TRAINING FOR COMBAT CONDITIONS

The trainer must realize that qualification is not an end but a step towards reaching combat requirements. To reach this goal, the gunner not only considers his position and the use of his weapon, but also some of the following combat conditions as well.

a. Most engagements will be within 300 meters; however, the gunner must still engage targets out to the maximum range of the machine gun.

b. Enemy personnel are seldom visible except when assaulting.

c. Most combat fire must be directed at an area where the enemy has been detected or where he is suspected of being but cannot be seen. Area targets consist of objects or outlines of men irregularly spaced along covered and concealed areas (ground folds, hedges, borders of woods).

d. Most combat targets can be detected by smoke, flash, dust, noise, or movement, but the targets are only visible for a moment.

e. Some combat targets can be engaged by using reference points, predetermined fire, or range card data.

f. The nature of the target and irregularities of terrain and vegetation may require a gunner to move from one position to another to place effective fire on the target. The most stable position for the gunner is the prone tripod-supported position.

g. Most combat targets have a low contrast outline and are obscured. Therefore, choosing an aiming point in elevation is difficult.

h. Time-stressed fire in combat can be divided into three types: a single, fleeting target that must be engaged quickly; distributed targets that must be engaged within the time they remain available; and a surprise target that must be engaged at once with instinctive, accurate fire.

SECTION II. PRELIMINARY GUNNERY

Once a soldier is proficient in the characteristics and mechanical training of the machine gun, he is ready to be trained on the four fundamentals of marksmanship. As the gunner learns the fundamentals, he should be required to manipulate the sights, use his body to shift and lay the sights on the target, use the T&E mechanism to lay on the target, conduct crew drill, and respond to fire commands. Dry-fire exercises are an excellent method for training to proficiency.

4-5. MARKSMANSHIP FUNDAMENTALS

The four fundamentals for firing are the same for all machine guns, they are *steady position, aim, breath control,* and *trigger control.*

a. **Steady Position**. In automatic fire, position is the most important aspect of marksmanship. If the gunner has a good zero, correctly aims his weapon, and properly applies a steady hold in firing a burst of automatic fire, the first round of that burst hits the target at the point of aim. However, this procedure is not necessarily true of the second and third rounds. The first round hits the aiming point the same as when a round is fired singularly. The recoil from the first and subsequent rounds progressively disturb the lay of the weapon with each round of the burst. The relationship between the point of impact of the first and subsequent rounds of the burst depends on the stability of the gunner's position. His body, directly behind the weapon, serves as the foundation, and his grip serves as a lock to hold the weapon against the foundation. The better the body alignment and the steadier the grip, the less dispersed the rounds of a burst of automatic fire will be.

b. **Aim.** To aim the machine gun, the gunner must align the sights, focus his eye, obtain a correct sight picture, control his breathing, and maintain trigger control.

(1) *Sight Alignment.* To obtain correct align, the gunner centers the front sight post in the aperture of the rear sight. For a correct sight picture, the gunner centers the target over the front sight post so that it appears to rest lightly on top of the sight. The aspects of obtaining an accurate initial burst through sight alignment and sight picture, trigger manipulation, and zeroing are the same for tripod training as for bipod training

(2) *Focus of the Eye.* A good firing position places the eye directly on line with the center of the rear sight. The gunner must focus on the tip of the front sight post. The natural ability of the eye to center objects in the rear sight and to seek the point of greatest light aids in providing correct sight alignment.

(3) *Sight Picture.* A correct sight picture has the target, front sight post, and rear sight aligned. The sight picture consists of sight alignment and placement of the aiming point on the target. The gunner aligns the front sight post in the center of the rear sight and then aligns the sights with the target. The top of the front sight post is aligned on the center base of the target (Figure 4-2).

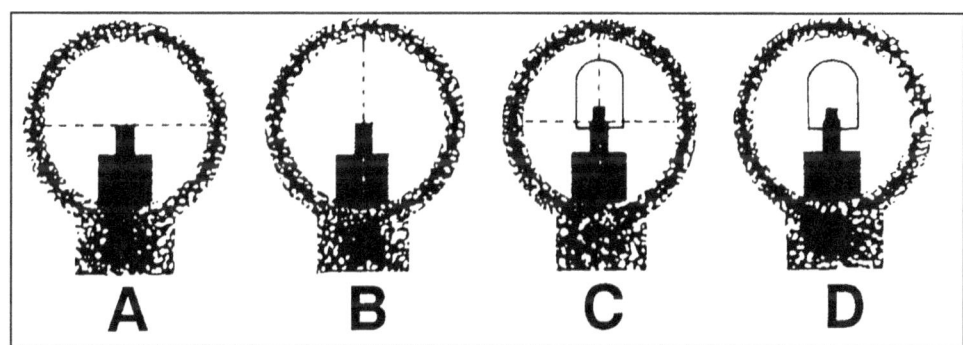

Figure 4-2. Sight picture.

c. **Breath Control.** When firing in bipod-mounted mode, two types of breath control are used. When firing single shots, as in zeroing, the gunner stops breathing after most of the air has been exhaled during the normal breathing cycle. He fires before he feels any discomfort. During automatic fire, ideally, the gunner exhales and stops his breath when pressing the trigger. He does not have time to take deep breaths between bursts. He must hold his breath before each burst or adapt his breathing by taking quick shallow breaths or taking deeper breaths between several bursts.

d. **Trigger Control.** Pressing the trigger straight to the rear and releasing it helps control the number of rounds in each burst and prevents disturbing the lay of the weapon. For this the gunner must learn how to manipulate the trigger so, that he may get the desired burst he wishes to obtain.

4-6. FIRING POSITIONS

The bipod-supported prone and fighting positions and the tripod-supported prone and fighting positions are covered in preliminary gunnery.

a. **Prone Position, Bipod-Supported.**

(1) Assume a prone position to the rear of the weapon (place the shoulder rest on your firing shoulder for the M249 and M60 only). An imaginary line drawn through the weapon should bisect the firing shoulder and buttock, and continue through the heel of your foot.

(2) Spread your legs a comfortable distance apart with your heels as close to the ground as possible, yet comfortable.

(3) Grasp the pistol grip with your firing hand. Place the fleshy end of the index finger resting lightly on the trigger. Place your nonfiring hand on the small of the stock with your thumb is curled underneath. Then slide your nonfiring hand forward until your little finger touches the receiver, so your aiming point will always be the same.

(4) Place your cheek against the forefinger of your nonfiring hand to form a stock weld. Try to position your nonfiring hand and cheek at the same spot on the stock each time you fire the weapon. The stock weld should provide for a natural line of sight through the center of the rear sight aperture to the front sight post and to the target. Relax your neck so that your cheek rests on your forefinger naturally.

(5) Apply a firm, steady pressure rearward and down, holding the weapon tightly into the hollow of your shoulder while aiming and firing.

(6) Keep your shoulders level and elbows about an equal distance from the receiver of the weapon (Figure 4-3).

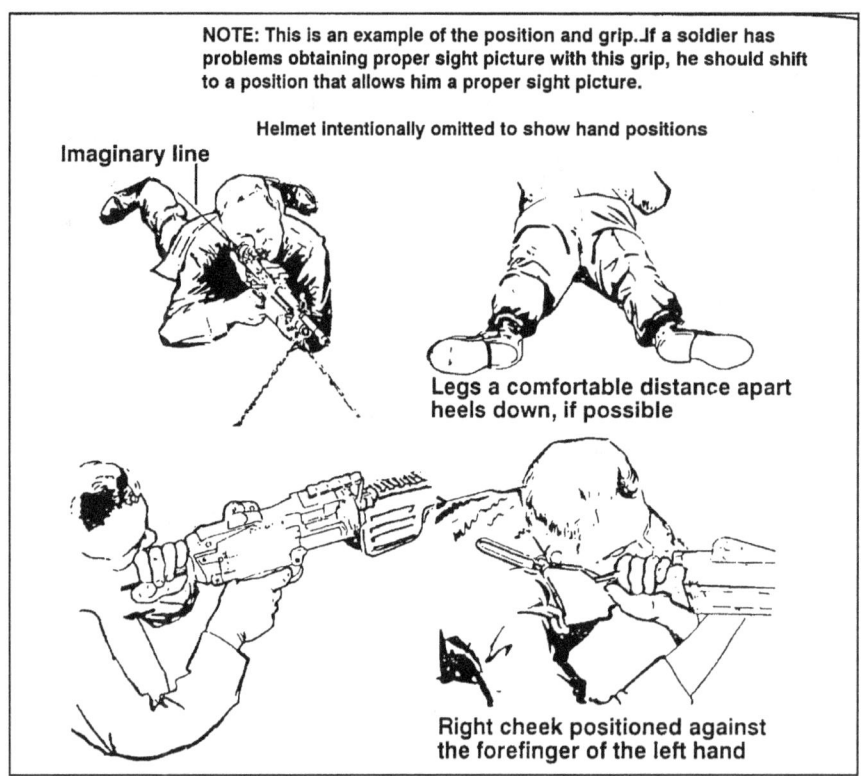

Figure 4-3. Prone position, bipod-supported.

NOTES: 1. The assistant gunner assumes a prone position along the left side of the gunner to load ammunition and observe.
2. Left-handed firing with the M249 and M60 is discouraged because the ejection pattern of some weapons is almost directly to the rear. When firing any machine gun using the tripod, the gunner must use his left hand to manipulate the T&E mechanism, therefore precluding the gunner from firing the machine gun left handed.
3. If a gunner has problems obtaining a proper sight picture, he should shift to a position that allows him to do so.

b. **Fighting Position, Bipod-Supported.** This is an excellent position that provides a stable firing platform. The depth of the fighting position and the support should be adjusted for the height and arm length of the gunner. This allows for a steadier position.

(1) Extend the bipod legs and place the machine gun in front of the position.

(2) Place your right (firing side foot) foot sideways against the rear of the fighting position and lean forward until your chest is squarely against the forward wall.

(3) Raise the folding shoulder rest and place it on your firing shoulder (M249 and M60 only). Keep your shoulders level or parallel to the ground.

(4) Grasp the pistol grip with your firing hand. place the fleshy end of the index finger resting lightly on the trigger. Place your nonfiring hand on the small of the stock and ensure that your thumb is curled underneath.

(5) Place your cheek against the forefinger of your nonfiring hand to form a stock weld. Try to position your nonfiring hand and cheek at the same spot on the stock each time you fire the weapon. The stock weld should provide for a natural line of sight through the center of the rear sight aperture to the front sight post and to the target. Relax your neck so that your cheek rests on your forefinger naturally.

(6) Apply a firm, steady pressure rearward and down, holding the weapon tight into the hollow of your shoulder while aiming and firing.

(7) Keep your shoulders level and elbows about an equal distance from the receiver of the weapon (Figure 4-4).

Figure 4-4. Fighting position, bipod-supported.

c. **Prone Position, Tripod-Supported.** The gunner assumes a prone position to the rear of the weapon (place the shoulder rest on your firing shoulder for the M249 and M60 only). An imaginary line drawn through the weapon should bisect the right shoulder and buttock and continue through the heel of his foot. When using the tripod, the assistant gunner assumes a prone position along the left side of the gunner to load ammunition and observe.

(1) The gunner, spreads his legs a comfortable distance apart with his heels as close to the ground as possible and still be comfortable.

(2) Grasps the pistol grip with his right hand with the fleshy end of his index finger resting lightly on the trigger. (The machine gun is not fired left-handed with the tripod because turning the traverse handwheel with the right hand is difficult.)

(3) Grasps the elevating handwheel with his left hand, palm down. Exerts a firm downward pressure with both hands while aiming and firing.

(4) Places both elbows on the ground between the tripod legs and his body. The position of his elbows raises or lowers his body in relation to the machine gun.

(5) Places his shoulder lightly against the stock without applying any pressure.

(6) Rests his cheek lightly (if at all) against the stock (Figure 4-5).

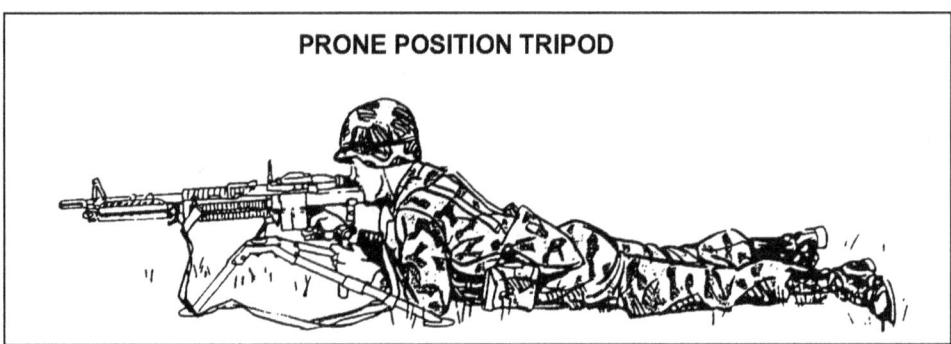

PRONE POSITION TRIPOD

Figure 4-5. Prone position, tripod-supported.

d. **Fighting Position, Tripod-Supported.** (Figure 4-6.) The gunner places his right (firing side) foot sideways against the rear of the fighting position and leans forward until his chest is squarely against the wall.

(1) The gunner, grasps the pistol grip with his firing hand with the fleshy end of his index finger resting lightly on the trigger.

(2) Places his left hand on the elevating handwheel, palm down, exerting a firm downward pressure to make either minor or major adjustments in deflection or elevation. (The weapon is stabilized by the support of the tripod.)

(3) Places his elbows on the inside and does not touch the tripod.

(4) Places little or no pressure against the stock of the gun.

(5) Rests his cheek lightly, if at all, against the stock.

Figure 4-6. Fighting position, tripod-supported.

4-7.   NIGHT FIRE

Although the same four fundamentals of marksmanship are used for night firing, adjustments must be made to accommodate the night vision devices.

a. **Bipod**.

(1) *Steady Position.* When firing unassisted, changes in head position and stock weld are necessary especially when using weapon-target alignment techniques. Normally, the gunner positions his head so that he can align the weapon on the target and look over the sights. In some cases, the lower part of his jaw makes firm contact with his nonfiring hand on the stock, with his eyes an inch or so above the sights. The key is to use the natural pointing ability to align the machine gun on the target. When using NVDs, the head position and stock weld must be altered to be able to use the device. Sometimes height of the NVD may make this impossible. NVDs alter the machine gun's weight and center of gravity. The gunner must compensate by exerting greater pressure and control with his firing hand on the pistol grip and his nonfiring hand on the stock.

(2) *Aim.* Various modifications are necessary when aiming the machine gun at night. When firing unassisted, the gunner uses off-center vision instead of pinpoint focus. Both eyes are open and focused downrange on the target and not on the sights. Rather than aim using the sights, the gunner looks over the sights and points the machine gun where he is looking. The normal tendency is to fire high so the gunner must improve weapon-target alignment by pointing slightly low to compensate. When using NVDs, the gunner uses the necessary aiming process to use the device.

(3) *Breath Control.* This fundamental is not affected by night firing conditions; however, wobble is more pronounced when using NVDs, because they magnify the field of view.

(4) *Trigger Control.* There is no change to this fundamental during night firing. The objective is to not disrupt alignment of the weapon with the target.

b. **Tripod.**

(1) *Steady Position.* When firing at predetermined targets with the weapon laid on each target, there are not differences in steady position at night as compared to day. However, firing at night at targets of opportunity requires modifications. The gunner is required to use weapon-target alignment techniques. He must align the weapon on the target and look over the sights. His head is higher and his lower jaw is lightly on the stock if at all. With night vision devices, the gunner must position his head so that his firing eye is in line with the device.

(2) *Aim.* For targets of opportunity, the gunner uses the same techniques as with a bipod during night firing except weapon-target alignment is achieved with the T&E mechanism.

(3) *Breath Control.* There are no changes in this fundamental.

(4) *Trigger Control.* There are no changes in this fundamental.

4-8.   NUCLEAR, BIOLOGICAL, CHEMICAL FIRE

The four fundamentals remain valid in an NBC environment, although some modifications may be needed to accommodate the equipment.

a. **Bipod**

(1) *Steady Position.* The bulk of overgarments may require adjustments to the position for stability and comfort. A consistent stock weld is difficult to maintain because of the shape of the protective masks. The gunner has to hold his head in an awkward position to see through the sight. If necessary, he may cant the weapon to overcome this situation. This procedure relieves the neck muscles and places the eye on line with the center of the rear sight.

(2) *Aim.* The gunner may have to rotate (cant) the machine gun to see through the rear sight aperture. He should rotate only enough to align the sights, and only if necessary. Ballistics cause rounds to impact low in the direction of the cant at long ranges. If canting at targets beyond 175 meters, the gunner must adjust his point of aim. The best technique is to aim at center base of the target initially and then make adjustments based on the strike of the rounds. Right-handed firers adjust point of aim to the right and high; left-handed firers to the left and high.

(3) *Breath Control.* Although breathing is somewhat restricted and more difficult while wearing the protective mask, the impact is negligible. Care must be taken, to avoid hyperventilating during burst fire. The amount of oxygen inhaled by taking quick shallow breaths or deeper breaths between bursts is significantly reduced.

(4) *Trigger Control.* Trigger control is affected when the gunner wears gloves. The effect cannot be accurately predicted for each soldier; therefore, practice and training under these conditions are required.

b. **Tripod.**

(1) *Steady Position.* Modifications are similar to those in bipod firing. There are two other points of importance. Manipulating the T&E with gloves on is more difficult because the feel of the handwheel differs. The gunner may not sense the same control as without gloves. Second, hearing is impaired. Together, reduced sense of touch and hearing impairment make T&E manipulations especially difficult. For these reasons, adjustments may be considerably slower.

(2) *Aim.* Unlike the bipod, the tripod does not allow the machine gun to be canted. This requires the gunner to position his head behind the stock to use the sight. Skilled gunners who make adjustments to the T&E quickly can confirm their sight picture and then look over the sights to observe the strike of the round while firing. This not only provides relief for the neck muscles but aids in making adjustments.

(3) *Breath Control.* Some considerations apply in the same way as with of the bipod; however, the stable platform of the tripod negates movement associated with breathing.

(4) *Trigger Control.* Like the bipod, control is different because the trigger feels different. Training familiarizes the gunner with the changes he must make while wearing gloves.

4-9. ENGAGEMENT OF MOVING TARGETS

The fundamentals used to hit moving targets are the same as those needed to hit stationary targets. However, the procedures to engage moving targets vary as the angle, speed, and range of the target varies. Targets moving directly at the gunner are engaged the same as a stationary target; there is no change in the application of the fundamentals. But fast-moving targets at varying ranges and angles do require changes in the application of steady position and aiming. (For aerial targets engagements, see Appendix C.)

a. **Leads.** To hit a moving target, the machine gun must be aimed ahead of the target far enough to cause the bullet and target to arrive at the same time at the same point. This distance is measured in target lengths. One target length as seen by the gunner is one lead. Leads are measured from the center of mass. Table 4-1 gives the amount of lead needed to hit a target moving at right angles, to the gunner, and at speeds and ranges indicated. The gunner makes adjustments as conditions change. If target speed is 7 1/2 mph, the amount of lead is half that shown on the table; at 30 mph, double that shown. The angle at which the target moves also changes the lead. If the target is moving on an oblique angle, only half the lead is required. For a target moving directly at the gunner, the aiming point is below the center base of the target depending on range and slope of the ground. For a target moving directly away from a gunner, the aiming point is above the center base of the target (Figure 4-7). Too much lead is better than too little because the target moves into the beaten zone, and observation of the strike of the rounds is easier in relation to the target.

SPEED	RANGE OF TARGET		
15 mph	300 meters	500 meters	900 meters
	1/2 X Target length	1 X Target length	2 X Target lengths

Table 4-1. Vehicle lead table.

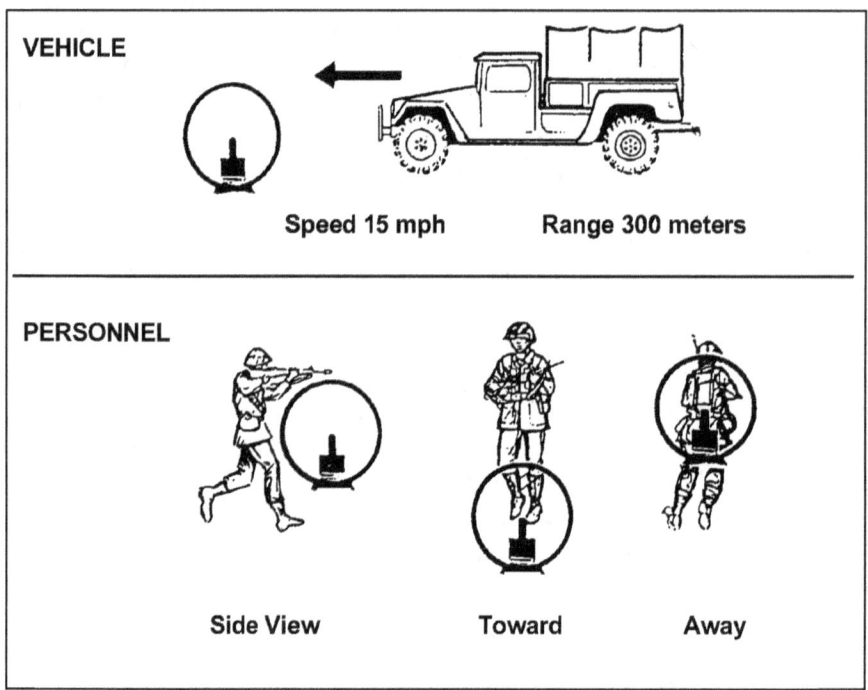

Figure 4-7. Moving-target aiming points.

NOTE: A soldier carrying a full combat load can run as fast as 8 mph for short distances on the battlefield.

b. **Tracking Techniques.** The gunner aims at a point ahead of the target equal to the estimated number of leads, maintains this lead by tracking the target (manipulates the weapon at the same angular speed as that of the target), and then fires. Tracking allows the gunner in position for a second burst if the first one misses.

c. **Trapping Techniques.** The gunner establishes an aiming point forward of the target and along the target path. He pulls the trigger as the target reaches the appropriate point in regard to lead.

d. **Position and Aim.**

(1) *Steady Position.* The gunner makes no change in position for targets moving directly toward or away from him. He manipulates the T&E mechanism to obtain the proper lead and sight picture. Some targets at varying speeds, angles, and ranges may require the gunner to reposition when in the prone position. The gunner redistributes his weight to his elbows and toes raising his body directly behind the weapon. He uses the T&E mechanism to traverse on to the target.

(2) *Aim.* The gunner uses the T&E mechanism to acquire the appropriate sight picture in relation to leading the target. He must quickly determine speed, angle, and range to the target, decide whether to track or trap, acquire lead, and engage the target. He uses the traversing handwheel to maintain lead.

(3) *Breath Control.* The gunner makes no change, but he must be quick to hold his breath because of the fleeting nature of moving targets.

(4) *Trigger Control.* The gunner makes no change in applying this fundamental.

e. **Bipod Techniques.** For targets moving to or from a gunner using a bipod, the same procedures are used. From a prone position, the gunner may be required to adjust his position quickly depending on range, angle, and speed of the target.

(1) *Steady Position.* If appropriate lead cannot be achieved by shifting his shoulders right or left (traverse) or by moving his elbows closer or farther a part (search), the gunner redistributes his weight to his elbows and toes and raises his body off the ground. Using his toes, the gunner shifts his body right or left in the opposite direction of the target and pivots on his elbows until the aiming point is well ahead of the target. The gunner rapidly assumes a steady position, obtains the sight picture, leads and engages the target. Trapping is the preferred technique. In order to apply this method, the bipod legs must move freely. When firing from a fighting position, the gunner must be flexible enough to track any target in his sector. If lead cannot be achieved, he slides the bipod legs in the appropriate direction (left or right) ahead of the target and continues as in the prone position. Trapping is still the preferred technique. If the terrain does not permit sliding the weapon left or right, the gunner lifts the bipod legs off the ground and places them where he can aim ahead of the target, reestablishes a steady position, and continues as before.

(2) *Aim.* The gunner determines angle, speed, and range quickly; acquires the appropriate lead; and engages the target. He aligns the front sight post in the proper position to lead the target. For targets moving directly away, he places the front sight post above center of mass. For targets moving directly at him, he aligns the front sight post below center of mass. For all other targets, he aligns the front sight with center base of the target applying the appropriate lead.

(3) *Breath Control.* The gunner must hold his breath quickly because of the fleeting nature of moving targets.

(4) *Trigger Control.* This is the same as for engaging stationary targets.

4-10. TRAVERSE AND SEARCH

The traverse technique moves the muzzle of the weapon to the left or right to distribute fire laterally. Search moves the muzzle up or down to distribute fire in depth.

a. **Tripod.**

(1) *Traverse.* To move the muzzle to the right, the gunner places his left hand on the traversing handwheel, thumb up, and pushes his thumb away from his body (right). To move the muzzle to the left, he pulls his thumb towards his body (left).

(2) *Search.* To move the muzzle up, the gunner grasps the elevating handwheel with his left hand and pushes his thumb away from his body (add). To move the muzzle down, he pulls his thumb towards his body (drop).

b. **Bipod.**

(1) *Traverse.* To make minor changes in direction, the gunner shifts his shoulders to the right or left to select successive aiming points in the target area. Major changes require him to redistribute his weight to his elbows and toes and raise his body off the ground. Using his toes, he shifts his body to the right or left to be in the opposite direction of the target, and pivots on his elbows until he is aligned with the target. The gunner rapidly assumes a steady position, obtains the proper sight picture, and engages the target.

(2) *Search.* To make changes in elevation, the gunner moves his elbows closer together to lower the muzzle or farther apart to raise the muzzle. He corrects gross errors in range by adjusting the range setting.

4-11. DIRECT LAY

The simplest, quickest, and most effective technique of delivering fire with the machine gun is to align the sights on the target and properly apply fire. This technique of fire is called *direct lay*.

4-12. APPLICATION OF FIRE

The gunner must aim, fire, and adjust on a certain point of the target. He always keeps the center of his beaten zone at the center base of the target for maximum effect from each burst of fire. When this procedure is done, bullets in the upper half of the cone of fire run through the target if it has height, and the bullets in the lower half of the beaten zone ricochet into the target.

4-13. FIRE ADJUSTMENT

The gunner initially sets his sights with the range to the target, lays on the target (sight alignment and sight picture on the center base of the target), fires a burst, and observes the strike of the rounds or flight of the tracers. When the initial burst is correct, he continues to fire until the target is covered. He must regain a good sight picture before each burst when using the bipod. When using the tripod, the gunner makes a rapid check of the sight picture after each traverse and search adjustment.

a. **Sight Corrections Method**. A gunner must observe and adjust fire rapidly to be effective. He observes bursts of fire by noting the strike of the rounds in the target area and the tracers in flight. The technique to adjust fire depends on time, range, and amount of adjustment. These factors assist the gunner in determining whether or not to make sight corrections or adjust position and point of aim. When the initial burst is not correctly placed, the gunner may change the elevation and windage on the sights and fire another burst on the target. This method is time-consuming, even for the well-trained soldier.

b. **Adjusted Aiming Point Method**. In this method of fire adjustment, the gunner uses his sight but does not make sight corrections. This method is quick. If the gunner misses the target with his initial burst, he must rapidly select a new aiming point the same distance from the target as the center of impact of the initial burst, but in the opposite direction. For example, if the initial burst is 20 meters beyond and 10 meters to the right of the target, the gunner rapidly selects an aiming point about 20 meters short and 10 meters to the left of the target, lays on that aiming point, and fires (Figure 4-8).

(1) When selecting a new aiming point from bipod mode, he may have to shift his shoulders slightly to the left or right for windage corrections. For elevation changes, he moves his elbows closer together (lowers the impact) or farther apart (raises the impact). For large corrections, he must move his elbows and realign his body to remain directly behind the weapon. He does this by redistributing weight to his elbows and toes and raises his body off the ground. He shifts his body using his toes, to the right or left, pivoting on his elbows until he is on line with the target. Then he assumes a steady position, obtains the sight picture, and engages the target.

(2) When selecting a new aiming point from tripod mode, the gunner may have to manipulate the T&E mechanism.

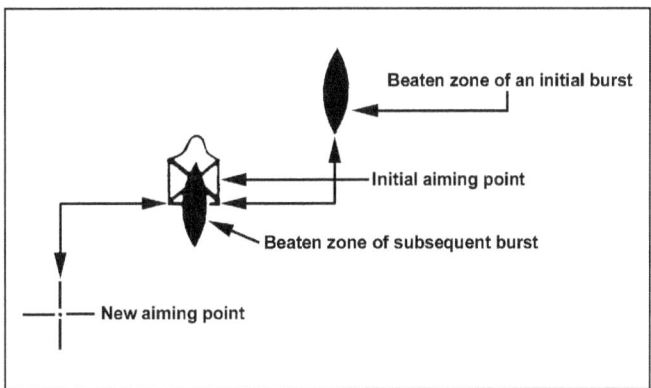

Figure 4-8. Adjusting aiming point method.

4-14. EFFECTS OF WIND

The effects of wind vary depending on changes in speed and direction. Wind is classified by the direction it is blowing in relationship to the firer and target line. The *clock system* is used to indicate wind direction and value (Figure 4-9).

a. **Clock System.** Winds that blow from the left (9 o'clock) or right (3 o'clock) are called *full-value winds*, because they have the most effect on the round. Winds that blow at an angle from the front or rear area are called *half-value winds*, because they have about one-half the effect on the round as full-value winds. Winds that blow straight into the gunner's face or winds that blow straight into the target are termed *no-value winds*, because their effect on the round is too small to be a concern. Effects of the wind increase as the range increases. (Figure 4-10) shows the effects of a 10-mph wind at varying ranges. A 20-mph wind doubles the effect. Winds at other than right angles have less effect. As indicated in Figure 4-10, wind has almost no effect up to 300 meters.

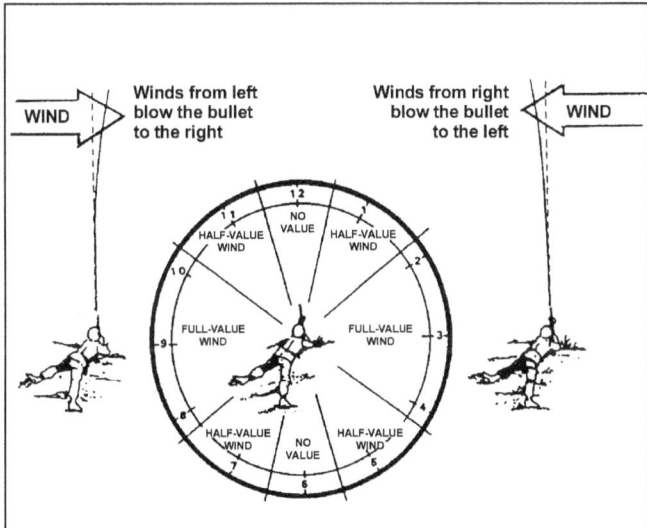

Figure 4-9. Clock method.

10-MILES PER HOUR WIND DRIFT	
RANGE IN METERS	INCHES (CM)
100	1 (2.54)
200	5 (12.70)
300	12 (30.48)
400	23 (53.42)
500	39 (49.06)
600	60 (152.04)
700	88 (223.52)
800	121 (307.34)
900	159 (403.86)
1,000 +	202 (513.08)

Figure 4-10. Effects of winds.

NOTE: When in doubt, the gunner aims the initial burst directly at the center base of the target and, using the techniques of observation and adjustment of fire, adjusts the fire onto the target.

b. **Wind Measurement**. Wind is highly variable and sometimes quite different at the firing position than at the target position. Even though the wind is blowing hard at the firing position, trees, brush, or terrain could protect the path of the round. The wind can vary by several miles per hour between the time a measurement is taken and when the round is fired. Therefore, training time should not be wasted trying to teach gunners an exact way to measure wind speed. They should know that even though wind can affect trajectory, it can be overcome by adjusting fire. A wind gauge can be used for precise measurement of wind velocity. When a gauge is not available, velocity is estimated by one of the following methods.

(1) *Observation Method.* The following information can assist in determining wind velocities.

(a) Winds under 3 mph can barely be felt, but the presence of slight wind can be determined by drifting smoke.

(b) Winds of 5 to 8 mph constantly move the leaves of trees.

(c) Winds of 8 to 12 mph raise dust and loose paper.

(d) Winds of 12 to 15 mph cause small trees to sway.

(2) *Pointing Method.* A piece of paper or other light material can be dropped from shoulder height. By pointing directly at the spot where it lands, the angle can be estimated. As shown in Figure 4-11, the angle is also divided by the constant number 4 to determine the wind speed in mph. However, this only indicates the conditions at the firing position; the conditions may be different at the target.

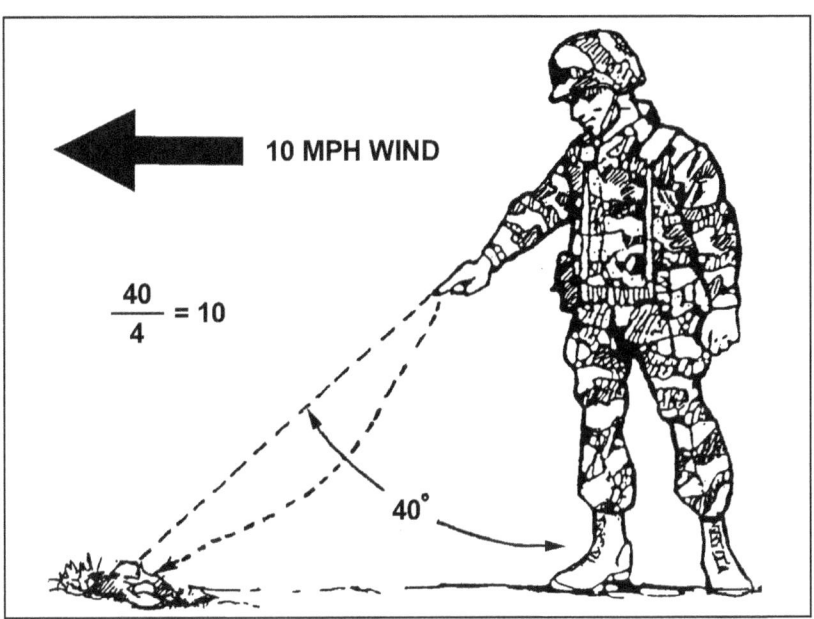

Figure 4-11. Pointing method.

4-15. FIRE COMMANDS

The standard fire commands are used as means of control during preliminary, basic, and advanced gunnery. The fire command must be explained to the gunner. The elements are given (as appropriate) before each dry-fire or live-fire exercise. The gunner takes action as directed and repeats each element as it is announced. (For a detailed explanation of fire commands, see Chapter 5.) When using the basic 10-meter range target, the fire command elements are as follows:

a. **Alert.** The alert is given as "Fire mission." Upon hearing the alert, the gunner loads his weapon and places the safety on "F".

b. **Direction.** Direction is given as FRONT since the targets appear to the gunner's front on the basic range.

c. **Description.** Description is given as PASTER NUMBER (pasters 1 through 8 as appropriate), at which time the gunner lays his weapon on the announced paster.

d. **Range.** The elevation on the rear sight assembly is always used on the basic range. This is announced as FIVE HUNDRED or SEVEN HUNDRED, at which time the gunner must ensure that his rear sight assembly has the correct elevation setting.

e. **Method of Fire.** Firing on the basic range is at a point target, so the method of fire is announced as FIXED. The gunner fires either single rounds or bursts at a rate slower than the sustained rate; therefore, the rate-of-fire element is omitted.

f. **Command to Open Fire.** This is announced as AT MY COMMAND. When the gunner is ready, he announces "Up." When all gunners are ready to fire, the command FIRE is given.

4-16. DRY-FIRE EXERCISES

Dry-fire exercises train the techniques of loading, unloading, immediate action, remedial action, fundamentals of marksmanship, sight settings, and T&E manipulation.

a. **Ammunition**. These exercises may be conducted using blank or dummy ammunition and should be conducted using fire commands when appropriate. If the blank firing attachment is used, safety restrictions for its use must be enforced. While the gunner performs the tasks, the assistant gunner—

- Checks the sight setting and initial lay.
- Checks the gunner's position.
- Ensures the gunner simulates firing before adjusting his position.
- Checks for proper body adjustment or manipulation of T&E.
- Critiques the gunner at the end of the exercise.

b. **Loading and Unloading Exercises**. The procedures for loading and unloading are prescribed in Chapter's 1, 2 and 3. They should be reinforced using dummy ammunition. This training instills confidence and proficiency in the operation of the weapon. It also provides training in clearing the weapon.

c. **Immediate Action and Remedial Action Exercise**. This exercise is conducted using linked dummy rounds and the basic machine gun target. The instructor should use salvage links to link the dummy rounds together. The gunner—

(1) Loads the weapon with dummy ammunition and aims at one of the aiming pasters on the basic machine gun target.

(2) Being conscious of the sight picture, pulls the trigger and the bolt goes forward (simulate firing the weapon). If the sight picture is disturbed, checks his position and grip, and maintains better control of the weapon.

(3) If he has a stoppage, applies immediate action procedures and continues to fire.

(4) If immediate action has failed, applies remedial action procedures and continue to fire.

d. **Operational Exercise**. The gunner aims and simulates firing each dummy round at the aiming paster on the basic machine gun target.

(1) Observes the sight picture through the feeding, locking, and firing cycle. (This provides feedback on his ability to maintain and hold the sight picture.)

(2) If at the completion of the firing cycle there is significant movement of the sight picture, his position is not steady enough or the tripod is not stable.

(3) Applies immediate action after firing each shot to extract and eject the dummy cartridge, and returns the bolt to the cocked position. Returns the cocking handle to the forward position.

> **WARNING**
>
> The M240B is carried loaded with the bolt locked to the *rear* in *tactical situations* where noise discipline is critical to the success of the mission. Trained gun crews are the only personnel authorized to load the M240B and only when command directs the crew to do so. During *normal training exercises*, the M240B is loaded and carried with the bolt in the *forward position*.

e. **Sight Setting and Sight Change Exercises**. These exercises are designed to train the gunner in the operation and adjustment of the rear sight, and making corrections in elevation and windage on the machine gun.

(1) For large adjustments in elevation (range), the gunner manipulates the rear sight to achieve different range settings. For fine adjustments in elevation, the gunner rotates the elevation knob for the machine gun.

(2) To make adjustments for windage, the gunner traverses the rear sight across the windage scale for the machine gun.

f. **Practice**. Before the dry-fire proficiency examination, soldiers should practice the tasks until they become proficient.

g. **Traversing and Searching Exercise**. After the gunner knows the principles of sighting and aiming and can assume a satisfactory firing position, he learns how to make minor and major body position changes to obtain an accurate initial lay. He practices shifting the direction of the weapon to successive points by moving his body. The basic machine gun target is placed 10 meters from the weapon for this exercise.

(1) Makes adjustments for large shifts in direction by using his elbows-and-toes technique described earlier. Makes small changes in direction by adjusting his shoulders.

(2) Makes major elevation changes by adjusting the range setting on the rear sight. Makes minor elevation changes by adjusting his elbows.

(3) Traverses and searches the target by sighting on the initial aiming paster (number 5 or 6) and then shifting to each of the other pasters in order (5 through 6 or its reverse).

(4) Upon receiving a fire command, the gunner repeats the instructions, sets the sights, lays the weapon on the designated paster, assumes the correct position, and reports *up*.

(5) At the command FIRE, the gunner simulates firing two single shots, then shifts to the next paster and simulates firing until the exercise is complete.

h. **T&E Manipulation Exercise**. After the gunner understands the principles of sighting and aiming and can assume a satisfactory firing position, he is instructed in manipulating the tripod-mounted machine gun to obtain an accurate initial lay. He is taught to shift the direction of the weapon to successive points with proficiency. The basic machine gun target is placed 10 meters from the weapon for this exercise.

(1) Makes large shifts in direction by releasing the traversing slide lock lever and moving the slide to the right or left. Makes minor changes in direction by using the traversing handwheel. (One click on the handwheel moves the strike of the round 1 cm on the target.)

(2) Adjusts for elevation by rotating the elevating handwheel with his left hand.

(3) Traverses and searches the target by laying on the initial aiming paster (number 5 or 6) and then shifts to each of the other pasters in order (5 through 6 or its reverse). (All major shifts in traverse are accomplished by loosening the traversing slide lockding lever.) When shifting from pasters number 7 through 8 or 8 through 7, uses the traversing handwheel.

(4) Upon receiving the command, the gunner repeats the instructions, sets the sights, lays the weapon on the designated paster, assumes the firing position, and reports UP.

(5) At the command FIRE, the gunner repeats the command, simulates firing two single shots, then shifts to the next paster and simulates firing until the exercise is completed.

i. **Dry-Fire Proficiency (Performance) Examination**. A gunner must demonstrate skill in all the tasks of the dry-fire proficiency examination before he is allowed to progress to 10-meter live firing. This examination emphasizes learning by doing. Proficiency is tested on a pass or fail basis. (The proficiency test is in Appendix B.)

j. **Remedial Training**. Remedial training must be given to soldiers who fail the performance objectives. Gunners who have passed the proficiency test may be used to assist in the training of soldiers having difficulty. Following retraining, the soldiers are retested in those tasks.

4-17. MULTIPURPOSE MACHINE GUN RANGE LAYOUT

The multipurpose machine gun range is used for conducting the 10-meter course as well as transition day, night, and integrated NBC firing. The firing area has 10 lanes. (Detailed setup and target configurations are described in TC 25-8. The layout is shown in Figure 4-12.) Personnel required for conducting the 10-meter range, as well as the transition firing, are the same, and they should perform the same duties for each training period. Local policy may dictate personnel requirements. The following are the minimum required personnel: OIC, NCOIC, safety officer or NCO, ammunition NCO, tower operator, lane NCOs, trainer and assistant gunners, or IAW TC 25-8. All personnel must adhere to safety rules IAW AR 385-63, local regulations, and Appendix D.

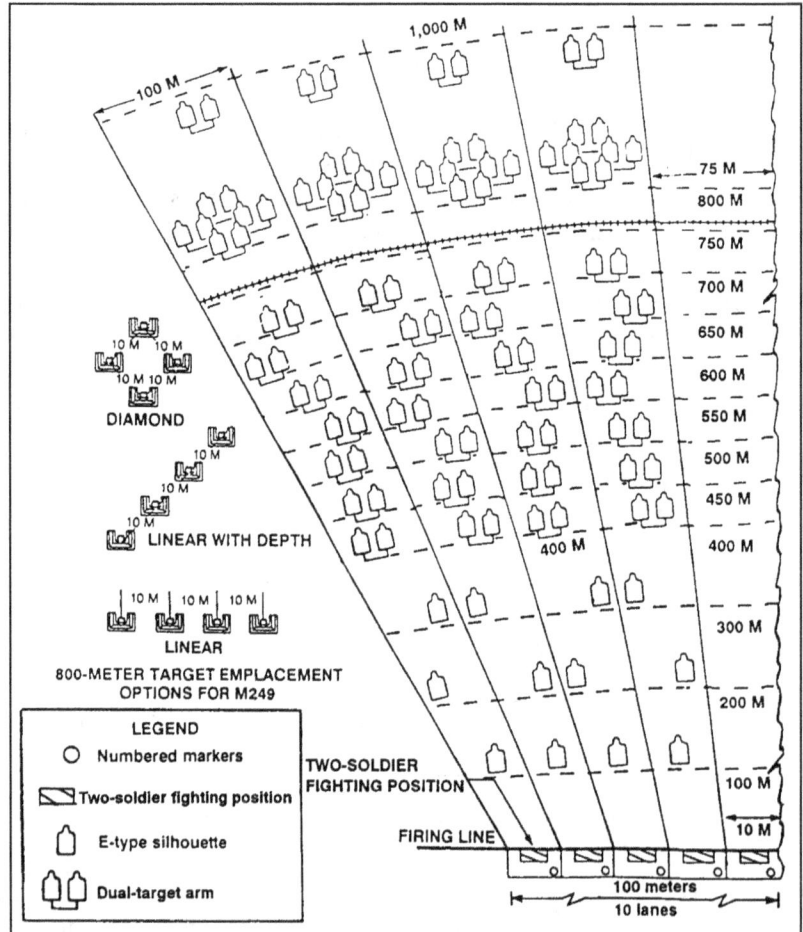

Figure 4-12. Multipurpose machine gun range layout.

NOTE: Targets beyond 800 meters are to be used with a machine gun optic and are not to be used during qualification without a machine gun optic.

4-18. BASIC MACHINE GUN TARGET

The basic machine gun target (FSN 6920-078-5128 and NSN 6920-00-078-5123) is used for the 10-meter firing exercise (Figure 4-13). The following explanation of the target, including the size of the aiming pasters and scoring spaces, aids in zeroing the machine guns and facilitates control during the 10-meter firing exercises. The target consists of four sections lettered A, B, C, and D. Each section has four point targets numbered 1, 2, 3, and 4; and two sets of area targets numbered 5 through 6 and 7 through 8. Each space is 4 cm wide and 5 cm high. The black aiming paster within the numbered scoring spaces is 1 cm square. The target is used to score one gunner—with one refire. Each gunner uses sections A, B and C. Sections C for qualification and section D for refire.

a. **Point Targets**. Point targets on the basic machine gun target are pasters 1 through 4 of sections A, B, C, and D. Firing at point targets exposes the gunner to zeroing techniques and controlled-burst fire techniques. Targets 1 through 4 can also be used for qualification.

b. **Area Targets**. Area targets on the basic machine gun target consist of pasters 5 through 6, and 7 through 8 of sections A, B, C, and D. Target group 5 through 6 provides the gunner with targets in depth and allows him to use a series of aiming points to disburse fire across the target by using the T&E mechanism. Target group 7 through 8 provides the gunner with linear targets with depth. This series of targets uses a series of aiming points to disburse fire across the target and in depth by using the T&E mechanism.

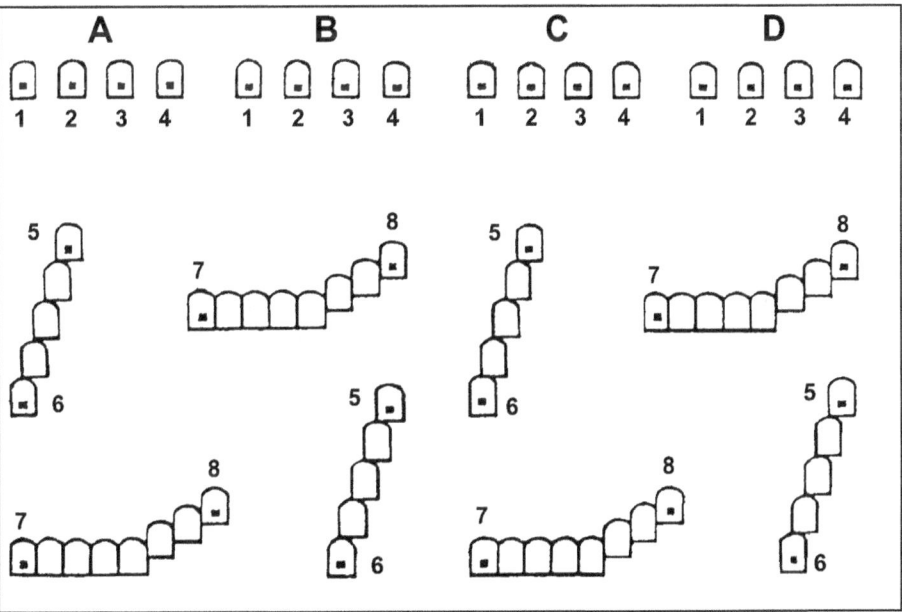

Figure 4-13. Basic machine gun target.

c. **Grid Square Overlay**. This device assists the gunner in zeroing his weapon at 10 meters, while using the basic machine gun target (Figure 4-14). The grid square overlay is used the same as an M16 25-meter zero target, except the material can be made of plastic or view graph transparency. Each square is equal to 1 cm.

1 CLICK = 1 CM. Turn the traversing handwheel to move the strike of the round left or right.
1 CLICK = 1 CM. Turn the elevation handwheel to move the strike of the round up or down.

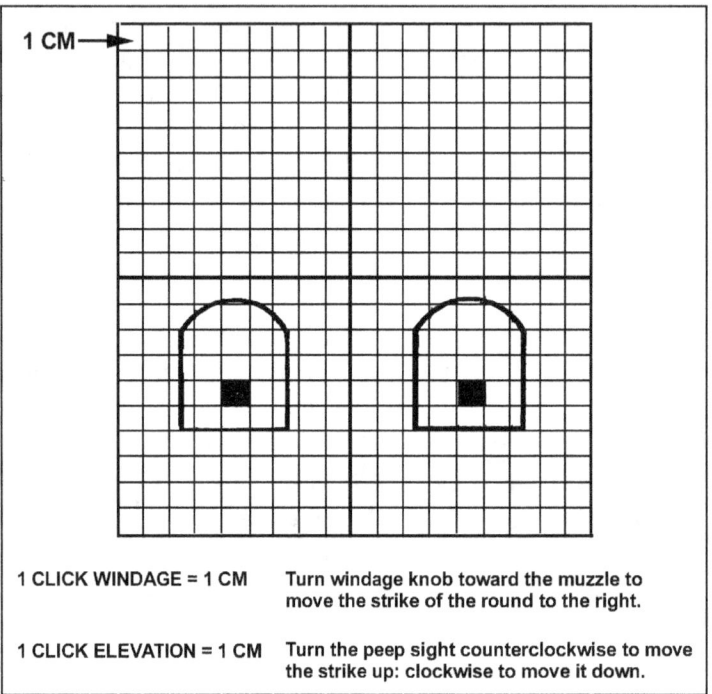

Figure 4-14. Grid square overlay.

(1) Sets the sights for 10-meter zeroing, then fires three single rounds to form a three-round shot group. Re-lays on the target using the T&E mechanism.

(2) After firing the three-round shot group (Figure 4-15), places the grid square overlay over the pasters (1 and 2) (Figure 4-16) and counts the number of clicks it will take for rounds to impact on the black aiming paster. (Corrections for Figure 4-16 would be turn the traverse handwheel to the right one click.)

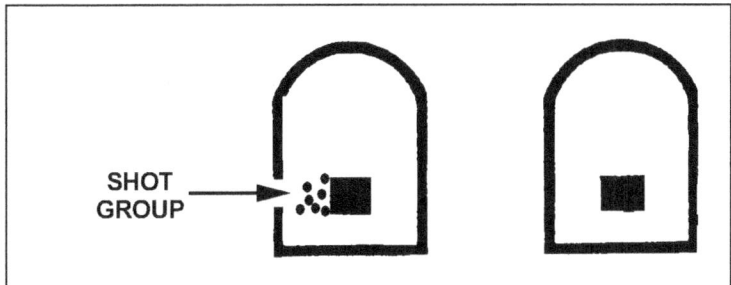

Figure 4-15. Shot group on basic machine gun target.

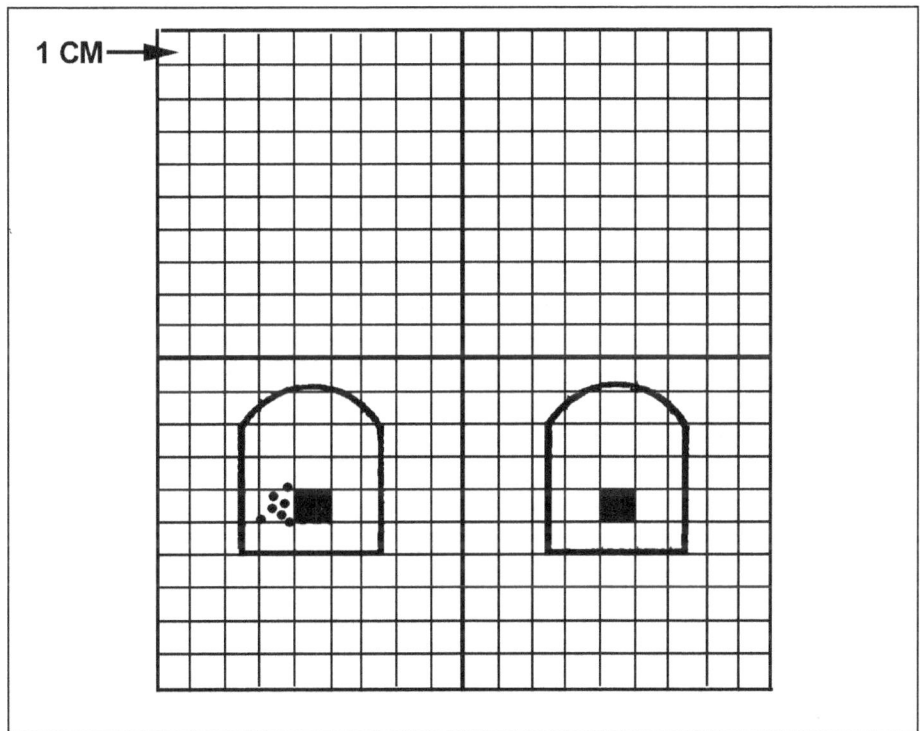

Figure 4-16. Overlay placed over pasters.

4-19. TARGET ANALYSIS

Targets are analyzed and scored to determine the gunner's proficiency and to reinforce the fundamentals of marksmanship. In a prone or fighting position firing with a zeroed weapon, a target is best analyzed by considering the common errors of machine gun marksmanship (Figure 4-17).

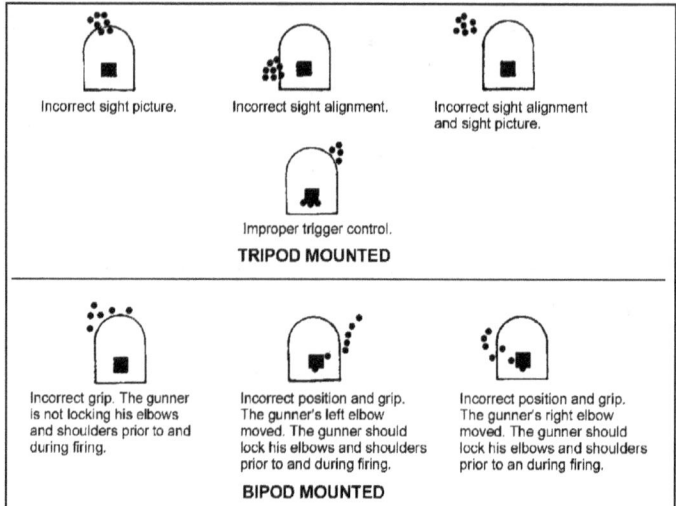

Figure 4-17. Common errors of marksmanship.

Section III. CREW DRILL

This section applies to all three machine guns and will be incorporated in *preliminary gunnery* and *basic gunnery*. The machine gun crew drill gives squad and platoon members training in the fundamentals of machine gun operation and confidence in their ability to put the machine gun into action with precision and speed. Rotation of duties during training ensures that every member becomes trained in the duties of each crew position. Precision is attained by learning and practicing correct procedures to include inspecting the machine gun before firing and observing safety procedures. Speed is acquired after precision has been developed. *Precision is never sacrificed for speed.*

4-20. PREPARATION

The crew drill will be conducted with preliminary gunnery and will be part of the 10-meter and transition firing practice and qualification, concurrently during other courses of fire, or anytime at the discretion of the unit commander. The organization for crew drill described in this section is for training crews in the fundamentals of machine gun operation; it is not the organization to be employed in every tactical situation.

    a. To instill realism and relate the crew drill to actual situations, the unit leader should vary his method of instruction. Possible approaches to this method of instruction include the following:

- Conduct the crew drill from the prone position.
- Initiate the crew drill from all types of tactical formations.
- Perform the crew drill in simulated tactical situations.

b. The crew drill, as discussed here, involves the leader and one machine gun crew. The machine gun crew consists of three members (a gunner, assistant gunner, and an ammunition bearer). There are two complete machine gun crews in the light headquarters section of infantry, air assault infantry platoons, and airborne infantry platoons.

c. All commands are given by a leader. This leader may be a team leader, squad leader, or someone placed in charge of the crew. The gunner and assistant gunner repeat all commands. After the machine gun is mounted, the assistant gunner transmits all signals from the leader to the gunner and from the gunner to the leader.

4-21. CREW EQUIPMENT

In addition to individual weapons and equipment, crew members carry equipment for both bipod and tripod training. The following is a suggested assignment of the equipment to the machine gun crew members:

a. **Day Time Equipment**.

(1) Leader (designated)—binoculars, compass.

(2) Gunner—machine gun, compass, MGO or AN/PAS-13, two bandoleers (with dummy ammunition).

(3) Assistant Gunner—binoculars, spare barrel case (spare barrel and accessories), traversing and elevating mechanism, pintle assembly, and three bandoleers (with dummy ammunition).

(4) Ammunition bearer—compass, tripod and four bandoleers (with dummy ammunition).

b. **Night Time Equipment**.

(1) Leader (designated)—AN/PVS-7B with 3XMAG, compass.

(2) Gunner—machine gun, compass, AN/PVS-4 or AN/PAS-13, two bandoleers (with dummy ammunition).

(3) Assistant Gunner—AN/PVS-14 with 3XMAG, spare barrel case (spare barrel and accessories), traversing and elevating mechanism, pintle assembly, and three bandoleers (with dummy ammunition).

(4) Ammunition bearer—AN/PVS-7B with 3XMAG, compass, tripod and four bandoleers (with dummy ammunition).

4-22. FORMATION (BIPOD OR TRIPOD)

The leader commands FORM FOR CREW DRILL. The crew forms in a file with five steps between each crew member in this order: gunner, assistant gunner, and ammunition bearer. The gunner is five steps from and facing the leader. When the crew members reach their positions, each assumes the prone position and is ready for the crew drill. (Figure 4-18, page 4-26.)

Figure 4-18. Crew in ready position.

4-23. CROSS-TRAINING PROCEDURES

Duties are rotated during the crew drill to train each soldier in the duties of all crew members. The command to rotate duties is FALL OUT, GUNNER. At this command, the gunner becomes the ammunition bearer, the assistant gunner becomes the gunner, and the ammunition bearer becomes the assistant gunner. When crew members have assumed their new positions, they call out their new duties in order: AMMUNITION BEARER, ASSISTANT GUNNER, GUNNER.

4-24. INSPECTION FOR BIPOD FIRE

An inspection of equipment is made at the beginning of each exercise.

a. **Command.** After the crew is formed for crew drill, the leader commands INSPECT EQUIPMENT BEFORE FIRING, BIPOD. At the command, each crew member inspects his equipment as explained below.

(1) *Inspection by Gunner.* The gunner inspects the ammunition first. He ensures that the ammunition is properly linked and free of dirt and corrosion, and that the double link is up (ready for loading). After he inspects the ammunition, he places the cloth slings over his shoulder (except for one bandoleer, which he prepares for loading). He then inspects the machine gun and takes his position parallel to the machine gun (his head on line with the feed tray). The night personnel also check the AN/PVS-4 or AN/PAS-13.

(a) Holding the machine gun with his left hand, using his right hand he lowers the bipod legs and then rest the machine gun on the bipod.

(b) Attaches the bandoleer to the machine gun.

(c) Places the safety on "F", pulls the cocking handle to the rear, places the safety on "S", returns the cocking handle to the forward position, raises the cover assembly.

(d) Calls for the cleaning rod and receives it from the assistant gunner.

(e) Crawls forward, then runs the cleaning rod through the barrel to ensure it is clear.

(f) Checks the flash suppressor for cracks.

(g) Checks the front sight for tightness and for damage to the blade.

(h) Checks the carrying handle to ensure that it can be positioned so it will not be in the way during aiming and firing.

(i) Ensures that the barrel is securely locked to the receiver.

(j) Returns the cleaning rod to the assistant gunner.

(k) Moves to the rear of the machine gun and checks the moving parts in the feed cover.

- Ensures that the feed cam is clean and properly lubricated.
- Pushes back and forth on the feed cam to check for freedom of movement.
- Pushes on the belt feed pawl to ensure that it has spring tension.
- Pushes on the cartridge guides to ensure that they a have spring tension.

(l) Pushes the belt holding pawl to ensure that it has spring tension.

(m)Lowers and latches the cover (without inserting the belt).

(n) Pulls the trigger to check the functioning of the safety.

(o) Places the safety on "F", pulls the cocking handle to the rear, pulls the trigger, eases the bolt forward manually with the cocking handle.

(p) Checks the rear sight.

(2) *Inspection by Assistant Gunner*. Remaining in a prone position, the assistant gunner begins by inspecting his ammunition. He takes the cleaning rod from the carrying case and assembles the cleaning rod. He then takes the traversing and elevating mechanism from the case and prepares it as follows. Night will also check AN/PVS-14 with 3X MAG.

(a) Rotates the elevating handwheel, exposing 1 1/2 inches or the width of two fingers) of threads above the elevating handwheel.

(b) Rotates the traversing slide sleeve, exposing 1 1/2 inches or the width of two fingers) of threads below the elevating handwheel.

(c) Centers the traversing mechanism.

(d) Checks the to ensure that the locking mechanism that attach to the machine gun are present and in working order.

(e) Replaces the traversing and elevating mechanism in on the case and removes the spare barrel from the spare barrel case.

(f) Checks the barrel.

(g) Checks the flash suppressor for cracks.

(h) Checks the front sight for tightness and for damage to the blade.

(i) Checks the pintle assembly for proper functioning.

(j) Places the spare barrel its case; disassembles the cleaning rod and returns it accessory pocket; and checks the ruptured cartridge extractor, bore brush, chamber brush, receiver brush, and heat protective mitten for serviceability.

(3) *Inspection by Ammunition Bearer*. Remaining in a prone position, the ammunition bearer inspects his ammunition as described above for gunner and assistant gunner. He then inspects the tripod, pintle assembly and T&E mechanism. Night personnel also check the AN/PVS-7 with the 3XMAG.

(a) Ensures that the front leg will unfold properly and the rear legs unfold and lock securely in place with the sleeve latch.

(b) Checks the sleeve latch to ensure that it has spring tension and will function.

(c) Checks the pintle assembly to ensure that it is locked into the pintle bushing and that the pintle rotates freely within the bushing.

(d) Checks to ensure that the T&E mechanism will lock on the traversing bar and move freely when unlocked for major changes in direction.

(e) Unlocks the pintle and T&E mechanism from the tripod and return to the assistant gunner.

(f) Folds the rear legs by unlocking the sleeve latch and folds the front leg so that the tripod is in the carrying position.

b. **Report**. When crew members have completed their inspection of the equipment, they call out their report, without command, starting from the rear.

(1) AMMUNITION BEARER CORRECT (or reports deficiencies).

(2) AMMUNITION BEARER AND ASSISTANT GUNNER CORRECT (or reports the ammunition deficiencies.

(3) GUNNER ALL CORRECT (or deficiencies found during the inspections).

4-25. PLACEMENT INTO ACTION (BIPOD)

To place the machine gun into action, the leader commands and signals MACHINE GUN TO BE MOUNTED HERE (pointing to the position where the machine gun is to be mounted), FRONT (pointing in the direction of fire), ACTION (raising fist to shoulder level and thrusting it several times in the direction of the selected position).

a. At the command ACTION, the gunner stands, grasps the carrying handle with his left hand, grasps the top of the stock with his right hand, raises the machine gun to a carrying position (muzzle to the front) and moves to the selected position.

b. Upon arrival at the position, the gunner places the machine gun on the ground. He then assumes a prone position to the rear of the machine gun, positions the carrying handle so that it will not interfere during aiming and firing, aligns the machine gun in the direction of fire, and set the rear sight. He places the safety on "F", pulls the bolt to the rear, places the safety on "S", and returns the cocking handle to the forward position. He then raises the feed cover, places the first round of ammunition in the cartridge feed tray groove, and closes the feed cover ensuring that the round does not slip out of the cartridge feed tray groove. He then places the machine gun to his shoulder and puts the safety on "F".

WARNING

The M240B is carried loaded with the bolt locked to the *rear* in *tactical situations* where noise discipline is critical to the success of the mission. Trained gun crews are the only personnel authorized to load the M240B and only when command directs the crew to do so. During *normal training exercises*, the M240B is loaded and carried with the bolt in the *forward position*.

---

c. The assistant gunner times his movements so that he arrives at the position as the gunner is assuming the prone position. He lies prone on his left hip, feet to the rear, and on the left side of the gunner. He places the spare barrel case parallel to the gun with the zippered side towards the machine gun. He opens the case and removes the spare barrel. He places the spare barrel on the case, muzzle to the front and even with the muzzle of the machine gun. (Figure 4-19.)

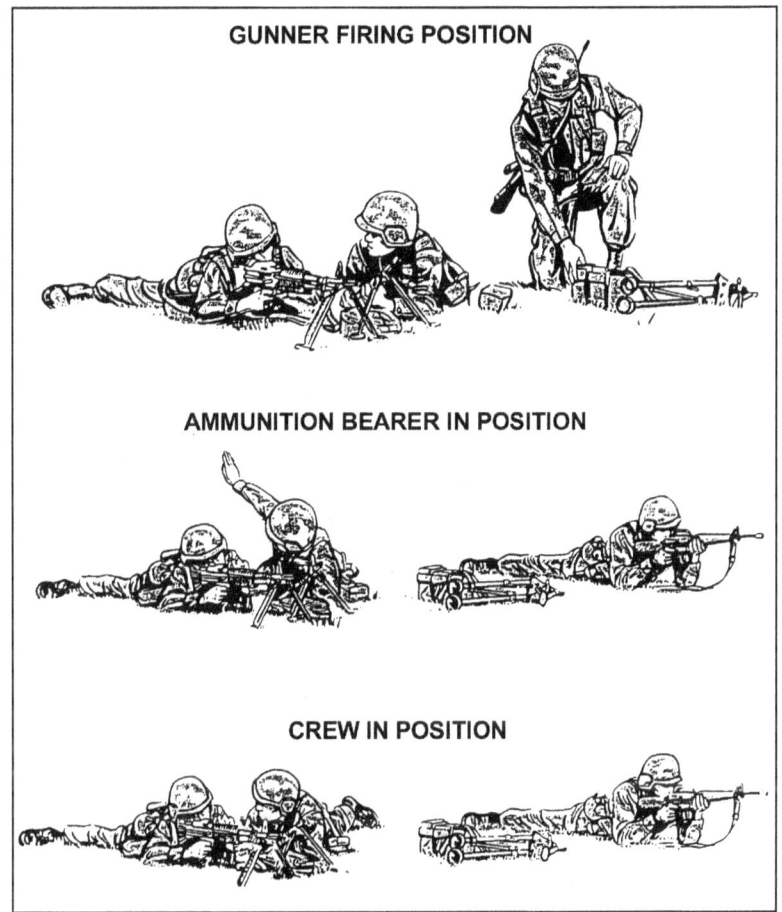

Figure 4-19. Crew members in firing position.

d. The ammunition bearer times his movements so that he arrives at the position as the assistant gunner is assuming the prone position. He places the folded tripod one step to the left of the muzzle of the machine gun and on line with the machine gun. He unslings his bandoleers and places them next to the folded tripod legs. He then lies prone 10 meters to the left and on line with the position, provides security, and prepares to fire into the target area with his rifle.

e. When ready to fire, the gunner puts the safety lever on "F" and reports UP. The assistant gunner signals READY to the leader.

4-26. PROCEDURES FOR CHANGING THE BARREL (BIPOD)

To ensure proficiency and speed in changing barrels, the barrel changing process is included in crew drill. When the gunner has reported UP and the assistant gunner has signaled READY, the leader commands CHANGE BARRELS.

a. The gunner ensures that the bolt is to the rear, puts the safety on "S", and puts the stock on the ground. Next, he moves his left hand to the top of the stock to ensure the weapon stays parallel to the ground. He puts his right hand under the handguard/forearm assembly help support the machine gun when the assistant gunner removes the barrel.

b. The assistant gunner (wearing the heat protective mitten) unlocks the barrel locking lever, removes the barrel, and places the barrel on the spare barrel case. He holds the spare barrel inserts it into the machine gun.

c. The gunner ensures that the barrel is lock and secured in the receive of the machine gun, moves the safety lever to "F", assumes the correct firing position, and reports UP. The assistant gunner signals READY to the squad leader.

4-27. REMOVAL FROM ACTION (BIPOD)

To take the machine gun out of action, the leader commands and signals OUT OF ACTION. The gunner and assistant gunner repeat the command.

a. At the command OUT OF ACTION, the ammunition bearer moves to the position, slinging his rifle. He picks up and slings the bandoleers that he previously left there. He gets the tripod and moves 15 steps to the rear of the machine gun. He lies prone, facing the position with the tripod in front of him.

b. The assistant gunner places spare barrel and the heat protective mitten in the spare barrel case. Before standing, he closes the spare barrel case enough to retain the spare barrel and the traversing and elevating mechanism. He moves 10 steps to the rear of the position and lies prone, facing the position. At this time, he fully closes the spare barrel case.

c. The gunner places the stock on the ground, ensures that the bolt is to the rear, places the safety on "S", and raises the feed cover. He removes the ammunition from the tray, puts it into the bandoleer, and closes the bandoleer. The gunner examines the chamber to ensure that it is clear; closes the feed cover; pulls the cocking handle to the rear; puts the safety on "F"; pulls the trigger, easing the bolt forward. Standing, he pivots on his right foot; without turning the machine gun, he raises it to his left hip and moves five steps to the rear. He visually checks to ensure that the ammunition bearer and the assistant gunner are in their positions. He lies prone, facing the position with the machine gun on his right. He folds the bipod legs alongside the barrel and reports UP to the squad leader.

4-28. INSPECTION FOR TRIPOD FIRE

The inspection of equipment for tripod training is the same as for bipod training except that the leader's command to start the inspection of equipment is INSPECT EQUIPMENT BEFORE FIRING TRIPOD. Also, the gunner inspects the bipod legs and folds them to their position alongside the barrel.

4-29. PLACEMENT INTO ACTION (TRIPOD)

The leader commands and signals MACHINE GUN TO BE MOUNTED HERE, FRONT, ACTION. (Figure 4-20.)

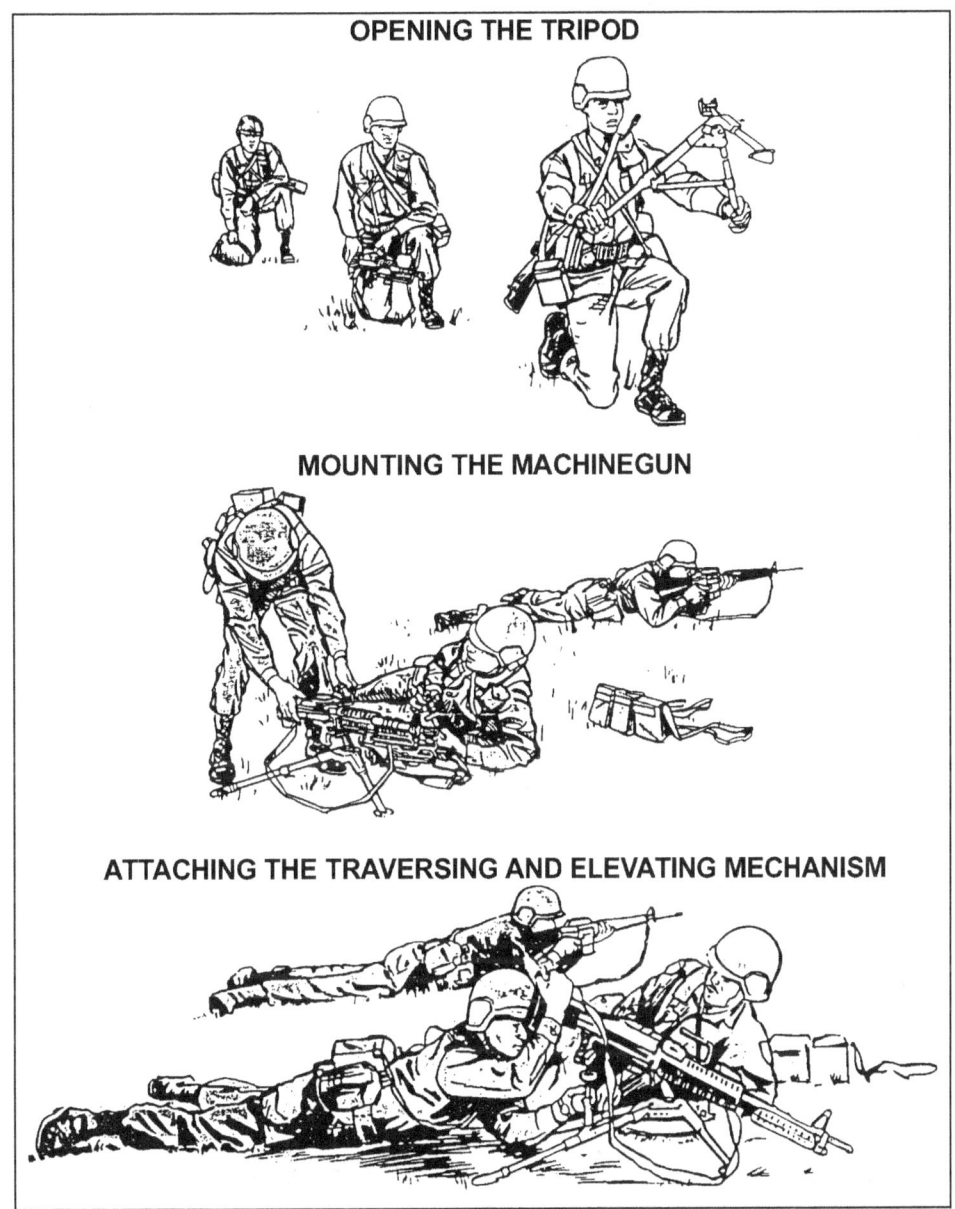

Figure 4-20. Placing the machine gun into action.

a. Upon the command ACTION, the ammunition bearer stands, holds the tripod with his right hand, and moves forward to the position. He kneels on his right knee and rests the shoes of the rear tripod legs on the ground, with the mount in a vertical position. Steadying the mount with his right hand near the tripod head, he raises the front leg with his left hand. He grasps the right shoe with his right hand and the left shoe with is left hand, and raises the tripod chest high. He separates the tripod legs with a quick jerk. Ensuring that the sleeve latch engages the sleeve, he places the tripod on the ground with the front leg pointing in the direction of fire. He rises to his feet and stamps the rear shoes into the ground. He then unslings his bandoleers and places them on line with the front leg of the tripod, one step to the left. He moves 10 meters to the left of the position, unslings his rifle, lies prone, provides security, and prepares to fire into the target area.

b. The assistant gunner times his movements and arrives at the position as the ammunition bearer leaves. He places the spare barrel case (zippered side towards the tripod) parallel to and on line with the spot where the muzzle of the machine gun will be when it is mounted. He lies on his left side, with his hip near the left tripod shoe. He unzips the spare barrel case and removes the spare barrel, mounting equipment necessary to mount the machine gun. He places the spare barrel on the spare barrel case with the muzzle forward.

c. The gunner times his movements and arrives at the position as the assistant gunner assumes the prone position. He stands, holds the carrying handle in his left hand and the stock in his right hand, and raises the gun to the carrying position (muzzle to the front). He mounts the machine gun on the tripod. He then positions the carrying handle to the right so it will not interfere with aiming and firing, raises the rear sight assembly, and lies prone.

d. The assistant gunner assists the gunner in mounting the machine gun to the tripod. They ensure that both the pintle and traversing and elevating mechanism are securely locked in place and working properly.

e. The gunner places the safety on "F", pulls the bolt to the rear, places the safety on "S", and returns the cocking handle to the forward position. The assistant gunner places the first round of ammunition in the tray groove and supports the belt, while the gunner closes the cover. The gunner takes the correct position and grip, places the safety on "F", and reports UP. The assistant gunner signals READY to the squad leader.

WARNING

The M240B is carried loaded with the bolt locked to the *rear* in *tactical situations* where noise discipline is critical to the success of the mission. Trained gun crews are the only personnel authorized to load the M240B and only when command directs the crew to do so. During *normal training exercises*, the M240B is loaded and carried with the bolt in the *forward position*.

4-30. PROCEDURES FOR CHANGING THE BARREL (TRIPOD)

When the gunner has reported UP and the assistant gunner has signaled READY, the leader commands CHANGE BARRELS.

a. The gunner ensures that the bolt is to the rear, puts the safety on "S". He also assists the assistant gunner in changing the barrel, if needed.

b. The assistant gunner (wearing the heat protective mitten) unlocks the barrel locking lever, removes the barrel, and places the barrel on the spare barrel case. He holds the spare barrel inserts it into the machine gun.

c. The gunner ensures that the barrel is lock and secured in the receiver of the machine gun, moves the safety lever to "F", assumes the correct firing position, and reports UP. The assistant gunner signals READY to the squad leader.

4-31. REMOVAL FROM ACTION (TRIPOD)

At the command OUT OF ACTION, the gunner ensures that the bolt is to the rear, places the safety on "S", and raises the cover. The assistant gunner removes the ammunition from the tray, returns it to the bandoleer, and closes the bandoleer. The gunner inspects the chamber to ensure that it is clear; closes the cover; pulls the cocking handle to the rear; puts the safety on "F"; pulls the trigger, easing the bolt forward. The gunner unlocks the rear of the machine gun from the tripod.

a. The assistant gunner will assist the gunner in dismounting the rear of the machine gun. He puts the spare barrel and heat protective mitten into the case and closes it enough to hold the contents. He stands, moves 10 steps to the rear of the position, and lies prone, facing to the front. After receiving all mounting equipment from the ammunition bearer, he puts it in the spare barrel case and fully closes the spare barrel case.

b. After the assistant gunner leaves, the gunner stands, lowers the rear sight, and holds the carrying handle with his left hand. With his right hand, he dismounts the front of the machine gun from the tripod. Holding the stock with his right hand, he pivots to his right as he raises the machine gun to the carrying position. He then moves five steps to the rear of the position and lies prone, facing to the front.

c. The ammunition bearer rises, slings his rifle, moves to the machine gun, and secures his bandoleers, timing his arrival so that the gunner and assistant gunner will be clear of the tripod. He grasps the tripod with his left hand and moves five steps to the rear of the position. He turns, facing the front, and kneels on his right knee. He places the tripod in a vertical position with the rear shoes on the ground and supports it with his right hand near the head of the tripod. At this time, he hands the assistant gunner all mounting equipment. He reaches up with his right hand down the right leg, and releases the sleeve latch. He then grasps the shoes and closes the tripod legs. He lowers the tripod to the ground, head to the left, lies prone behind it, and reports UP.

4-32. PRONE POSITION

Machine gun crew drill, as it is described in the preceding paragraphs, is an excellent training vehicle for the machine gun crew. A continuation or second phase of the crew drill is outlined in this paragraph. It should be used only as a technique for adding realism to training.

a. **Inspecting Equipment Before Firing.** The inspection of equipment for crew drill from the prone position is the same as that for bipod training and tripod training.

b. **Placing the Machine Gun Into Action.** The leader commands and signals MACHINE GUN TO BE MOUNTED HERE, FRONT, ACTION in the same manner as for bipod training. The procedures for bipod training are the same with one exception—crew members do not get to their feet and movements are executed in the low crawl. Once in position, all actions are performed from the prone position.

c. **Training With the Tripod.** Upon the command ACTION, the ammunition bearer crawls forward to the designated position and extends the front leg of the tripod. Grasping the rear legs firmly, he emplaces the front leg. Applying downward pressure, he emplaces the rear legs. He then crawls to a position about 10-meters to the left of the machine gun and gets into a good firing position with his rifle.

(1) The assistant gunner crawls forward, timing his movement to arrive as the ammunition bearer leaves. Positioning himself on the left side and facing the tripod, he

places the spare barrel case alongside the tripod, unzips the case, and removes the spare barrel and mounting equipment.

(2) The procedures for mounting the machine gun on the tripod remain the same except all are performed in a prone position and all movements are in the low crawl.

d. **Taking the Machine Gun Out of Action.** The procedures for taking the machine gun out of action remain the same except all are performed in a prone position and all movements are in the low crawl.

Section IV. BASIC GUNNERY

In basic marksmanship, the gunner applies the fundamentals in live-fire exercises during day and night. This includes 10-meter zeroing, 10-meter firing, field zeroing, transition firing, and record firing.

4-33. ZERO

Zeroing aligns the sights with the barrel so that the point of aim equals the point of impact. Ten-meter zeroing is for conducting 10-meter fire only and has no further application. (Zeroing at range or field zeroing is the gunner's battlesight zero and must be recorded.) Remember to zero both barrels of the machine gun.

a. **10-Meter Zero, Set the Sights (Mechanical Zero).** The gunner indexes or places the range scale on a range of 500 meters. He assumes a prone position and sights on the target.

b. **Three-Round Group.** The gunner fires three single rounds loaded individually at the center base of the aiming points on the basic machine gun marksmanship target. He fires the three rounds without making any adjustments to the sights. The shot group must be about a 4-cm circle or smaller to establish the center of the group in relation to the center base of the aiming paster.

c. **Grid Square Overlay.** For a more accurate adjustment, the gunner moves downrange and places the grid square overlay over pasters 1 and 2. He ensures that he aligns the overlay with the pasters and squares.

(1) Counts the number of squares it will take to move the shot group to the aiming paster.

(2) Upon completion, returns to the firing line to make corrections to the weapon. (Figure 4-21 illustrates a zero group size on which adjustments can be made and a group that is too loose for adjustments [bipod mode].) If a group is too loose, the gunner checks his position and group.

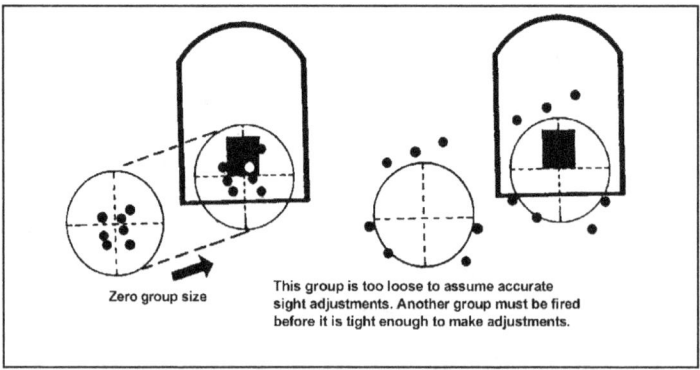

Figure 4-21. Zero group size.

d. **Windage Correction**. If the center of the group is to the left or right of the black aiming paster, the gunner must correct for windage.

e. **Elevation Correction**. If the center of the shot group is above or below of the black aiming paster, the gunner must correct for elevation.

f. **Confirmation**. The gunner fires another three-shot group (loaded singly) after making his corrections for windage and elevation. If the center of the group is still off the aiming point, he adjusts further until the group is centered on the point of aim.

g. **Recording of Zero**. There is no reason to record the 10-meter zero, because it applies only to firing at the 10-meter basic machine gun target.

NOTE: Remember to zero both barrels.

> **WARNING**
>
> The M240B is carried loaded with the bolt locked to the *rear* in *tactical situations* where noise discipline is critical to the success of the mission. Trained gun crews are the only personnel authorized to load the M240B and only when command directs the crew to do so. During *normal training exercises*, the M240B is loaded and carried with the bolt in the *forward position*.

4-34. FIELD ZERO

A gunner must know how to zero the machine gun at distance. He should select a known distance target between 300 and 700 meters. As the range increases, it becomes more difficult to determine where the center of the beaten zone is in relation to the target. Therefore, the 500-meter target on the transition range is recommended because of the ease of determining adjustments.

a. **Setting of the Sights**. The gunner uses the same procedures as for 10-meter zeroing except that he places the rear sight on the range to the target. The recommended range is 500 meters.

b. **Burst**. Fire a burst of 5 to 7 rounds for the M249 or 7 to 9 for the M60/M240B. The gunner assumes a good stable position and fires bursts of 5 to 7 rounds for the M249 or 7 to 9 for the M60/M240B at the center base of the target and notes where the burst strikes.

c. **Correction for Windage**. If the center of the beaten zone is to the left or right of the target, he corrects for windage. He adjusts the windage accordingly.

d. **Correction for Elevation**. If the center of the beaten zone is high or low in relation to the target, he corrects for elevation. Because determining that relationship is difficult, the gunner relies on trial and error to gain sufficient experience in making reliable estimates. He makes corrections in the same manner as 10-meter zeroing.

e. **Confirmation**. After making corrections for windage and elevation, the gunner fires confirming bursts of 5 to 7 rounds for the M249 or 7 to 9 rounds for the M60/M240B. If the target is not hit, he repeats the procedures.

f. **Recording of Zero.** Upon confirming the zero, the gunner records it by counting the number of clicks he moved the sight for windage and elevation from the initial setting.

4-35. 10-METER FIRING

The 10-meter firing trains the gunner to apply the fundamentals of machine gun marksmanship in live-fire exercises. It familiarizes the soldier with the weapon's characteristics, noise, and recoil. It instills in the soldier confidence in his weapon. Each gunner learns to zero his machine gun, conducts crew drill, controlled-burst fire at point targets, and uses traverse and search techniques of fire at area targets. The 10-meter firing is conducted on a 10-meter range or a multipurpose range using the basic machine gun target. These exercises are fired with the machine gun on the bipod from both the prone position and the fighting position and with the tripod from prone and fighting positions. The 10-meter firing exercises are for practice as well as part of record qualification. All 10-meter firing exercises are recorded and scored to provide the gunner an assessment of his performance. The 10-meter firing is conducted IAW Firing Table I (Table 4-2, page 4-42). There are ten tasks.

a. **Task 1—Zero Bipod.** The gunner fires single shots to determine his weapon's zero for 10 meters. This task reinforces the dry-fire experience and allows the gunner to practice loading, while providing the most accurate and tight shot group obtainable. (A1 and A2)

b. **Task 2—Controlled-Burst Fire Bipod Fixed.** Using point targets, the gunner fires bursts of 5 to 7 rounds for the M249 or 7 to 9 rounds for the M60/M240B. This task exposes the gunner to automatic fire and the action of the weapon and at the same time introduces trigger control. (A3 and A4)

c. **Task 3—Controlled-Burst Fire Bipod Fixed.** This task requires the gunner to make body position to engage area targets in depth, to use controlled-burst firing, and to use a series of aiming points to disburse fire across the target. (A5 and A6)

d. **Task 4—Controlled-Burst Fire Bipod Fixed.** This task requires the gunner to make position changes to engage linear targets with depth, to use controlled-burst firing, and to use a series of aiming points to disburse fire across the target. (A7 and A8)

e. **Task 5—Zero Tripod.** The gunner fires single shots to determine his weapon's zero for 10 meters. This task reinforces the dry-fire experience and allows the gunner to practice loading, while providing the most accurate and tight shot group obtainable. (B1 and B2)

f. **Task 6—Controlled-Burst Fire Tripod.** Using point targets, the gunner fires bursts of 5 to 7 rounds for the M249 or 7 to 9 rounds for the M60/M240B. This task exposes the gunner to automatic fire and the action of the weapon and at the same time introduces trigger control. (B1 through B4)

g. **Task 7—Traverse and Search Fire.** This task requires the gunner to make position changes or manipulate the T&E mechanism to engage linear targets with depth, to use controlled-burst firing, and to use a series of aiming points to disburse fire across the target. (B7 through B8)

h. **Task 8—Traverse and Search Fire.** This task requires the gunner to make body position changes or manipulate the T&E mechanism to engage area targets in depth, to use controlled-burst firing, and to use a series of aiming points to disburse fire across the target, while wearing a protective mask and gloves. (B5 through B6)

i. **Task 9—Search and Traverse Fire Qualification**. This task requires the gunner to make position changes or manipulate the T&E mechanism to engage area targets in depth during timed conditions. (C5 through C6)

j. **Task 10—Traverse and Search Fire Qualification**. This task requires the gunner to engage area targets with width and depth, while making position changes or manipulating the T&E mechanism during timed conditions. (C7 through C8)

4-36. 10-METER CONDUCT OF FIRE

The gunners are instructed on the objectives and fundamentals of firing from the bipod and tripod-supported prone or fighting positions, on fire commands used on the basic range, on the basic machine gun marksmanship target, and on analyzing and scoring the target. The unit is organized in firing orders based on range constraints. Each firing order should consist of a gunner and an assistant gunner. The assistant gunner assists the gunner during prefire checks and zeroing. The assistant gunner also relays signals to the tower operator, checks the gunner's position, and assists him. During qualification, an assistant gunner is not used. The ten tasks are fired in the following manner:

a. **Task 1—Bipod, Zero.**

(1) The tower operator gives the command MACHINE GUN TO BE MOUNTED HERE (weapon squad leader's pointing to the firing points on the 10-meter line), FRONT (weapon squad leader's pointing to the 10-meter targets), ACTION.

(2) At the command ACTION the machine gun crew conducts, placing the machine gun into action (bipod mode)

(3) The gunner prepares the rear sight for zeroing and checks the front sight.

(4) The gunner assumes a good position.

(5) The tower operator instructs the gunner to prepare a single round.

(6) The following fire command is given. The gunner and assistant gunner repeat each element of the fire command as it is given.

> FIRE MISSION (The gunner loads and moves the safety to "F".)
>
> FRONT (The gunner focuses on the target or target area.)
>
> PASTER A ONE (The gunner locates target.)
>
> FIVE HUNDRED (The gunner adjusts sights and acquires the sight picture.)
>
> FIXED, ONE ROUND (The gunner is given the method of fire.)
>
> COMMENCE FIRING (The gunner fires on command from tower operator, but when ready.)

NOTE: Throughout all firing exercises, the gunner performs the appropriate tasks during each element of the fire command. The number of rounds fired is used instead of the rate for METHOD OF FIRE. This is for control. (Omitting the rate specifies RAPID fire, which is not desirable for the tasks.)

WARNING

The M240B is carried loaded with the bolt locked to the *rear* in *tactical situations* where noise discipline is critical to the success of the mission. Trained gun crews are the only personnel authorized to load the M240B and only when command directs the crew to do so. During *normal training exercises*, the M240B is loaded and carried with the bolt in the *forward position*.

---

(7) The gunner loads one round, obtains the proper sight picture, and gives an UP to the assistant gunner.

(8) The assistant gunner relays the READY signal to the tower operator.

(9) The tower operator gives the command COMMENCE FIRING.

(10) The gunner engages paster A1 with three-single shots when he is ready.

(11) The gunner moves downrange to observe, mark, and triangulate the shot group. He makes adjustments as needed.

(12) Steps 3 through 10 are repeated, but the gunner fires at paster A2 firing a single round, then he adjusts.

NOTE: If the gunner should zero his weapon using 9 rounds, he uses the remaining 3 rounds to confirm his zero. If he is unable to zero with 12 rounds, he is removed from the firing line for remedial training.

WARNING

The M240B is carried loaded with the bolt locked to the *rear* in *tactical situations* where noise discipline is critical to the success of the mission. Trained gun crews are the only personnel authorized to load the M240B and only when command directs the crew to do so. During *normal training exercises*, the M240B is loaded and carried with the bolt in the *forward position*.

---

b. **Task 2—Bipod, Controlled-Burst Fire, Fixed.**

(1) The tower operator instructs the gunner to prepare two 7-round belts (M249) or two 9-round belts (M60/M240B).

(2) When the fire command is given, the gunner and assistant gunner repeat each element as it is given.

    FIRE MISSION
    FRONT
    PASTER A THREE
    FIVE HUNDRED
    FIXED, FIVE- TO SEVEN-ROUND BURSTS (M249) or SEVEN- TO NINE-ROUND BURSTS (M60/M240B).
    AT MY COMMAND

(3) The gunner acquires the proper sight picture and gives an UP to the assistant gunner.

(4) The assistant gunner relays the READY signal to the tower operator.

(5) The tower operator gives the command to FIRE.

(6) The gunner fires the first burst of 5 to 7 rounds (M249) or 7 to 9 rounds (M60/M240B) at paster A3.

(7) Steps 2 through 6 are repeated, but the gunner fires at paster A4.

c. **Task 3—Bipod, Controlled-Burst Fire, Fixed.**

(1) The tower operator instructs the gunner to prepare a 14-round belt (M249) or 18-round belt (M60/M240B).

(2) When the fire command is given, the gunner and assistant gunner repeat each element as it is given.

FIRE MISSION
FRONT
PASTER A FIVE
FIVE HUNDRED
TRAVERSE AND SEARCH, FIVE- TO SEVEN-ROUND BURSTS (M249) OR
SEVEN- TO NINE-ROUND BURSTS (M60/M240B)
AT MY COMMAND

(3) The gunner acquires the proper sight picture and gives an UP to the assistant gunner.

(4) The assistant gunner relays the READY signal to the tower operator.

(5) The tower operator gives the command to FIRE.

(6) The gunner fires the first burst of 5 to 7 (M249) OR 7 TO 9 (M60/M240B) rounds at paster A5.

(7) Steps 2 through 6 are repeated, but the gunner fires at paster A6.

d. **Task 4—Bipod, Controlled-Burst Fire, Fixed.**

(1) The tower operator instructs the gunner to prepare 14-round belt (M249) or 18-round belt (M60/M240B).

(2) When the fire command is given, the gunner and assistant gunner repeat each element as it is given.

FIRE MISSION
FRONT
PASTER A SEVEN
FIVE HUNDRED
TRAVERSE AND SEARCH, FIVE- TO SEVEN-ROUND BURSTS (M249) or
SEVEN- TO NINE-ROUND BURSTS (M60/M240B)
AT MY COMMAND

(3) The gunner acquires the proper sight picture and gives an UP to the assistant gunner.

(4) The assistant gunner relays the READY signal to the tower operator.

(5) The tower operator gives the command to FIRE.

(6) The gunner fires the first burst of 5 to 7 rounds (M249) or 7 to 9 rounds (M60/M240B) at paster A7.

(7) Steps 2 through 6 are repeated, but the gunner fires at paster A8.

(8) The gunner and assistant gunner moves downrange to observe and analyze his target and shot groups.

(9) The Tower operator gives the following command when the gunner and assistant gunner return from downrange. OUT OF ACTION.

(10) At the command OUT OF ACTION the machine gun crew conducts, taking the machine gun out of action (bipod mode)

e. **Task 5—Tripod, Zero.** If the gunner should zero his weapon in 9 rounds, he uses the remaining 3 rounds to confirm his zero. If he is unable to zero in 12 rounds, he is removed from the firing line for remedial training.

(1) The tower operator gives the command MACHINE GUN TO BE MOUNTED HERE (weapon squad leaders point to the firing points on the 10-meter line), FRONT (weapon squad leader points to the 10-meter targets), ACTION.

(2) At the command ACTION the machine gun crew conducts, placing the machine gun into action (tripod mode)

(3) The gunner prepares the rear sight for zeroing and checks the front sight.

(4) The gunner assumes a good tripod position.

(5) The tower operator instructs the gunner to prepare a single round.

(6) The following fire command is given. The gunner and assistant gunner repeat each element of the fire command as it is given.

> FIRE MISSION (The gunner loads and moves the safety to "F".)
> FRONT (The gunner focuses on the target or target area.)
> PASTER B ONE (The gunner locates target.)
> FIVE HUNDRED (The gunner adjusts sights and acquires the sight picture.)
> FIXED, ONE ROUND (The gunner is given the method of fire.)
> COMMENCE FIRING (The gunner fires on command from tower operator, but when ready.)

(7) The gunner loads one round, obtains the proper sight picture, and gives an UP to the assistant gunner.

(8) The assistant gunner relays the READY signal to the tower operator.

(9) The tower operator gives the command COMMENCE FIRING.

(10) The gunner engages paster B1 with three single shots when he is ready.

(11) The gunner moves downrange to observe, mark, and triangulate the shot group. He makes adjustments as needed.

(12) Steps 3 through 10 are repeated, but the gunner fires at paster B2 firing a single round, then he adjusts.

f. **Task 6—Tripod, Controlled-Burst Fire, Traverse.**

(1) The tower operator instructs the gunner to prepare a 28-round belt (M249) or 36-round belt (M60/M240B).

(2) When the fire command is given, the gunner and assistant gunner repeat each element as it is given.

> FIRE MISSION
> FRONT
> PASTERS B ONE THROUGH B FOUR
> FIVE HUNDRED
> FIXED, FIVE TO SEVEN-ROUND BURSTS (M249) or SEVEN- TO NINE-ROUND BURSTS (M60/M240B)
> AT MY COMMAND

(3) The gunner acquires the proper sight picture and gives an UP to the assistant gunner.

(4) The assistant gunner relays the READY signal to the tower operator.

(5) The tower operator gives the command to FIRE.

(6) The gunner engages pasters B1 through B4, firing 5- to 7-round bursts (M249) or 7 to 9 round bursts (M60/M240B) at each paster, using traverse technique.

g. **Task 7—Tripod, Controlled-Burst Fire, Traverse and Search**.

(1) The tower operator instructs the gunner to prepare a 56-round belt (M249) or 63-round belt (M60/M240B).

(2) When the fire command is given, the gunner and assistant gunner repeat each element as it is given.

FIRE MISSION
FRONT
PASTERS B SEVEN THROUGH B EIGHT
FIVE HUNDRED
TRAVERSE AND SEARCH, FIVE- TO SEVEN-ROUND BURSTS (M249) or
SEVEN- TO NINE-ROUND BURSTS (M60/M240B)
AT MY COMMAND

(3) The gunner acquires the proper sight picture and gives an UP to the assistant gunner.

(4) The assistant gunner relays the READY signal to the tower operator.

(5) The tower operator gives the command to FIRE.

(6) The gunner engages pasters B7 through B8, firing a 5- to 7-round bursts or 7- to 9-round bursts at each paster, using traverse and search technique.

h. **Task 8—Tripod, Controlled-Burst Fire, Search and Traverse.**

(1) The tower operator instructs the assistant gunner to prepare a 35-round belt (M249) or 45-round belt (M60/M240B).

(2) When the fire command is given, the gunner and assistant gunner repeat each element as it is given

FIRE MISSION
FRONT
PASTERS B FIVE THROUGH B SIX
FIVE HUNDRED
TRAVERSE AND SEARCH, FIVE- TO SEVEN-ROUND BURSTS (M249) or
SEVEN- TO NINE-ROUND BURSTS (M60/M240B)
AT MY COMMAND

(3) The gunner acquires the proper sight picture and gives an UP to the assistant gunner.

(4) The assistant gunner relays the READY signal to the tower operator.

(5) The tower operator gives the command to FIRE.

(6) The gunner engages pasters B5 through B6, firing a three round burst at each paster, using search and traverse technique.

(7) The gunner and assistant gunner moves downrange to observe and analyze his targets.

i. **Task 9—Tripod, Qualification, Search and Traverse Fire.** On completion of all firing, the firing line is cleared and the instructors or safeties move downrange and score the targets. The firer will not score his own target.

(1) The tower operator instructs the assistant gunner to prepare a 35-round belt (M249) or 45-round belt (M60/M240B).

(2) When the fire command is given, the gunner and assistant gunner repeat each element as it is given

> FIRE MISSION
> FRONT
> PASTERS C FIVE THROUGH C SIX
> FIVE HUNDRED
> TRAVERSE AND SEARCH, FIVE- TO SEVEN-ROUND BURSTS (M249) or
> SEVEN- TO NINE-ROUND BURSTS (M60/M240B)
> AT MY COMMAND

(3) The gunner acquires the proper sight picture and gives an UP to the assistant gunner.

(4) The assistant gunner relays the READY signal to the tower operator.

(5) The tower operator gives the command to FIRE.

(6) The gunner engages pasters B5 through B6, firing a 5- to 7- round bursts (M249) or 7- to 9-round bursts (M60/M240B) at each paster, using search and traverse technique. The gunner has 30 seconds to engage as many pasters as he can during the time allowed.

j. **Task 10—Tripod, Qualification, Traverse and Search.** On completion of all firing, the firing line is cleared and the instructors or safeties move downrange and score the targets. The firer will not score his own target.

(1) The tower operator instructs the gunner to prepare a 56-round belt (M249) or 72-round belt (M60/M240B).

(2) When the fire command is given, the gunner and assistant gunner repeat each element as it is given.

> FIRE MISSION
> FRONT
> PASTERS C SEVEN THROUGH C EIGHT
> HUNDRED
> TRAVERSE AND SEARCH, FIVE- TO SEVEN-ROUND BURSTS (M249) or
> SEVEN- TO NINE-ROUND BURSTS (M60/M240B)
> AT MY COMMAND

(3) The gunner acquires the proper sight picture and gives an UP to the assistant gunner.

(4) The assistant gunner relays the READY signal to the tower operator.

(5) The tower operator gives the command to FIRE.

(6) The gunner engages pasters C7 through C8, firing 5- to 7-round bursts (M249) or 7- to 9-round bursts (M60/M240B) at each paster, using traverse and search technique. The gunner has 45 seconds to engage as many pasters as he can during the time allowed.

(7) The tower operator gives the following command when the gunner and assistant gunner return from downrange. OUT OF ACTION.

(8) At the command OUT OF ACTION the machine gun crew conducts, taking the machine gun out of action (tripod mode)

TASK	TIME	RDS M249	RDS M60/ M240B	TYPE	TARGET	TYPE FIRE
	**BASIC (10-METER) FIRE** **PRONE OR FIGHTING POSITION, BIPOD OR TRIPOD,** **PRACTICE AND QUALIFICATION**
1	No limit	12	12	Ball	Pasters A1 and A2	12 single rd (zero).
2	No limit	14	18	Ball	Pasters A3 and A4	5- to 7-rd bursts (M249) or 7- to 9-rd bursts (M60/ M240B) for each paster.
3	No limit	14	18	Ball	Pasters A5 and A6	5- to 7-rd bursts (M249) or 7- to 9-rd bursts (M60/ M240B) for each paster.
4	No limit	14	18	Ball	Pasters A7 and A8	5- to 7-rd bursts (M249) or 7- to 9-rd bursts (M60/ M240B) for each paster.
5	No limit	12	12	Ball	Pasters B1 and B2	12 single rd (zero).
6	No limit	28	36	Ball	Pasters B1 thru B4	5- to 7-rd bursts (M249) or 7- to 9-rd bursts (M60/ M240B) for each paster.
7	No limit	56	72	Ball	Pasters B7 thru B8	5- to 7-rd bursts (M249) or 7- to 9-rd bursts (M60/ M240B) for each paster traverse and search.
8	No limit	35	45	Ball	Pasters B5 thru B6	5- to 7-rd bursts (M249) or 7- to 9-rd bursts (M60/ M240B) for each paster.
*9	30 seconds	35	45	Ball	Pasters C5 thru C6	5- to 7-rd bursts (M249) or 7- to 9-rd bursts (M60/ M240B) for each paster.
*10	45 seconds	56	72	Ball	Pasters C7 thru C8	5- to 7-rd bursts (M249) or 7- to 9-rd bursts (M60/ M240B) for each paster.

NOTE: The unit commander determines the position to be used. A summary of the ammunition requirements is on page 4-54.
*Indicates qualification tasks.

Table 4-2. Firing Table I—Basic (10-meter) fire.

> **WARNING**
>
> The M240B is carried loaded with the bolt locked to the *rear* in *tactical situations* where noise discipline is critical to the success of the mission. Trained gun crews are the only personnel authorized to load the M240B and only when command directs the crew to do so. During *normal training exercises*, the M240B is loaded and carried with the bolt in the *forward position*.

4-37. 10-METER FIRING, QUALIFICATION

The first phase of qualification consists of firing tasks 2 through 8 of Firing Table I for practice, and tasks 9 and 10 of Firing Table I for record. Before firing, all soldiers must be familiar with the tasks, the time allowed, the ammunition allowances, the procedures to follow in the event of a stoppage, and the penalties imposed.

a. **Time and Ammunition**. Each gunner completes zeroing before record firing. Individual fire commands are given for each task. Task 9 is fired in 30 seconds, and task 10 is fired in 45 seconds.

b. **Stoppages**. If a stoppage occurs, the gunner must apply immediate action. If the stoppage is reduced, he continues to fire the course.

(1) If a stoppage occurs that cannot be reduced by immediate action, the gunner raises his hand and awaits assistance.

(2) Once the stoppage is reduced, the gunner completes firing beginning with the next task.

(3) If a stoppage is caused by an error on the part of the gunner, additional time is not permitted. The gunner receives the score he earned before the stoppage occurred.

(4) If it is necessary to replace the machine gun, the gunner must zero the new weapon. The gunner can fire the exercise again.

(5) Gunners who cannot fire a task or cannot complete firing in the time allowed (because of malfunctions) can finish the exercise in an *alibi run* after all other gunners complete firing. They fire only those tasks they failed to engage because of the malfunction.

c. **Penalties**. Five points are deducted from the score of any gunner who fails to stop firing at the command or signal to cease fire. If a gunner fires at the wrong target or exercise, he loses the points for those rounds. A gunner whose target was fired upon by another gunner is permitted to refire the exercise.

d. **Scoring**. When scoring the 10-meter target, the trainer scores all scoring pasters (C5 through C6 and C7 through C8). One point is given for each round impacting within the scoring space. The maximum point value is 7 points (M249) or 9 points (M60/M240B) for each paster. Rounds touching the line on the paster are considered a HIT. When firing C5 though C6, the gunner engages 5 scoring pasters with 35 rounds. (M249) or 45 rounds (M60/M240B) The maximum possible is 35 points (M249) or 45 points (M60/M240B). When firing pasters C7 through C8, the gunner engages 8 scoring pasters with 56 rounds (M249) or 72 rounds (M60/M240B). The maximum possible is 56 points (M249) or 72 points (M60/M240B). Gunners do not score their own targets when firing for qualification. During qualification firing, at least 63 points (M249) or 81 points

(M60/M240B) must be achieved on Firing Table I. DA Form 85-R is used to record scores (Figure 4-23). (See paragraph 4-42).

e. **Position**. Based on his METL, the commander selects either the bipod-supported prone or fighting position for table A only. For qualification the position will be either tripod-supported prone or tripod-supported fighting position table B for practice and table C for qualification.

4-38. TRANSITION FIRE

Transition firing provides the gunner the experience necessary to progress from 10-meter firing to field firing at various types of targets at longer ranges. The gunner experiences and learns the characteristics of fire, field zeroing, and range determination, and engaging targets in a timed scenario. He uses the adjusted aiming-point method of fire adjustment. Transition firing is conducted on a machine gun transition range or the MPRC. These exercises are fired with the bipod prone or fighting position. Transition firing is fired and scored for practice and qualification to provide feedback to the gunner. Firing Table II consists of eight tasks (Table 4-3, page 4-47).

a. **Range Facilities**. The transition range should consist of several firing lanes. Each lane should be 10 meters wide at the firing line and 100 meters wide at a range of 800 meters. Ideally, each lane has a fighting position with an adjacent prone firing position.

b. **Targets** (Card board: NSN 6920-00-795-1806 and plastic: 6920-00-071-4780). The E-type silhouette targets are used—single and double are needed for qualification. The double represents an enemy automatic weapon, which for the gunner is a priority target (Figure 4-22). The targets are at various ranges that a gunner might engage. All targets should be plainly seen from the firing positions. Electrical targets are desirable.

c. **Stoppage**. The same procedures used in Firing Table I qualification firing are used (page 4-42).

d. **Penalties**. The same procedures used in Firing Table I qualification firing are used (page 4-42).

e. **Scoring**. Ten points are given for each target hit, whether hit on the first or second burst. The total possible points are 110. The gunner must hit at least 7 (70 points) targets out of 11 exposures to qualify. DA Form 85-R is used to record scores Figure 4-23 (see paragraph 4-42).

f. **Position**. Based on his METL, the commander selects either the bipod-supported prone or bipod-supported fighting position for qualification.

Figure 4-22. Single and double E-type silhouette targets.

4-39. TRANSITION CONDUCT OF FIRE, BIPOD

The unit is organized in firing orders based on range constraints. Each firing order should consist of a gunner and an assistant gunner. The assistant gunner assists the gunner during prefire checks and zeroing. He also relays signals to the tower operator, checks the gunner's position, and assists him during qualification in target detection and adjustments. The bipod-supported prone or fighting positions are used. The eight tasks are fired in the following manner.

a. **Task 1—Field Zero, 500-Meter, Double E-Type Silhouette.**

(1) The tower operator gives the command MACHINE GUN TO BE MOUNTED HERE (weapon squad leader's pointing to the firing points on the transition line), FRONT (weapon squad leader's pointing to the targets), ACTION.

(2) At the command ACTION the machine gun crew conducts, placing the machine gun into action (bipod mode)

(3) The gunner prepares the rear sight for field zeroing and checks the front sight blade. He sets the range to the zero target on the range scale. The preferred range is 500 meters.

(4) The gunner assumes a good position.

(5) The tower operator instructs the assistant gunner to prepare a 28-round belt (M249) or 36-round belt (M60/M240B).

(6) When the fire command is given, the gunner and assistant gunner repeat each element as it is given.

> FIRE MISSION
> FRONT
> TARGETS: TROOPS IN THE OPEN
> THREE HUNDRED
> FIXED, FIVE- TO SEVEN-ROUND BURST (M249) or SEVEN- to NINE-ROUND BURST (M60/M240B)
> AT MY COMMAND

(7) The gunner loads one 28-round belt of ammunition (M249) or 36-round belt of ammunition (M60/M240B), obtains the proper sight picture, and gives an UP to the assistant gunner.

(8) The assistant gunner relays the READY signal to the tower operator.

(9) The tower operator gives the command FIRE.

(10) The gunner fires a 5- to 7-round burst (M249) or 7- to 9-round burst (M60/M240B) at the target when ready.

(11) The gunner observes the beaten zone. If the rounds miss the target, he makes adjustments for windage and elevation.

(12) After adjustments have been made, the gunner repeats steps 8 through 9 with the remaining rounds until rounds are impacting on the target. He records his zero.

b. **Task 2—400-Meter, Double E-Type Silhouette.**

(1) The tower operator instructs the gunner to load one 154-round belt.

(2) When the fire command is given, the gunner and assistant gunner repeat each element as it is given. It is only given once for tasks 2 through 8.

> FIRE MISSION
> FRONT
> TARGET: TROOPS IN THE OPEN

ONE HUNDRED TO EIGHT HUNDRED METERS
FIXED, FIVE- TO SEVEN-ROUND BURST (M249) or SEVEN- TO NINE-ROUND BURST (M60/M240B)
AT MY COMMAND

(3) The gunner gives an UP to the assistant gunner.

(4) The assistant gunner gives the READY signal to the tower operator.

(5) The tower operator gives the command FIRE.

(6) The gunner scans the sector.

(7) A 400-meter, double E-type target is exposed for 10 seconds.

(8) The gunner determines the range, places the proper setting on the rear sight, assumes the proper position, obtains the correct sight alignment and sight picture, and fires a 5- to 7-round burst (M249) or 7- to 9-round burst (M60/M240B).

(9) If the gunner fails to hit the target, he fires another 5- to 7-round burst (M249) or 7- to 9-round burst (M60/M240B) using the adjusted aiming point method of fire adjustment.

c. **Task 3—500-Meter, Double E-Type Silhouette.**

(1) The gunner and assistant gunner continues to scan the sector.

(2) A 500-meter, double E-type target is exposed for 10 seconds.

(3) The gunner determines the range, places the proper setting on the rear sight, assumes the proper position, obtains the correct sight alignment and sight picture, and fires a 5- to 7-round burst (M249) or 7- to 9-round burst (M60/M240B).

(4) If the gunner fails to hit the target, he fires another 5- to 7-round burst (M249) or 7- to 9-round burst (M60/M240B) using the adjusted aiming point method of fire adjustment.

d. **Task 4—600-Meter, Single E-Type Silhouette.**

(1) The gunner and assistant gunner continues to scan the sector.

(2) A 600-meter, single E-type target is exposed for 20 seconds.

(3) The gunner determines the range, places the proper setting on the rear sight, assumes the proper position, obtains the correct sight alignment and sight picture, and fires a 5- to 7-round burst (M249) or 7- to 9-round burst (M60/M240B).

(4) If the gunner fails to hit the target, he fires another 5- to 7-round burst (M249) or 7- to 9-round burst (M60/M240B) using the adjusted aiming point method of fire adjustment.

e. **Task 5—800-Meter, Single E-Type Silhouette.**

(1) The gunner and assistant gunner continues to scan the sector.

(2) A 800-meter, single E-type target is exposed for 30 seconds (total of six targets).

(3) The gunner determines the range, places the proper setting on the rear sight, assumes the proper position, obtains the correct sight alignment and sight picture, and fires a 5- to 7-round burst (M249) or 7- to 9-round burst (M60/M240B).

(4) If the gunner fails to hit the target, he fires another 5- to 7-round burst (M249) or 7- to 9-round burst (M60/M240B) using the adjusted aiming point method of fire adjustment.

f. **Task 6—400-Meter, Single E-Type Silhouette; and 600-Meter, Double E-Type Silhouettes**.

(1) The gunner and assistant gunner continue to scan the sector.

(2) A 400-meter single E-type target and a 600-meter double E-type target are exposed for 30 seconds.

(3) The gunner determines the range, places the proper setting on the rear sight, assumes the proper position, obtains the correct sight alignment and sight picture, and fires a 5- to 7-round burst (M249) or 7- to 9-round burst (M60/M240B) at each target.

(4) If the gunner fails to hit the target, he fires another 5- to 7-round burst (M249) or 7- to 9-round burst (M60/M240B) using the adjusted aiming point method of fire adjustment at each target.

g. **Task 7—700-Meter and 800-Meter, Double E-Type Silhouettes**.

(1) The gunner and assistant gunner continue to scan the sector.

(2) A 700-meter and a 800-meter double E-type targets are exposed for 45 seconds (total of four targets at 700 meters and six targets at 800 meters).

(3) The gunner determines the range, places the proper setting on the rear sight, assumes the proper position, obtains correct sight alignment and sight picture, and fires a 5- to 7-round burst (M249) or 7- to 9-round burst (M60/M240B) at each target.

(4) If the gunner fails to hit the target, he fires another 7-round burst using the adjusted aiming point method of fire adjustment at each target.

h. **Task 8—400-Meter, Single E-Type Silhouette, and 500-Meter, 600-Meter, Double E-Type Silhouettes**.

(1) The gunner and assistant gunner continue to scan the sector.

(2) The 400-meter single E-type silhouettes, and 500- and 600-meter double E-type silhouettes are exposed for 45 seconds (total of two targets at 400 meters, four targets at 500 meters, and six targets at 600 meters).

(3) The gunner determines the range, places the proper setting on the rear sight, assumes the proper position, obtains correct sight alignment and sight picture, and fires a 5- to 7-round burst (M249) or 7- to 9-round burst (M60/M240B) at each target.

(4) If the gunner fails to hit the target, he fires another 5- to 7-round burst (M249) or 7- to 9-round burst (M60/M240B) using the adjusted aiming point method of fire adjustment at each target.

BIPOD TRANSITION FIRE PRONE OR FIGHTING POSITION PRACTICE AND QUALIFICATION							
TASK	TIME	RDS M249	RDS M60/ M240B	TYPE	TARGET	RANGE	TYPE FIRE
1	No limit	28	36	X 4:1	Double E	500	Fixed, 5- to 7-rd burst (M249) or 7- to 9-rd burst (M60/M240B) (field zero)
*2	5 seconds	14	18	X 4:1	Double E	400	Fixed, 5- to 7-rd burst (M249) or 7- to 9-rd burst (M60/M240B)
*3	10 seconds	14	18	X 4:1	Double E	500	Fixed, 5- to 7-rd burst (M249) or 7- to 9-rd burst (M60/M240B)
*4	5 seconds	14	18	X 4:1	Double E	600	Fixed, 5- to 7-rd burst (M249) or 7- to 9-rd burst (M60/M240B)
*5	10 seconds	14	18	X 4:1	Double E	800	Fixed, 5- to 7-rd burst (M249) or 7- to 9-rd burst (M60/M240B)
*6	20 seconds	28	36	X 4:1	Single E Double E	400 600	Fixed, 5- to 7-rd burst (M249) or 7- to 9-rd burst (M60/M240B)
*7	20 seconds	28	36	X 4:1	Double E Double E	700 800	Fixed, 5- to 7-rd burst (M249) or 7- to 9-rd burst (M60/M240B)
*8	25 seconds	42	54	X 4:1	Single E Double E Double E	400 500 600	Fixed, 5- to 7-rd burst (M249) or 7- to 9-rd burst (M60/M240B)
NOTE: The unit commander determines the firing position. A summary of the ammunition requirements is on page 4-53. *Indicates qualification tasks. **X** Indicates ball and tracer 4:1 mix.							

Table 4-3. Firing Table II—Bipod transition fire.

4-40. TRANSITION FIRE, LIMITED VISIBILITY

Night or limited visibility firing requires the soldier to apply the fundamentals of gunner marksmanship while using nightsights. This training instills confidence in the machine gunner. Each soldier learns how to engage targets using nightsight. He learns to mount the sight, boresight the weapon at 10-meters, and zero the aided vision devices (IAW Appendix G for that device) at 10-meters using a 10-meter (M16A2) zero target. Finally, he learns to detect and engage a series of undetermined targets at various ranges with the aided vision device. Night firing exercises can be conducted during daylight with the AN/PVS-4 when the daylight cover is used. These exercises are for instructional, practice and qualification purposes. The commander can use this training to assess his unit's METL. Night firing is conducted on the same 10-meter range and transition range or a multipurpose machine gun range used for Firing Tables I and II. The tasks and conduct of fire in Firing Table III are the same as in Firing Table II. Therefore, a conduct of fire is not necessary.

a. **Time and Ammunition**. Table 4-4, Firing Table III (page 4-51) outlines ammunition requirements.

b. **Stoppage**. The same procedures that are used in Firing Table II, page 4-49.

c. **Penalties**. No penalties are used.

d. **Scoring**. No points are given when the target is hit on the first or second hit, only a hit or miss. The gunner must hit 6 out of 11 targets in order to be a qualified gunner. The gunner must have qualified on both the 10-meter and transition in order to advance to this step. DA Form 85-R, provided in the back of this manual, can be used to record the number of hits.

e. **Conditions**. Table 4-3, Firing Table III is used for engaging targets out to 400 meters under ideal moonlight or during daylight conditions. If visibility is limited because of a lack of ambient light, commanders may use field-expedient means to identify targets.

NOTE: The commander may lower the ranges by 100 meters when the ambient conditions do not allow the gunners to engage targets at extended ranges.

f. **Targets**. Single E-type silhouette targets and double E-type silhouette targets are used.

g. **Position**. Based on his METL, the commander selects either the bipod-supported prone position or bipod-supported fighting position.

h. **Conduct of Fire**. Limited visibility is the same as Firing Table II. The only difference is time and distance of the targets to be engaged and firing the scanning, walking and IR discipline exercise.

4-41. AN/PVS-4 ZERO
Refer to Appendix G and the appropriate TM for this piece of equipment.

CAUTION
When mounting the AN/PVS-4 to the mounting bracket, make sure the hole for the screw in the AN/PVS-4 is aligned and flush against the bracket screw. If not, it will strip the threads on the screw, and the AN/PVS-4 cannot be used with the M249 machine gun.

			TRANSITION FIRE, LIMITED VISIBILITY			
TASK	**TIME**	**RDS M249**	**RDS M60/ M240B**	**TYPE**	**TARGET**	**TYPE FIRE**
1	No limit	6	6	X 4:1	25-meter zero at 10 meters	6-single rounds
2	No limit	18	18	X 4:1	25-meter zero at 10 meters	18-single rounds
3	No limit	28	36	X 4:1	500	Fixed, 5- to 7- rd bursts (M249) or 7- to 9-rd bursts (M60/M240B)
*4	10 seconds	14	18	X 4:1	200	Fixed, 5- to 7- rd bursts (M249) or 7- to 9-rd bursts (M60/M240B)
*5	15 seconds	14	18	X 4:1	400	Fixed, 5- to 7- rd bursts (M249) or 7- to 9-rd bursts (M60/M240B)
*6	10 seconds	14	18	X 4:1	100	Fixed, 5- to 7- rd bursts (M249) or 7- to 9-rd bursts (M60/M240B)
*7	15 seconds	14	18	X 4:1	300	Fixed, 5- to 7- rd bursts (M249) or 7- to 9-rd bursts (M60/M240B)
*8	25 seconds	28	36		200 400	Fixed, 5- to 7- rd bursts (M249) or 7- to 9-rd bursts (M60/M240B)
*9	25 seconds	28	36		100 300	Fixed, 5- to 7- rd bursts (M249) or 7- to 9-rd bursts (M60/M240B)
*10	30 seconds	42	56	X 4:1	100, 200 400	Fixed, 5- to 7- rd bursts (M249) or 7- to 9-rd bursts (M60/M240B)

NOTE: The unit commander determines the position to be used. A summary of the ammunition requirements is on page 4-53.

* Indicates qualification tasks.   X Indicates ball and tracer 4:1 mix

Table 4-4. Firing Table III—Transition fire, limited visibility.

4-42. QUALIFICATION STANDARDS

Qualification with the M249, M60/M240B machine gun consists of achieving the minimum standards for 10-meter day and transition day firing tables. One point is allowed for each round impacting within the scoring space (maximum of 7 points [M249] or 9 points [M60/M240B] for each space) for Firing Table I. For Firing Table II, 7 points (M249) or 9 points (M60/M240B) are allowed for each target hit whether the target is hit on the first or second burst. For Firing Table III, place an X in the hit column and place an O in the miss column. The maximum possible score for Firing Table I is 91 points (M249), 117 points (M60/M240B). A minimum of 63 points (M249), 81 points (M60/M240B) is required. The maximum score for Firing Table II is 110 points; at least

70 points must be scored on this table to qualify. The maximum possible score for Firing Table III is 11 hits. A minimum of 7 hits is required. The combined minimum total score is 133 (M249), 151 (M240B); the combined maximum total score is 201 points (M249), 227 points (M240B). The overall ratings are as follows:

	M249	M60/M240B
EXPERT	182 to 201	206 to 227
GUNNER 1st CLASS	158 to 181	180 to 205
GUNNER 2nd CLASS	133 to 157	151 to 179
UNQUALIFIED	0 to 132	0 to 150

The trainer uses DA Form 85-R (Scorecard for M249, M60/M240B Machine Gun) for recording the gunner's performance on the machine gun qualification range. The instructions for completing the scorecard are on its reverse side. For an example of a completed form, see Figure 4-23. A blank locally reproducible form is in the back of this manual. The instructions are on the back of the form explaining how to fill out the form:

Use the following procedures to fill out the M249, M60/M240B scorecard:

1. **NAME:** Enter the gunner's last name, first name, middle initial, and rank.

2. **SSN:** Enter the gunner's social security number.

3. **UNIT:** Enter the gunner's unit designation.

4. **DATE:** Enter the date of firing.

5. **LANE:** Enter the lane number for the gunner's firing point.

6. **RECORD:** Tasks used for record and qualification are Firing Table I, tasks 9 through 10; Firing Table II, tasks 2 through 8; and Firing Table III, tasks 4 through 10.

7. **HIT/MISS:** For Table I, tasks 9 through 10, enter the number of rounds impacting within target spaces (maximum of 7 [M249] or 9 [M60/M240B] per space). For Table II, tasks 2 through 8, and Table III, tasks 4 through 10, enter an X for a hit and an O for a miss (regardless of whether the target is hit on the first or second burst).

8. **TOTAL HITS/ POINTS:** For Table I, tasks 9 through 10, give 1 point for each round impacting within a scoring space.
For Table II, tasks 2 through 8, give 10 points for each target hit.
For Table III, tasks 4 through 10, enter the number of targets hit (no points awarded).

9. **TOTAL SCORE:** Add points from Tables IV and V. Use the following qualification levels*:

	M249	M60/M240B
EXPERT GUNNER	182-201	206-227
GUNNER 1ST CLASS	158-181	180-205
GUNNER 2D CLASS	133-157	151-179
UNQUALIFIED	0-132	0-150

* The gunner must score 63 points (M249), 81 points (M60/M240B) on Table I, 70 points on Table II, and 6 hits on Table III to meet the minimum score for each.

The following is a summary of ammunition required:

	M249	M60/M240B	TYPE
Table I, Practice	185	231	Ball
Table I, Record	91	117	X4:1
Table II, Practice	182	236	X4:1
Table II, Record	154	200	X4:1
Table III, Practice	360	460	X4:1
Table III, Record	154	200	X4:1

NOTE: See DA Pam 350-38 for STRAC ammunition requirements.

SCORECARD FOR M249, M60/M240B MACHINE GUNS

For use of this form, see FM 3-22.68; the proponent agency is TRADOC.
See back of this form for instructions.

PRIVACY ACT STATEMENT

AUTHORITY: 10 USC 30129(g) Executive Order 9397.

PRINCIPAL PURPOSE: Records individual's performance on record fire range.

ROUTINE USES: Evaluate individual's proficiency and basis for determination of award of proficiency badge: SSN is used for positive identification purposes only.

DISCLOSURE: Voluntary, individuals not providing information cannot be rated/scored on a mass basis.

NAME: PVT DAVID JONES
SSN: 123-45-6789
UNIT: C Co 2/45TH IN
DATE (YYYYMMDD): 12 DEC 02
LANE: 3

TABLE I (10-METERS)

TASK	RANGE (meters)	TIME	HITS
1*	10	N/A	N/A
2*	10	N/A	N/A
3*	10	N/A	N/A
4*	10	N/A	N/A
5*	10	N/A	N/A
6*	10	N/A	N/A
7*	10	N/A	N/A
8*	10	N/A	N/A
9	10	40 SEC	30
10	10	50 SEC	52
TOTAL HITS (POINTS)			82

TABLE II (DAY TRANSITION)

TASK	RANGE (meters)	TIME	*PRACTICE HIT	MISS	**QUALIFY HIT	MISS
1*	500	N/A	N/A	N/A	N/A	N/A
2**	400	10 SEC	X		X	
3**	500	15 SEC	X		X	
4**	600	20 SEC	X	O	X	O
5**	800	30 SEC	X			
6**	400 / 600	30 SEC	X X		X X	
7**	700 / 800	45 SEC	X X	O	X X	O
8**	400 / 500 / 600	45 SEC	X X X		X X X	
**TOTAL POINTS						100

TABLE III (LIMITED VISIBILITY)

TASK	RANGE (meters)	TIME	*PRACTICE HIT	MISS	**QUALIFY HIT	MISS
1*	10	N/A	N/A	N/A	N/A	N/A
2*	10	N/A	N/A	N/A	N/A	N/A
3*	500	N/A	N/A	N/A	N/A	N/A
4	200	10 SEC	X		X	
5	400	15 SEC	X			O
6	100	10 SEC		O	X	
7	300	15 SEC	X		X	
8	200 / 400	25 SEC	X X	O	X X	
9	100 / 300	25 SEC	X X X		X X X	
10	100 / 200 / 400	30 SEC	X X X	O	X X X	
TOTAL HITS		9				

TOTAL SCORE

CHECK APPROPRIATE WEAPON

EXPERT	FIRST CLASS	SECOND CLASS
☑ M249 182-201	☐ M249 158-181	☐ M249 158-181
☐ M60/M240B 206-227	☐ M60/M240B 180-205	☐ M60/M240B 180-205

* NONSCORED TASKS
*** 10 POINTS PER HIT

OIC SIGNATURE: John Smith
GRADER: Paul Davis
RATING: EXPERT

DA FORM 85-R, OCT 2002   DA FORM 85, SEP 62, IS OBSOLETE.

Page 1 of 2
USAPA V1.00ES

Figure 4-23. Example of a completed DA Form 85-R.

CHAPTER 5
COMBAT TECHNIQUES OF FIRE

Technique of fire is the method of delivering and controlling effective fire. The machine gunners must be trained in the standard methods of applying fire. This chapter discusses combat techniques of fire, application of fire on the battlefield, and advanced gunnery. Before the machine gun can be employed to its full potential, the soldier must know and be trained on characteristics of fire, classes of fire, types of targets, and application of fire.

Section I. CHARACTERISTICS OF FIRE

Each gunner must know the effects of rounds when fired. Factors influencing the path and strike of rounds are not limited to applying the fundamentals. They include the velocity of the round, gravity, terrain, atmospheric conditions, and the innate differences between each round.

5-1. TRAJECTORY

The trajectory is the path of the round in flight (Figure 5-1). The gunner must know the machine gun trajectory to effectively fire the weapon throughout its full range. The path of the round is almost flat at ranges up to 300 meters; then it begins to curve, and the curve becomes greater as the range increases.

5-2. MAXIMUM ORDINATE

Maximum ordinate is the highest point the trajectory reaches between the muzzle of the weapon and the base of the target. It always occurs about two-thirds of the distance from the weapon to the target. The maximum ordinate increases as the range increases (Figure 5-1).

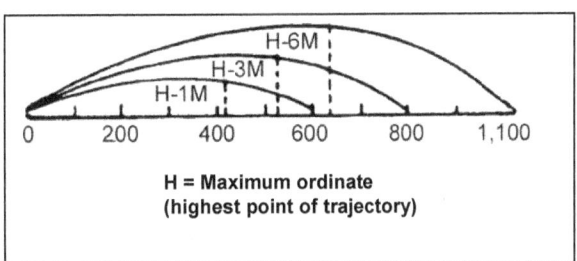

Figure 5-1. Trajectory and maximum ordinate.

5-3. CONE OF FIRE

When several rounds are fired in a burst from any machine gun, each round takes a slightly different trajectory. The pattern these rounds form on the way to the target is called a cone of fire (Figure 5-2, page 5-2). This pattern is caused primarily by vibration of the machine gun and variations in ammunition and atmospheric conditions.

5-4. BEATEN ZONE

The beaten zone (Figure 5-2) is the elliptical pattern formed by the rounds striking the ground or the target. The size and shape of the beaten zone changes when the range to the target changes or when the machine gun is fired on different types of terrain. On uniformly sloping or level terrain, the beaten zone is long and narrow. As the range to the target increases, the beaten zone becomes shorter and wider. When fire is delivered on terrain sloping down and away from the machine gun, the beaten zone becomes longer. When fire is delivered on rising terrain, the beaten zone becomes shorter. The terrain has little effect on the width of the beaten zone.

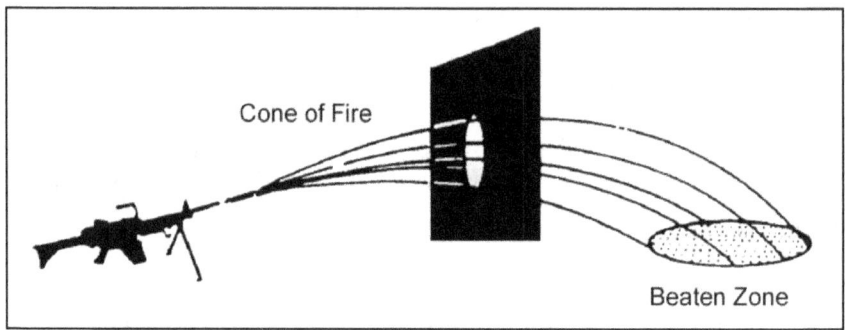

Figure 5-2. Cone of fire and beaten zone.

5-5. DANGER SPACE

The danger space is the space between the machine gun and the target where the trajectory does not rise above 1.8 meters (the average height of a standing soldier). This space includes the area of the beaten zone. When the machine gun is fired on level or uniformly sloping terrain at a target less than 700 meters away, the trajectory does not rise above the average height of a standing soldier. When targets are engaged on level or uniformly sloping terrain at ranges greater than 700 meters, the trajectory rises above the average height of a standing soldier, therefore, not all the distance between the machine gun and the target is danger space.

Section II. CLASSES OF FIRE

Machine gun fire is classified with respect to the ground, the target, and the weapon.

5-6. RESPECT TO THE GROUND

Fire with respect to the GROUND (Figure 5-3) includes grazing and plunging fires.

    a. **Grazing Fire**. Grazing fire occurs when the center of the cone of fire does not rise more than 1 meter above the ground. When firing on level or uniformly sloping terrain, the gunner can obtain a maximum of 600 meters of grazing fire.

    b. **Plunging Fire**. Plunging fire occurs when the danger space is confined to the beaten zone. Plunging fire also occurs when firing at long ranges, from high ground to low ground, into abruptly rising ground, or across uneven terrain, resulting in a loss of grazing fire at any point along the trajectory.

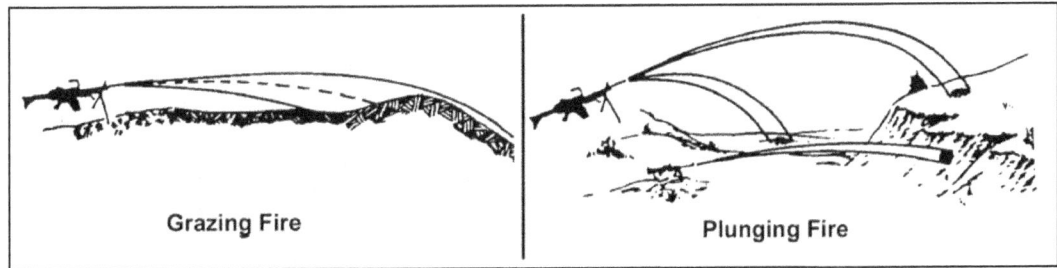

Figure 5-3. Classes of fire with respect to the ground.

5-7. RESPECT TO TARGET

Fire with respect to the TARGET includes frontal, flanking, oblique, and enfilade fires.

a. **Frontal Fire.** Frontal fire is when the long axis of the beaten zone is at a right angle to the front of the target. An example is when firing at the front of a target (Figure 5-4).

b. **Flanking Fire.** Flanking fire is firing at the side of a target (Figure 5-4).

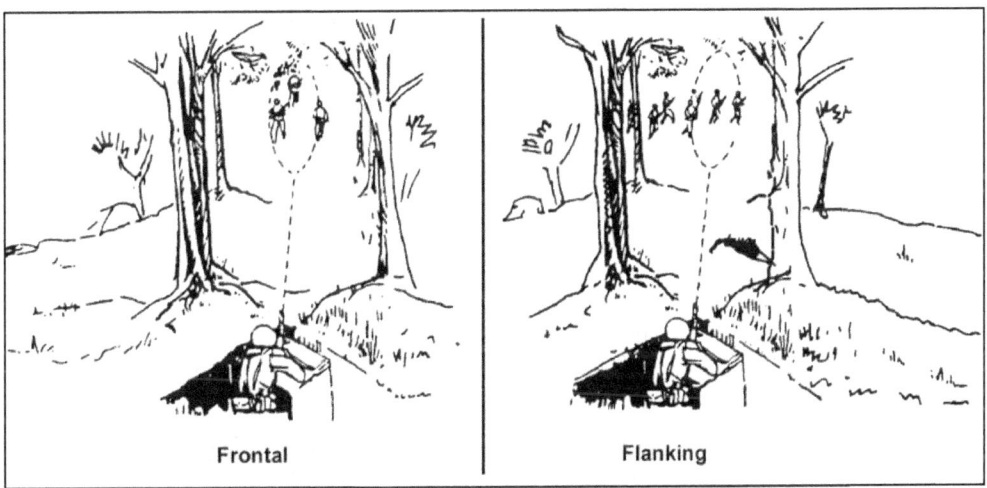

Figure 5-4. Frontal fire and flanking fire.

c. **Oblique Fire.** Oblique fire is when the long axis of the beaten zone is at an angle other than a right angle to the front of the target (Figure 5-5).

d. **Enfilade Fire.** Enfilade fire is when the long axis of the beaten zone coincides or nearly coincides with the long axis of the target. This type of fire is either frontal or flanking. It is the most desirable type of fire with respect to a target, because it makes maximum use of the beaten zone (Figure 5-5, page 5-4).

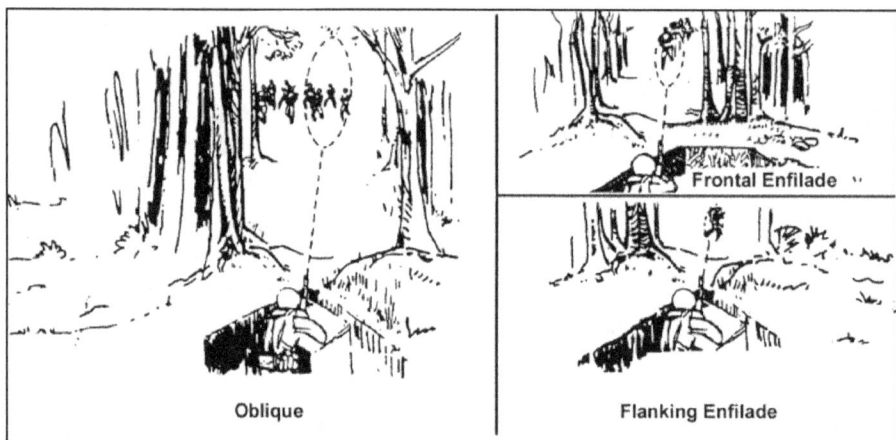

Figure 5-5. Oblique fire and enfilade fire.

5-8. RESPECT TO MACHINE GUN

Fire with respect to the machine gun (Figure 5-6) includes fixed, traversing, searching, and traversing and searching, and free-gun fires.

a. **Fixed Fire.** Fixed fire is fire delivered against a point target when the depth and width of the beaten zone covers the target. Fixed fire also means only one aiming point is necessary to provide coverage of the target.

b. **Traversing Fire.** Traversing fire is fire distributed in width by successive changes in direction. The gunner selects successive aiming points throughout the width of the target. These aiming points must be close enough to ensure adequate coverage but not so close as to waste ammunition.

c. **Searching Fire.** Searching fire is fire distributed in depth by successive changes in elevation. The gunner selects successive aiming points in depth. The changes made in each aiming point will depend on the range and slope of the ground.

d. **Traversing and Searching Fire.** Traversing and searching fire is fire distributed in width and depth by successive changes in direction and elevation. Combining traversing and searching provides good coverage of the target. Adjustments are made in the same manner as described for traversing and searching fire.

e. **Free-Gun Fire.** Free-gun fire is fire delivered against targets requiring rapid major changes in direction and elevation that cannot be applied with the T&E mechanism. To deliver this type of fire, the gunner removes the T&E mechanism from the traversing bar on the tripod, allowing the weapon to be moved freely in any direction.

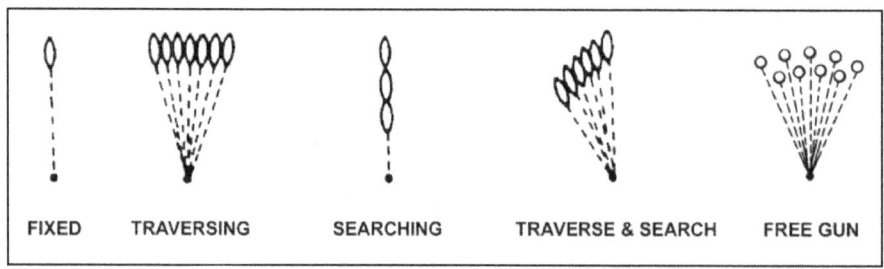

Figure 5-6. Classes of fire with respect to the machine gun.

Section III. APPLICATION OF FIRE

Application of fire consists of the methods the gunner uses to cover a target area. Training these methods of applying fire can be accomplished only after the soldiers have learned how to recognize the different types of targets they may find in combat, how to distribute and concentrate their fire, and how to maintain the proper rate of fire. Normally, the gunner is exposed to two types of targets in the squad or platoon sector: enemy soldiers and supporting automatic weapons. These targets have priority and should be engaged immediately.

5-9. TYPES OF TARGETS

Targets presented to the gunner in combat are usually enemy troops in various formations, which require distribution and concentration of fire. Targets with width and depth must be thoroughly covered by fire.

a. **Point Targets**. Point targets require the use of a single aiming point. Examples of point targets are enemy soldiers, bunkers, weapons emplacements, and lightly armored vehicles. Fixed fire is delivered at point targets.

b. **Area Targets**. Area targets may have considerable width and depth and may require extensive traversing and searching fire. These include targets in which the exact location of the enemy is unknown. The following are varieties of area targets likely to be engaged.

(1) *Linear Targets*. Linear targets have sufficient width to require successive aiming points (traversing fire). The beaten zone effectively covers the depth of the target area (Figure 5-7). Traversing fire is delivered at linear targets.

(2) *Deep Targets*. Deep targets require successive aiming points (searching fire) (Figure 5-8, page 5-6). Searching fire is delivered at deep targets.

(3) *Linear Targets with Depth*. Linear targets with depth have sufficient width requiring successive aiming points in which the beaten zone does not cover the depth of the target area. A combined change in direction and elevation (traversing and searching) is necessary to effectively cover the target with fire (Figure 5-9, page 5-6). Traversing and searching fire are delivered at linear targets with depth.

Figure 5-7. Linear target.

Figure 5-8. Deep target.

Figure 5-9. Linear targets with depth.

5-10. DISTRIBUTION, CONCENTRATION, AND RATE OF FIRE

The size and nature of the target determine how the gunner applies his fire. He must manipulate the machine gun to move the beaten zone throughout the target area. The rate of fire must be controlled to adequately cover the target but not waste ammunition or destroy the barrel.

a. Distributed fire is delivered in width and depth such as at an enemy formation.

b. Concentrated fire is delivered at a point target such as an automatic weapon or an enemy fighting position.

c. The rates of fire that can be used with the machine gun are sustained, rapid, and cyclic. These rates enable leaders to control and sustain fire and prevent the destruction of barrels. More than anything else, the size of the target and ammunition supply dictate the selection of the rate of fire.

(1) *Sustained Fire*. Sustained fire for the M249 is 85 rounds per minute in bursts of 3 to 5 rounds. The M60 and M240B are 100 rounds per minute in bursts of 6 to 9 rounds. The gunner pauses 4 to 5 seconds between bursts. The barrel should be changed after firing at sustained rate for 10 minutes. This is the normal rate of fire for the gunner.

(2) *Rapid Fire*. Rapid fire for the M249, M60, and M240B gunner is 200 rounds per minute in bursts of (6 to 8 M249) 10 to 12 rounds. The gunner pauses 2 to 3 seconds

between bursts. The barrel should be changed after firing at a rapid rate for 2 minutes. This procedure provides for an exceptionally high volume of fire, but for only a short period.

(3) *Cyclic Fire.* Cyclic fire uses the most ammunition that can be used in 1 minute. The cyclic rate of fire with the machine gun is achieved when the trigger is held to the rear and ammunition is fed into the weapon uninterrupted for one minute. Normal cyclic rate of fire for the M249 is 850 rounds, M60 is 550 rounds, and for the M240B it is 650 to 950 rounds. Always change the barrel after firing at cyclic rate for 1 minute. This procedure provides the highest volume of fire that the machine gun can fire, but this adversely affects the machine gun, and should only be fired in combat under emergency purposes only.

5-11. TARGET ENGAGEMENT

The gunner engages targets throughout his sector. He must know how to effectively engage all types of targets either by himself or in conjunction with another gunner.

a. **Single Gunner.**

(1) *Point Target.* When engaging a point target, the gunner uses fixed fire (Figure 5-10). If the target moves after the initial burst, the gunner adjusts fire onto the target by following its movement.

Figure 5-10. Engagement of point target.

(2) *Area Target.* When engaging an area target, the gunner fires in the center of mass, then traverses and searches to either flank (Figure 5-11, page 5-8). Upon reaching the flank, he reverses direction and traverses and searches in the opposite direction. A leader may indicate the width and depth of the target.

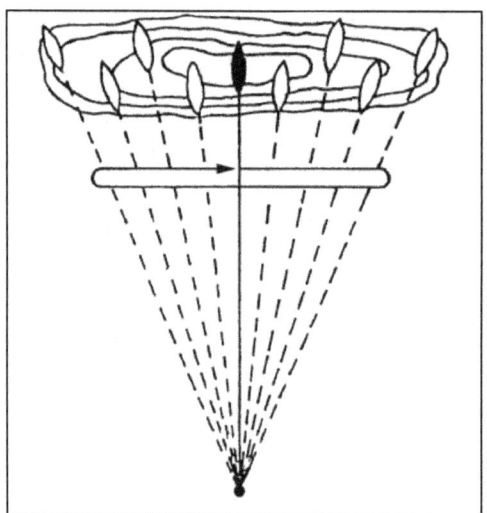

Figure 5-11. Engagement of area target.

(3) *Linear Target*. When engaging a linear target, the gunner traverses the machine gun to distribute fire evenly onto the target. He must cover the entire width of a linear target. The initial point of aim is on the midpoint. The gunner then manipulates to cover the rest of the target. If a linear target is hard to identify, a leader may designate the target by using a reference point (Figure 5-12). When this method is used, the leader determines the center of mass of the target and announces the number of meters from the reference point that will cause the gunner to aim on the center of mass. The reference point may be within or adjacent to the target (Figure 5-13). However, the reference point should be on line with the target for the best effect. After the command to fire has been given, the leader maintains and controls the fire by subsequent fire commands.

**Figure 5-12. Engagement of hard-to-identify linear targets
with a reference point outside the target area.**

(4) *Deep Target*. When engaging a deep target, the gunner must use searching fire. If the range is announced, he initially aims on the midpoint of a deep target unless another portion of the target is more critical or presents a greater threat. The gunner then searches

down to one aiming point in front of the near end and back up to one aiming point beyond the far end. If a deep target is hard to identify, use the reference points to designate the center of mass. The extent (depth) of the target is always given in meters.

(5) *Linear Target With Depth.* When engaging a linear target with depth, the gunner uses traversing and searching fire. He begins engagement at the midpoint of the target unless another portion of the target is more critical or presents a greater threat. He traverses and searches to the near flank, then back to the far flank. When engaging hard-to-identify linear targets with depth, he designates the flanks and midpoint with rifle fire. The reference-point method is not used because at least two reference points are required to show the angle of the target.

Figure 5-13. Engagement of hard-to-identify targets with a reference point within the target area.

b. **Pair of Gunners.**

(1) *Area Targets.* When using a pair of machine guns to engage area targets, the gunner on the right fires on the right half, and the gunner on the left fires on the left half. The point of initial aim and adjustment for both gunners is on the midpoint. After adjusting fire on the center of mass, both gunners distribute fire by applying direction and elevation changes that give the most effective coverage of the target area. The right gunner traverses to the right, applies the necessary amount of search, and fires a burst. He traverses and searches up and down until the right flank of the area target has been reached. The left gunner traverses and searches to the left flank in the same way. Both gunners then reverse the direction of manipulation and return to the center of mass, firing a burst after each combined direction and elevation change (Figure 5-14, page 5-10).

Figure 5-14. Engagement of area targets with a pair of gunners.

(2) *Linear Targets*. When using a pair of machine guns to engage a linear target, the target is divided at midpoint with the gunner on the right of the target firing on the right half, and the gunner on the left of the target firing on the left half (Figure 5-15).

(a) Both gunners aim on the midpoint initially. After adjusting on the midpoint, the gunner on the right traverses right, firing a burst after each change in direction until the rounds reach one aiming point beyond the right flank (this ensures complete target coverage). The gunner on the left traverses to the left flank in the same way the gunner on the right did. Both gunners then reverse their directions and return to the midpoint. The gunner must select aiming points for each burst rather than "spray" the target area.

Figure 5-15. Engagement of linear targets with a pair of gunners.

(b) If one part of the target is a greater threat, fire can be concentrated on the greater threat by dividing the target unevenly. This special division of the target is done with fire commands. To preclude confusion, the gunners initially aim on the midpoint regardless of the special division to be made.

(3) *Deep Targets*. When using a pair of machine guns to engage a deep target, the initial point of aim is also on the midpoint for both gunners. Normally, the gunner on the right has the near half and the gunner on the left has the far half. Since enfilade fire is being used, they do not adjust on the midpoint of the target, because the long beaten zone compensates for any range errors. After the initial burst, the gunner on the right searches down to one aiming point in front of the near end of the target, and the gunner on the left searches up to one aiming point beyond the far end. Both gunners then reverse their direction of search and return to the midpoint (Figure 5-16).

Figure 5-16. Engagement of deep targets with a pair of gunners.

(4) *Linear Target With Depth*. When using a pair of machine guns to engage a linear target with depth, the initial point of aim and the extent of manipulation for both gunners is the same as those prescribed for linear targets (Figure 5-17).

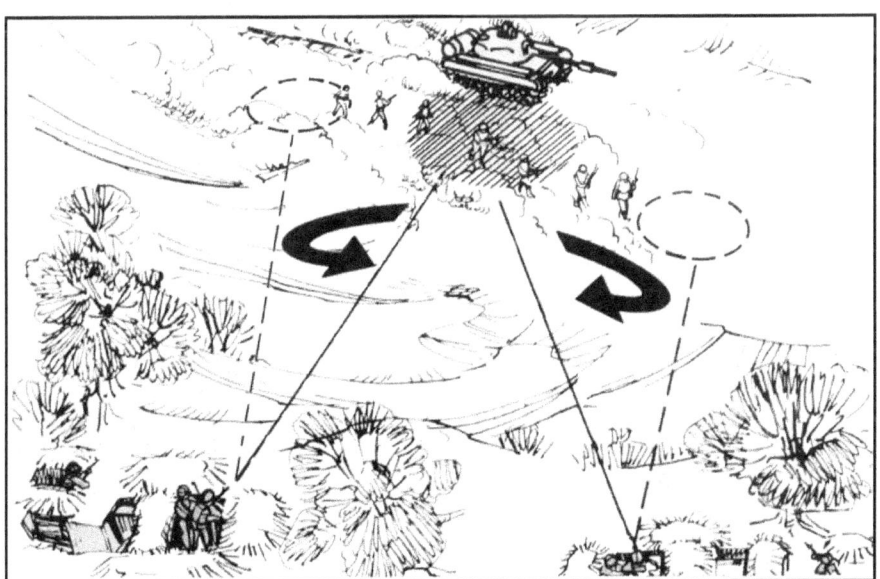

Figure 5-17. Engagement of linear target with depth with a pair of gunners.

5-12. TARGET ENGAGEMENT DURING LIMITED VISIBILITY

Gunners have problems detecting and identifying targets during limited visibility. The leader's ability to control the fires of his weapons is also reduced, therefore, he may instruct the gunners to fire without command when targets present themselves.

a. Gunners should engage targets only when they can identify the targets, unless ordered to do otherwise. For example, if one gunner detects a target and engages it, the other gunner observes the area fired upon and adds his fire only if he can identify the target or if ordered to fire.

b. Tracer ammunition helps a gunner engage targets during limited visibility and should be used, if possible. If firing unaided, gunners must be trained to fire low at first and adjust upward. This overcomes the tendency to fire high.

c. When two or more gunners are engaging linear targets, linear targets with depth, or deep targets, they do not engage these targets as they would when visibility is good. With limited visibility, the center and flanks of these targets may not be clearly defined; therefore, each gunner observes his tracers and covers what he believes to be the entire target.

5-13. OVERHEAD FIRE

Fire delivered over the heads of friendly soldiers is called overhead fire. It is used during training ONLY AFTER SOLDIER SAFETY IS CHECKED AND VERIFIED. The terrain and visibility dictate when overhead fire can be delivered safely. (See AR 385-63 for a complete summary of training safety requirements.) Overhead fire is delivered with any machine gun mounted on a tripod because the machine guns provide greater stability and accuracy, and because vertical mil angles can be measured by using the elevating mechanism.

DANGER

OVERHEAD FIRE CANNOT BE SAFELY DELIVERED ON A TARGET AT GREATER THAN 850 METERS FROM THE MACHINE GUN, AND IT IS NOT DELIVERED OVER LEVEL OR UNIFORMLY SLOPING TERRAIN. IT CAN CAUSE DEATH OR INJURY.

---

a. Ideally, overhead fire is delivered when there is a depression in the terrain between the machine gun position and the target. The depression should place the gunner's line of aim well above the heads of friendly soldiers.

b. The squad leader normally controls overhead fire. He lifts or shifts the fire when the friendly soldiers reach an imaginary line, parallel to the target, where further fire would cause casualties to friendly soldiers. This imaginary line is called the "safety limit." The leader of the friendly soldiers may direct lifting of fire by prearranged signals transmitted by radio, wire, or visual means. The safety limit can be determined by observing the fire or by using the gunner's rule (Figure 5-18).

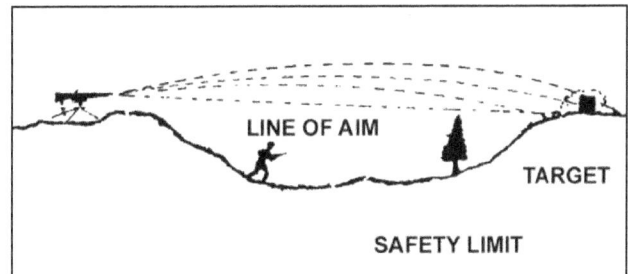

Figure 5-18. Overhead fire safety limit.

(1) To determine the safety limit by observation, the leader uses binoculars to see how close the fire is to advancing friendly soldiers.

(2) A safety limit can be selected by using the gunner's rule before the weapon is fired. The accuracy and safety of this method depends on the machine gun being zeroed and the range to the target being known. The gunner's rule is used only when the target is between 350 and 850 meters from the machine gun. The gunner's rule consists of the following procedure.

(a) Determine the range to the target and set the range on the rear sight.

(b) Aim the machine gun to hit the target.

(c) Set the rear sight to 1,000 meters.

(d) Depress the muzzle 10 mils by using the elevating handwheel (one click equals 1 mil).

(e) Look through the rear sight and note the point where the new line of aim strikes the ground. (An imaginary line drawn through this point and parallel to the target is the safety limit.)

(f) Reset the range to the target on the rear sight, aim on the target, and prepare to fire.

(g) Cease or shift fire when soldiers reach the safety limit.

c. The following safety measures MUST be applied when delivering overhead fire.

(1) Firmly emplace the tripod mount.

(2) Use field-expedient depression stops to prevent the muzzle from accidentally being lowered below the safety limit.

(3) Do not deliver overhead fire through trees.

(4) Inform commanders of friendly soldiers when fire is to be delivered over their heads.

(5) Ensure that all members of the crew are aware of the safety limit.

(6) Do not deliver overhead fire if the range from the machine gun to the target is less than 350 meters or more than 850 meters.

(7) Do not use a barrel that is badly worn.

(8) During training exercises, do not aim any machine gun where their trajectories will cross at a point directly over the heads of friendly soldiers. See AR 385-63 and local safety regulations concerning overhead fire.

5-14. DEFILADE POSITIONS

A machine gun is in defilade when the weapon and its crew are completely behind terrain that masks them from the enemy (usually on the reverse slope of a hill). Fire, from a defilade position, is controlled by an observer (the leader or a member of the crew who can see the target) that is in a position near the machine gun. (Figure 5-19.)

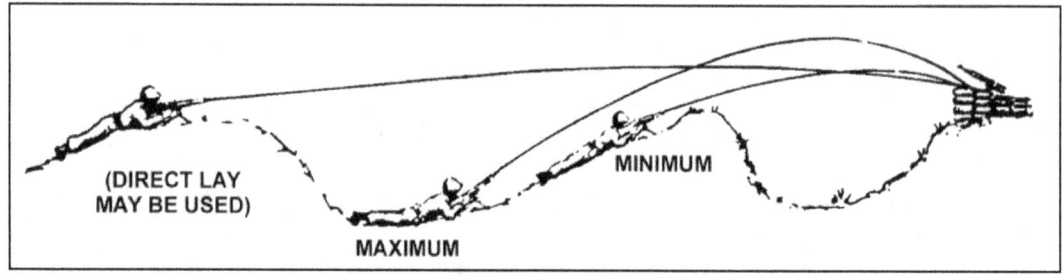

Figure 5-19. Defilade positions.

a. The machine gun must fire up and over the hill. Its fire must be observed and adjusted by a crewmember that can observe the target from a position on a flank or to the rear of the weapon (on higher ground). A defilade position allows little opportunity to engage new targets. The tripod mount is used when firing from defilade, because the gunner can measure vertical angles with it. This makes changes in elevation for adjusting fire easier, and if data is determined during daylight, the crew can fire from the same position after dark. A machine gun is in partial defilade when it is positioned just back of the crest of a hill, so that the crest provides some protection from enemy direct-fire and the machine guns are still able to engage its target by direct-lay techniques.

(1) *Advantages.*

- The crew has cover and concealment from enemy direct-fire weapons.
- The crew has some freedom of movement near the position.
- Control and supply are easier.
- The smoke and flash of the machine gun are hidden from the enemy.

(2) *Disadvantages.*

- Rapidly moving ground targets are hard to engage, because adjustment of fire must be made by using an observer.
- Targets close to the mask usually cannot be engaged.
- Final protective line is hard to understand.

b. The essential elements in the engagement of a target from a defilade position are mask clearance, direction, and adjustment of fire. If possible, a minimum mask clearance (minimum elevation) is determined for the entire sector of fire, however, a mask clearance for each target may be necessary (due to the slope of the mask). The elevation readings obtained using the methods below give the minimum elevation for the sector or target(s). The minimum elevation should be recorded on a range card.

(1) If the mask is 300 meters or less from the machine gun position, the gunner places a 300-meter range setting on the rear sight, aims on the top of the mask and adds 3 mils (clicks) of elevation with the elevating handwheel.

(2) If the mask is over 300 meters from the machine gun position, the gunner places the range setting to the mask on the rear sight, aims on the top of the mask, and adds 3 mils (clicks) of elevation.

c. The observer places himself to the rear of the machine gun on the gun-to-target line and in a position where he can see the machine gun and the target. He aligns the machine gun for general direction by directing the gunner to shift the machine gun until it is aligned on the target. A prominent terrain feature or landmark visible to the gunner through his sights is selected as an aiming point. This aiming point should be at a greater range than the target and at a higher elevation. When laying the machine gun on the aiming point, the range setting on the rear sight must correspond to the range to the target. (Figure 5-20.)

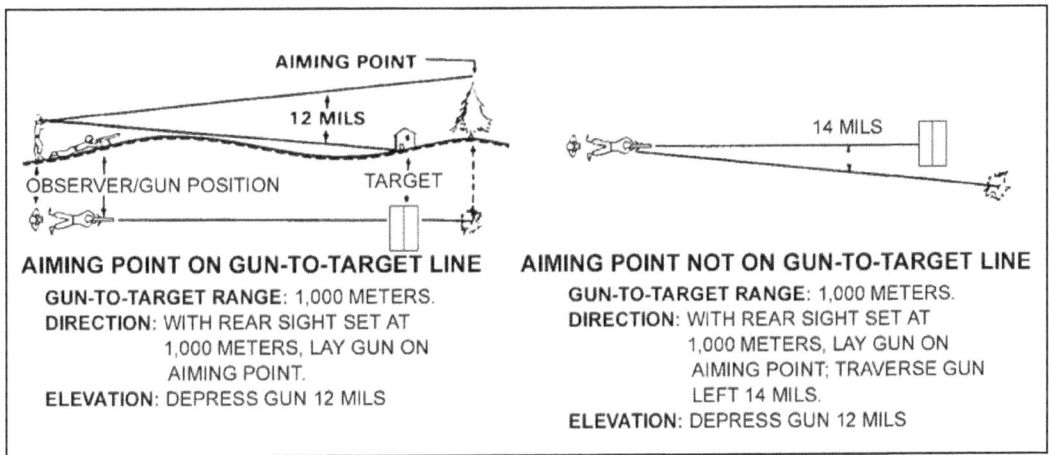

Figure 5-20. Observer adjusting fire.

(1) If the aiming point is on the gun-to-target line, the gun is laid on the aiming point and is thereby aligned for direction.

(2) If the aiming point is not on the gun-to-target line, the horizontal distance in mils is determined using the best means available (usually binoculars) and announced to the gunner. This measured distance is then set with the traversing handwheel.

d. The observer measures the vertical distance from the aiming point to the base of the target using the best means available and directs the gunner to depress the muzzle of the machine gun the number of mils measured. The machine gun should now be laid to hit the target.

Section IV. PREDETERMINED FIRES

Predetermined fires organize the battlefield for the gunners. They allow the leader and gunner to select potential targets or target areas that will most likely be engaged or that have tactical significance. This includes dismounted enemy avenues of approach, likely positions for automatic weapons, and probable enemy assault positions. The gunners do this by using sectors of fire, final protective lines, or a principal direction of fire and selected target areas. This preparation maximizes the effectiveness of the machine gun during good as well as limited visibility. It enhances fire control by reducing the time required to identify targets, determine range, and manipulate the weapon onto the target. Abbreviated fire commands and previously recorded data enable the gunner to aim or adjust fire on the target quickly and accurately. Selected targets should be fired on in daylight whenever practical to confirm data. The range card identifies the targets and provides a record of firing data.

5-15. TERMINOLOGY

Several terms are associated with predetermined fire that every gunner needs to know.

a. **Sector of Fire**. A sector of fire is an area to be covered by fire that is assigned to an individual, a weapon, or a unit. Gunners are normally assigned a primary and a secondary sector of fire.

b. **Final Protective Fire**. An FPF is an immediately available prearranged barrier of fire to stop enemy movement across defensive lines or areas.

c. **Final Protective Line**. An FPL is a predetermined line along which grazing fire is placed to stop an enemy assault. If an FPL is assigned, the machine gun is sighted along it except when other targets are being engaged. An FPL becomes the machine gun's part of the unit's final protective fires. An FPL is fixed in direction and elevation; however, a small shift for search must be employed to prevent the enemy from crawling under the FPL and to compensate for irregularities in the terrain or the sinking of the tripod legs into soft soil during firing. Fire must be delivered during all conditions of visibility.

d. **Principal Direction of Fire**. A PDF is a direction of fire assigned priority to cover an area that has good fields of fire or has a likely dismounted avenue of approach. It also provides mutual support to an adjacent unit. Machine guns are sighted using the PDF if an FPL has not been assigned. If a PDF is assigned and other targets are not being engaged, machine guns remain on the PDF. A PDF has the following characteristics.

(1) It is used only if an FPL is not assigned; it then becomes the machine gun's part of the unit's final protective fires.

(2) When the target has width, direction is determined by aiming on one edge of the target area and noting the amount of traverse necessary to cover the entire target.

(3) The gunner is responsible for the entire wedge-shaped area from the muzzle of the weapon to the target, but elevation may be fixed for a priority portion of the target.

e. **Grazing Fire**. A good FPL covers the maximum area with grazing fire. Grazing fire can be obtained over various types of terrain out to a maximum of 600 meters. To obtain the maximum extent of grazing fire over level or uniformly sloping terrain, the gunner sets the rear sight at 600 meters. He then selects a point on the ground that he estimates to be 600 meters from the machine gun, and he aims, fires, and adjusts on that point. To prevent enemy soldiers from crawling under grazing fire, he searches (downward) by lowering the muzzle of the weapon. To do this, the gunner separates his elbows.

f. **Dead Space.** The extent of grazing fire and the extent of dead space may be determined in two ways. In the preferred method, the machine gun is adjusted for elevation and direction. A member of the squad then walks along the FPL while the gunner aims through the sights. In places where the soldier's waist (midsection) falls below the gunner's point of aim, dead space exists. Arm-and-hand signals must be used to control the soldier who is walking and to obtain an accurate account of the dead space and its location. Another method is to observe the flight of tracer ammunition from a position behind and to the flank of the weapon.

g. **Fire Control**. Predetermined targets, including the FPL or PDF, are engaged on order or by SOP. The signal for calling for these fires is normally stated in the defense order. Control these predetermined targets by using arm-and-hand signals, voice commands, or pyrotechnic devices. Gunners fire the FPL or PDF at the sustained rate of fire unless the situation calls for a higher rate. When engaging other predetermined targets, the sustained rate of fire is also used unless a different rate is ordered.

h. **Primary Sector of Fire**. The primary sector of fire is the area to be covered by an individual or unit.

i. **Secondary Sector of Fire**. The secondary sector of fire is the same area covered by the same individual or unit after it has moved to a different location.

5-16. RANGE CARD

The standard range card (DA Form 5517-R) provides a record of firing data and aids defensive fire planning. (See FM 7-8 for a reproducible copy of this form.) Its use enhances fire control and rapid engagement of predetermined targets. It is also used in estimating ranges to other targets within the sector of fire. Each gunner makes two copies—one for his position and one for the squad leader. The squad leader uses his copy to prepare his sector sketch. The range card is prepared immediately upon occupation and is constantly revised. Each range card contains the following:

- Weapon symbol (Figure 5-21, page 5-18).
- Sector of fire.
- PDF or FPL.
- Range, azimuth, and number label to predetermined targets.
- Dead space.
- Distance and azimuth from a known point or eight-digit grid coordinate (reference point).
- Magnetic north arrow.
- Data section.

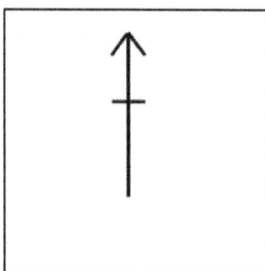

Figure 5-21. M249/M60 and M240B machine gun symbol.

a. **Procedures.** The machine gun is placed in the tripod-supported mode in the position it will be fired. The machine gun symbol is sketched on the range card pointing toward the most dangerous target in the sector.

(1) If using the FPL, the gunner aims the machine gun along the FPL. This procedure will also be either the left or right limit of the sector of fire. To set the limit, he slides the T&E mechanism all the way to the left or right end of the traversing bar. Then, he moves the tripod until the barrel lines up on the FPL. The sector of fire with the FPL along one limit is now prepared. The FPL is always labeled target number 1.

(2) To determine the range for all targets in the sector, the gunner ensures each circle, except the first one, represents 100 meters. Since the lowest setting on the M249 and M60 is 300 meters and the M240B is 200 meters, the first circle represents 200 or 300 meters. He indicates this on the range card in the data section just below the circles. On the top half of the range card, the gunner draws the left or right limits from the weapon position to the maximum effective range of the machine gun.

(3) If the FPL is assigned, the machine gun symbol is drawn along that line (left or right limit) (Figure 5-22). The extent of grazing fire is determined. A shaded blade is sketched on the inside of the FPL to represent the extent of the grazing fire. If there is dead space along the FPL, it is shown by breaks in the shaded area. The ranges to the *near* and *far* edges of the dead space are recorded above the FPL, and the *extent* of the grazing fire is recorded along the FPL. The magnetic azimuth of the FPL is determined and recorded below the shaded blade representing the FPL. The elevation reading and other data are recorded in the data section.

(4) If an FPL is not assigned, the gunner locks the T&E mechanism on 0 on the traversing bar scale and shifts the tripod until the muzzle points to the PDF. The machine gun symbol is sketched in the center of the left and right limits pointing in the direction of the PDF (Figure 5-23, page 5-20).

(5) The opposite primary sector limit is drawn. If a target is along this line, the target information is added to the data section. If the opposite side of the traversing bar cannot be used to mark the opposite side of the primary sector, a direction reading must be recorded in the sketch section.

(6) Next, the left and right limits of the secondary sector are drawn using a broken line. The area between the primary and secondary sector is labeled dead space.

(7) An arrow is drawn in the magnetic north block (upper right hand corner) pointing in the direction of magnetic north.

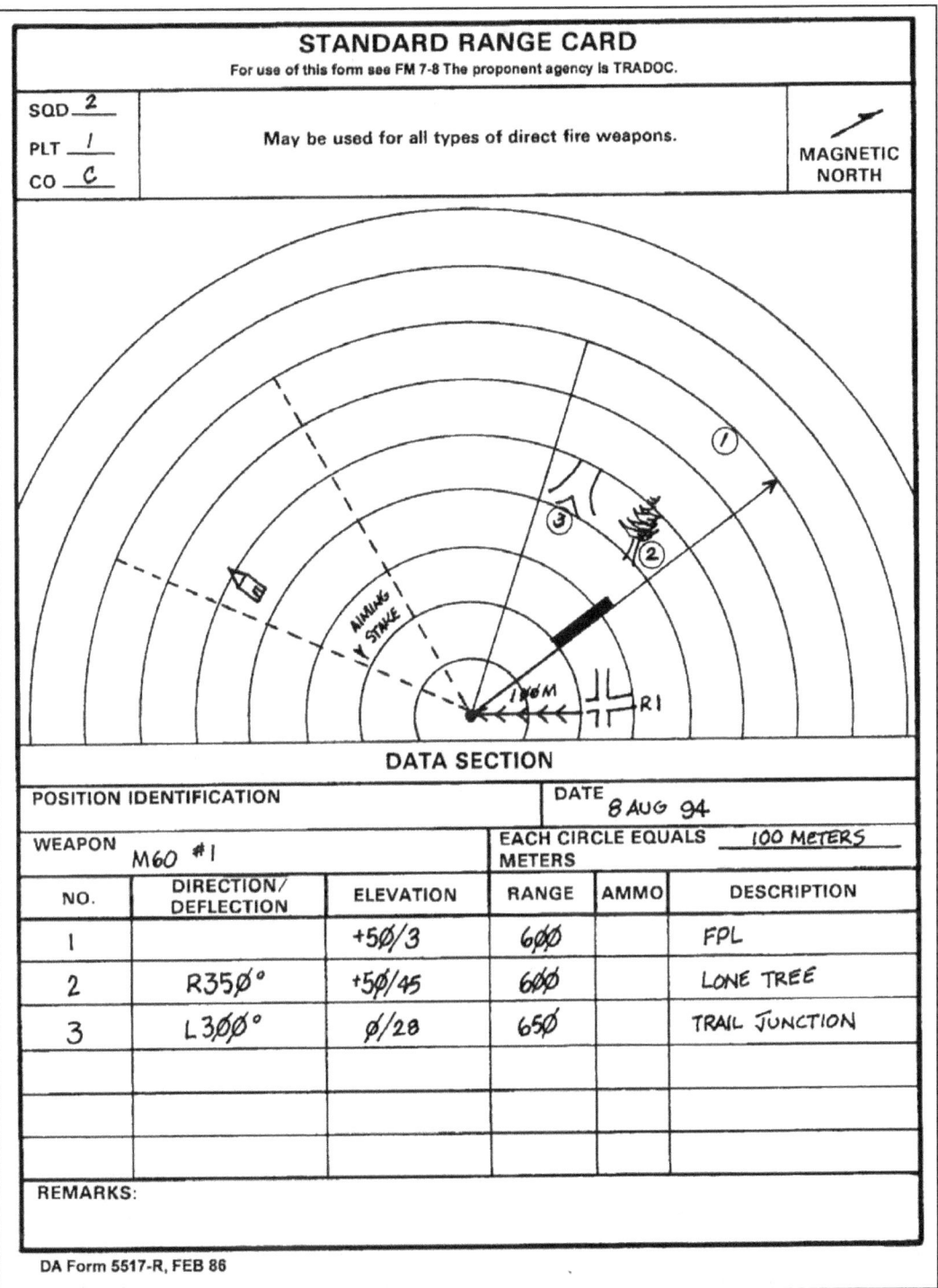

STANDARD RANGE CARD
For use of this form see FM 7-8 The proponent agency is TRADOC.

SQD __2__
PLT __1__
CO __C__

May be used for all types of direct fire weapons.

MAGNETIC
NORTH

DATA SECTION

POSITION IDENTIFICATION			DATE 8 AUG 94		
WEAPON M60 #1			EACH CIRCLE EQUALS 100 METERS METERS		
NO.	DIRECTION/ DEFLECTION	ELEVATION	RANGE	AMMO	DESCRIPTION
1		+50/3	600		FPL
2	R350°	+50/45	600		LONE TREE
3	L300°	0/28	650		TRAIL JUNCTION
REMARKS:					

DA Form 5517-R, FEB 86

Figure 5-22. Final protective line.

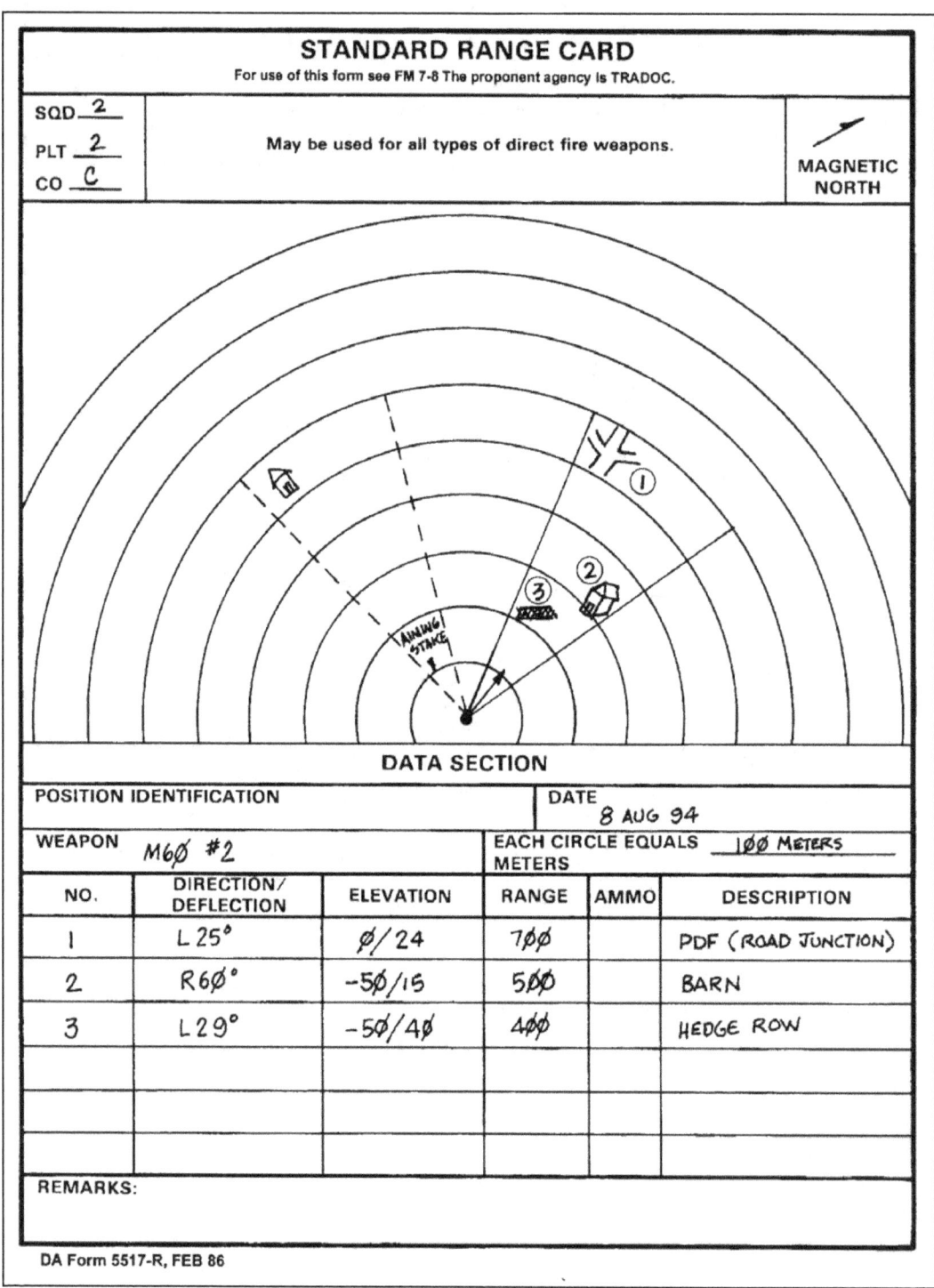

STANDARD RANGE CARD

For use of this form see FM 7-8 The proponent agency is TRADOC.

SQD _2_

PLT _2_

CO _C_

May be used for all types of direct fire weapons.

MAGNETIC NORTH

DATA SECTION

POSITION IDENTIFICATION

DATE
8 AUG 94

WEAPON _M6Ø #2_

EACH CIRCLE EQUALS _1ØØ METERS_ METERS

NO.	DIRECTION/ DEFLECTION	ELEVATION	RANGE	AMMO	DESCRIPTION
1	L 25°	Ø/24	7ØØ		PDF (ROAD JUNCTION)
2	R6Ø°	-5Ø/15	5ØØ		BARN
3	L29°	-5Ø/4Ø	4ØØ		HEDGE ROW

REMARKS:

DA Form 5517-R, FEB 86

Figure 5-23. Principal direction of fire.

(8) The position is oriented with a prominent terrain feature (recognizable on a map) by obtaining a magnetic azimuth to or from the terrain feature to the position. A line is

drawn between these two points. Arrow barbs are drawn along this line pointing in the direction the magnetic azimuth was taken. The magnetic azimuth is recorded in mils or degrees below the line. If a prominent terrain feature is not available, identify the position by using an eight-digit grid coordinate. The grid coordinate is recorded below the position on the range card.

(9) The gunner's number, unit designation (SQD, PLT, CO), and date are recorded in the upper left-hand corner. For security, do not use a unit designation higher than a company.

(10) Targets within the sector are identified. A symbol is drawn to represent the target in the appropriate place within the sector of fire. Targets in the primary sector are shown by numbers and enclosed in circles. An FPL, when assigned, is always labeled target Number 1. Other targets are assigned subsequent numbers in order of tactical importance.

(a) Wide targets in the primary sector are usually engaged in the center; however, the initial burst can be positioned anywhere the leader designates. The gunner measures the target width and records it in the data section; for example, TW-20 (target width is 20 mils). The gunner lays on the point on the target where the initial burst will be placed, and traverses to one edge of the target, while counting the clicks. He records the number of clicks he traverses and the direction he moves the muzzle; for example, TW-20/R7 (target width, 20 mils; right 7 clicks). After the initial burst, the gunner traverses 7 clicks to the right edge of the target and back to the left 20 clicks to cover the target area. To lay on the left edge of the target, the gunner records TW-20/R20.

(b) When field expedients are used with the machine gun to engage targets, they are sketched above the drawing of the target. Predetermined targets in the secondary sector are sketched on the range card and ranges to these targets are recorded below the targets but not in the data section. Field expedients should be used for targets in the secondary sector.

b. **Field Expedients**. When laying the machine gun for predetermined targets, the gunner can use field expedients as a means of engaging targets when other sources are not available. These methods are not as effective as the traversing bar and T&E mechanism method.

(1) *Base Stake Technique*. A base stake is used to define sector limits and may provide the lay for the FPL or predetermined targets along a primary or secondary sector limit. This technique is effective in all visibility conditions. The gunner uses the following steps:

(a) Defines the sector limits by laying the gun for direction along one sector limit and by emplacing a stake along the outer edge of the folded bipod legs. Rotates the legs slightly on the receiver, so that the gunner takes up the "play". Uses the same procedure for placing a stake along the opposite sector limit.

(b) Lays the machine gun along the FPL by moving the muzzle of the machine gun to a sector limit. Adjusts for elevation by driving a stake into the ground, so that the top of the stake is under the gas cylinder extension, allowing a few mils of depression to cover irregularities in the terrain.

(c) Lays the machine gun to engage other targets within a sector limit, in a primary sector by using the procedure described previously, except keeps the elevation fixed.

(2) *Notched-Stake or Tree-Crotch Technique*. The gunner uses the notched-stake or tree-crotch technique (Figure 5-24, page 5-22) with the bipod mount to engage

predetermined targets within a sector or to define sector limits. This technique is effective during all conditions of visibility, and it requires little additional material. The gunner uses the following steps:

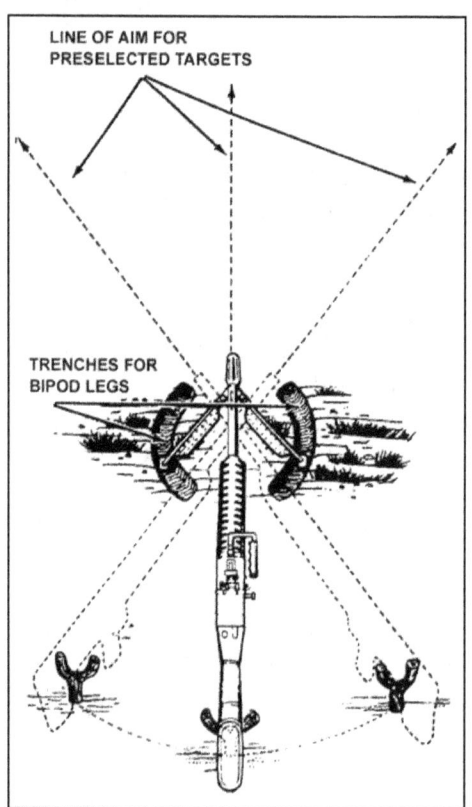

Figure 5-24. Notched-stake or tree-crotch technique.

(a) Drives either a notched stake or tree crotch into the ground where selected targets are anticipated. Places the stock of the machine gun in the nest of the stake or crotch and adjusts the weapon to hit the selected targets and to define his sector limits.

NOTE: If notched stakes and crotches are not available, tent poles can be used. It requires four poles for the left and right limits and additional poles for target areas. The gunner drives two poles in the ground in the shape of an X and then places the stock within that X as described with stakes and crotches.

(b) Digs shallow, curved trenches or grooves for the bipod feet. (These trenches allow for rotation of the bipod feet as the gunner moves the stock from one crotch or stake to another.)

(3) *Horizontal Log or Board Technique.* This technique is used with the bipod or tripod mount to mark sector limits and engage wide targets. This technique is good for all visibility conditions. It is best suited for flat, level terrain. The gunner uses the following steps:

(a) Using a bipod-mounted machine gun, places a log or board beneath the stock of the weapon, so that the stock can slide across it freely. Digs shallow, curved trenches or grooves for the bipod feet to allow rotation of the feet as he moves the stock along the log or board. (The gunner may mark the sector limits by notching or placing stops on the log or board. The gunner uses the bipod firing position and grip.)

(b) Using a tripod-mounted machine gun, places a log or board beneath the barrel, positioning it so that the barrel, when resting on the log or board is at the proper elevation to obtain grazing fire. Marks the sector limits, when appropriate, as described for the bipod in the preceding paragraph. (This technique is used only if a T&E mechanism is not available.)

Section V. FIRE CONTROL

Fire control includes all actions of the leader and soldiers in planning, preparing, and applying fire on a target. The leader selects and designates targets. He also designates the midpoint and flanks or ends of a target, unless they are obvious to the gunner. The gunner fires at the instant desired. He then adjusts fire, regulates the rate of fire, shifts from one target to another, and ceases fire. When firing, the gunner should continue to fire until the target is neutralized or until signaled to do otherwise by the leader.

5-17. METHODS OF FIRE CONTROL

The noise and confusion of battle may limit the use of some of these methods; therefore, the leader must select a method or combination of methods that will accomplish the mission.

a. **Oral**. This can be an effective method of control, but sometimes the leader may be too far away from the gunner, or the noise of the battle may make it impossible for him to hear. The primary means of the oral fire control method is the issuance of a fire command.

b. **Arm-and-Hand Signals**. This is an effective method when the gunner can see the leader. All gunners must know the standard arm-and-hand signals. The leader gets the gunner's attention and then points to the target. When the gunner returns the READY signal, the leader commands FIRE.

c. **Prearranged Signals**. These are either visual or sound signals such as casualty-producing devices, pyrotechnics, whistle blasts, or tracers. These signals should be included in SOPs. If the leader wants to shift fire at a certain time, he gives a prearranged signal such as smoke or pyrotechnics. Upon seeing the signal, the gunner shifts his fire to a prearranged point.

d. **Personal Contact**. In many situations, the leader must issue orders directly to individual soldiers and is used more than any other method by small-unit leaders. The leader must use maximum cover and concealment to keep from disclosing the position or himself.

e. **Range Cards**. When using this method of fire control, the leader must ensure all range cards are current and accurate. Once this is accomplished, the leader may designate certain targets for certain weapons with the use of limiting stakes or with fire commands. He should also designate no-fire zones or restricted fire areas to others. The key factor, in this method of fire control, is that gunners must be well-disciplined and pay attention to detail.

f. **Standing Operating Procedures**. SOPs are actions to be executed without command that are developed during the training of the squads. Their use eliminates many commands and simplifies the leader's fire control. SOPs for certain actions and commands can be developed to make gunners more effective. Some examples follow:

(1) *Observation*. The gunners continuously observe their sectors.

(2) *Fire*. Gunners open fire without command on appropriate targets that appear within their sectors.

(3) *Check*. While firing, the gunners periodically check with the leader for instructions.

(4) *Return Fire*. The gunners return enemy fire without order, concentrating on enemy automatic weapons.

(5) *Shift Fire*. Gunners shift their fires without command when more dangerous targets appear.

(6) *Rate of Fire*. When gunners engage a target, they initially fire at the rate necessary to gain and maintain fire superiority.

(7) *Mutual Support*. When two or more gunners are engaging the same target and one stops firing, the other increases the rate of fire and covers the entire target. When only one gunner is required to engage a target and the leader has alerted two or more, the gunner not firing aims on the target and follows the movements of the target. This is so that he can fire instantly should the other machine gun malfunction or cease fire before the target has been eliminated.

5-18. FIRE COMMANDS

A fire command is given to deliver effective fire on a target quickly and without confusion. When the leader decides to engage a target that is not obvious to the squad, he must provide them with the information they need to effectively engage the target. He must alert the soldiers; give a target direction, description, and range; name the method of fire; and give the command to fire. There are initial fire commands and subsequent fire commands.

a. **Initial Fire Commands.** Initial fire commands are given to adjust onto the target, change the rate of fire after a fire mission is in progress, interrupt fire, or terminate the alert.

b. **Elements**. Fire commands for all direct-fire weapons follow a pattern that includes similar elements. There are six elements in the fire command for the machine gun: alert, direction, description, range, method of fire, and command to open fire. The gunners repeat each element of fire command as it is given.

(1) *Alert*. This element prepares the gunners for further instructions. The leader may alert both gunners in the squad and may have only one fire, depending upon the situation. To alert and have both gunners fire, the leader announces, "Fire mission." If he desires to alert both gunners but have only one fire, he announces,"Gun number one, fire mission." In all cases, upon receiving the alert, the gunners load their machine guns and place them on FIRE.

(2) *Direction*. This element indicates the general direction to the target and may be given in one or a combination of the following methods.

(a) Orally. The leader orally gives the direction to the target in relation to the position of the gunner (for example, FRONT, LEFT FRONT, RIGHT FRONT).

(b) Pointing. The leader designates a small or obscure target by pointing with his finger or aiming with a weapon. When he points with his finger, a soldier standing behind him should be able to look over his shoulder and sight along his arm and index finger to locate the target. When aiming his weapon at a target, a soldier looking through the sights should be able to see the target.

(c) Tracer Ammunition. Tracer ammunition is a quick and sure method of designating a target that is not clearly visible. When using this method, the leader should first give the general direction to direct the gunner's attention to the target area. To prevent the loss of surprise when using tracer ammunition, the leader does not fire until he has given all elements of the fire command except the command to fire. The leader may fire his individual weapon. The firing of the tracer(s) then becomes the last element of the fire command, and it is the signal to open fire.

NOTE: Soldiers must be aware that with the night vision device, temporary blindness "white out" may occur when firing tracer ammunition at night or when exposed to other external light sources. Lens covers may reduce this effect.

EXAMPLE
FIRE MISSION
FRONT
FIVE HUNDRED
WATCH MY TRACER(S)

(d) Reference Points. Another way to designate obscure targets is to use easy-to-recognize reference points. All leaders and gunners must know terrain features and the terminology used to describe them (FM 21-26). When using a reference point, the word "reference" precedes its description. This is done to avoid confusion. The general direction to the reference point should be given.

EXAMPLE

FIRE MISSION
FRONT
REFERENCE: BUNKER, CENTER MASS
TARGET: TROOPS EXTENDING SHORT ONE HUNDRED, OVER
     ONE HUNDRED
FOUR HUNDRED
FIRE

(Sometimes the reference point may be outside the target area).

EXAMPLE

FIRE MISSION
FRONT
REFERENCE: BUNKER, RIGHT FOUR FINGERS, CENTER MASS
TARGET: TROOPS EXTENDING SHORT ONE HUNDRED, OVER
    ONE HUNDRED
THREE HUNDRED
SEARCH
AT MY COMMAND
FIRE

(Sometimes a target must be designated by using successive reference points).

EXAMPLE

GUN NUMBER ONE, FIRE MISSION
RIGHT FRONT
REFERENCE: RED-ROOFED HOUSE, LEFT TO HAYSTACK, LEFT TO
    BARN

(Finger measurements can be used to direct the gunner's attention to the right or left of reference points).

EXAMPLE

FIRE MISSION
LEFT FRONT
REFERENCE: CROSSROADS, RIGHT FOUR FINGERS

(3) *Description.* The target description creates a picture of the target in the minds of the gunners. To properly apply their fire, the soldiers must know the type of target they are to engage. The leader should describe it briefly. If the target is obvious, no description is necessary.

(4) *Range.* The leader always announces the estimated range to the target. The range is given, so the gunner knows how far to look for the target and what range setting to put on the rear sight. Range is announced in meters; however, since the meter is the standard unit of range measurement, the word "meters" is not used. With machine gun's, the range is determined and announced to the nearest hundred or thousand (in other words, THREE HUNDRED, or ONE THOUSAND).

EXAMPLE

FIRE MISSION
FRONT
REFERENCE: KNOCKED-OUT TANK, LEFT TWO FINGERS
TARGET: TROOPS
THREE HUNDRED

(5) Method of Fire. This element includes manipulation and rate of fire. Manipulation prescribes the class of fire with respect to the weapon. It is announced as

FIXED, TRAVERSE, SEARCH, or TRAVERSE AND SEARCH. Rate controls the volume of fire (sustained, rapid, and cyclic). Normally, the gunner uses the sustained rate of fire. The rate of fire is omitted from the fire command. The method of fire for the machine gun is usually 3- to 5-round bursts (M249) and 6- to 9-round bursts (M60/M240B).

EXAMPLE

FIRE MISSION
FRONT
REFERENCE: KNOCKED-OUT TANK, LEFT TWO FINGERS
TARGET: TROOPS
THREE HUNDRED
TRAVERSE

(6) *Command to Open Fire*. When fire is to be withheld so that surprise fire can be delivered on a target or to ensure that both gunners open fire at the same time, the leader may preface the command to commence firing with AT MY COMMAND or AT MY SIGNAL. When the gunners are ready to engage the target, they report READY to the leader. The leader then gives the command FIRE at the specific time desired.

EXAMPLE

FIRE MISSION
FRONT
TROOPS
FOUR HUNDRED
AT MY COMMAND or AT MY SIGNAL (The leader pauses until the gunners are ready and fire is desired.)
FIRE (The gunners fire on prearranged signal.)

If immediate fire is required, the command FIRE is given without pause and the gunners fire as soon as they are ready.

c. **Subsequent Fire Commands**. These fire commands are used to make adjustments in direction and elevation, to change rates of fire after a fire mission is in progress, to interrupt fires, or to terminate the alert. If the gunner fails to properly engage a target, the leader must promptly correct him by announcing or signaling the desired changes. When these changes are given, the gunner makes the corrections and resumes firing without further command.

(1) Adjustments in direction and elevation with the machine gun are always given in meters; one finger is used to indicate 1 meter and so on. Adjustment for direction is given first. For example: RIGHT ONE ZERO METERS or LEFT FIVE METERS. Adjustment for elevation is given next. For example: ADD FIVE METERS or DROP ONE FIVE METERS. These changes may be given orally or with arm-and-hand signals.

(2) Changes in the rate of fire are given orally or by arm-and-hand signals.

(3) To interrupt firing, the leader announces "Cease fire," or he signals to cease fire. The gunners remain on the alert. They resume firing when given the command FIRE.

(4) To terminate the alert, the leader announces "Cease fire, end of mission."

d. **Doubtful Elements and Corrections**. When the gunner is in doubt about any element of the fire command, he replies "Say again range, target." The leader then announces "The command was," repeats the element in question, and continues with the fire command.

(1) When the leader makes an error in the initial fire command, he corrects it by announcing "Correction," and then gives the corrected element.

> **EXAMPLE**
> FIRE MISSION
> FRONT
> TROOPS
> SIX HUNDRED
> CORRECTION
> THREE HUNDRED
> TRAVERSE
> AT MY COMMAND

(2) When the leader makes an error in the subsequent fire command, he may correct it by announcing "Correction," and then repeating the entire subsequent fire command.

> **EXAMPLE**
> LEFT FIVE METERS, DROP ONE METER
> CORRECTION
> LEFT FIVE METERS, DROP ONE HUNDRED METERS

e. **Abbreviated Fire Commands**. Fire commands need not be complete to be effective. In combat, the leader gives only the elements necessary to place fire on a target quickly and without confusion. During training, however, he should use all of the elements to get gunners in the habit of thinking and reacting properly when a target is to be engaged. After the gunner's initial training in fire commands, he should be taught to react to abbreviated fire commands, using one of the following methods.

(1) *Oral*. The leader may want to place the fire of one machine gun on an enemy machine gun.

> **EXAMPLE**
> GUN NUMBER ONE, FIRE MISSION
> MACHINE GUN
> FOUR HUNDRED
> FIRE

(2) *Arm-and-Hand Signals*. Battlefield noise and the distance between the gunner and the leader often make it necessary to use arm-and-hand signals to control fire (Figure 5-25). When an action or movement is to be executed by only one of the gunners, a preliminary signal is given to that gunner only. The following are commonly used signals for fire control.

THE READY SIGNAL

ADJUSTING FIRE WITH THE BIPOD-MOUNTED GUN

CEASE FIRE

COMMENCE FIRING

ADJUSTING FIRE WITH THE TRIPOD-MOUNTED GUN

Figure 5-25. Arm-and-hand signals.

(a) Ready. The gunner indicates that he is ready to fire by yelling "Up" or having the assistant gunner raise his hand above his head toward the leader.

(b) Commence Firing or Change Rate of Firing. The leader brings his hand (palm down) to the front of his body about waist level, and moves it horizontally in front of his body. To signal an increase in the rate of fire, he increases the speed of the hand movement to signal slower fire, and he decreases the speed of the hand movement.

(c) Change Direction or Elevation. The leader extends his arm and hand in the new direction and indicates the amount of change necessary by the number of fingers extended. The fingers must be spread, so the gunner can easily see the number of fingers extended. Each finger indicates 1 meter of change for the weapon. If the desired change is more than 5 meters, the leader extends his hand the number of times necessary to indicate the total amount of change. For example, *right nine* would be indicated by extending the hand once with five fingers showing and a second time with four fingers showing for a total of nine fingers.

(d) Interrupt or Cease Firing. The leader raises his arm and hand (palm outward) in front of his forehead and brings it downward sharply.

(e) Other Signals. The leader can devise other signals to control his weapons. A detailed description of arm-and-hand signals is given in FM 21-60.

Section VI. RANGE DETERMINATION

During combat, ranges are seldom known. Poor visibility and damp ground often make adjustment of fire by observation difficult if not impossible. Therefore, correct range determination is critical for accurate effective fire. Range estimation and lateral distance measurements are two methods used to determine the range to the target.

5-19. RANGE ESTIMATION

Range estimation is determining the distance between two points. In most situations, one of these points is the gunner's own position; the other point may be a target or prominent terrain feature. The gunner must accurately determine the range to set the sights and effectively fire on a target with the first burst.

a. Not only does the accurate estimation of range affect marksmanship, but it is also required in the reporting of information and the adjustment of artillery and mortar fire (Table 5-1).

FACTORS AFFECTING RANGE ESTIMATION	FACTORS CAUSING UNDERESTIMATION	FACTORS CAUSING OVERESTIMATION
The clearness of outline and details of the target.	When most of the target is visible and offers	When only a small portion of the target is small in relation to its surroundings.
Nature of terrain or position of the gunner.	When looking across a depression that is mostly hidden from view.	When looking across a depression that is totally visible.
	When looking downward form high ground.	When looking from low ground toward high ground.
	When looking down a straight, open road or along a railroad.	When vision is narrowly confined as in streets, draws, or forest trails.
	When looking over uniform surfaces like water, snow, desert, or grain fields.	

Table 5-1. Factors of range estimation.

FACTORS AFFECTING RANGE ESTIMATION	FACTORS CAUSING UNDERESTIMATION	FACTORS CAUSING OVERESTIMATION
Light and atmosphere.	In bright light or when the sun is shining from behind the gunner.	In poor light such as dawn and dusk; in rain, snow, fog; or when the sun is in the gunner's eyes.
	When the target is in sharp contrast with the silhouette because of its size, shape, or color. When seen in the clear air of high altitudes.	When the target blends into the background or terrain.

Table 5-1. Factors of range estimation (continued).

b. There are several methods of estimating range. They include measuring distance on a map, pacing the distance between two points, and using an optical range finder. The gunner does not usually have a map and rarely has access to an optical range finder. He can pace the distance between two points if the enemy is not within range. Firing rounds to determine the range is not desirable, since it may reveal your position to the enemy. Most of the time, the gunner must use techniques that do not require equipment and can be used without exposing himself or revealing his position. There are two methods that meet these requirements: the appearance-of-objects and the 100-meter-unit-of-measure.

(1) *Appearance-of-Objects Method.* This method is a means of estimating range by the size and other characteristic details of the object.

(a) This is a common method of determining distances and is used most often. For example, a motorist trying to pass another car must judge the distance of oncoming vehicles based on his knowledge of how vehicles appear at various distances. In this example, the motorist is not interested in precise distances but only in having enough road space to safely pass the car. Suppose, however, the motorist knew that at a distance of 1 kilometer, an oncoming vehicle appeared to be 1 centimeter between headlights. Then, anytime he saw other oncoming vehicles that fit these dimensions, he would know they were about 1 kilometer away. This technique can be used by a gunner to estimate ranges on the battlefield. If the gunner knows the characteristic size and detail of men and equipment at known ranges, he can compare these characteristics to similar objects at unknown ranges. When characteristics match, so does the range.

(b) To use the appearance-of-objects method with any degree of accuracy, the gunner must know the characteristic details of objects as they appear at various ranges. For example, the gunner should study the appearance of a man standing at a range of 100 meters. He fixes the man's appearance firmly in his mind, carefully noting details of size and the characteristics of uniform and equipment. Next, he studies the same man in a kneeling position and then in a prone position. By comparing the appearance of the man at known ranges from 100 to 500 meters, the gunner can establish a series of mental images that will help determine range on unfamiliar terrain. Training should also be conducted in the appearance of other familiar objects such as weapons or vehicles. Because the successful use of this method depends upon visibility, anything that limits visibility (such as weather, smoke, or darkness) will also limit the effectiveness of this method.

(2) *100-Meter-Unit-of-Measure Method.* To use this method, the gunner visualizes a distance of 100-meters on the ground. For ranges up to 500-meters (Figure 5-26), he determines the number of 100-meter increments between the two points he wishes to measure. Beyond 500-meters (Figure 5-27), he selects a point halfway to the target, determines the number of 100-meter increments to the halfway point, and then doubles it to find the range to the target.

(a) During training, the gunner must become familiar with the effect that sloping terrain has on the appearance of a 100-meter increment. Terrain that slopes upward gives the illusion of longer distance, and observers have a tendency to overestimate the 100-meter increment. Terrain that slopes downward gives the illusion of shorter distance. In this case, the gunner's tendency is to underestimate the 100-meter increment and thus underestimate the range.

(b) Proficiency in the 100-meter-unit-of-measure method requires constant practice. When training in this technique, the gunner should make frequent comparisons between the range as determined by the himself and by pacing or other accurate means of measurement. The best training technique is to pace the range after he has visually determined it. In this way, he discovers the actual range for himself, which makes a much greater impression than if he is told the correct range.

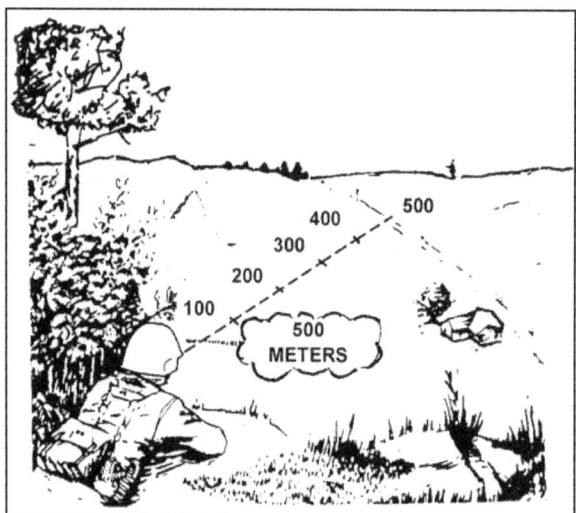

Figure 5-26. Applying the 100-meter-unit-of-measure method for ranges up to 500 meters.

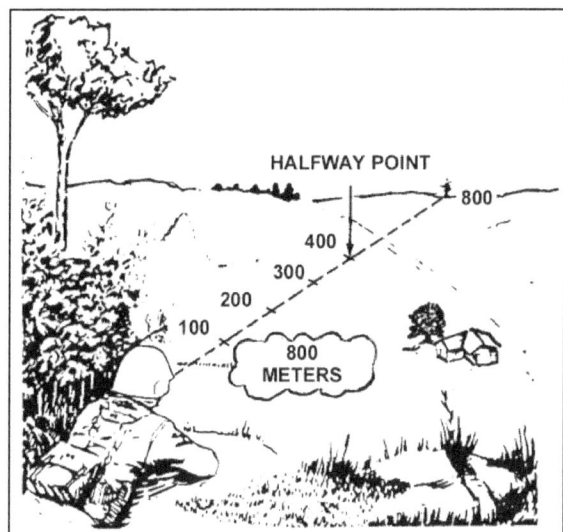

Figure 5-27. Applying the 100-meter-unit-of-measure method for ranges up to 800 meters.

(c) A limitation of the 100-meter-unit-of-measure method is that its accuracy is directly related to the amount of terrain visible to the gunner. This is particularly true at greater ranges. If a target appears at a range of 500 meters or more and the gunner can only see a portion of the ground between himself and the target, it becomes difficult to use the 100-meter-unit-of-measure method of range estimation with any degree of accuracy.

(3) *Combination of Methods*. Under ideal conditions, either the appearance-of-objects method or 100-meter-unit-of-measure method is an effective method of estimating range. However, ideal conditions rarely exist on the battlefield, so the gunner must use a combination of methods. The terrain might limit the use of the appearance-of-objects method. For example, a gunner may not be able to see all the terrain out to the target; however, he may see enough to get a general idea of the distance. A slight haze may obscure many of the target details, but the gunner should still be able to judge its size. By carefully considering the ranges estimated by both methods, an experienced gunner should arrive at a figure close to the true range. The best way to reduce errors using these two methods is to train often.

5-20. LATERAL DISTANCE MEASUREMENT
In addition to estimating range accurately, the gunner needs a quick method of measuring lateral distance (right or left) from a reference point to a target. When the machine gun is tripod-mounted, width can be measured by aiming on a point, manipulating the traversing handwheel, and counting the clicks from one point of aim to another point of aim. Each click equals 1 mil and is equivalent to 1 meter at 1,000 meters, or half a meter at 500 meters. When the machine gun is bipod-mounted, the gunner can use his fingers to measure the lateral distance between a reference point and a target. He extends his arm with his palm outward, lowers his fingers, and locks his elbow. Then, he closes one eye, raises his index finger, and sights along its edge, placing the edge of his finger so that it

appears to be along the flank of the target or reference point. The gunner fills the space remaining between the points by raising his fingers until the space is covered. He states the measurement from the reference point to the target as being one or more fingers, depending upon how many fingers are raised to cover this distance.

Section VII. ADVANCED GUNNERY

Once the gunner masters the four fundamentals of marksmanship in the prone position and fighting position, he needs practice in engaging targets that will most likely replicate the battlefield. The advanced gunnery field firing exercise for the gunner exposes him to different types of targets at various ranges to simulate combat conditions.

5-21. OBJECTIVES

The objectives of this training are to reinforce the fundamentals and increase the effectiveness of the gunner by building his confidence (*not for qualification*). He must acquire targets quickly and deliver an accurate volume of fire.

5-22. ORGANIZATION

The unit is assembled in the bleachers, given the training objectives, a range briefing, and a safety briefing. Gunners are then organized into firing orders with a gunner and an assistant gunner. (Concurrent training stations must be set up for those soldiers not on the firing line.)

5-23. AMMUNITION

This exercise requires 392 rounds of 7.62-mm linked ammunition (zero is included). The gunner is allotted two 7-round bursts for each target and fires twice.

5-24. FIRING SEQUENCE

The sequence of firing is to be conducted IAW Firing Table IV (Table 5-2). Commanders may score their soldiers to determine their most proficient gunners, to assess the marksmanship program, and to encourage competition.

    a. **Task 1, Field Zeroing the 500-Meter, Single E-Type Silhouette.** The gunner is allocated 28 rounds of ammunition.

    b. **Task 2, Engage Single E-Type Silhouettes From the Prone and Fighting Position, Bipod Supported (Point Targets) at Various Ranges.** The gunner will use his NBC equipment (Mask and Gloves). Targets are at 100, 200, 250, 300, and 400 meters. The gunner is allocated 70 rounds of ammunition.

    c. **Task 3, Engage Double E-Type Silhouettes (Automatic Weapon Positions) at Various Ranges.** Targets are at 250, 300, 400, 500, and 600 meters. The gunner is allocated 70 rounds of ammunition.

    d. **Task 4, Engage Linear E-Type Silhouettes (Troops on Line) at Various Ranges.** The gunner uses his NBC equipment (Mask and Gloves). Targets are at 300 and 600 meters. The gunner is allocated 28 rounds of ammunition.

> **WARNING**
>
> The M240B is carried loaded with the bolt locked to the *rear* in *tactical situations* where noise discipline is critical to the success of the mission. Trained gun crews are the only personnel authorized to load the M240B and only when command directs the crew to do so. During *normal training exercises*, the M240B is loaded and carried with the bolt in the *forward position*.

TASK	RANGE (M)	TIME	TOTAL ROUNDS PER INDIVIDUAL	TARGET	AMMO	TYPE FIRE
1	500	No limit	28	E-type silhouette	4:1	Zeroing 7-round bursts
2*	100 200 250 300 400	60 seconds	70	Single E-type silhouette	4:1	7-round bursts
3	250 300 400 500 600	120 seconds	70	Single E-type silhouette	4:1	7-round bursts
4*	300 600	120 seconds	28	Linear target Single E-type 1 meter apart	4:1	7-round bursts
* Indicates tasks fired with protective mask and gloves as a minimum.						

Table 5-2. Firing Table II.

5-25. ALTERNATE FIRING POSITIONS

All gunners must master the bipod-supported prone firing fighting position, and tripod-supported prone firing position to be effective. But it is also equally important that they know other positions. Each gunner must be trained to assume different positions quickly during various combat conditions. The situation determines the appropriate position. The gunner must establish his position so that he can effectively observe and engage the target yet minimize his exposure to enemy fire.

a. **Positions.** The underarm firing position and the hip firing position are used.

(1) *Underarm Firing Position.* This position is used almost exclusively when moving in and around the objective during the assault (Figure 5-28). To assume this position, the gunner—

(a) Puts the bipod legs and rear sight down for instant use in the prone position if necessary.

(b) Faces the target with his feet spread about shoulder width apart.

(c) Places his left foot in front of the right with most of his weight on his left foot.

(d) Bends both legs at the knees and leans forward at the waist.

(e) With his right hand, firmly grasps the pistol grip, and with his right forearm holds the stock firmly against the side of his body at a point between his armpit and waist.

(f) With his left hand, grasps the handguard firmly.

(g) Points his left foot in the direction of the target while his right foot provides stability.

(h) Depresses the muzzle of the machine gun slightly so the strike of rounds can be observed. (This reduces shooting high and takes advantage of ricochets.)

(i) Leans toward the target before and during firing.

Figure 5-28. Underarm firing position.

(2) *Hip Firing Position.* This position is used when closing with the enemy, when a heavy volume of fire in the target area is required, and when rapid movement is not necessary (Figure 5-29). The only differences between this position and the underarm position are that the gunner—

(a) Holds the rear of the stock firmly against the forward position of his right thigh.

(b) Extends his arms fully downward.

Figure 5-29. Hip firing position.

b. **Alternate Firing Position Exercises**. The assault fire exercise challenges the gunner. It consists of point and area targets during a variety of conditions replicating the battlefield. These exercises, which involve fire and maneuver, must be carefully controlled for safety purposes.

(1) *Objectives*. This exercise gives the gunner practice on engaging targets as quickly as possible, using any of the alternate firing positions.

(2) *Organization*. The unit is assembled in the bleachers, given instructions, and briefed on training that will be conducted while they are on the range. After the briefing, they are organized into firing orders and moved to firing lanes. Lanes are conducted and used IAW local range policies.

(3) *Ammunition*. This exercise requires a total of 168 rounds of 7.62-mm linked ammunition. The gunner is allowed two bursts per exposure, and he is also required to conduct at least one rapid reload during the exercise and the gunner will fire this twice. The commander has the option of when the rapid reload may take place. Ammunition is configured into two belts of any size that requires the gunner to reload.

(4) *Firing Sequence*. The sequence of firing is conducted IAW Firing Table V (Table 5-3). The suggested sequence of firing is as follows.

(a) Task 1, Dry Fire Walk-Through. Upon his arrival at the firing position, the gunner walks through his respective lane to become familiar with the targets. No ammunition is fired at this time. When he returns, he draws his ammunition.

NOTE: Commanders ensure that ammunition is used in such a manner that the gunner is required to rapidly reload sometime during his movement phases.

(b) Task 2, Engage Single E-Type Silhouette from the Hip-Firing Position. After being issued the ammunition, the gunner begins his movement. When targets are exposed, he uses the hip-firing technique. He is given a single exposed target at a distance of 25 meters, with an exposure time of 5 seconds.

(c) Task 3, Engage Single E-Type Silhouettes from the Underarm-Firing Position. As the gunner continues to move through the course, he is given two single exposed E-type silhouettes at distances of 50 and 25 meters, where he engages each silhouette using the underarm-firing position. The exposure time for each target is 5 seconds.

(d) Task 4, Engage Single E-Type Silhouettes from the Underarm or Hip-Firing Position. Once the gunner reaches this point, he is be given three single exposed E-type silhouettes at distances of 25, 50, and 75 meters. The exposure time for each target is 5 seconds.

NOTE: The commander may integrate firing under NBC conditions for selected tasks while negotiating the course, or he may conduct the course during limited visibility unaided.

TASK	RANGE (M)	TIME	TOTAL ROUNDS PER INDIVIDUAL	TARGET	AMMO	TYPE FIRE
1	NA	No limit	NA	NA	NA	NA
2	25	5 seconds	14	Single E-type silhouette	4:1	7-round bursts
3	50	10 seconds	28	Single E-type silhouette	4:1	7-round bursts
4	25 50 75	15 seconds	42	Single E-type silhouette	4:1	7-round bursts

Table 5-3. Firing Table VIII.

5-26. MOVEMENT, SPEED, AND ALIGNMENT

The gunner must keep up with the other soldiers of the assaulting element through individual movement techniques. To do this, he moves as rapidly as possible, consistent with his ability to fire accurately and maintain alignment.

5-27. RELOADING

The gunner must reload rapidly to avoid lulls in the firing. This can be achieved by practicing and by applying the following techniques.

a. Before the assault, the gunner conducts prefire checks on the machine gun. He inspects ammunition to ensure that it is clean and serviceable, and he checks the box for serviceability.

b. During the assault, the gunner must continue moving forward and reload as rapidly as possible. The sling allows the gunner to reload using both hands.

CHAPTER 6
TRAIN-THE-TRAINER PROGRAM

This chapter helps the leader develop a good train-the-trainer program. The goal of this program is to certify qualified machine gun trainers and achieve a high state of combat readiness. Knowledgeable, small-unit leaders and trainers are the key to any successful marksmanship training program; however, the entire leadership must be involved in the execution of training to standard. An effective train-the-trainer program reflects the priority, emphasis, and interest of the leaders and trainers to see that execution of training to standard is achieved.

The objectives of the train-the-trainer program are to develop in every machine gun trainer the confidence, willingness, knowledge, and skills required to consistently train their soldiers to be effective in combat.

6-1. MISSION-ESSENTIAL TASK LIST
The unit's combat mission is considered when establishing training priorities. This not only applies to the tasks selected but to the conditions under which the tasks are to be preformed. The tasks for the METL are developed for both defensive and offensive operations. Machine gun marksmanship will be a critical individual, crew and leader task. Each commander should develop a METL and organize a training program that devotes adequate time to conduct marksmanship training.

6-2. TRAINER ASSESSMENT
The leaders are also involved in determining the proficiency of potential trainers by reviewing the following information.
   a. **Selection.** Trainers should be selected from the most highly qualified soldiers available within the unit. These soldiers should be knowledgeable of the machine guns, a high degree of proficiency in applying the fundamentals, and demonstrate a motivated attitude for marksmanship training. The leaders must ensure that a high level of proficiency is maintained. Knowledgeable trainers are the key to any successful training program.
   b. **Trainer Course.** Once the leaders have identified these soldiers possessing the required knowledge, skills, and motivation in machine gun marksmanship, they must then ensure this knowledge can be effectively taught to other soldiers.
   c. **Training.** There are several available means that may be used in the progression of trainer training or that can easily be tailored to the certain needs of the command. The more time and training initially invested, the better the trainer will be. The leaders should periodically evaluate each trainer and replace any that loses his motivation or desire. To maintain interest in the program, leaders should have a way of promoting competition and awards the best trainer.

6-3. ASSISTANT TRAINERS AND CADRE COACHES
Assisting the trainer and coaching a soldier to fire the machine gun are highly technical jobs that must be done well. The most valuable soldiers in the program are those who not only have obtained a high standard, but those who can effectively teach this knowledge to

others. Once the individual is consistent in this train-the-trainer program, he can then develop into a competent assistant trainer. It is worth the effort to train these individuals to become a successful assistant trainer, because experience has shown that such training also develops leadership ability.

a. The primary responsibility of assistant trainers is to train individuals in the effective use of the machine gun. In addition, assistant trainers are responsible for enforcing safety regulations. They must maintain strict discipline on the firing lane at all times and constantly enforce compliance with the range regulations and training guidance.

b. To be an assistant trainer, a soldier must know the principles of accurate firing and coaching techniques, and he must have the following qualifications as well.

(1) *Knowledge*. The assistant trainer must know this manual. He must be prepared to accurately answer any question on the subject of marksmanship. Then, he must develop his ability to observe the actions of the soldier quickly and to correct them with sound recommendations.

(2) *Patience*. Gunners can be persuaded to accept the principles and procedures by patient repetition and demonstration.

(3) *Understanding*. The assistant trainers that have good "firing lane manners" enhance the success of training. Training new gunners is stressful to the soldiers and the trainers. The soldier may be sensitive to abruptness, impatience, or a lack of sympathy with his difficulties; and he will immediately react unfavorably to evidence of such attitude on the part of the coach.

(4) *Consideration*. Most soldiers, even those who do not fire well, enjoy firing and begin with a positive interest in their performance on the range. If the assistant trainer is considerate of his pupils' feelings from the beginning and encourages them throughout their training, he will find training a pleasant and rewarding duty.

(5) *Ability to Maintain Respect*. When a soldier is assigned the duties of assistant trainer, he too is an expert and should receive the same respect as the primary trainer. The assistant trainer must retain that respect throughout his contact with students by showing a thorough knowledge of his subject in a dignified manner.

(6) *Alertness*. Even the most capable student may forget or neglect some essential point in his instruction in the excitement of firing on the range. The assistant trainer must always be alert and patiently correct him as often as necessary. He must keep the gunners encouraged throughout the instruction by making the most of all progress. The assistant trainer must not allow his students to become discouraged or to lose interest.

(7) *Helpful Attitude*. When assisting on the range, as in most other lines of instruction, a combative, hard-boiled attitude is rarely effective.

(8) *Ability to Provide Encouragement*. The assistant trainer can encourage his soldiers by convincing them there is no mystery about good firing: The weapon and ammunition are mechanically developed for accuracy. The assistant trainer is there to assist the gunner and to help him gain the experience that produces a good marksman.

6-4. PROGRAM PHASES

Since firing is a learning process, certain prerequisites must be satisfied before a trainer passes from one phase of marksmanship to another. The trainer must qualify with the machine gun (the trainer must pass all tasks and qualify on the 10-meter and transition fire) that he will be teaching to the machine gunners in his unit. To obtain maximum results on the battlefield, the machine gunners are trained in the fundamentals before they engage a combat target. The phases of the train-the-trainer program are to develop this structure in the most progressive manner. They are sequenced to train-the-trainer in teaching tasks necessary to produce a quality machine gunner and a machine gun team.

a. **Preliminary Gunnery.** The machine gunners must receive this training before live firing. It is during this phase that sound foundations of good firing principles are constructed, reviewed, and reinforced. The degree of proficiency obtained or retained by the machine gunners depends on the foundation built during this phase. Correct firing and good safety habits must become natural. Drilling of the fundamentals and continued leader emphasis will bring the greatest return in the shortest time. Proper firing is a physical skill, which must be learned. When practiced, the process becomes a learned skill that will be retained. However, good firing is a perishable skill. All machine gunners must periodically familiarize themselves with the fundamentals regardless of their years of marksmanship experience. Even experienced machine gunners will develop a deficiency in applying certain fundamentals (for example, overconfidence).

b. **Basic Gunnery.** This training teaches the trainers how to qualify, plan, set up, and conduct 10-meter and transition firing exercises on the available ranges.

c. **Advanced Gunnery.** This training teaches the trainer how to develop teamwork among the machine gun teams. This training also gives them confidence in their ability to deliver a large volume of accurate fire against targets. During this phase, the trainer is responsible for the conduct of assault firing exercises. These exercises consist of assault fire, NBC assault fire, and field fire on available ranges.

6-5. TRAINING TASKS

This paragraph assists trainers in effectively training soldiers assigned to any machine gun team. It explains the tasks, organization, equipment needed, and instruction sequence for the three phases of gunnery. However, unit SOPs or post regulations may direct increases or decreases in these prescribed requirements.

a. **Phase I, Preliminary Gunnery Training**. This phase covers the basics that each trainer must know to teach the general care and maintenance of the machine gun.

(1) *Task 1: (071-312-3025) Disassemble the Machine Gun.* The trainer stresses that this task is not done hurriedly, because the soldiers may damage parts of the machine gun.

(a) Equipment Needed. A table is needed for placement of the machine gun so that the soldiers may better see the removal of parts of the gun. Nomenclature charts or mats are material aids in explaining mechanical training, and they help the gunners learn the nomenclature of parts.

(b) Class Organization. One assistant trainer is assigned for each group if possible; otherwise, assistant trainers are placed where they can supervise assigned groups.

(c) Sequence of Training. The trainer presents a brief history of the machine guns. He stresses the combat role it has played and the mission it is assigned. He emphasizes the purpose, scope, and importance of the instruction to be presented. He gives a brief description of the operation, general data, and exterior nomenclature of the machine gun. Assistant trainers should clear and disassemble the machine gun as the trainer explains the procedures. The gunners then practice until they become skilled in disassembly and can demonstrate this task to standards to either the trainer or assistant trainers. This practice often encourages the gunners to practice during free time and develops their individual skill and initiative.

(2) *Task 2: (071-025-0001) Perform Operator Maintenance on the Machine Gun.* The subtasks are inspect, clean, and lubricate.

(a) Equipment Needed. The trainer needs one cleaning rod and one dummy round for each machine gun, bore cleaner, (one cleaning reamer, one combination regulator scraper, one combination scraper and extractor tool), lubricating oil, patches, and rags. The trainer displays all the available cleaning materials, lubricants, and rust preventatives.

(b) Class Organization. One assistant trainer is assigned for each group if possible; otherwise, the assistant trainers are placed where they can supervise assigned groups.

(c) Sequence of Training. The trainer emphasizes meticulous cleaning, lubrication, inspection, and preventive maintenance to ensure performance. The care and cleaning period is used to further the gunner's knowledge of the nomenclature and skill in disassembly. The trainer emphasizes inspection, care, and preventive maintenance during combat conditions, which is the final test of the weapon maintenance program. Practical work is conducted. The trainer points out the differences in care and cleaning following an NBC attack. He emphasizes the importance of frequent inspection as a means of ensuring proper maintenance of the machine guns.

(3) *Task 3: (071-312-4025) Assemble the Machine Gun.*

(a) Equipment Needed. A table is needed for placement of the machine gun so that the soldiers may better see the removal of the parts. Nomenclature charts or mats are material aids in explaining mechanical training, and they help the gunners to learn the nomenclature of parts.

(b) Class Organization. One assistant trainer is assigned for each group if possible; otherwise, assistant trainers are placed where they can supervise assigned groups.

(c) Sequence of Training. Assistant trainers should assemble the machine gun as the trainer explains the procedures. The gunners practice until they become proficient in assembly and can demonstrate this task to standards to either the trainer or assistant trainer.

(4) *Task 4: (071-312-4026) Explain the Operation of the Machine Gun.*

(a) Equipment Needed. One machine gun placed on a table; one belt of six dummy rounds (5.56-mm or 7.62-mm linked), and a cleaning rod for each gunner.

(b) Class Organization. One assistant trainer is assigned for each group if possible; otherwise, assistant trainers are placed where they can supervise assigned groups.

(c) Sequence of Training. The trainer explains and the assistant trainer demonstrates loading, unloading, and clearing the machine gun. The trainer stresses the safety factors involved. The assistant trainer demonstrates letting the bolt go forward when the barrel is out of the machine gun. (Damage could be done to the chamber or the face of the bolt if the barrel is left in.)

(5) *Task 5: (071-312-3026) Explain the Functioning of the Machine Gun.*

(a) Equipment Needed. One machine gun for each gunner as in previous mechanical training instruction. Graphic training aids are useful if the class is about platoon size; otherwise, GTAs may be made available for study and discussion during breaks.

(b) Class Organization. One assistant trainer is assigned for each group if possible; otherwise, assistant trainers are placed where they can supervise assigned groups.

(c) Sequence of Training. Functioning is divided into eight steps—feeding, chambering, locking, firing, unlocking, extracting, ejecting, and cocking. The assistant trainer duplicates each demonstration on the machine gun with each group. Functioning is taught by seeing how the parts work, rather than by memorizing the text. The trainer tests retention of the training by asking questions concerning the steps of functioning.

(6) *Task 6: (071-312-3029) Explain Malfunction, Stoppage, Immediate Action, and Remedial Action.*

(a) Equipment Needed. A table is needed for placement of the machine gun so that the soldiers may better see the removal of parts. Nomenclature charts or mats are material aids in explaining mechanical training, and they help the gunners learn the nomenclature of parts.

(b) Class Organization. One assistant trainer is assigned for each group if possible; otherwise, assistant trainers are placed where they can supervise assigned groups.

(c) Sequence of Training. Malfunction and stoppages charts may be used as a guide in presenting instruction. These charts may be available from the local Training Support Center or the trainer can use tables of the appropriate chapters for the machine gun. The trainer stresses precision in detecting the cause and reducing stoppages. As the gunners progress, the trainer has them concentrate on speed in applying immediate action and other methods of reducing a stoppage. He stresses safety precautions in connection with a hangfire or cook off.

(7) *Task 7: (071-312-3030) Explain the Procedures for Sight Adjustments and Mechanical Zero.*

(a) Equipment Needed. A table is needed for placement of the machine gun so that the soldiers may better see the removal of parts. Nomenclature charts or mats are material aids in explaining mechanical training, and they help the gunners learn the nomenclature of parts, plus tripod. (Front sight adjustment tool for the M240B.)

(b) Class Organization. One assistant trainer is assigned for each group if possible; otherwise, assistant trainers are placed where they can supervise assigned groups.

(c) Sequence of Training. Assistant trainers demonstrate, while trainers describe the proper techniques to mechanically zero the machine gun. The trainer then describes sight adjustments. The trainer emphasizes the number of clicks in relation to the targets for M240B only.

(8) *Task 8: (071-020-0006) Explain the M122 or M122A1 Tripod with Appropriate Mounting Equipment.*

(a) Equipment Needed. One machine gun mounted on an M122 or M122A1 tripod complete with appropriate mounting equipment placed on a table. GTAs and film strips if available.

(b) Class Organization. One assistant trainer is assigned for each group if possible; otherwise, assistant trainers are placed where they can supervise assigned groups.

(c) Sequence of Training. The assistant trainers demonstrate, while the trainers describe the general nomenclature, data, functioning, and operation of the tripod with the appropriate mounting equipment.

(9) *Task 9: (071-020-0006) Place the Machine Gun Into Operation on the M122 or M122A1 Tripod with Appropriate Mounting Equipment Using Crew Exercises.*

(a) *Equipment Needed.* Basic TOE and individual equipment.

(b) Class Organization. Gunners are divided into three-man crews. To aid control and supervision, equipment is aligned with engineer tape or wire with the gunners in files behind the equipment.

(c) Sequence of Training. Assistant trainers demonstrate, while trainers explain how to place the machine gun into operation on the tripod with the appropriate mounting equipment. The crew drill is the first step in developing teamwork. Precision is a must for each crewmember. Crewmembers practice their duties with precision. Speed is increased as precision is attained. In advanced training, speed drills create interest and stimulate competition, while developing teamwork and testing individual crew performance. A well-trained crew can place the machine gun into action or take it out of action in 25 seconds.

(10) *Task 10: (071-312-3025) Demonstrate Fundamentals of Marksmanship.*

(a) Equipment Needed. One machine gun and a basic machine gun target for each firing lane on a range of suitable training area equipped with a prone and fighting position.

(b) Class Organization. The maximum number of required gunners is on the firing line or suitable training area.

(c) Sequence of Training. The trainer conducts conference, demonstration, and practical work on the fundamentals of marksmanship (steady position, aim, breath control, trigger control).

(11) *Task 11: (071-312-3026) Demonstrate Fundamentals of Firing Positions.*

(1) *Equipment Needed.* One machine gun and a basic machine gun target for each firing lane on a range of suitable training area equipped with a prone and fighting position.

(2) *Class Organization.* The maximum number of required gunners is on the firing line or suitable training area.

(3) *Sequence of Training.* The trainer conducts conference, demonstration, and practical work on the fundamentals of marksmanship (steady position, aim, breath control, trigger control).

(12) *Task 12: (071-312-3027) Demonstrate Fundamentals of Traverse and Search.*

(a) Equipment Needed. One machine gun and a basic machine gun target for each firing lane on a range of suitable training area equipped with a prone and fighting position.

(b) Class Organization. The maximum number of required gunners is on the firing line or suitable training area.

(c) Sequence of Training. The trainer conducts conference, demonstration, and practical work on the fundamentals of marksmanship (steady position, aim, breath control, trigger control).

(13) *Task13: (071-312-3031) Demonstrate Fundamentals of Engaging Night, NBC, and Moving Targets.*

(a) Equipment Needed. One machine gun, one night vision sight, one protective mask with gloves for each gunner, and a basic machine gun target for each firing lane on a range of suitable training area equipped with a prone and fighting position.

(b) Class Organization. The maximum number of required gunners is on the firing line or suitable training area.

(c) Sequence of Training. The trainer conducts conference, demonstration, and practical work on the fundamentals of marksmanship (steady position, aim, breath control, trigger control).

(14) *Task 14: (071-025-0007) Demonstrate Fire Commands.*

(a) Equipment Needed. One machine gun and a basic machine gun target for each firing lane on a range of suitable training area equipped with a prone and fighting position. GTAs and film strips if available.

(b) Class Organization. The maximum number of required gunners is on the firing line or suitable training area.

(c) Sequence of Training. The trainer conducts conference, demonstration, and practical work on the fundamentals of marksmanship (steady position, aim, breath control, trigger control), plus, the trainer gives the fire commands. (See Chapter 5.)

(15) *Task 15: (071-025-0007) Execute Dry-Fire Exercises.*

(a) Equipment Needed. One machine gun and a basic machine gun target for each firing lane on a range of suitable training area equipped with a prone and fighting position.

(b) Class Organization. The maximum number of required gunners is on the firing line or suitable training area.

(c) Sequence of Training. The trainer conducts conference, demonstration, and practical work on the fundamentals of marksmanship (steady position, aim, breath control, trigger control), plus, the trainer give the fire commands. (See Chapter 4.)

b. **Phase II, Basic Gunnery Training.** The information learned in this phase is essential to the development of the trainer who is to conduct the 10-meter firing, day transition firing, day NBC firing, and night transition instructional firing for the machine gun. The trainer must be qualified or certified on Phase I before moving to Phase II.

(1) *Task 16: (071-312-3031) Conduct 10-Meter Firing.*

(a) Equipment Needed. One machine gun and basic machine gun target (10-meter) for each firing lane; stopwatches; patches; and cleaning rods. Sound equipment is desirable during firing.

(b) Class Organization. The maximum number of required gunners is on the firing line with the remainder receiving concurrent instruction in the rear training area.

(c) Sequence of Instruction. The unit is assembled, given instructions, and briefed on the training that will be conducted while they are on the range. The trainer conducts conference, demonstration, and practical work on emplacing the machine gun on the firing lane. He places emphasis on preparation of the machine gun for firing, including safety checks. The interval between the two portions of the control command should be sufficient to permit the execution of the command and to allow the assistant gunner to perform his duties. Assistant gunners are required to perform their duties quickly and precisely. During practice, the trainer must ensure that the gunner is in the proper position before he is permitted to shoot. The OIC controls all firing. If space permits, all personnel are placed on the firing line. After the briefing, they are organized into firing orders and moved to firing lanes. Lanes are conducted IAW local range policies. Firing is conducted as described in Chapter 4. Concurrent training stations:

- Mechanical training.
- Care and cleaning.
- Any other machine gun subjects in which additional training is needed.

(2) *Task 17: (071-312-3031) Conduct Daytime Transition Fire on the Multipurpose Machine Gun Range.*

(a) Equipment Needed. Requires one machine gun for each firing lane, single and double E-type silhouette targets, and cleaning rods. Sound equipment is desirable during firing.

(b) Class Organization. Preferably, one gunner and one assistant gunner for each firing lane. Personnel not required in the operation of the range should receive concurrent training in rear area.

(c) Sequence of Instruction. The unit is assembled, given instructions, and briefed on the training that will be conducted while they are on the range. Before the conference and demonstration of firing, the trainer briefly reviews range estimation and techniques of adjustment. He also explains the characteristics of machine gun fire and their effect on field targets. The machine guns are zeroed at a known distance on the transition range. The gunner receiving the instruction should do the zeroing. The lane NCO requires the gunner to be in the correct position before letting him fire. The assist gunner helps the gunner in locating the targets and aids him in hitting the targets. The acting safety NCO may assist the assist gunner in locating the targets, but he is not permitted to aid in range estimation or fire adjustment. After the gunners complete this exercise, the gunner and assist gunner rotates duties. After completion of both gunner and assist gunner, the next gun team moves up. The OIC controls all firing. If space permits, all personnel are placed on the firing line. After the briefing, they are organized into firing orders and moved to firing lanes. Lanes are conducted IAW local range policies. Firing is conducted as described in Chapter 4. Concurrent training stations:

- Mechanical training.
- Care and cleaning.
- Any other machine gun subjects in which additional training is needed.

(3) *Task 18: (071-010-0006) Demonstrate Fundamentals of Engaging NBC Targets.*

(a) Equipment Needed. One machine gun, protective mask and gloves for every gunner, and a basic machine gun target (10-meter) for each firing lane on a range of suitable training area equipped with a prone and fighting position.

(b) Class Organization. The maximum number of required teams is on the firing line or suitable training area.

(c) Sequence of Training. The unit is assembled, given instructions, and briefed on the training that will be conducted while they are on the range. The trainer conducts conference, demonstration, and practical work on the fundamentals of marksmanship (steady position, aim, breath control, trigger control) while wearing the protective mask and gloves. (Same as Task 16.) After the briefing, they are organized into firing orders and moved to firing lanes. Lanes are conducted IAW local range policies. Firing is conducted as described in Chapter 4, Firing Tables I or IV. Concurrent training stations, using sand tables, charts, diagrams, or terrain, are set up to review rapid reloading techniques while wearing a protective mask and gloves:

- Mechanical training.
- Care and cleaning.
- Any other machine gun subjects in which additional training is needed.

(4) *Task 19: (071-025-0007) Conduct NBC Familiarization Transition Fire.*

(a) Equipment Needed. Requires protective mask and gloves, one machine gun, and appropriate ammunition for each firing lane, single and double E-type silhouette targets, and cleaning rods. Sound equipment is desirable during firing.

(b) Class Organization. Preferably, one gunner and one assistant gunner for each firing lane. Personnel not required in the operation of the range should receive concurrent training in rear area.

(c) Sequence of Instruction. The unit is assembled, given instructions and briefed on the training that will be conducted while they are on the range. The trainer conducts conference, demonstration, and practical work on the fundamentals of marksmanship (steady position, aim, breath control, trigger control) while wearing the protective mask and gloves. (Same as Task 16.) After the briefing, they are organized into firing orders and moved to firing lanes. Lanes are conducted IAW local range policies. Firing is conducted as described in Chapter 4, Firing Tables II or V. Concurrent training stations, using sand tables, charts, diagrams, or terrain, are set up to review rapid reloading techniques while wearing a protective mask and gloves:

- Mechanical training.
- Care and cleaning.
- Any other machine gun subjects in which additional training is needed.

(5) *Task 20: (071-010-0001) Conduct Nighttime Transition Fire.*

(a) Equipment Needed. One machine gun for each firing lane with appropriate night vision sight, and appropriate ammunition for each firing lane, single and double E-type silhouette targets, and cleaning rods. Sound equipment is desirable during firing.

(b) Class Organization. The firing area should have seating for the entire group during conferences. After the conference, the group is divided into small groups for practical work under the control of the assistant trainers. The OIC controls all firing. If space permits, all personnel are placed on the firing line. Requirements for the various exercises should be simple and progressive. If possible, the trainer selects terrain for the subject; otherwise, he applies the subject to the terrain.

(c) Sequence of Instruction. The unit is assembled, given instructions, and briefed on the training that will be conducted while they are on the range. Before the conference and demonstration, the trainer conducts the preparatory exercises of mounting the night vision sight and seating, boresighting, and zeroing procedures for the sight. He should also review and discuss range estimation, techniques of fire, adjustment, and characteristics of the machine gun fire. The machine gun should be zeroed to the sight using the night fire procedures in Chapter 4, Firing Tables III or VI. The acting safety NCO for each lane requires the gunner to be in the correct position before letting him fire. The OIC controls all firing. If space permits, all personnel are placed on the firing line. At the completion of the exercise, the next gunner moves up. After the briefing, they are organized into firing orders and moved to firing lanes. Lanes are conducted IAW local range policies. Firing is conducted as described in Chapter 4. Firing Tables III or VI. Concurrent training stations:

- Mechanical training.
- Care and cleaning
- Any other machine gun subjects in which additional training is needed.

c. **Phase III, Advanced Gunnery Training**. This training phase enables the trainer to develop his advanced skills. (See Chapter 5.)

(1) *Task 21: (071-025-0007) Conduct Day Assault Fire.*

(a) Equipment Needed. One machine gun and appropriate ammunition for each firing lane.

(b) Class Organization. The multipurpose machine gun transition range is used if the installation has one. *If need be, the lanes are modified so that the gunner has a trail of at least 150 meters in front of the weapon position.* The training area should have seating for the entire group during conferences. After the conferences, the group is divided into firing orders. If the group is large, two firing orders are placed on the firing line and all other personnel go to the concurrent training area for practical work under the control of the assistant gunners. The OIC controls all firing. If the group is small, all personnel go to the firing line at once. Requirements for the various exercises should be simple and progressive. If possible, the trainer selects terrain for the subject; otherwise, he applies the subject to the terrain.

(c) Sequence of Instruction. The unit is assembled, given instructions, and briefed on the training that will be conducted while they are on the range. After the briefing, they are organized into firing orders and moved to firing lanes. Lanes are conducted IAW local range policies. Firing is conducted as described in Chapter 5. Concurrent training stations, using sand tables, charts, diagrams, or terrain, are set up to review rapid reloading techniques. The OIC controls all firing. If space permits, all personnel are placed on the firing line.

- Underarm-firing position.
- Hip-firing position.
- Rapid reloading techniques.
- Any other machine gun subjects in which additional training is needed.

(2) *Task 22: (071-025-0009) Conduct NBC Assault Fire With the Machine Gun.*

(a) Equipment Needed. Requires protective mask and gloves, one machine gun, and appropriate ammunition for each firing lane.

(b) Class Organization. The maximum number of required gunners is on the firing line with the remainder receiving concurrent instruction in the rear training area.

(c) Sequence of Instruction. The unit is assembled, given instructions, and briefed on the training that will be conducted while they are on the range. After the briefing, they are organized into firing orders and moved to firing lanes. Lanes are conducted IAW local range policies. Firing is conducted as described in Chapter 5. Concurrent training stations, using sand tables, charts, diagrams, or terrain, are set up to review rapid reloading techniques while wearing a protective mask and gloves:

- Underarm-firing position while wearing a protective mask and gloves.
- Hip-firing position while wearing a protective mask and gloves.
- Rapid reloading techniques while wearing a protective mask and gloves.
- Any other machine gun subjects in which additional training is needed.

6-6. TRAINER CERTIFICATION PROGRAM

The certification program standardizes procedures for certifying and sustaining the proficiency of trainers. Their technical expertise must be continuously refreshed and updated, and leaders must manage it closely. One of the goals of the program is for the trainer to know the training mission.

a. **Training Base**. The training base can expect the same personnel changes as any other organization. Soldiers assigned as machine gun trainers have varying experience and knowledge of training procedures and methods. Therefore, the trainer certification program must address these variables. As a minimum, formal records document the trainer's progress in the certification program. All machine gun trainers must complete the three phases of machine gun training, and they must update their training quarterly.

b. **Certification Program Outline**. All trainers must attend, then conduct, all phases of the train-the-trainer program. Certified trainers have demonstrated the ability to train soldiers, to diagnose and correct problems, and to achieve standards. Those who fail to attend or fail any phase of the diagnostic examination will be assigned to subsequent training. The personnel designated to present instruction must complete the phases of the program in the prescribed sequence.

(1) *Phase I, Program Orientation*. In order for leaders to certify trainers, the trainers must visit training sites and ranges and demonstrate an understanding of—

- The certification program concept.
- The unit's marksmanship training outline and strategy.
- Issued reference materials and when to use which.

(2) *Phase II, Preliminary Gunnery*. During Phase II, the trainer must demonstrate his mastery of the fundamentals of marksmanship. He should complete within two weeks after completing Phase I. Leaders should review the following fundamentals. They record and maintain the results of this review on a trainer's progression sheet IAW the unit SOP:

- Characteristics.
- Capabilities.
- Disassembly.
- Cleaning, lubrication, and inspection.
- Assembly.
- Range determination and estimation.
- Classes of fire.
- Application of fire.
- Fire commands.
- Loading.
- Unloading.
- Immediate actions.
- Sight manipulations.
- Traverse and search.

(3) *Phase III, Basic Gunnery*. During this phase, the trainer must first qualify with the machine gun, then he must set up and conduct firing on the various ranges. He must brief leaders, explaining the targets as well as zeroing and scoring procedures. He explains the purpose of transition firing, field-zero procedures, range layout, and the conduct of training on the transition range. This briefing validates that he has the knowledge

necessary to conduct training. Leaders add the results of this interview to the trainer's progression sheet.

(4) *Phase IV, Advanced Gunnery.* This is the final test of the trainer's ability to train. He must set up a range and train at least one person. If ammunition is available, he conducts a firing exercise. If ammunition is not available, he is judged based on the quality of training.

APPENDIX A
UNIT TRAINING PROGRAM

This appendix provides guidance for conducting unit training as part of preliminary marksmanship training for each machine gun. The training program prepares the unit for war by enabling leaders and soldiers to develop and sustain proficiency in machine gun tasks. It does this by integrating individual training and evaluation with battle drills and other collective tasks.

A-1. FOCUS
An effective unit training program focuses on three battlefield variables: nature of the target (moving or stationary, single or multiple); nature of the firer (stationary or moving); and conditions (full or limited visibility, with or without protective mask, day or night).

A-2. STRUCTURE
This proposed training program is subdivided into the following periods:
   a. Introduction.
   b. Preliminary marksmanship training and dry fire.
   c. Proficiency (performance) examination.
   d. 10-meter zero practice and qualification.
   e. Transition range, field zero, and practice fire.
   f. Transition range qualification fire.
   g. Night zero and instructional fire.
   h. Night qualification firee.

A-3. PERIODS

After a brief description of the machine gun, soldiers receive the following instruction:

   a. **Period 1--Introduction**.

DISASSEMBLY AND ASSEMBLY	TIME ALLOWED	
	HRS	MIN
Disassembly.		25
Operator maintenance:		
Inspection		10
Cleaning		10
Lubrication		10
Assembly		25
Disassembly and assembly (practice exercise--optional)		50
SUBTOTAL (including practice exercise):	2	10

CHARACTERISTICS OF FIRE	TIME ALLOWED	
	HRS	MIN
Burst fire		15
Trajectory and beaten zone		15
Engagements of targets:		
Point		10
Area		10
SUBTOTAL:		50
TOTAL:	3	0

b. **Period 2--Preliminary Marksmanship Training and Dry Fire.** After a brief description of the training to be conducted, soldiers receive the following instructions on the bipod, tripod, and mounting equipment:

TECHNIQUES OF FIRE	TIME ALLOWED	
	HRS	MIN
Position and grip, aiming, trigger manipulation, and T&E manipulation.		40
Loading ammunition.		15
Reducing stoppages and clearing the weapon.		5
SUBTOTAL:	1	10
DRY-FIRE PRACTICE	TIME ALLOWED	
	HRS	MIN
Aiming and firing sequence.		30
Sight setting and sight changes.		30
Zeroing procedures.	1	
SUBTOTAL:	2	
TOTAL:	3	10

c. **Period 3--Proficiency (Performance) Examination.** During this period, leaders use the proficiency examination to test and evaluate tasks learned during Periods 1 and 2.

PROFICIENCY (PERFORMANCE) EXAMINATION	TIME ALLOWED	
	HRS	MIN
TOTAL:	1	

d. **Period 4--10-Meter Zero Practice and Qualification**.

INSTRUCTIONAL SUBPERIODS	TIME ALLOWED	
	HRS	MIN
Preliminary marksmanship training including the aiming, sight picture, trigger control, bipod and tripod positions, and T&E manipulation.	1	
Function checks, loading, immediate action, clearing, and range safety.		15
Introduction to the 10-meter firing (includes zeroing and practice and qualification on the 10-meter target, and scoring of the target).		15
Zero firing.	1	
Practice day Table I.	1	
Qualification day Table I.	1	
TOTAL:	4	30

e. **Period 5—Transition Range, Field Zero, and Practice Fire**.

TRANSITION RANGE PRACTICE FIRE	TIME ALLOWED	
	HRS	MIN
Introduction to field firing (includes the transition range organization and operation).		15
Fire standard qualification course for practice (IAW with procedures in Chapter 4).	3	45
TOTAL:	4	

f. **Period 6—Transition Range Qualification Fire**. Soldiers fire the standard qualification course for record IAW procedures in Chapter 4.

TRANSITION RANGE QUALIFICATION FIRE	TIME ALLOWED	
	HRS	MIN
TOTAL:	4	

g. **Period 7—Night Zero, Instructional Fire, and Night Qualification Fire**.
Soldiers receive instruction on mounting, placing the night vision device into operation,
boresighting, and zeroing the device once it is seated. They fire the standard night course
as Period 4, except a night vision device is mounted on the weapon.

NIGHT ZERO, INSTRUCTIONAL FIRE, NIGHT QUALIFICATION FIRE	TIME ALLOWED	
	HRS	MIN
TOTAL:	4	

A-4. HOURS
The unit training program requires a total of 23 hours and 40 minutes:

SUMMARY OF HOURS	TIME ALLOWED	
	HRS	MIN
Period 1	3	
Period 2	3	10
Period 3	1	
Period 4	4	30
Period 5	4	
Period 6	4	
Period 7	4	
TOTAL:	23	40

A-5.   AMMUNITION

This paragraph summarizes ammunition required for the unit training program. Leaders should check STRAC requirements in DA Pamphlet 350-38.

   a.   **M249 Machine Gun**. See Table A-1.

TABLE	ROUNDS	TYPE
I Practice	185	Ball
I Record	91	Ball
II Practice	182	4:1
II Record	154	4:1
III Practice	371	4:1
III Record	154	4:1

Table A-1. M249 ammunition requirements.

   b.   **M60 and M240B Machine Guns**. See Table A-2.

TABLE	ROUNDS	TYPE
I Practice	231	Ball
I Record	117	Ball
II Practice	236	4:1
II Record	200	4:1
III Instructional	460	4:1
III Record	200	4:1

Table A-2. M60 and M240B ammunition requirements.

APPENDIX B
PROFICIENCY (PERFORMANCE) EXAMINATION

A proficiency examination determines if a soldier can perform all the tasks taught in the dry-fire training. This appendix is a guide for administering the examination to gunners.

B-1. DRY-FIRE PROFICIENCY EXAMINATION
The examination is a practical nonfiring exercise given during the last period of instruction on the machine gun before range firing. It may be held indoors if there are available facilities. The soldier must demonstrate techniques for the following tasks:
- General disassembly and assembly.
- Placement of direction and elevation readings on the T&E mechanism.
- Immediate action.
- Field zeroing.
- Engagement of a linear and a deep target.

B-2. CONDUCT OF THE EXAMINATION
Leaders can use the following schedule or modify it to fit their unit's training.
- Orientation, instructions, breakdown, and movement—15 minutes.
- Five stations—30 minutes each.
- Two breaks—10 minutes each.
- Four movement periods—5 minutes each.
- Total time—3 hours, 25 minutes.

B-3. STATION 1: PERFORM GENERAL DISASSEMBLY AND ASSEMBLY
This station normally has 11 setups. Each has one tripod-mounted machine gun with cover raised, bolt forward, and safety on the "F" position. This is placed on a mat to keep the parts free of dirt.

a. The following statement should be read at this station:

"DURING THIS PERIOD, YOU WILL BE ORGANIZED INTO THREE GROUPS AND REQUIRED TO DISASSEMBLE AND ASSEMBLE THE MACHINE GUN. THERE WILL BE ONE MACHINE GUN AND ONE GRADER FOR EVERY TWO GUNNERS. EACH GROUP WILL BE ALLOWED EIGHT MINUTES TO COMPLETE GENERAL DISASSEMBLY AND ASSEMBLY. IF YOU HAVE ANY TROUBLE, RAISE YOUR HAND AND THE GRADER WILL ASSIST YOU. THE TWO GROUPS NOT BEING TESTED WILL REMAIN TO THE REAR OF THE STATION WITH THEIR BACKS TOWARDS THE WORKING AREA UNTIL THEY ARE CALLED."

b. A scoresheet, like the example in Figure B-1, should be used in grading individual performance.

c. As each group completes this station, each grader should assemble the individuals he graded and gives them a thorough critique (6 minutes).

STATION 1: CHECKLIST
PERFORM GENERAL DISASSEMBLY AND ASSEMBLY
1. Cleared the machine gun using the procedures prescribed.
2. Disassembled the machine gun as prescribed for that machine gun.
    a. Removed the buttstock and buffer assembly.
    b. Removed the driving spring rod assembly.
    c. Removed the bolt and operating rod assembly. (Bolt is not separated from operating rod)
    d. Removed the trigger housing assembly.
    e. Removed the cover assembly.
    f. Removed the feed tray.
    g. Removed the barrel assembly hand heat shield.
    h. Removed the handguard from the receiver.
3. Assembled the machine gun as prescribed for that machine gun.
    a. Replaced the handguard on the receiver.
    b. Replaced the barrel assembly and heat shield.
    c. Replaced the cover assembly and feed tray.
    d. Replaced the trigger assembly.
    e. Replaced the bolt and operating rod assembly.
    f. Replaced the driving spring rod assembly.
    g. Replaced the buttstock, pulled the bolt to the rear, closed the cover, and pulled the trigger.
4. Completed task in 8 minutes.

TASK: GENERAL DISASSEMBLY AND ASSEMBLY	GO	NO GO
1. Cleared the machine gun using the procedures prescribed.		
2. Disassembled the machine gun as prescribed for that machine gun.		
a. Removed the buttstock and buffer assembly.		
b. Removed the driving spring rod assembly.		
c. Removed the bolt and operating rod assembly. (Bolt is not separated from operating rod.)		
d. Removed the trigger housing assembly		
e. Removed the cover assembly.		
f. Removed the feed tray.		
g. Removed the barrel assembly hand heat shield.		
h. Removed the handguard from the receiver.		
3. Assembled the machine gun as prescribed for that machine gun.		
a. Replaced the handguard on the receiver.		
b. Replaced the barrel assembly with the heat shield.		
c. Replaced the cover assembly and feed tray.		
d. Replaced the trigger assembly.		
e. Replaced the bolt and operating rod assembly.		
f. Replaced the driving spring rod assembly.		
g. Replaced the buttstock, pulled the bolt to the rear, closed the cover, and pulled the trigger.		
4. Completed task in 8 minutes.		

Figure B-1. Example format for Station 1 scoresheet.

B-4.   STATION 2: PLACE DIRECTION AND ELEVATION READINGS ON THE T&E MECHANISM

This station normally has 11 setups. Each has one tripod-mounted machine gun complete with pintle and platform group and traversing-and-elevating mechanism.

a.   For the first direction reading, the grader should ensure that the traversing slide is an even 5-mil graduation on the traversing bar. The gunner is required to place 1 to 4 mils on the traversing handwheel; for example, L242. This requires the gunner to center the traversing mechanism before he can place the next direction reading on it. The second direction reading should be in the opposite direction; for example, R240. The second elevation reading should also be a major change: +50/32 to -50/17.

b.   The following statement should be read at this station:

"DURING THIS PERIOD, YOU WILL BE ORGANIZED INTO THREE GROUPS AND REQUIRED TO PLACE TWO SETS OF READINGS ON THE TRIPOD-MOUNTED MACHINE GUN. A GRADER WILL CHECK YOUR FIRST SET OF READINGS BEFORE YOU PLACE THE SECOND SET ON THE TRIPOD-MOUNT MACHINE GUN. YOU WILL BE ALLOWED EIGHT MINUTES AT THIS STATION. IF YOU HAVE ANY TROUBLE, RAISE YOUR HAND AND THE GRADER WILL ASSIST YOU. THE TWO GROUPS NOT BEING TESTED WILL REMAIN TO THE REAR OF THE STATION WITH THEIR BACKS TOWARDS THE WORK AREA UNTIL THEY ARE CALLED."

c.   A scoresheet, like the example in Figure B-2, should be used in grading individual performance.

d.   As each group completes this station, each grader should assemble the individuals he graded and gives them a thorough critique (6 minutes).

STATION 2: CHECKLIST
PLACE DIRECTION AND ELEVATION READINGS ON THE T&E MECHANISM

1.   Placed first set of readings on the T&E mechanism.
    a.   Centered the traversing handwheel.
    b.   Placed direction reading on T&E mechanism.
    c.   Placed elevation reading on T&E mechanism.
2.   Placed second set of readings on the T&E mechanism.
    a.   Placed direction reading on T&E mechanism.
    b.   Placed elevation reading on T&E mechanism.
3.   Completed task in 8 minutes.

TASK: PLACE DIRECTION AND ELEVATION READINGS ON THE T&E MECHANISM	GO	NO GO
1. Placed first set of readings on the T&E mechanism.		
a. Centered the traversing handwheel.		
b. Placed direction reading on T&E mechanism.		
c. Placed elevation reading on T&E mechanism.		
2. Placed second set of readings on T&E mechanism.		
a. Placed directing reading on T&E mechanism.		
b. Placed elevation reading on T&E mechanism.		
3. Completed task in 8 minutes.		

Figure B-2. Example format for Station 2 scoresheet.

B-5.   STATION 3: PERFORM IMMEDIATE ACTION
This station normally has six setups. Each has a cleaning rod and a bipod-mounted machine gun with bolt forward, cover closed, and safety on "F" position.

   a.   The grader should ask the individual to perform immediate action as he would if a round were in the chamber and would not fire providing the barrel was not hot enough to cause a cook off.

   b.   The following statement should be read at this station:
   "DURING THIS PERIOD, YOU WILL BE ORGANIZED INTO FIVE GROUPS AND REQUIRED TO GO THROUGH THE STEPS OF IMMEDIATE ACTION AND REMEDIAL ACTION WITH THE MACHINE GUN. YOU WILL BE ALLOWED FIVE MINUTES. IF YOU HAVE ANY TROUBLE, RAISE YOUR HAND AND A GRADER WILL ASSIST YOU. THE GROUPS NOT BEING TESTED WILL REMAIN TO THE REAR OF THE STATION WITH THEIR BACKS TOWARDS THE WORK AREA UNTIL THEY ARE CALLED."

   c.   A scoresheet, like the example in Figure B-3, should be used in grading individual performance.

   d.   As each group completes this station, each grader assembles the individuals that he graded and gives them a thorough critique (5 minutes).

STATION 3: CHECKLIST
PERFORM IMMEDIATE ACTION
1. Pulled the cocking handle to the rear.
2. Observed a round, cartridge or linked being extracted from the machine gun.
3. Returned cocking handle to the forward position.
4. Attempted to fire the machine gun.
5. If the machine gun did not fire, pulled the cocking handle to the rear, locking the bolt assembly to the rear.
6. Place the safety on "S" and returned cocking handle to the forward position.
7. If machine gun was hot, kept it pointed downrange and waited 15 minutes, then performed remedial action. If machine gun was cold, performed remedial action.
8. Completed the task in 5 minutes.

TASK: IMMEDIATE ACTION	GO	NO GO
1. Pulled the cocking handle to the rear.		
2. Observed a round, cartridge or linked being extracted from the machine gun.		
3. Returned cocking handle to the forward position.		
4. Attempted to fire the machine gun.		
5. If the machine gun did not fire, pulled the cocking handle to the rear, locking the bolt assembly to the rear.		
6. Placed the safety on "S" and returned the cocking handle to the forward position.		
7. When machine gun was hot, kept it pointed downrange, waited 15 minutes, then performed remedial action. When machine gun was cold, performed remedial action.		
8. Completed the task in 5 minutes.		

Figure B-3. Example format for Station 3 scoresheet.

B-6. STATION 4: PERFORM FIELD ZEROING

This station normally has six setups. Each has a bipod-mounted machine gun with tools needed.

a. The grader tells each individual the range (500 meters) to the target and has him simulate the firing of a 7-round burst (M249) or 9-round burst (M60/M240B). The grader then tells the individual what corrections for deflection and elevation (in meters) are needed to hit the target. The gunner is then graded on his actions.

b. The following statement should be read at this station:

"DURING THIS PERIOD, YOU WILL BE ORGANIZED INTO FIVE GROUPS AND REQUIRED TO GO THROUGH THE STEPS OF FIELD ZEROING. YOU WILL BE ALLOWED FIVE MINUTES TO PERFORM AND EXPLAIN YOUR ACTIONS TO THE GRADER. IF YOU HAVE ANY PROBLEM, ASK YOUR GRADER. THE GROUPS NOT BEING TESTED WILL REMAIN TO THE REAR OF THE STATION WITH THEIR BACKS TOWARDS THE WORK AREA UNTIL THEY ARE CALLED."

c. A scoresheet, like the example in Figure B-4, should be used in grading individual performance.

d. As each group completes this station, each grader assembles the individuals that he graded and gives them a thorough critique (5 minutes).

STATION 4: CHECKLIST
PERFORM FIELD ZEROING
1. Placed the range setting on 500 meters.
2. Made corrections for deflection.
3. Made corrections for elevation.
4. Simulated firing the second burst and hitting the target.
5. Completed task in 5 minutes.

TASK: FIELD ZEROING	GO	NO GO
1. Placed the range setting on 500 meters.		
2. Made corrections for deflection.		
3. Made corrections for elevation.		
4. Simulated firing the second burst and hitting the target.		
5. Completed task in 5 minutes.		

Figure B-4. Example format for Station 4 scoresheet.

B-7. STATION 5: ENGAGE A LINEAR AND A DEEP TARGET
This station normally has six setups. Each should have a punchboard-type training aid or a blackboard and chalk.

a. The individual is required to show his point of initial lay, direction of manipulation, and extent of manipulation for a linear (single machine gun) and a deep target (pair of machine guns). The individual is also asked what rate of fire he would use to engage these targets if the rate were not stated in the fire command.

b. The following statement should be read at this station:
"DURING THIS PERIOD, YOU WILL BE ORGANIZED INTO FIVE GROUPS AND REQUIRED TO EXPLAIN HOW TO ENGAGE DIFFERENT TARGETS WITH THE MACHINE GUN EMPLOYED SINGLY AND IN PAIRS. YOU WILL BE ALLOWED FIVE MINUTES FOR SIMULATED ENGAGEMENT OF TWO TYPES OF TARGETS. IF YOU HAVE ANY QUESTIONS, ASK YOUR GRADER. THE GROUPS NOT BEING TESTED WILL REMAIN TO THE REAR OF THE STATION WITH BACKS TOWARDS THE WORK AREA UNTIL THEY ARE CALLED."

c. A scoresheet, like the example in Figure B-5, should be used in grading individual performance.

d. As each group completes this station, each grader assembles the individuals that he graded and gives them a thorough critique (5 minutes).

STATION 5: CHECKLIST
ENGAGE A LINEAR AND A DEEP TARGET
1. Engaged a linear target (single machine gun).
    a. Used initial point of aim.
    b. Manipulated T&E mechanism.
    c. Used sustained rate of fire.
2. Engaged a deep target (pair of machine guns).
    a. Used initial point of aim.
    b. Manipulated T&E mechanism.
    c. Used sustained rate of fire.
3. Completed task in 5 minutes.

TASK: ENGAGE A LINEAR AND A DEEP TARGET	GO	NO GO
1. Engaged a linear target (single machine gun).		
a. Used initial point of aim.		
b. Manipulated T&E mechanism.		
c. Used sustained rate of fire.		
2. Engaged a deep target (pair of machine guns).		
a. Used initial point of aim.		
b. Manipulated T&E mechanism.		
c. Used sustained rate of fire.		
3. Completed task in 5 minutes.		

Figure B-5. Example format for Station 5 scoresheet.

APPENDIX C
AERIAL DEFENSE

This appendix describes the use of machine guns in an air defense role, including the concept and two techniques for applying lead. Also discussed are the rules of engagement and firing positions.

C-1. PASSIVE AND ACTIVE MEASURES

A unit can take passive and active measures to defend itself against enemy air attack. Although volume fire is the key, there is a need to coordinate fires.

a. Passive measures are those that help the unit identify enemy aircraft before the aircraft locates the unit, make the unit difficult to locate, and make the unit less vulnerable when attacked. The unit must develop and practice camouflage as a passive measure. Concealment from the air must be considered when selecting routes, transportation means, or defensive positions. The use of air guards is important to give the unit time to react. Air guards should cover interlocking sectors of visible airspace.

b. Active measures for appropriate reactions to an air attack should be prescribed in unit SOPs. Each of the two techniques for applying lead is based on delivering a heavy volume of fire ahead of the target. The idea is to have every soldier in the unit engage the target. To achieve volume fire, soldiers armed with machine guns should fire at the cyclic rate.

c. If an aircraft is attacking his position, the soldier sees the aircraft in a head-on or diving view. To engage this aircraft, the soldier would fire slightly above the nose of the aircraft. Adjacent positions would see the aircraft in a crossing view. To engage the aircraft, these units would have to apply a proper lead. The method of applying lead depends on the technique used.

(1) *Football-Field Technique.* When engaging high-performance aircraft (those flying in excess of 200 mph), gunners should apply a one-football-field lead in front of the target and fire at the rapid rate until the target passes through the tracer stream. If the target is a low-performance aircraft, such as a helicopter, with a speed of 200 mph or less, gunners should apply half a football-field lead in front of the target, firing the cyclic rate. With all soldiers firing, a curtain of fire is formed because of slight differences in each soldier's estimate of the distance and lead.

(2) *Reference-Point Technique.* The unit leader designates terrain features as reference points. Upon spotting enemy aircraft, the leader commands, ENEMY AIR, REFERENCE POINT 1. At this time, the gunner points his weapon at reference point 1, elevates the weapon to about 45 degrees above the ground, and fires on command. Once he sights the target, he can make minor adjustments to align his fire on the target.

C-2. USE OF TRACERS

When planning for air defense, the leader should consider the use of tracers so that the gunner can observe the tracer stream and better align his fire on the target. A unit may engage an attacking aircraft without command. If an aircraft is not attacking, the unit may not fire on it unless ordered to do so.

C-3. FIRING POSITION

When firing the machine gun in an air defense role, the gunner should fire from a protected position, if possible. When not in a fighting position, he must position the weapon so that he has some type of support. In an emergency, another soldier can provide a firing support.

APPENDIX D
RANGE SAFETY

This appendix recommends safety precautions for the ranges described in this manual, but it does not replace AR 385-63 or local regulations. Range safety requirements vary because of the varied requirements of the courses of fire.

D-1. SAFETY PRECAUTIONS
The following safety precautions must be observed during all marksmanship training:

a. Display a red flag (red light for night firing) at the entrance to the range or in some other prominent location on the range during firing.

b. Always assume that weapons are loaded until they have been thoroughly examined and found to contain no ammunition and barrel is clear.

c. Mark firing limits with red-and-white-striped poles that are visible to all firers.

d. Never place obstructions in the muzzles of weapons about to be fired.

e. Keep all weapons in a prescribed area and proper safeguards when not in use.

f. Do not permit smoking near ammunition, explosives, or flammables.

g. Wear hearing-protection devices during firing.

D-2. RANGE PROCEDURES
The range can be a dangerous place, especially if safety procedures are not followed. Everyone must stay alert and adhere to the following precautions:

a. **Before Firing.**

(1) Close all prescribed roadblocks and barriers, and post necessary guards.

(2) Check all weapons to ensure that they are clear of ammunition and obstructions, and that the cover-feed mechanism assemblies are *up* to show they are cleared.

(3) Brief all personnel on the firing limits of the range and firing lanes.

(4) Obtain range clearance from the installation range-control office.

(5) Check the downrange area before firing to ensure that all personnel and equipment are clear of the area.

(6) Keep a complete first-aid kit on the range.

(7) Locate medical personnel on or near the range where they can be contacted quickly.

(8) Have all weapons checked by an officer or noncommissioned officer to ensure that they are operational.

(9) Do not handle weapons except on command from the tower operator or the officer in charge.

(10) Draw ammunition and issue it only on command of the officer in charge. When two or more lots of ammunition are used for firing, the officer in charge must ensure that the lots are separated and properly marked so that identification can be made by lot numbers in case of an accident or malfunction.

(11) Protect all ammunition from the direct rays of the sun.

(12) Do not allow anyone to move forward of the firing line without permission of the tower operator, safety officer, or officer in charge.

b. **During Firing.**

(1) Immediately order "CEASE FIRE" if an unsafe condition is noted during firing. Do not resume firing until directed to by the officer in charge.

(2) During firing, all personnel on the range must be aware of the danger in moving forward of the firing line to score their targets. Before the firing line is clear and anyone is allowed forward, the officer in charge or the safety officer will clear all weapons.

(3) The safety officer or NCO inspects each weapon that was fired on the firing line by making sure the bolt is locked to the rear and the safety is on. He makes sure each barrel is clear by running a cleaning rod through the barrel until he can see the end of the rod in the receiver. He performs the safety check.

c. **When Firing During Darkness.**

(1) Check the downrange area before firing to ensure that all personnel and equipment are clear of the area. This is accomplished by asking three times over a public address system, "IS THERE ANYONE DOWNRANGE?" Always pause each time to permit a response.

(2) Use a blinking red light in addition to the red flag. Display it at the entrance to the range or at some other prominent location.

(3) Mount two red lights on the striped poles marking the right and left limits of fire. They must be visible to all firers.

(4) Do not allow anyone to move from his position until told to do so by the officer in charge.

d. **After Firing.**

(1) Have safety personnel inspect all weapons to ensure that they are clear, and check to determine if the soldiers have any brass, links, or live ammunition.

(2) When weapons have been cleared, keep them in a prescribed area with the bolt forward and safety on.

APPENDIX E
EMPLOYMENT

Despite their Post-Civil War development, modern machine guns did not exhibit their full potential in battle until World War I. Although the machine gun has changed, the role of the machine gunner has not. The mission of machine guns in battle is to deliver fires when and where the leader wants them in both the offense and defense. Machine guns rarely, if ever, have independent missions. Instead, they provide their unit with accurate, heavy fires to accomplish the mission. This appendix provides information on three machine guns: the M249 light machine gun and the M60 and M240B general-purpose machine guns.

E-1. TACTICAL ORGANIZATION OF THE MACHINE GUN

The accomplishment of the mission demands an efficient machine gun crew who can fulfill all assigned missions. Each leader considers the mission and organizes machine guns to deliver firepower and fire support to any area or point needed to accomplish the assigned mission. Such organization takes time to achieve and reduces the flexibility of the unit.

E-2. MACHINE GUN IN THE ATTACK

The potential increase of air and ground attacks on the unit demands every possible precaution for maximum security while on the move. Where this situation exists, the machine gun crew must be thoroughly trained in the hasty delivery of antiaircraft fire and of counterfires against enemy ground forces. The distribution of the machine guns in the formation is critical. The machine gun crew is constantly on the alert, particularly at halts, ready to deliver fire as soon as possible. If the leader expects a halt to exceed a brief period, he carefully chooses machine gun positions to avoid unduly tiring the machine gun crew. If he expects the halt to extend for a long period, he can have the machine gun crew take up positions in support of the unit. They cover the direction from which he expects enemy activity as well as the direction the unit came from. He selects positions that permit the delivery of fire in the most probable direction of attack, such as into valleys, draws, ridges, and spurs. He chooses positions that offer obstructed fire.

a. **Machine Gun in the Offense.**

(1) *General Discussion.* Successful offensive operations result from the employment of fire and maneuver. Each is essential and greatly depends upon the other. Without the support of covering fires, maneuvering in the presence of enemy fire can result in disastrous losses. Covering fires, especially those that provide fire superiority, allow maneuvering in the offense. However, fire superiority alone rarely wins battles. The primary objective of the offense is to advance, occupy, and hold the enemy position.

(2) *Machine Gun.* The machine gun delivers an accurate, high-volume rate of fire on fairly large areas in a brief time. It is a great power to have on any offensive operation. When accurately placed on the enemy position, machine gun fires secure the essential element of fire superiority for the duration of the firing. Troops advancing in the attack should take full advantage of this period to maneuver to a favorable position from which

to facilitate the last push against the enemy. In addition to casualties, machine gun fire destroys the enemy's confidence and neutralizes his [actions in the?] defense.

(3) *Early Entry*. The early entry of machine guns in the offense is, with rare exceptions, highly desirable. Their continued action up to the moment of the assault enhances the probability of success. One desirable feature for employment of machine guns in the offense requires a proper handling of the ammunition for each machine gun. The other feature is to determine the actions of the machine gun crew to handle their weapon on the battlefield in order to deliver fire with the objective to support the maneuver unit at the time it is needed, regardless of physical difficulties encountered

(a) The machine guns seldom accompany the maneuver element. The gun's primary mission is to provide covering fire. The machine guns are only employed with the maneuver element when the area or zone of action assigned to the assault or company is too narrow to permit proper control of the guns. The machine guns are then moved with the unit and readied to employ on order from the leader and in the direction needing the supporting fire.

(b) Where the area or zone of action is too wide to allow proper coverage by the machine guns, the unit is assigned additional machine guns or personnel from within the battalion to permit the unit to accomplish its assigned mission. The machine guns are assigned a zone or a sector to cover and they move with the maneuver element.

(c) Under certain terrain conditions and for proper control, the machine guns move with the unit and are assigned a zone or sector to cover.

(d) When machine guns move with the unit undertaking the assault, the unit brings its machine guns to provide additional firepower. These weapons are fired either from the bipod or in an assault mode, from the hip or underarm position. They target enemy automatic weapons anywhere on the unit's objective. Once the enemy's automatic weapons have been destroyed, or if there are none, the gunners distribute their fire over their assigned zone or sector. In terms of engagement ranges, the machine gun in the assault engages within 300 meters of its target and frequently at point blank ranges.

c. **Machine Gun in a Base-of-Fire Element**. Machine guns organic to the company can help battalion machine guns lay the base of fire. In this case, the leader positions and controls the fires of all machine guns in the element. Machine gun targets include key enemy weapons or groups of enemy targets either on the objective or attempting to reinforce or counterattack. In terms of engagement ranges, machine guns in the base-of-fire element may find themselves firing at targets within 800 meters of the target. These ranges are simply a practical average. The nature of the terrain and desire to achieve some standoff, leads the leader to the correct tactical positioning of the base-of-fire element.

E-3.   MACHINE GUN IN THE DEFENSE

Machine gun fire is distributed in width and depth in a defensive position. The leader can use machine guns to subject the enemy to increasingly devastating fire from the initial phases of his attack, and to neutralize any partial successes the enemy might attain by delivering intense fires in support of counterattacks. The machine gun's tremendous firepower is what enables the unit to hold ground. This is what makes them the backbone or framework of the defense.

a. The units' defense centers around the platoon's machine guns. The platoon leader sites the rifle squad to protect the machine guns against the assault of a dismounted enemy formation. The machine gun provides the requisite range and volume of fire to cover the squad front in the defense.

b. The primary requirement of a suitable machine gun position in the defense is that the machine gun be able to accomplish its specific missions. Secondarily, the position should be accessible and afford cover and concealment. Machine guns are sited to protect the front, flanks, and rear of occupied portions of the defensive position, and to be mutually supporting. Attacking troops usually seek easily traveled ground that provides cover from fire. This is not to say that they will avoid marshes, rough grounds, wooded areas, or any other type of terrain. Every machine gun should have three positions: primary, alternate, and supplementary. All of these positions should be chosen by the leader to ensure his sector is covered and that the machine guns are protected on their flanks.

c. The leader sites his machine gun to cover the entire sector or to overlap sectors with the other machine gun. The engagement range of a leader's weapon may extend from the last 300 meters where the enemy begins his assault to point-blank range. Machine gun targets include enemy automatic weapons and command and control elements.

E-4. MACHINE GUN ON A SECURITY MISSION

Security includes all command measures to protect against surprise, observation, and annoyance by the enemy. The principal security measures against ground forces include employment of security patrols and detachments covering the front flanks and rear of the units' most vulnerable areas. The composition and strength of these detachments depends on the size of the main body, its mission, and the nature of the opposition expected. The presence of machine guns with security detachments augments their firepower to effectively delay, attack, and defend, by virtue of their inherent firepower. When the machine guns are used as part of the security detachments in battalion trains or larger, the proportion of machine guns in such a detachment varies according to the situation. The main mission of the machine gun is to protect and defend through both defensive and offensive missions. For defense, the unit's main mission is to position the machine guns throughout the assigned area. For offense, the second mission, after a successful delay against an enemy attack, the unit expands its security outpost as needed to prevent another enemy attack.

APPENDIX F
TRAINING AIDS AND DEVICES

Training aids and devices must be included in a marksmanship program. This appendix lists those that units can make from materials most units have on-hand.

F-1. TRAINING DEVICES AND EXERCISES
The marksmanship training devices in this appendix are available to aid in sustainment training when used with the appropriate training strategies. These devices are beneficial when ammunition is limited for training or practice. Some training devices are complex and costly, but others are relatively simple and cheap to make. Devices and aids can be used alone or in combination. Individuals or squads can sustain or practice basic marksmanship skills and fundamentals with devices and aids.

F-2. FIRST SIGHTING AND AIMING EXERCISE
The purpose of the first sighting and aiming exercise is to teach the correct alignment of the sights on a target.

    a. **Equipment Needed**:

        One—sighting bar complete for each machine gun crew.

        One—sighting target that measures 1 inch X 2 inches X 48 inches long. The sighting target is secured 5 1/2 inches away from one end (it should be moveable). The eyepiece is secured on the other end. The peep sight is secured 20 1/2 inches from the sighting target and 22 inches from the eyepiece (Figure F-1).

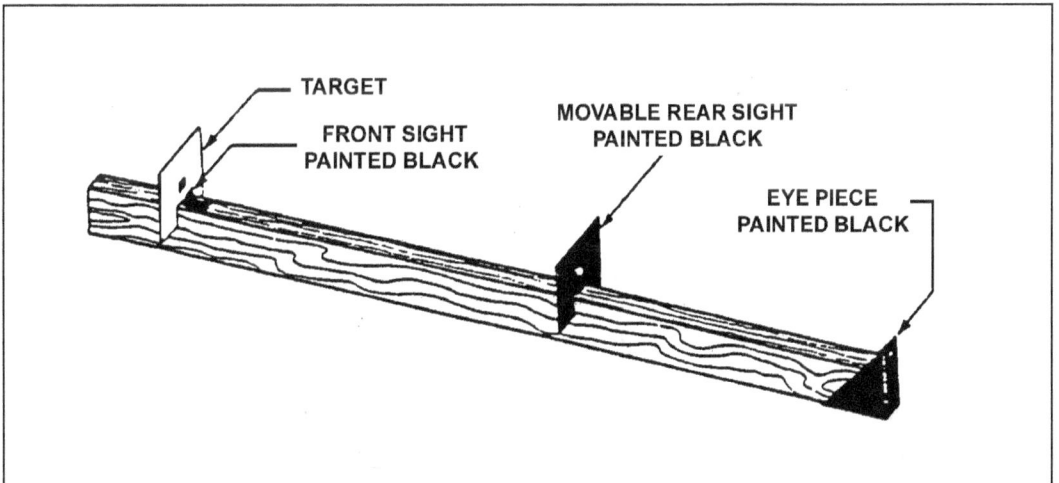

Figure F-1. Sighting bar.

    b. **Conduct**. The instructor shows a sighting bar to the machine gun crews, points out its parts, and explains its use as follows:

    (1) The sighting bar is used to assist in detecting small errors and in explaining them to the crews undergoing instruction.

(2) The front and rear sights on the sighting bar represent enlarged machine gun sights.

(3) The gunner looks through the eyepiece in such a position that he sees the sights in exactly the same alignment as the instructor does. Although there is no eyepiece on the machine gun, the use of an eyepiece on the sighting bar assists the gunners in learning how to align the sights properly when using the machine gun.

(4) The attachment of the removable target to the end of the sighting bar provides a simple method of readily aligning the sights on the target.

(5) Using a blackboard or a chart, the instructor explains and illustrates the correct sight alignment.

(6) A gunner from each crew adjusts the sights of the sighting bar and movable target to correctly align the sights on the target.

F-3. SECOND SIGHTING AND AIMING EXERCISE
The purpose of the second sighting and aiming exercise is to apply the preceding lesson to actual alignment of the machine gun sights on a target 25 meters away.

   a. **Equipment Needed:**

      One—Machine gun.

      One—Basic machine gun target placed 25 meters away, with the reverse (blank) side showing.

      One—Sighting target, 24 inches long 1 inch X 1 inch, a 3-inch square piece of wood painted black with a small 1/4-inch hole in the center (Figure F-2).

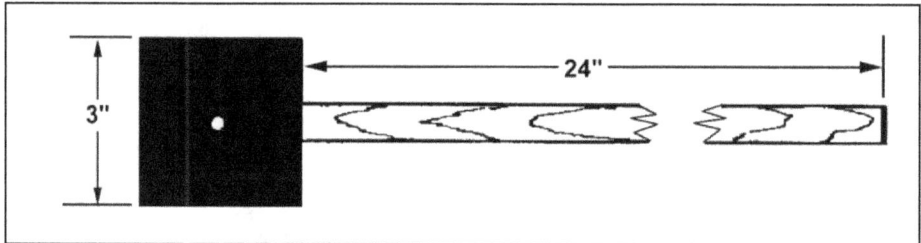

Figure F-2. Sighting target.

   b. **Conduct.** The instructor takes a normal position behind the machine gun, keeping his body and hands clear of the gun so that the eye is in the correct position for aiming.

(1) The gunner takes a position near enough to observe the instructor.

(2) The assistant gunner stands near the instructor to transmit signals to the ammunition bearer.

(3) The ammunition bearer is provided with the 3-inch sighting target and is posted as the marker at the blank target, which is 25 meters away from the gun.

(4) The instructor, through improvising signals transmitted through the signalman, directs the marker to move the sighting target until it correctly aligns with the sights, and then commands: HOLD.

(5) The marker complies, holding the sighting target in place on the blank target. The gunner and assistant gunner then look through the sights.

(6) The instructor explains that, in aiming, the gunner's eye should first focus on the target, to ensure that he is aiming at the proper target. His eye then focuses on the top of

the front sight, to ensure that the line-of-sight established passes through the center of the peep sight and over the top of the center of the front sight.

(7) After the gunner and assistant gunner look through the sight, the instructor directs the marker (ammunition bearer) to move the sighting target out of alignment. He then requires the gunner to direct the marker to move the sighting target until it is in correct alignment with the sights.

(8) The instructor checks the alignment made by the gunner and points out any errors. When the instructor believes the gunner is proficient, the assistant gunner begins his exercise.

F-4. THIRD SIGHTING AND AIMING EXERCISE

The purpose of the third sighting and aiming exercise is to show the importance of uniform and correct aiming and to instill in the gunners a sense of exactness. This exercise can be used to check the consistency of the aiming and placement of a three-round shot group in a dry-fire environment.

   a. **Equipment Needed**:

   One—Machine gun.

   One—Basic machine gun target placed at a distance of 25 meters away with the reverse (blank) side showing.

   One—Sighting target (24 inches long 1 inch X 1 inch, a 3-inch square piece of wood painted black and a small 1/4-inch hole in the center) (Figure F-2).

   b. **Conduct**. The instructor takes a normal position behind the machine gun, keeping his body and hands clear of the gun so that the eye is in the correct position for aiming.

(1) The gunner takes a position near the instructor to observe.

(2) The assistant gunner stands near the instructor to transmit signals to the ammunition bearer.

(3) The ammunition bearer is provided with a 3-inch sighting target and is posted as the marker at the blank target, which is 25 meters away from the gun.

(4) The instructor, improvising signals, transmits through the signalman to direct the marker to move the sighting target until it is in correct alignment with the sights and then commands: MARK.

(5) The marker complies, holding the sighting target in place on the blank target. The marker marks the position by inserting the tip of a pencil through the 1/4-inch hole in the center of the target. The marker marks the first dot with a number 1, second with a 2 and the third with a 3, ensuring the marker moves the target after every mark. All three dots should fit inside a 4-cm circle.

(6) The instructor explains that, in aiming, the gunner's eye should first be focused on the target to ascertain that he is aiming at the proper target. His eye is then focused on the top of the front sight to ensure the line of sighting established is a line through the center of the peep sight and over the top of the center of the front sight.

(7) The gunner and assistant gunner, without touching the gun, repeat the operation until three dots have been made and numbered.

(8) The instructor now explains the errors noted in the three sight alignments and the probable shape of the shot group formed by joining the three dots. Repeat as many times as needed until the gunner and assistant gunner can put seven rounds inside a 4-cm circle. The grader marks the first dot with a number 1, the second with a number 2 and the third

with a number 3. He makes sure the grader moves the target after every mark. When the instructor believes the gunner is proficient, the assistant gunner begins his exercise.

(9) The marker traces the three dots on a sheet of paper and connects them with lines. He writes the gunner's name at the bottom of the sheet and gives the paper to the squad leader.

F-5. MACHINE GUN T&E MANIPULATION DRILLS

The purpose of these exercises is to teach and instill confidence in the gunner in properly using his T&E. These exercises are conducted on a 25-meter line.

a. **Equipment Needed:**

One—Machine gun.

One—4-foot X 8-foot sheet of plywood. Paint the plywood white with black ruled lines of 1/8-inch width horizontally and vertically. The horizontal lines are 2 inches apart, starting 1 inch from the top and the bottom. The vertical lines are 3 inches apart, with 1 inch on either side.

(1) Label the horizontal lines starting from the top with 1, 3 and so on skipping every other line. Label the vertical lines along the middle horizontal line starting at the left; for example, A, B, C and so on (Figure F-3).

(2) When using the night vision sight, cut out a 4-cm-square circle from every four squares across and down. The squares or circles can be cut in any order the unit leader desires.

(3) Set up the machine 25 meters away from the target. Center the machine gun on the target.

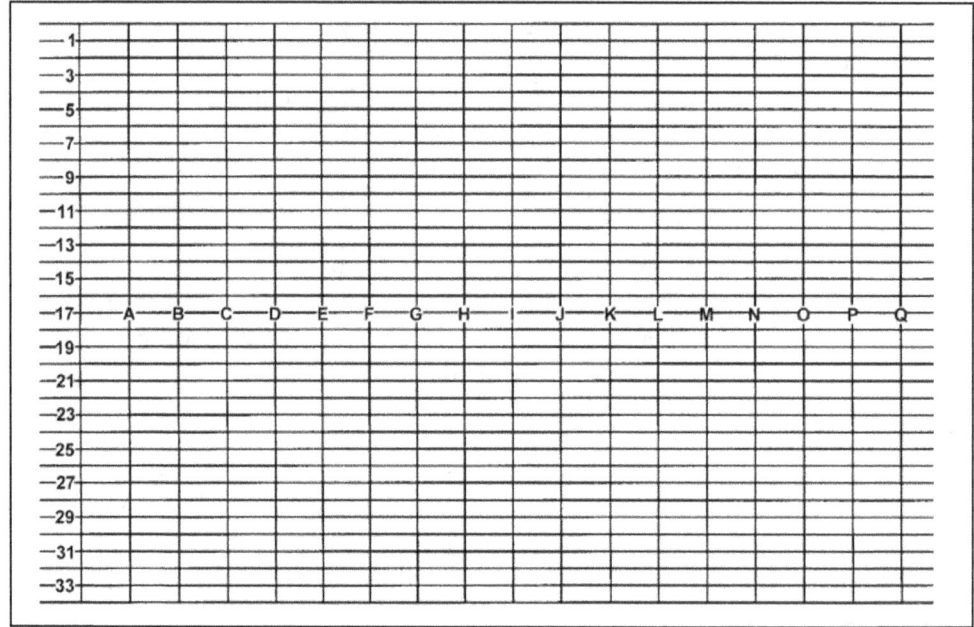

Figure F-3. Manipulator for T&E drills.

b. **Conduct.**

(1) The gunner is given the command to aim at vertical line B and horizontal line 4. The next command is RIGHT 150 mils; ADD 50 mils. The instructor then asks the gunner where he is aiming.

(2) Lay on the horizontal line 15 and vertical line O. The next command is, LEFT 100 mils; ADD 10 mils. The instructor then asks the gunner where he is aiming now.

(3) The leader or instructor can have as many of these types of questions set up, until he feels the gunner is proficient at this task.

F-6. TRAVERSE AND SEARCH EXERCISE

The purpose of the traverse and search exercise is to teach the gunner how to aim and point on a silhouette target and maintain that aim while the target is moving.

a. **Equipment Needed:**

One—Machine gun.

One—Basic machine gun target placed at a distance of 25 meters away with the reverse (blank) side showing.

One—Marking silhouette measures 1 inch X 1/2 inch X 22 inches long (wood).

One—F-type silhouette (reduced by half its size) measuring 7 1/2 inches long X 3 3/4 high (Chapter 4).

b. **Conduct.** The instructor shows the target to the machine gun crews. He points out its parts and explains its use as follows:

(1) The gunner takes a normal position behind the machine gun. The gunner is required to aim at a prescribed point on the silhouette target and to maintain that aim during the uniform movement of the target.

(2) The assistant gunner takes a normal position next to the gunner. The assistant gunner assists the gunner in maintaining the point of aim.

(3) The ammunition bearer is located 25 meters away behind the basic machine gun target with the target. The bearer moves the target back and fourth, up and down in any direction he wants. The movement should be consistent and not uniform, so that the gunner and assistant gunner can get proper training. The speed that the ammunition bearer moves depends on the instructor.

(4) The instructor watches the gunner and determines if the gunner or assistant gunner is properly doing the exercise by telling the ammunition bearer to stop and hold. He informs the gunner or assistant gunner to stand.

(5) The instructor positions himself behind the gun and looks through the sights to see where the gunner or assistant gunner was aiming. The instructor now explains the errors noted. When the instructor believes the gunner is proficient, the assistant gunner begins his exercise.

F-7. ENGAGEMENT SKILLS TRAINER

The engagement skills trainer (EST) 2000 (Figure F-4, page F-6) is a home station, indoor, multipurpose, multilane, small arms simulator. The EST augments and substitutes individual, crew, and static-squad collective training. Using projected imagery and laser-light technologies, the EST 2000 provides weaponry that simulates the same physical, functional, operational characteristics, and capabilities of service weapons. Weaponry for the EST 2000 includes the M16A2 rifle, M4 carbine, M9 pistol, M249 automatic rifle/light machine gun, M60, M240B and M2 machine guns, MK 19 grenade machine gun, M136 AT4, M1200 shotgun, and M203 grenade launcher.

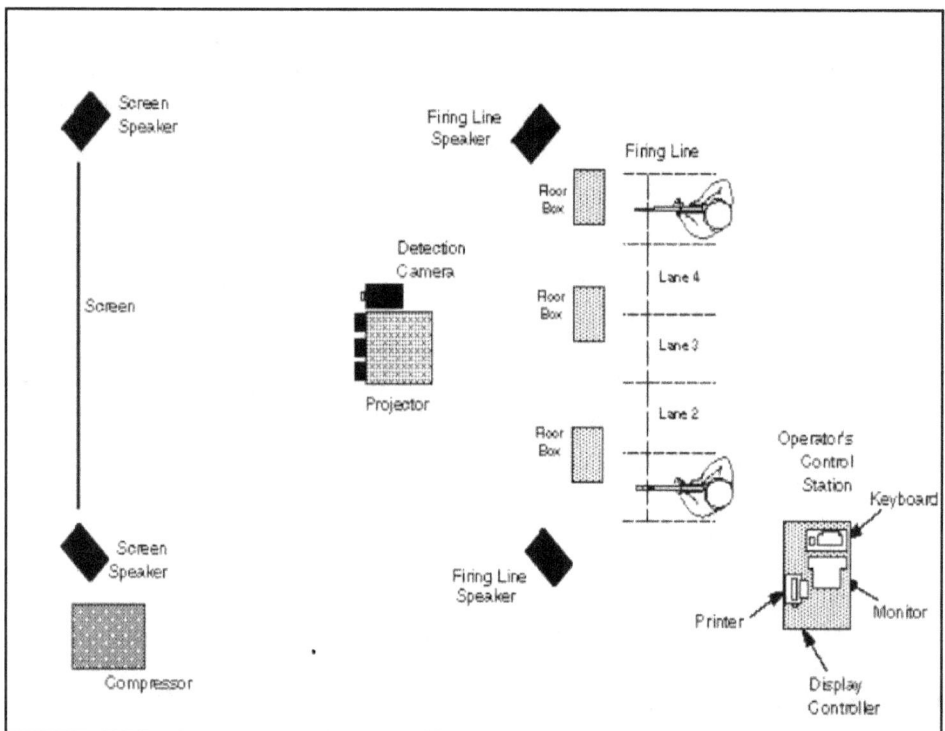

Figure F-4. EST 2000.

a. The EST 2000 is a modular system with an operational size of 35 feet by 35 feet by 8 feet high for a 10-lane system. Training programs include standard Army courses of fire, "shoot-don't shoot" decision training, and static-squad or element collective defensive training for infantry, scouts, engineers, military police, and CS or CSS. Basis of issue is one 15-lane EST 2,000 for each OSUT or BCT battalion supporting Initial Entry Training (IET) and one 10-lane EST 2,000 for each brigade-size element for Active and Reserve Component units for sustainment training.

b. The following tables (Tables F-1, F-2, and F-3) show the capabilities and limitations for each training program:

MARKSMANSHIP TRAINING PROGRAM	
209 marksmanship exercises, from zeroing through record-fire courses.	
Capabilities	**Limitations**
Train and sustain M16A2 rifle skills.	No qualification. No weather effects.
Train and sustain M4 carbine skills.	No qualification. No weather effects.
Train and sustain shotgun skills.	No qualification. No nonlethal munitions training.
Train and sustain M9 pistol skills.	No qualification. No weather effects.
Train and sustain light MG skills.	No maneuver training.
Train and sustain AR skills.	No maneuver training.
Train and sustain MMG skills.	No maneuver training.
Train and sustain M2 HB MG skills.	No maneuver training.
Train and sustain M203 GL skills.	No maneuver training. No nonlethal munitions.
Train and sustain MK 19 grenade MG skills.	No maneuver training.
Train antiarmor weapons employment.	No maneuver training.

Table F-1. Marksmanship training capabilities and limitations.

COLLECTIVE TRAINING PROGRAM	
178 squad tactical exercises against varying enemy targets, in terrain that varies from woodlands, desert, urban, and mountains that are typical of terrain found throughout the world.	
Capabilities	**Limitations**
Train and sustain defensive operations.	No offensive operations.
Train and sustain overwatch operations.	Nontactical interaction.
Train and sustain passage of lines.	Overwatch only.
Train and sustain ambush operations.	Limited eye points. Restricted interaction with on-screen CGI forces.
NOTE: No effects of weather and firing position distances under squad leader and fire-team leader control.	

Table F-2. Collective training capabilities and limitations.

"SHOOT-DON'T SHOOT" TRAINING PROGRAM	
40 "shoot-don't shoot" judgmental exercises.	
Capabilities	**Limitations**
Train and test rules of engagement.	No shoot back. No nonlethal training mode.
Train target selection under stress.	No shoot back.
Train target engagement under stress.	No shoot back.
Train verbal skills to deescalate.	No direct adversary reactions.

Table F-3. "Shoot-don't shoot" training capabilities and limitations.

c. The EST trains many skills, but it is not intended to replace live qualification or MILES force-on-force tactical training. Its many capabilities are clearly definable, but its limitations preclude total elimination of training ammunition resources. Training on the EST is planned to save ammunition resources, both at the assistant gunner and secondary firer positions and in peripheral training exercises such as protective mask and night-fire small-arms training. The EST 2000 enhances moving target training exercises. Sometimes shortages of range facilities or environmentally safe range resources prevent training in night, moving, and protective mask. The EST 2000 is the only three-mode training device capable of conducting realistic range operations while sustaining STRAC standards for individual weapons training, sustaining collective tactical skills and training, and sustaining judgmental engagements for the peace-keeping role of today's forces.

APPENDIX G
ADVANCED OPTICS AND LASERS

The newest systems greatly increase the night firing accuracy of all crew-served machine guns. They primarily enhance the gunner's ability to engage targets with great effectiveness to ranges of or beyond 1,000 meters. This appendix describes the AN/PAQ-4C, AN/PEQ-2A, laser systems. It also describes the AN/PAS-13 thermal sight and the M145 (MGO) telescope. Information for mounting, boresighting, and zeroing procedures for each weapon is also given.

Section I. ZERO PROCEDURES

An established day/night advanced marksmanship program equipped with training strategies and proposed qualification standards has been developed. Before beginning a night marksmanship program, soldiers must qualify on their assigned weapons during daylight conditions as outlined in the previous chapters of this manual and TMs. However, this appendix implements the new night qualification standards to compliment current Army training strategies. Commanders should follow these training strategies and abide by the qualification standards set forth to the best of their abilities. Although some courses of fire at first may seem redundant or inappropriate, numerous tests show that these training strategies work, and the qualification standards are achievable, if the strategy is followed.

G-1. BORE LIGHT

The bore light is an accurate means of zeroing weapons and the most aided vision equipment without the use of ammunition. Time and effort are applied to ensure a precise boresight, which in turn saves time and ammunition. Table G-1 outlines weapon/aided vision device combinations that can be zeroed using the bore light with the M249/M60/M240B weapons. With optics, a 25-meter zero must follow boresighting. The precise boresighting of a laser allows the soldier to directly engage targets without a 25-meter zero.

	M249	**M60**	**M240B**
MGO	X	X	X
AN/PAQ-4C	X	X	X
AN/PEQ-2A	X	X	X
AN/PAS-13	X	X	X

Table G-1. Weapon/aided vision device combinations.

a. **Intent**. Align the bore of the weapon to the optic, laser, or iron sight being fired to reduce or eliminate the time and ammunition it currently requires to live fire zero.

b. **Special Instructions**. Here are some special instructions the gunner should follow:

- Zero the bore light.
- Use only approved 10-meter offsets from Picatinny Arsenal (noted on offset).

- Ensure the proper 10-meter offset is used for the weapon configuration.
- Ensure boresighting is conducted 10 meters from the end of the barrel.
- Ensure weapon and offset is stabilized or the boresight will not be accurate.
- Ensure filters for aiming lasers are installed to reduce blooming.

b. **Observables.** The gunner should do the following:

- Confirm that the bore light spins on itself when zeroed at 10 meters.
- Boresight using the official and proper offsets only.
- Confirm that the weapon and offset are not moving during the boresighting procedure.
- Confirm that the bore light is centered on the circle of the offset.
- Confirm that the aiming device is aimed at the center of the crosshair on the offset.

DANGERS

PERMANENT INJURY COULD OCCUR WHEN DOING THE FOLLOWING:

1. **STARE INTO THE VISIBLE LASER BEAM.**
2. **LOOK INTO THE VISIBLE LASER BEAM THROUGH BINOCULARS OR TELESCOPE.**
3. **POINT THE VISIBLE LASER BEAM AT MIRROR-LIKE SURFACES.**
4. **SHINE THE VISIBLE LASER BEAM INTO OTHER INDIVIDUALS' EYES.**

WARNINGS

1. **Make sure the weapon is CLEAR and on SAFE before using the bore light.**
2. **Ensure that the bolt is locked in the forward position.**
3. **When rotating the bore light to zero it, ensure the mandrel is turning counterclockwise (from the gunner's point of view) to avoid loosening the bore light from the mandrel.**

G-2. CONCEPT

Boresighting is a simple procedure that can save time and ammunition only if the procedures outlined in this section are strictly followed. The bore light is a visible laser that is aligned with the barrel of the designated weapon. Then using a 10-meter offset, boresight the weapon with any optic, laser, or iron sight that you are assigned to fire. This procedure is accomplished by simply ensuring that the visible laser of the bore light is in line with the barrel by zeroing the bore light to the weapon, and then placing the visible laser of the bore light in a designated spot on the 10-meter offset. Once this procedure is accomplished, simply move the aiming point of the aiming device to the cross hair on the 10-meter offset. The weapon system is now boresighted and you are ready to engage targets or conduct a 25-meter zero. With optics, such as the MGO, TWS, and PVS-4, the bore light will put you on paper at 25 meters, thus reducing time and ammunition trying to locate rounds during the 25-meter zeroing. With lasers, the bore light allows you to boresight and then engage targets, eliminating the 25-meter zeroing procedures all together.

G-3. ZERO of BORE LIGHT TO WEAPON

Before boresighting the weapon system, make sure the bore light is first zeroed to the weapon. Take a flashlight and shine it through the barrel of the weapon and at 10 meters mark the spot that the flashlight is shining on. Then, without moving the weapon, fire one round. The impact of the round and the mark made with the flashlight should be the same. This procedure is the same principle used when zeroing the bore light to the weapon. This procedure is nothing more than aligning the visible laser with the barrel of the weapon, which would then hit the same area that the flashlight hit.

```
CAUTION
Do not over adjust the laser at soldiers.
```

G-4. STABILIZE

Stabilization of the weapon is crucial. The weapon can be stabilized on a tripod or using the bipod as a field-expedient method. The weapon does not have to be perfectly level with the ground when boresighting the weapon. Every barrel is different; therefore, with every weapon, steps (d) through (f) must be done to ensure that the bore light is zeroed to that barrel. If the bore light is zeroed, then go directly to the boresighting procedures.

a. Attach the 5.56-mm or 7.62-mm mandrel to the bore light.

b. Insert the mandrel into the muzzle of the weapon. The bore light is seated properly when no further travel of the mandrel into the muzzle is permitted and the mandrel spins freely.

c. Stabilize the weapon so that it will not move. The commands of *Start Point* and *Half Turn* are given to ensure clear communication between the soldier by the weapon and the soldier by the offset.

(1) *10 Meters.* 10 meters can be measured with the 10-meter cord that comes with the bore light or simply pace off eleven paces.

(2) *Zeroing Mark.* The zeroing mark (Figure G-1) is nothing more than a small dot drawn on a piece of paper, tree bark, or the bore light reference point on the 10-meter offset.

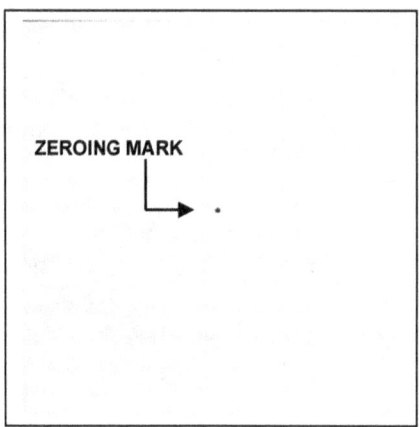

ZEROING MARK

Figure G-1. Example of a zeroing mark.

(3) *Start Point*. Rotate the bore light until the battery compartment is facing upward and the adjusters are on the bottom. This position of the bore light and where the visible laser is pointing is identified as the start point (Figure G-2).

Figure G-2. Bore light in the START-POINT position.

(4) *Half Turn*. Rotate the bore light until the battery compartment is down and the adjusters are on top. This technique allows for easy access to the adjusters and helps with communication and stabilization of the weapon while conducting the boresighting procedures. This position of the bore light and where the visible laser is pointing is identified as the half turn position (Figure G-3).

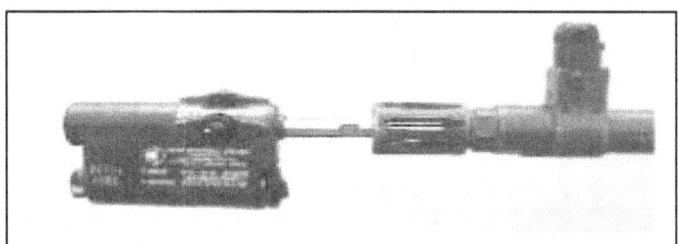

Figure G-3. Bore light in the HALF-TURN position.

(5) *Reference Point*. The reference point is the point that is about half way between the *start point* and the *half-turn* point (Figure G-4).

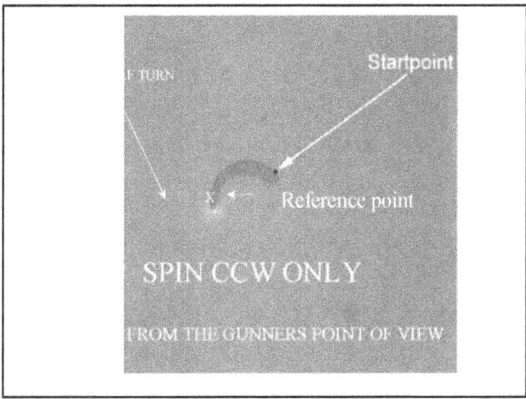

Figure G-4. Example of a start point, half-turn point, and reference point.

d. Turn the bore light on and spin it until it is in the ***start point*** position. Get a zeroing mark and mark a dot on it. Place the zeroing mark about 10 meters from the end of the barrel so that the visible laser strikes the zeroing mark.

e. Slowly rotate the bore light 360 degrees, while watching the visible laser made by the bore light. If the visible laser stops on the zeroing mark, the bore light is zeroed to the weapon.

f. If the bore light does not stop on the zeroing mark, then elevation and windage adjustments must be made to the bore light.

g. From the ***start point***, realign the zeroing mark with the visible laser and rotate the bore light 180 degrees into the *half turn* position. Then identify the *reference point*. Using the adjusters on the bore light move the visible laser to the reference point. Rotate the bore light back to the *start point*; move the zeroing mark to the visible laser. If the visible laser cannot be located once the bore light has been spun into the *half turn* position, start this procedure again at 2 meters instead of 10 meters. Once the visible laser is adjusted to the *reference point* at 2 meters, then start the procedure again at 10 meters.

h. Repeat step g until the visible laser spins on itself.

G-5. BORESIGHT TARGET OFFSET
Appendix H shows the most current 10-meter boresight target offsets. The 10-meter boresight offset grids are 1-centimeter squares, unlike the 25-meter zero targets. Some boresight target offsets are not available at this print. For more information, contact the infantry proponent at C co, 2/29 IN at Fort Benning, GA. Stability of the weapon is *crucial* in boresighting. Place the weapon in the *Bolt Forward* position during boresighting procedures. Do not cant the weapon left or right during this process. Two soldiers (a firer and a target holder) are required to properly boresight a weapon.

a. **Firer.** The firer's primary duty is to zero the bore light and make all adjustments on the aided vision device being used.

b. **Target Holder.** The target holder secures the 10-meter boresight target straight up and down 10 meters from the bore light and directs the firer in making the necessary adjustments to the aiming device. The target holder *must* wear night vision goggles when boresighting infrared aiming lasers.

NOTE: Weapon stabilization is crucial, orientation is irrelevant.

Section II. AN/PAQ-4C AIMING LIGHT

The AN/PAQ-4 aiming light projects an infrared laser beam, which cannot be seen with the naked eye but can be seen with night vision devices. This aiming light works with the AN/PVS-7B/C/D goggles and AN/PVS-14. The AN/PAQ-4C mounts on various weapons with mounting brackets and adapters.

G-6. EQUIPMENT DATA AND DESCRIPTION

The AN/PAQ-4 aiming light (Figure G-5) is activated by rotating the ON/OFF switch lever or the button on the optional cable switch. Either switch connects power from two AA batteries to an internal electronic circuit, which produces the infrared laser. Internal lenses focus the infrared light into a narrow beam. Rotating the mechanical adjusters with click detents controls the direction of the beam. These adjusters are used to zero the aiming light to the weapon. Once zeroed to the weapon, the aiming light projects the beam along the line of fire of the weapon. The optical baffle prevents off-axis viewing of the aiming light beam by the enemy.

a. **Data**. The AN/PAQ-4 aiming light includes the following equipment data:

Optics:	100 percent parallax free, anti-reflective coated lens system.
Length (sight):	14 centimeters (5.5 inches)
Weight:	164 grams (5.78 ounces)
Height:	3 centimeters (1.2 inches)
Width:	6.5 centimeters (2.5 inches)
Range:	Beyond 600 meters. (Actual range depends on light level and night vision device used for observation.)
Battery life:	100-hour operating (ON) time for AA batteries in temperatures above 0 degrees centigrade (32 degrees Fahrenheit); 36-hours for temperatures below 0 degrees centigrade (32 degrees Fahrenheit).

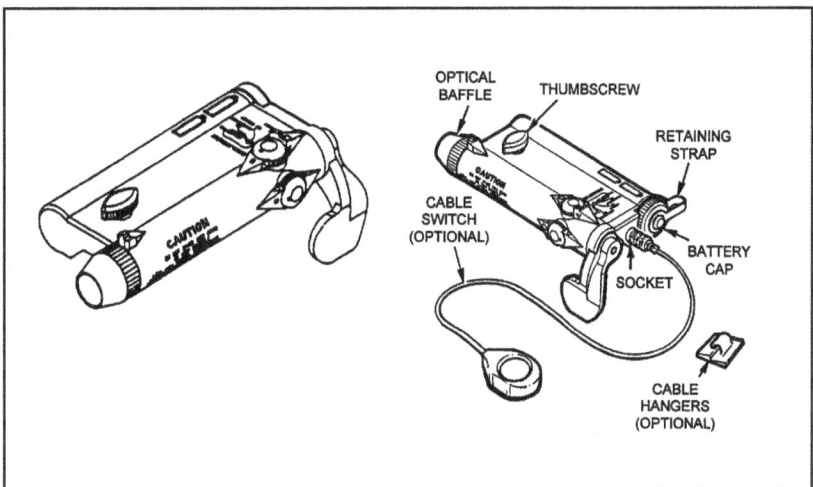

Figure G-5. AN/PAQ-4 aiming light.

c. **M249 Machine Gun.**

(1) *Mounting Procedures.* The gunner uses the AN/PVS-4 mounting bracket when mounting the AN/PAQ-4 on the M249 machine gun.

> **CAUTION**
> When mounting an AN/PAQ-4 to the mounting bracket, make sure that the hole for the screw in the AN/PAQ-4 is aligned and flush against the bracket screw. If not, the screw will strip the threads in the screw hole of the AN/PAQ-4 and prevent use with the M249.

(a) Install the AN/PVS-4 mounting bracket by first placing the mounting bracket on top of the feed cover mechanism assembly so that the two forked ends are secured around the headless pins. Next, remove the screw cover behind the rear sight assembly, and screw the bracket knob in until it is tight.

(b) Install the bracket adapter (Figure G-6).

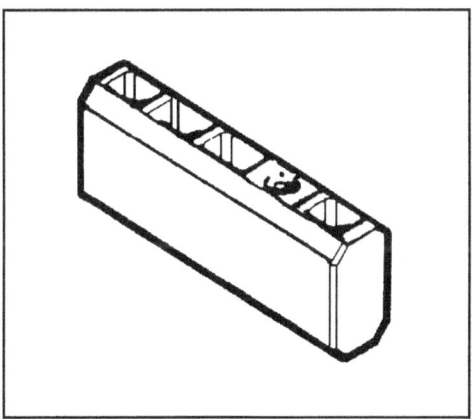

Figure G-6. Bracket adapter.

(c) Attach the AN/PAQ-4 on the bracket adapter (Figure G-7).

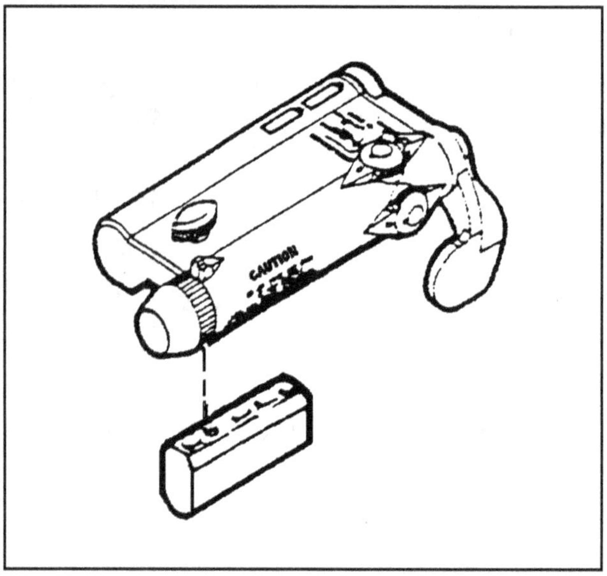

Figure G-7. Attaching bracket adapter to aiming light.

(d) Attach the AN/PAQ-4 to the AN/PVS-4 mounting bracket by first positioning the AN/PAQ-4 on top of the bracket so the spacer of the AN/PAQ-4 is aligned with the mounting knob of the bracket. Then, turn the mounting knob clockwise until the AN/PAQ-4 is tight.

WARNING
Do not store the AN/PAQ-4 with batteries installed.

---

(2) *Dismounting Procedures.*

(a) Detach the AN/PAQ-4 from the AN/PVS-4 mounting bracket. Turn the mounting knob counterclockwise until the AN/PAQ-4 is loose. Remove the AN/PAQ-4 and spacer from the bracket.

(b) Remove the spacer from the AN/PAQ-4.

(c) Remove the AN/PVS-4 mounting bracket. Unscrew the bracket knob until the rear of the bracket is loose. Replace the screw cover behind the rear sight assembly. Remove the two forked ends from the headless pins and lift up on the mounting bracket to remove it from the feed cover mechanism assembly.

c. **M60 Machine Gun.**

(1) *Mounting Procedures.* The gunner uses the AN/PVS-4 mounting bracket when mounting the AN/PAQ-4 on the M60 machine gun.

CAUTION

When mounting an AN/PAQ-4 to the mounting bracket, make sure that the hole for the screw in the AN/PAQ-4 is aligned and flush against the bracket screw. If not, the screw will strip the threads in the screw hole of the AN/PAQ-4 and prevent use with the machine gun.

(a) On the M60 machine gun bracket (Figure G-8), remove the M60 hinge pin latch and hinge pin from the over assembly by pressing on the latch (open end of pin) with an empty cartridge case, and separates the latch and pin. Place the pin and latch in the aiming guides on the left side of the mounting bracket and press together.

(b) Position the mounting bracket assembly on top of the machine gun cover so that the holes in the front of the bracket align with the cover assembly pinholes.

(c) Insert the longer hinge pin supplied with the bracket through the bracket and cover assembly, and secure it by inserting the hinge pin latch.

(d) Loosen the wing nuts on both leg clamps and positions the clamps under the cover assembly. Secure the mounting bracket by tightening the wing nuts firmly. Place the split washer is placed next to the wing nut and the flat washer is placed next to the bracket.

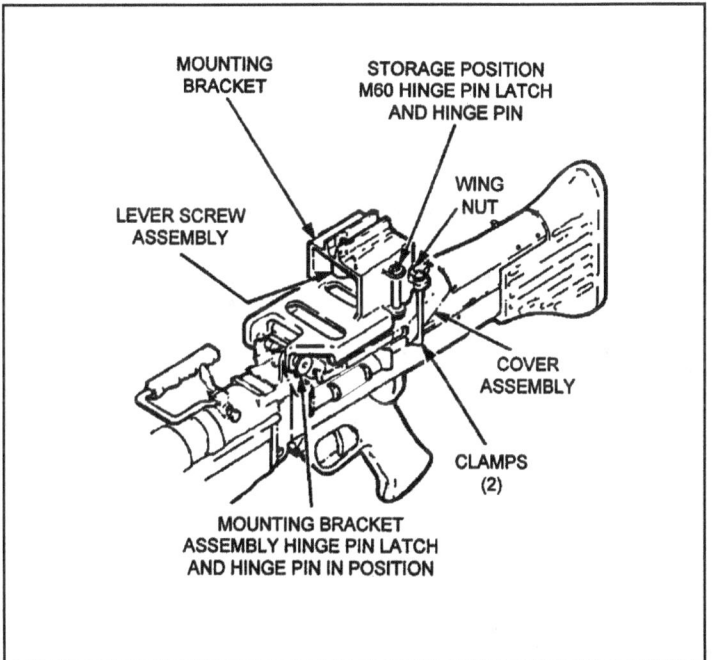

Figure G-8. Installation of M60 mounting bracket.

(f) Install the sight on the M60 mounting bracket assembly by positioning it in the groove on top of the bracket so that the scribe line on the bracket is aligned with the scribe line on the sight-mounting adapter. Tighten the lever screw assembly to secure the sight to the bracket. Use an empty cartridge case placed over the lever arm to increase leverage as the screw is tightened.

(2) *Dismounting Procedures.*

(a) Unscrew the lever screw assembly by turning it counterclockwise and remove the AN/PAQ-4 from the mounting bracket. Use an empty cartridge case placed over the lever arm for increased leverage if necessary.

(b) Loosen the wing nuts on both leg clamps.

(c) Push down on the longer hinge pin latch with an empty cartridge case and remove the hinge pin and latch.

(d) Remove the mounting bracket from the machine gun.

(e) Remove the M60 hinge pin and latch from the left side of the bracket by pushing on the hinge pin latch and pulling out the hinge pin.

(f) Replace the M60 hinge pin and latch.

(g) Remove the batteries when storing the sight.

d. **M240B Machine Gun.**

(1) *Mounting Procedures.* Before zeroing and qualifying with the AN/PAQ-4, the gunner must mount the sight onto his weapon. The M240B machine gun has a rail mount already attached to the cover assembly.

(a) Install the sight on the M240B rail mount by loosening the mounting knob located on the left side.

(b) Position the sight in a slot on the rail mount. Any slot can be used as long as the mount does not hang over the edge of the rail.

(c) Hand tighten the knob (clockwise) on the mount until a clicking noise is heard (two clicks).

(d) Places the sight in the same slot after zeroing to ensure that the sight retains its zero.

WARNING
Do not store the AN/PAQ-4 with batteries installed.

---

(2) *Dismounting Procedures.* Loosen the mounting knob on the left side of the bracket, then lift up on the sight to remove it from the M240B machine gun.

(a) Adjust the bore light, if necessary. Move the target to a distance of 2 meters. Mark the location of the laser dot. Slowly rotate the bore light one half turn. Note the new location of the laser dot. Adjust the windage and elevation until the laser dot moves halfway back to its original location. Continue the procedure until the laser dot remains stationary (or spins upon itself within 1 centimeter) when the bore light is rotated. Move the target to a distance of 10 meters and recheck the boresight.

(b) Boresight the AN/PAQ-4 to the weapon. Select the target (boresight offset) for the appropriate weapon and the AN/PAQ-4. Position the weapon so the bore light strikes the small dot on the boresight target. Zero the AN/PAQ-4 by turning both windage and elevation knobs (for the pointer and illuminator) fully clockwise until they stop. Rotate counterclockwise three turns and align the white dot on the adjuster with the center of the front adjuster flange (Figure G-9).

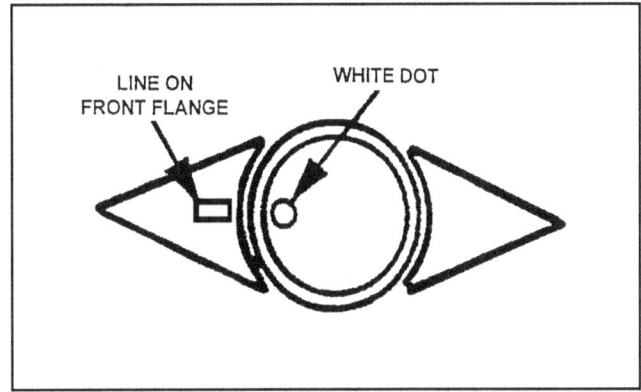

Figure G-9. Adjuster alignment.

G-7. BORESIGHT AND ZERO PROCEDURES

The following procedures are used to boresight and zero the M249, M60, and M240B machine guns using the AN/PAQ-4C aiming light.

a. **Boresight**. Check the alignment of the bore light.

(1) Place the appropriate mandrel with the bore light attached in the muzzle of the weapon.

(2) Turn on the bore light so that the laser dot strikes the target (offset) 10 meters away.

(3) Slowly rotate the bore light one-half turn (180 degrees) while watching the dot made by the laser on the target area.

(4) If the dot remains stationary, the laser is boresighted. Go to step 3 and use the appropriate boresight target for the weapon being boresighted.

(5) If the dot rotates in a circle, adjust the windage, elevation, or both until the dot remains stationary or rotates on itself no more than 1 cm. Go to step 2.

b. **25-Meter Zero**. The gunner chooses the appropriate strike zone from TM 11-5855-309-12&P, and draws it on the 25-meter zero target. He follows the procedures above and zeroes the weapon with the AN/PAQ-4. He fires a total of three rounds (one at a time) before triangulating the shot group. Once the weapon is zeroed on the 25-meter zero range, the gunner follows the procedures outlined below for field zeroing to obtain an accurate zero.

c. **Field Zero**. If the adjustment screws are turned too far, they will break. If the laser is side-mounted, the elevation and windage knobs will switch roles.

(1) Assume a good prone bipod-supported position. Fire a seven-round burst at the target. Note the burst pattern on the ground in relation to the target.

(2) Correct for windage (if rounds are impacting to the right or left of the target). Note that each click of the windage knob sight moves the group on the target mil (1/2 mil equals 6 inches at 300 meters or 10 inches at 500 meters).

(3) Correct for elevation (if rounds are impacting over or short of the target).

After making corrections on the sight, fire a confirming burst. If the target is not hit with the confirming burst, repeat the above procedures. Treat each subsequent burst as if it were the initial burst.

(2) Prepare the sight for field zeroing and check the sight. The preferred range is 300 meters.

G-8. TRAINING STRATEGIES

Two training strategies have been devised to adequately train soldiers in the use of the infrared aiming laser devices. The *night initial* training strategy is used for soldiers who have little or no previous experience with night vision goggles or with units beginning a night training program. The *night sustainment* training strategy is for soldiers who are familiar with night vision goggles and with units who have already implemented a night training program. The night initial training strategy is conducted over a two- to three-day time frame and consists of the following:

a. **Day 1**.

(1) *Night Vision Goggles Training With Terrain Walk When Firing Aiming Lasers*. Soldiers are given in-depth instruction on the proper use and fit of night vision goggles, to include characteristics and capabilities, maintenance, and mounting procedures. At night, soldiers conduct a terrain walk to become more familiar and build confidence using the night vision goggles.

(2) *Aiming Device Training*. Soldiers receive familiarization training on the aiming device. This training covers operation and characteristics, maintenance procedures, and mounting procedures.

(3) *Fundamentals of Firing*. This includes body position, foxhole, and prone. Soldiers review and practice firing positions and fundamentals of marksmanship and any changes that occur when using this aiming device.

b. **Day 2 to 3**.

(1) *Weapon and Equipment*. Inspect the weapon and aiming device to ensure the aiming device is mounted securely to the weapon. A review of clearing or misfire procedures is important. Let the soldiers use dummy rounds to practice correcting malfunctions with their eyes closed or during limited visibility.

(2) *Boresight Aiming Device to Weapon*. Each soldier boresights the weapon and aiming device at a range of 10 meters. If a bore light is not available, then 25-meter zero the weapon and sight by using the specified zeroing procedure for that weapon/sight combination. For course of fire, refer to Table 4-4 in Chapter 4 for a description of the aiming laser and AN/PVS-4 firing table. MGO and TWS will fire the day qualification table.

c. **Field Fire I**. Perform dry-fire exercise with no ammunition:

(1) Assume a stable, prone firing position. Fire the weapon maintaining sight alignment and sight picture. Pull the trigger correctly by pulling straight to the rear and releasing the trigger. Pull the trigger to the rear and say to yourself, "*fire a burst of seven*." After the word "*seven*," let go of the trigger.

(2) Apply correct traversing and searching techniques. Traversing means moving the muzzle of the weapon to the left or to the right to distribute fire laterally. Shift the shoulder slightly to the right or left for minor changes. For major changes, move the elbows and align the body directly behind the weapon. Searching means moving the muzzle of the weapon up or down to distribute fire in depth. To make changes in elevation, move the elbows closer or farther apart.

(3) The following targets are used for field fire I:
- 200-meter target single E-type silhouettes.
- 300-meter target single E-type silhouettes.
- 400-meter target double E-type silhouettes.
- 500-meter target double E-type silhouettes.
- 200-meter single E-type and 500-meter double E-type silhouettes.
- 300-meter single E-type and 400-meter double E-type silhouettes.
- 200-meter single E-type silhouettes.
- 400-meter double E-type silhouettes.
- 600-meter double E-type silhouettes.

d. **Field Fire II**. Perform a timed, dry-fire exercise on a transition range. This familiarizes the gunner with acquiring targets on a timed exercise. It also allows the soldier and the point safety time to make any corrections on-sight, or the body position and grip before the qualification table.

(1) Assume a stable, prone firing position. Fire the weapon maintaining sight alignment and sight picture. Pull the trigger correctly. Pull straight to the rear and release. Pull the trigger to the rear and say to yourself, *"fire a burst of seven."* After the word *"seven,"* let go of the trigger.

(2) Apply correct traversing and searching techniques. Traversing means moving the muzzle of the weapon to the left or to the right to distribute fire laterally. Shift the shoulder slightly to the right or left for minor changes. For major changes, move the elbows and align the body directly behind the weapon. Searching means moving the muzzle of the weapon up or down to distribute fire in depth. To make changes in elevation move the elbows closer or farther apart.

(b) The following targets are used for field fire II:
- 200-meter target single E-type silhouettes (15 seconds).
- 300-meter target single E-type silhouettes (20 seconds).
- 400-meter target double E-type silhouettes (25 seconds).
- 500-meter target double E-type silhouettes (30 seconds).
- 200-meter single E-type silhouettes (40 seconds).
- 500-meter double E-type silhouettes (40 seconds).
- 300-meter single E-type silhouettes (35 seconds).
- 400-meter double E-type silhouettes (35 seconds).
- 200-meter single E-type silhouettes (50 seconds).
- 400-meter double E-type silhouettes (50 seconds).
- 600-meter double E-type silhouettes (50 seconds).

e. **Night Record Qualification**. Perform live-fire exercises with ammunition. Engage targets on a transition range timed. This exercise measures the gunner's ability to engage targets during a timed exercise (154 rounds of A064 4x1 mix 5.56-mm linked M249, 154 rounds of A131 4x1 mix 7.62-mm linked M60 and M240B):

(1) Assume a stable, prone firing position. Fire the weapon maintaining sight alignment and sight picture. Pull the trigger correctly. Pull straight to the rear and release. Pull the trigger to the rear and say to yourself, *"fire a burst of seven."* After the word *"seven,"* let go of the trigger.

(2) Apply correct traversing and searching techniques. Traversing means moving the muzzle of the weapon to the left or to the right to distribute fire laterally. Shift the

shoulder slightly to the right or left for minor changes. For major changes, move the elbows and align the body directly behind the weapon. Searching means moving the muzzle of the weapon up or down to distribute fire in depth. To make changes in elevation move the elbows closer or farther apart.

(3) Use observation and adjustment of fire. Observe machine gun fire by noting the strike of the projectiles in the target area. When firing the bipod-mounted gun, adjust fire by changing body position.

(4) Apply the adjusted aiming point method. The adjusted aiming point method is a means of rapidly and accurately adjusting fires without making sight adjustment. If the initial burst misses the target, select a new aiming point on the ground. The aiming point should be the same distance from the target as the initial burst's center of impact.

(5) The following targets are used for night record qualification with the AN/PVS-4 and the aiming lasers. TWS and MGO will fire the day record fire table:

- 200-meter target single E-type silhouettes (10 seconds).
- 300-meter target single E-type silhouettes (15 seconds).
- 400-meter target double E-type silhouettes (15 seconds).
- 500-meter target double E-type silhouettes (25 seconds).
- 200-meter single E-type silhouettes (35 seconds).
- 500-meter double E-type silhouettes (35 seconds).
- 300-meter single E-type silhouettes (30 seconds).
- 400-meter double E-type silhouettes (30 seconds).
- 200-meter single E-type silhouettes (45 seconds).
- 400-meter double E-type silhouettes (45 seconds).
- 600-meter double E-type silhouettes (45 seconds).

Section III. AN/PEQ-2A TARGET POINTER/ ILLUMINATOR/AIMING LIGHT

The AN/PEQ-2A target pointer/illuminator/aiming light (TPIAL) (Figure G-11) is a Class IIIB laser that emits a highly collimated beam of infrared light for precise aiming of the weapon as well as a separate infrared illuminating beam with adjustable focus. A safety block is provided for training purposes (blue side), which limits the operator from selecting the high power modes (black side).

G-9. DESCRIPTION

This paragraph gives a description of the AN/PEQ-2A along with its accessories (Figure G-10). This paragraph also describes how to install and operate the AN/PEQ-2A. The TPIAL projects an infrared laser beam that cannot be seen with the eye but can be seen with night vision devices. It is capable of projecting a much wider infrared illuminating beam from an integral illuminator. The TPIAL works with night vision goggles and mounts on various weapons with mounting brackets and adapters. Leaders use the AN/PEQ-2A in the hand-held mode to illuminate and designate targets.

a. **Data**.

Weight:	7.5 ounce (with 2 AA batteries)
Length:	16.26 centimeters (6.4 inches)
Width:	7.12 centimeters (2.8 inches)
Height:	3.05 centimeters (1.2 inches)
Range:	600 meters in low power (eye safe)
	2,000 meters in high power (non-eye safe)
Output Power:	
Aiming laser	25 meters wide (+- 10 percent)
Illuminator	30 meters wide (+50, -20 percent)
Beam Divergence:	
Aiming laser	5 meter rad
Illuminator	1.0 to 115 meter rad
Batteries:	Two 1.5-volt AA batteries

b. **Components**. (See Figure G-10.)

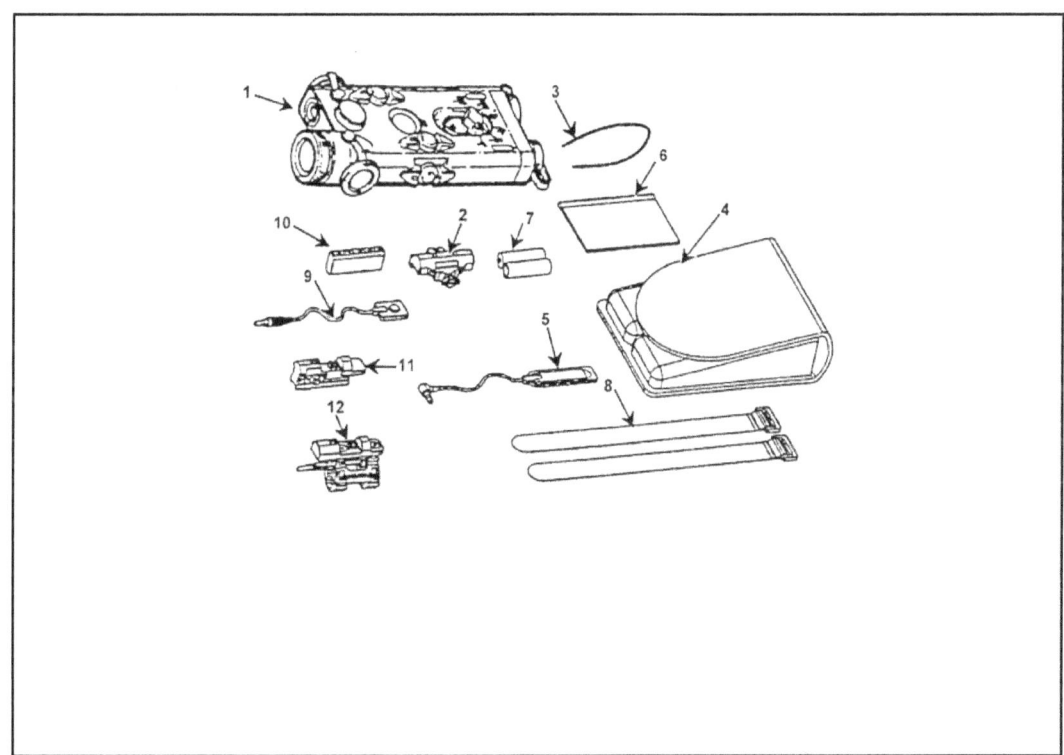

Figure G-10. AN/PEQ-2A with accessories.

(1) TPIAL assembly with safety block.
(2) Rail.
(3) Neck cord.
(4) Textile bag.
(5) Cable switch, 12-inch, membrane.
(6) Operator's manual.

(7) Batteries 1.5V AA.

(8) Strap, retention.

(9) Cable Switch, 20-inch, button.

(10) Bracket Adapter.

(11) Training extender (Army only).

(12) M4/M16A2 bracket assembly.

G-10. OPERATION

This paragraph describes how to operate the AN/PEQ-2A, to include battery installation, safety block installation, the button switch, the cable switch, the mode switch, and boresight adjusters.

a. **Battery Installation** (Figure G-11). Unscrew the battery caps and install two AA batteries. Orient the batteries as indicated by the markings on the AN/PEQ-2A body.

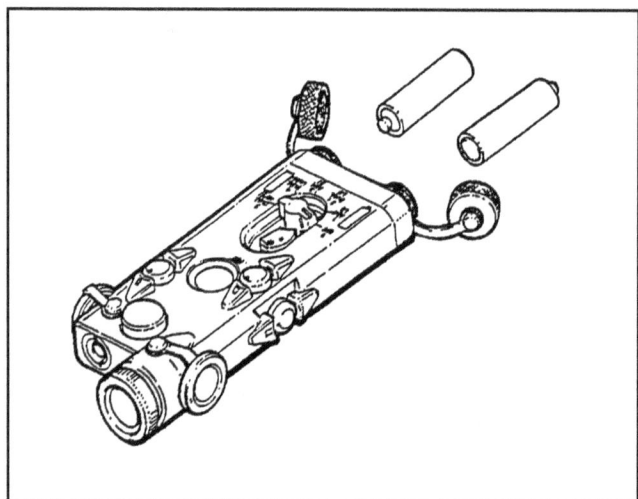

Figure G-11. AN/PEQ-2A battery installation.

b. **Safety Block Installation** (Figure G-12). The safety block installed in the training mode (blue side up) prevents the operator from accessing the non-eye safe modes (AIM HI, DUAL LO/HI, DUAL HI/HI). A .050 hex head Allen wrench is needed to unscrew the block from the body and reinstall it in the tactical mode (black side up).

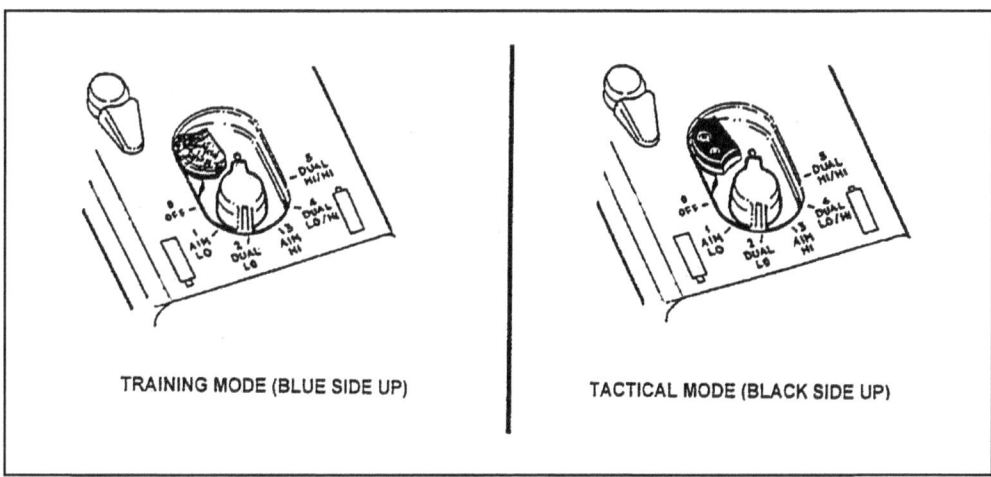

TRAINING MODE (BLUE SIDE UP)　　　TACTICAL MODE (BLACK SIDE UP)

Figure G-12. Safety block installation.

c. **Mode Selector**. The mode selector is used to set the mode in which the AN/PEQ-2A operates when the cable-switch button or the push button is depressed. The mode selector has six positions (Table G-2).

KNOB POSITION	OPERATION
0 OFF	The AN/PEQ-2A does not operate.
1 AIM LO	The aiming beam operates at low power.
2 DUAL LO	The aiming beam operates at low power and the illuminating beam operates at low power.
3 AIM HI	The aiming beam operates at high power.
4 DUAL LO/HI	The aiming beam operates at low power and the illuminating beam operates at full power.
5 DUAL HI/HI	The aiming beam operates at high power and the illuminating beam operates at full power.

Table G-2. Mode selector positions.

d. **Button Switch** (Figure G-13, page G-18). The button switch is used when the AN/PEQ-2A is hand held. Pressing the button switch operates the AN/PEQ-2A in the operational mode set by the mode selector. When the button is released, the AN/PEQ-2A turns off. A green LED is incorporated into the body of the AN/PEQ-2A to indicate that the AN/PEQ-2A is ON. Whenever the AN/PEQ-2A is activated, the green LED lights and stays lit until the unit is turned OFF. If continuous operation of the AN/PEQ-2A is desired, pressing the button switch twice in rapid succession latches the AN/PEQ-2A to ON. The AN/PEQ-2A remains on until the push button is pressed a third time.

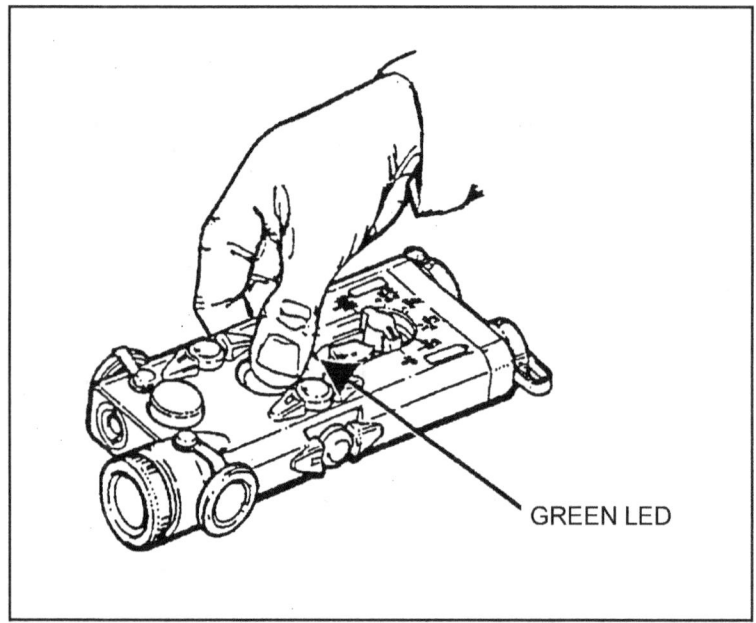

Figure G-13. Operation of the button switch.

e. **Cable Switch**. The cable switch (Figure G-14) is used when the AN/PEQ-2A is mounted on a weapon. The switch plugs into the back of the AN/PEQ-2A assembly. Pressing the button or pad at the end of the cable switch causes the AN/PEQ-2A to turn on in the operational mode selected by the mode select switch. When the button is released, the AN/PEQ-2A turns off. If continuous operation of the AN/PEQ-2A is desired, pressing the cable switch twice in rapid succession latches the AN/PEQ-2A to ON. The AN/PEQ-2A remains on until the push button is pressed a third time. When the cable switch plug is installed in the AN/PEQ-2A, it automatically locks into place. To remove the switch, pull back on the plug sleeve and pull the plug out. DO NOT TRY TO REMOVE THE PLUG BY PULLING ON THE CABLE.

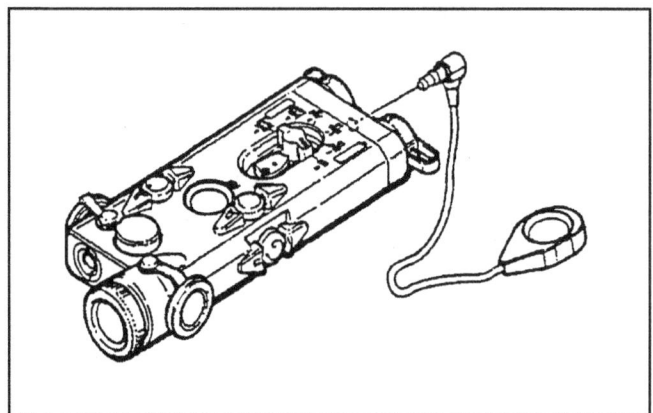

Figure G-14. Installation of the cable switch.

f. **Focus Knob** (Figure G-15). The focus knob is used to vary the spread of the illumination beam based on the range and size of the area to be illuminated.

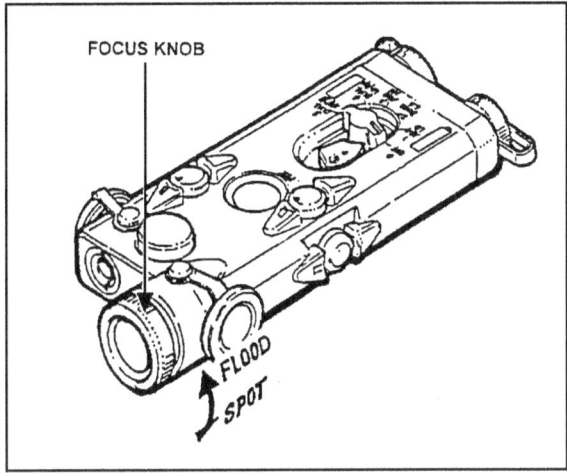

Figure G-15. Using the focus knob.

g. **Lens Cap** (Figure G-16).

(1) The *black lens cap* blocks the AN/PEQ-2A illuminator or aiming laser beam should the device be activated. To use the black lens cap, pull it from its stored location on the side of the AN/PEQ-2A and stretch it over the front of the focus knob or aiming beam so that it fits snugly in place.

(2) The *diffuser lens cap* enables the illuminator or aiming laser to emit in a 45-degree cone (10 feet at 10 feet). To use the diffuser lens cap, pull it from its stored location on the side of the AN/PEQ-2A and stretch it over the front of the focus knob or aiming beam so that it fits snugly in place.

(3) The *neutral density lens cap* enables the AN/PEQ-2A illuminator or aiming laser to be operated in low power. To use the neutral density lens cap, pull it from its stored location on the side of the AN/PEQ-2A and stretch it over the front of the focus knob or aiming beam so that it fits snugly in place.

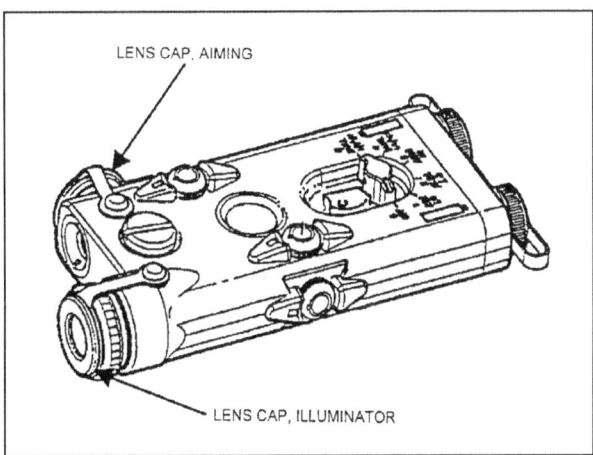

Figure G-16. Installing the lens caps.

h. **Adjusters** (Figure G-17). The AN/PEQ-2A is equipped with boresight adjusters for zeroing the aiming beam and illumination beam. The AN/PEQ-2A adjusters move the beams in true horizontal and vertical directions. When zeroing the AN/PEQ-2A, it is best to zero the aiming beam to the weapon and then align the illumination beam to the aiming beam.

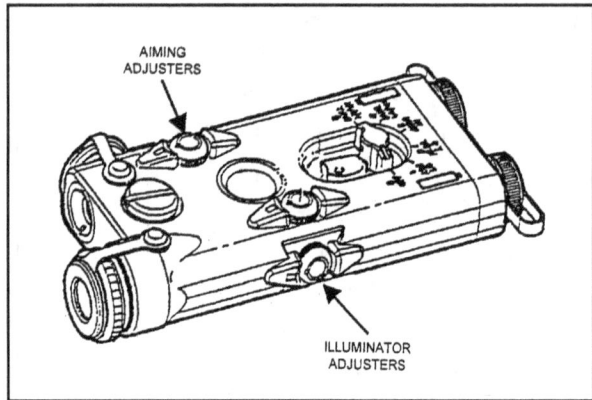

Figure G-17. Boresight adjusters for both aiming and illumination beams.

G-11. MOUNT/DISMOUNT PROCEDURES

This paragraph describes the mounting procedures for the AN/PEQ-2A (M249, M60, M240B). Reverse the procedures to dismount the AN/PEQ-2A.

a. **TWS Mounting Bracket.** (See Figure G-18.)

(1) Attach the rail grabber (3) (P/N 12598120) to the AN/PEQ-2A (4).

(2) Loosen the knob on the AN/PEQ-2A rail grabber.

(3) Select the slot on rail (5) for mounting. Any slot may be used as long as the mount does not hang over the edge of the rail.

(4) Place the bar of the rail grabber (3) in the slot of the rail (5) and hand tighten the knob on mount until a clicking noise can be heard.

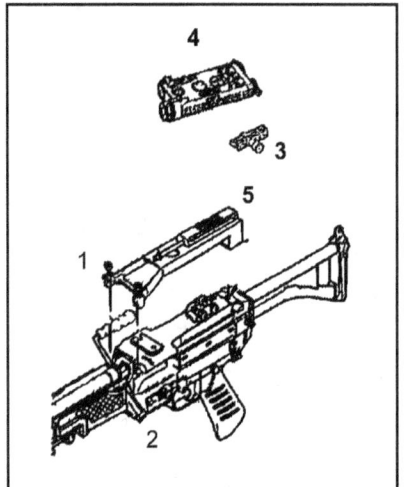

**Figure G-18. Mounting the AN/PEQ-2A
to the M249 using TWS bracket.**

b. **M60 Machine Gun.**

(1) Remove the M60 hinge pin latch and hinge pin from the cover assembly. Place the pin latch in the aiming guides on the left side mounting bracket and press together.

(2) Place the mounting bracket on top of the machine gun cover so that the holes in the front of the bracket align with the cover assembly pinholes.

(3) Insert the longer hinge pin supplied with the bracket through the bracket and cover assembly and secure by inserting the hinge pin latch.

(4) Turning counterclockwise loosen the wing nuts on both leg clamps and position the leg clamps under the cover assembly. Secure the mounting bracket by tightening the wing nuts firmly. The split washer should be next to the wing nut and the flat washer next to the bracket.

(5) Place the bracket adapter in the AN/PEQ-2A mounting groove flush with the front of the AN/PEQ-2A. Tighten the thumbscrew clockwise.

(6) Position the AN/PEQ-2A with the bracket adapter on the M60 mounting bracket mounting groove. Align the front edge of the bracket adapter and the front edge of the groove. Tighten the lever screw assembly (Figure G-19).

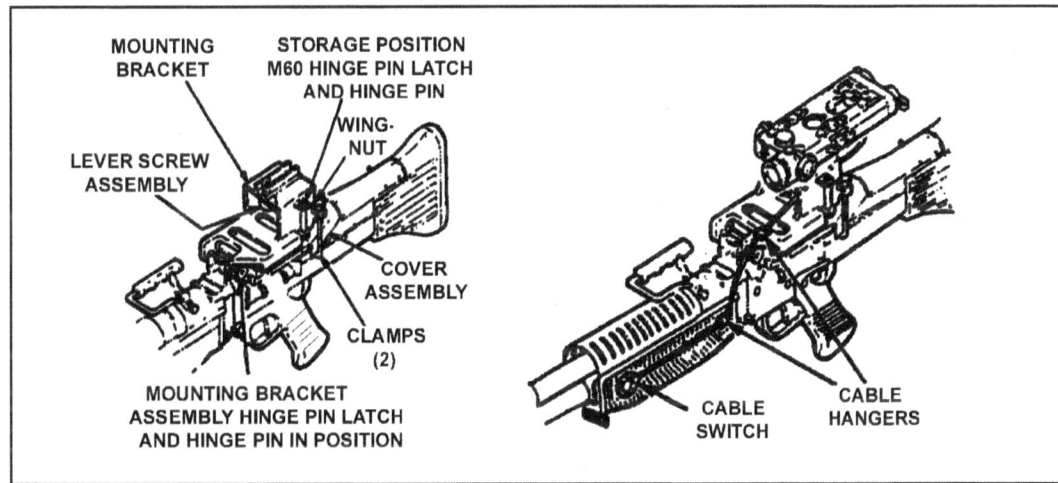

Figure G-19. Mounting the AN/PEQ-2A to the M60 machine gun.

c. **M240B Machine Gun.**

(1) Mount the AN/PEQ-2A 1 on the top cover rail (see arrow) using the AN/PEQ-2A bracket adapter and a standard rail grabber. The unit armorer preassembles the rail grabber and the bracket adapter.

(2) Mount the bracket adapter to the AN/PEQ-2A using the thumbscrew on the AN/PEQ-2A.

(3) Loosen the clamping knob until the rail grabber has sufficient space to fit over the top cover rail. Tighten the clamping knob until two clicks are heard.

(4) Place the AN/PEQ-2A at a position on the rail that is the most convenient for the operator. If however the AN/PEQ-2A is removed from the rail, the operator must take note of the position at which the device was zeroed, and then return the device to the same position to ensure the zero is retained.

(5) Install the remote switch in a convenient location using the provided cable hangers (Figure G-20).

Figure G-20. Mounting the AN/PEQ-2A to the M240B machine gun.

WARNING
Eye damage can occur if the laser is handled carelessly. The danger area is 15 meters in the training mode and 220 meters in the tactical mode.

(6) To dismount the devices for each weapon, reverse the procedures.

G-12. FUNDAMENTALS OF MARKSMANSHIP
The fundamentals of machine gun marksmanship for the M249, M60 and M240B machine guns are the same as with the AN/PAQ-4 (paragraph G-7). To use the maximum effective range of the AN/PEQ-2A, the safety block must be removed and the AN/PEQ-2A placed in high power. Because the laser is non-eye safe in the tactical mode (high power), batteries for the AN/PEQ-2A are issued to the firers on the firing line only when the weapon is oriented down range.

a. **Boresight Procedures**. Follow the procedures outlined in paragraph G-6 to boresight the machine gun and the AN/PEQ-2A.

b. **Zero Procedures**. Follow the procedures outlined in paragraph G-6 to zero and field zero the machine gun and the AN/PEQ-2A. (Refer to TM 11-5855-308-12&P for further information on zeroing procedures and zeroing targets with designated strike zones.)

c. **Sight Adjustments**. Sight adjustments for the aiming light and illuminator beam are the elevation adjustment screw (1 click at 25 meters equals 4 millimeters) (clockwise equals up) and the windage adjustment screw (1 click at 25 meters equals 4 millimeters) (clockwise equals right).

(1) The adjustment screws will break if they are turned too far.

(2) If the laser is side-mounted, the elevation and windage knobs will switch roles.

G-13. TRAINING STRATEGIES

Training strategies are the same for all weapons that use the AN/PAQ-4 except for the use of the illuminating beam. The illuminating beam allows soldiers to detect targets at ranges up to 2,000 meters (dependent upon terrain and weather constraints) in the high-power mode (tactical mode). Remember that the laser is not eye-safe in the tactical mode. In the low-power mode, targets can be engaged out to 600 meters during ideal limited visibility conditions (for example, 75 percent illumination, no rain or fog). The tactical mode should only be used on the M60 machine gun, and M240B machine gun.

Section IV. AN/PAS-13 (V2) MEDIUM WEAPON THERMAL SIGHT

The AN/PAS-13 (V2) medium-weapon, thermal sight (MWTS) (Figure G-21) is silent, lightweight, compact, and durable battery-powered thermal imaging sensors that operate with low battery consumption.

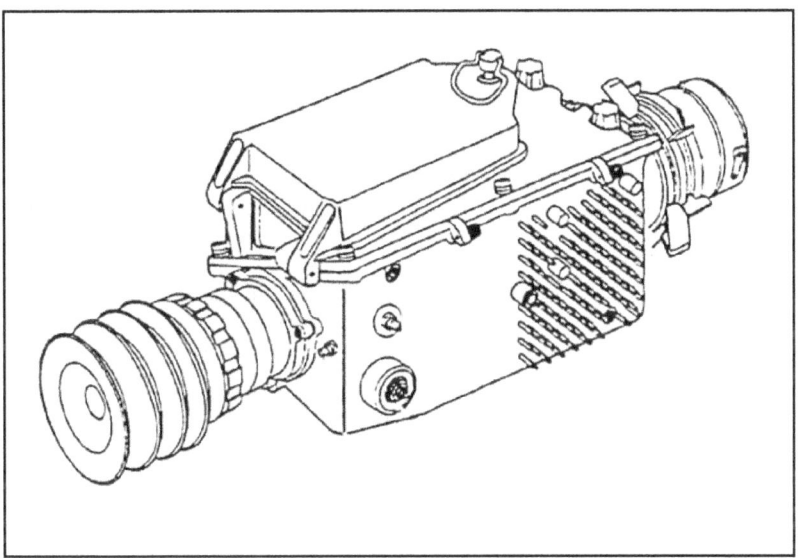

Figure G-21. Model of the medium-weapon thermal sight.

G-14. DESCRIPTION

The MWTS is capable of target acquisition under conditions of limited visibility such as darkness, smoke, fog, dust, and haze. The MWTS operates at night and during the daytime. Infrared light is received through the telescope, detected by an IR sensor, converted to digital data, processed, and then displayed for the user. The MWTS is composed of two functional groups: the telescope and the basic sensor.

    a. **Telescope.** The telescope receives IR light emitting from an intended target and its surroundings. The telescope magnifies and projects the IR light on the scanner on the basic sensor (Figure G-22, page G-24).

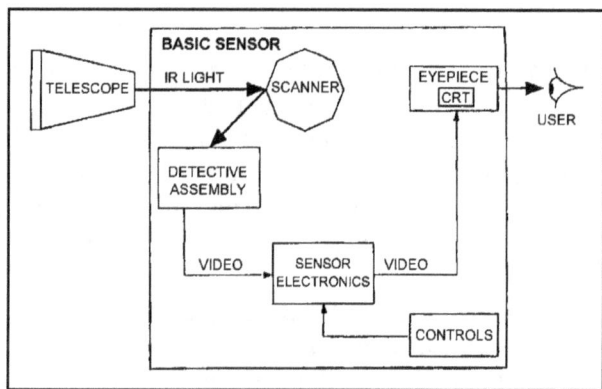

Figure G-22. MWTS configurations.

b. **Basic Sensor**. The scanner reflects the IR light received from the telescope on the detective assembly. The detective assembly senses the IR light and converts it to video. The sensor's electronics condition the video for display on the LED array. The LED array illuminates the IR image along with the reticle. The light from the LED array is reflected off the scanner to form an image at the eyepiece. The only difference between the MWTS and the HWTS are the telescopes, which are different magnifications and hold different reticles. The basic sensor on the two models is the same. The MWTS fits the M249, M60, and the M240B machine gun. (Figure G-23).

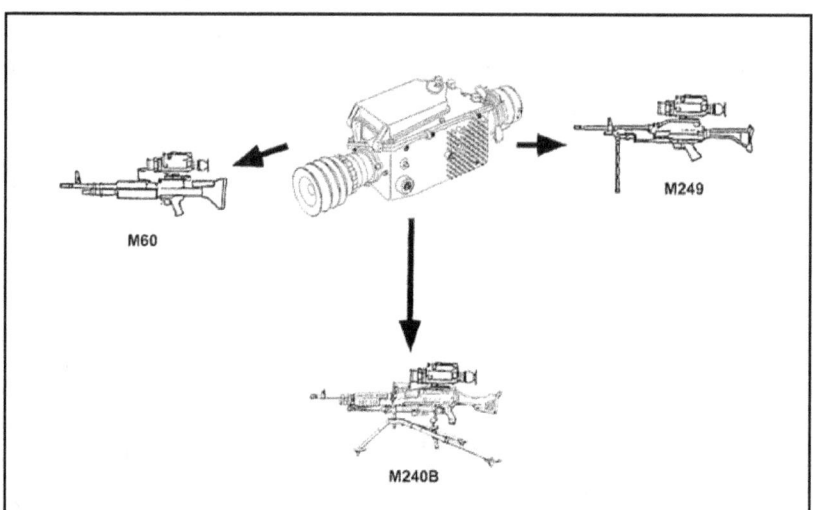

Figure G-23. Medium-weapon thermal sight.

c. **Data**. The following is the equipment data for the medium-weapon thermal sight.
- Field of view (FOV):
  - Narrow—9 degrees
  - Wide—15 degrees
- Telescope magnification:
  - Narrow FOV—3.3X

Wide FOV—2X
- Length—15.5 inches
- Width—6.25 inches
- Height—6.25 inches
- Weight—4.1 pounds
- Power consumption:
    ON mode—12.0 watts
    STANDBY mode—5.5 watts
- Battery life:
    71 percent STANDBY mode—10 hours
    EMERGENCY mode—3.5 hours

G-15. OPERATION

The MWTS has three modes of operation: STANDBY, ON, and EMERGENCY. Figure G-24, page G-26, shows controls and indicators.

a. **Modes.**

(1) *STANDBY Mode.* When the system is first turned on, the MWTS begins a cool-down period of about 2 minutes. After the cool-down period, the MWTS enters the STANDBY mode. During the STANDBY mode, power is not applied to the scanner or display to extend the life of the battery.

(2) *ON Mode.* When the MWTS is in the STANDBY mode and pressure is applied to the eyecup, the MWTS switches to the ON mode, and a switch engages to provide power to the scanner and display. After a three-second delay, the system is fully operational.

(c) EMERGENCY mode. When switched to the EMERGENCY mode, the MWTS continuously applies power to the entire system. This mode allows the operator to bypass the 3-second delay experienced when switching from the STANDBY to the ON mode. Since power is applied to the entire system while in the emergency mode, battery life is greatly reduced.

b. **Controls and Switches.**

(1) The CONTRAST CONTROL (1) adjusts the contrast of the thermal scene. When turned fully clockwise to AUTO, contrast is automatically set.

(2) The EMERGENCY CONTROL (2) overrides the eyecup switch and turns entire system on, which places the MWTS in the EMERGENCY mode.

(3) The BRIGHTNESS CONTROL (3) is a nine-position rotary switch with an off detent position (turned fully counterclockwise). The purpose is to turn the system on or off and adjust the brightness of the eyepiece display.

(4) The FOCUS RING (4) adjusts the telescope focus from 20 meters to infinity. It requires a manual adjustment and affects both the wide and narrow fields of view.

(5) The FIELD OF VIEW RING (5) is located on the telescope. It has a wide and a narrow field of view. The wide FOV is for using low magnification during target detection, and the narrow FOV is for using high magnification during recognition and engagement.

(6) The RETICLE SELECT SWITCH (6) selects one of the available reticles depending on the MWTS model (medium or heavy). It must be held for 2 seconds to enable reticle changes. After 2 seconds, release the switch to cycle to the next reticle. This control is disabled after 10 seconds of inactivity.

(7) The RETICLE ADJUST SWITCH (7) adjusts the reticle aiming features in azimuth and elevation. It is used during zeroing, and it must be held for 2 seconds to allow changes to be made. After 2 seconds, each press moves the reticle aiming features one increment. This control is also disabled after 10 seconds of inactivity.

(8) The BLACK/WHITE POLARITY SWITCH (8) selects the polarity of the thermal image displayed on the raster. The initial setting is WHITE HOT. The polarity switch affects the appearance of the target.

(9) The EYECUP (9) controls STANDBY/ON when the system is on. When forward pressure is applied to the eyecup, the system is in the ON mode. When the pressure is removed for longer than 30 seconds, the system returns to the standby mode.

(10) The DIOPTER FOCUS RING (10) adjusts the focus of the raster and indicators to the operator's eye. It ranges from +2 to -6 diopters.

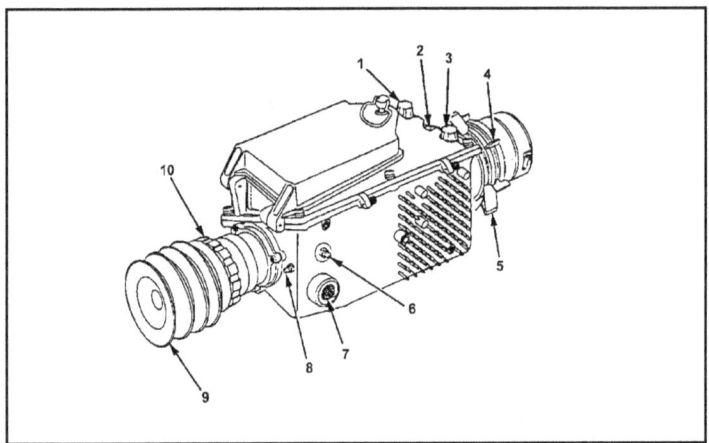

Figure G-24. MWTS controls and indicators.

c. **Eyepiece Indicators** (Figure G-25). Eyepiece indicators illuminate as follows:

(1) NOT COOL (11) when the detectors are not cool enough for proper operation.

(2) WHT HOT/BLK HOT (12) polarity.

(3) EMER (13) during emergency mode operation.

(4) LOW (14) when battery power has about 15 minutes of useful power left with go-to-war batteries.

(5) RETICLE SELECT/FOV (15) identifies which reticle is currently selected and indicates wide FOV or narrow FOV as selected by the FOV.

(6) ELEVATION INDICATOR (16) indicates the elevation zeroing adjustment of the reticle. It also displays the number of increments the reticle is UP (U) or (D) DOWN from the center zero position.

(7) NFOV/WFOV (17) indicates wide FOV or narrow FOV.

(8) ZOOM (18) indicates the zoom mode is selected.

(9) RET ADJ (19) indicates the reticle adjustment mode is selected.

(10) RET SEL (20) indicates the reticle select mode is selected.

(11) AZIMUTH INDICATOR (21) indicates the azimuth zeroing adjustment of the reticle. It also displays the number of increments the reticle is left (L) or right (R) from the center zero position.

(12) SENSOR COOLING (22) is displayed when the power is turned on, the indicator displays about a 2-minute cool-down period. After cool-down, the current reticle is displayed.

(13) The COOLDOWN PERIOD INDICATORS blink the first 10 seconds after the system is turned on. After 10 seconds, the NOT COOL indicator is lit and the POLARITY, EMERGENCY, and LOW BATTERY indicators function normally. The DISPLAY RASTER displays the thermal image with a superimposed reticle.

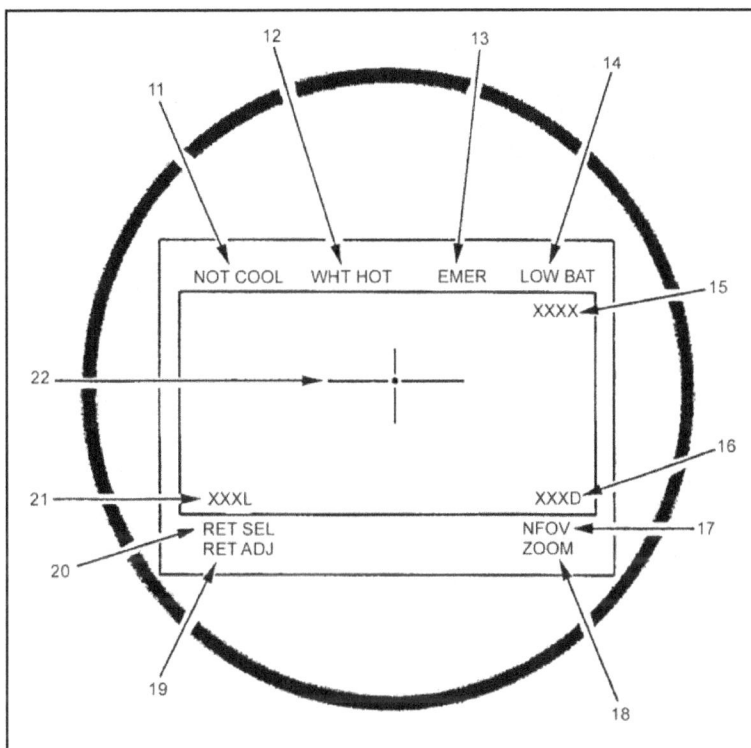

Figure G-25. Eyepiece indicators.

CAUTION

When raising or lowering the cover with the MWTS installed, avoid slamming the MWTS into the heat shield or slamming the cover closed.

---

d. **M249 Machine Gun.**

(1) *Mounting Procedures.* Before zeroing and qualifying with the AN/PAS-13, the gunner must mount the sight on the weapon (Figure G-26, page G-28).

(a) Open the cover of the weapon.

(b) Rotate the hook-retaining pin downward (over the top of the hinge pin) and remove the retaining clip from the left side of the hinge pin.

(c) Remove the weapon's hinge pin. **Do not lose the retaining clip.**

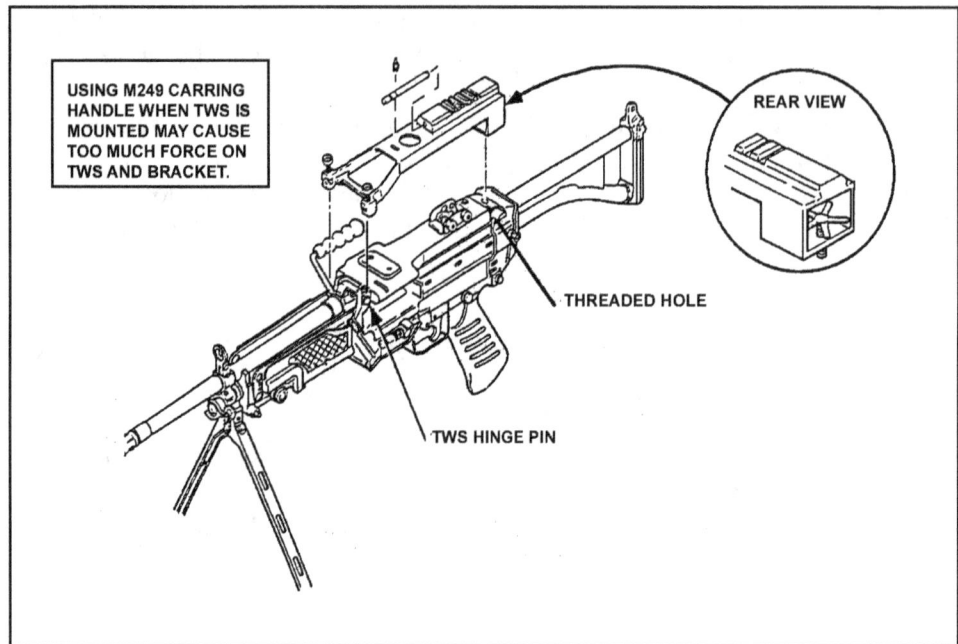

Figure G-26. Mounting the MWTS on the M249.

(d) Remove the retaining clip from the M249 mounting bracket (Figure G-27).

(e) Remove the MWTS hinge pin from the mounting bracket and replace it with the M249 hinge pin (Figure G-28, page G-29). Secure it to the mounting bracket by replacing the retaining clip (the one from the mounting bracket).

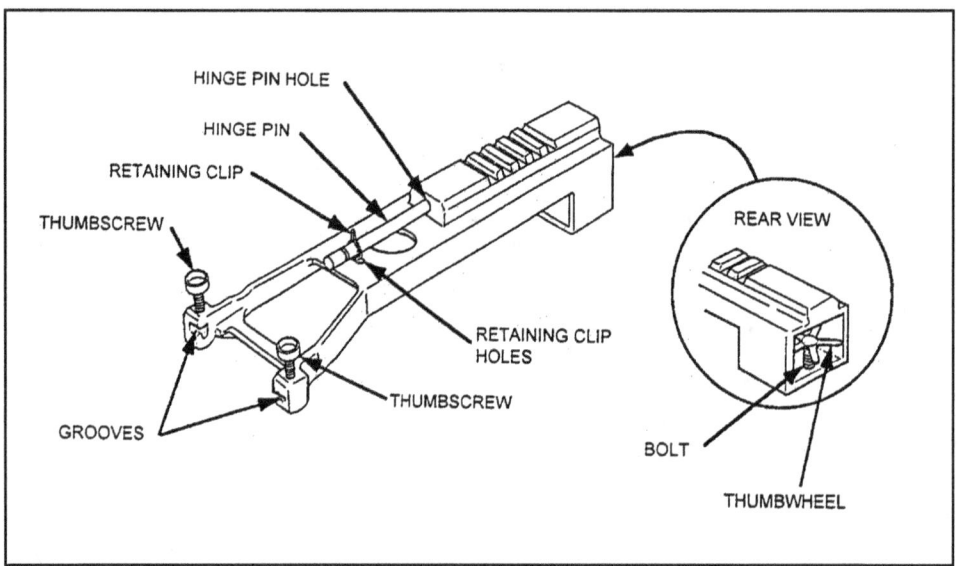

Figure G-27. M249 bracket.

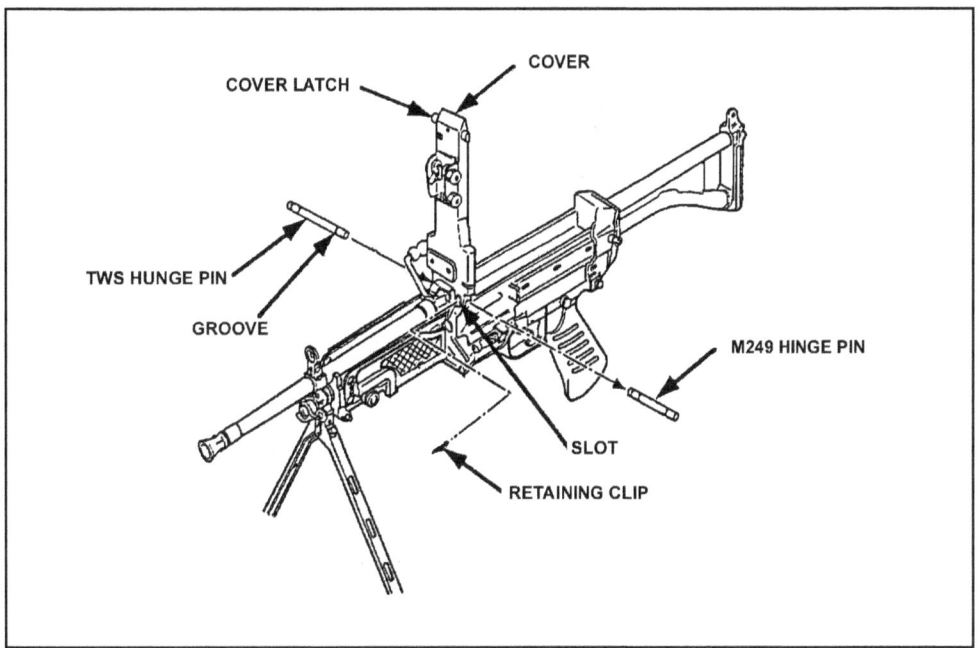

Figure G-28. M249 hinge pin replacement.

(f) Replace the cover of the M249 so that the slot in the cover lines up with the holes in the receiver group.

(g) Push the MWTS hinge pin through the slot and the spring.

(h) Secure the MWTS hinge pin by rotating the hook-retaining pin upward (over the hinge pin) and replacing the retaining clip on the left side of the pin. Close the cover of the weapon.

(i) Place the grooves on the front of the bracket over the edges of the MWTS hinge pin and rotate the bracket downward onto the cover. Ensure that the thumb wheel on the rear of the mounting bracket lines up with the threaded hole on the cover of the weapon.

(j) Secure the mounting bracket to the cover by tightening the thumbscrews and the thumb wheel.

(k) Select a slot on the rail of the bracket and place the bar of the MWTS mount in the slot. Hand-tighten the knob on the MWTS mount until it clicks at least twice.

(2) *Dismounting Procedures.*

(a) Loosen the knob on the MWTS mount until it is free of the rail and remove the MWTS.

(b) Unscrew the thumb wheel and thumbscrews and remove the mounting bracket from the weapon.

(c) Open the cover of the weapon and remove the retaining clip from the MWTS hinge pin.

(d) Rotate the hook-retaining pin downward (over the top of the hinge pin) and remove the MWTS hinge pin.

(e) Remove the M249 hinge pin from the mounting bracket and replace it with the MWTS hinge pin. Secure it with the MWTS retaining clip.

(f) Place the cover of the M249 on top of the weapon, aligning the holes in the cover with the slot in the receiver.

(g) Replace the M249 hinge pin to the weapon.

(h) Secure the M249 hinge pin by replacing the retaining clip and rotating the hook-retaining pin upward (over the top of the hinge pin).

CAUTION

Failure to move the MWTS to the rear before opening the feed tray causes damage to the MWTS. Push in on the cam release and push the MWTS to the rear. To return the MWTS to the firing position, push in on the cam release and slide the MWTS forward. When raising or lowering the cover with the MWTS installed, avoid slamming the MWTS into the heat shield or slamming the cover closed.

---

e. **M60 Machine Gun.**

(1) *Mounting Procedures.* Before zeroing and qualifying with the AN/PAS-13, the gunner must mount the sight on the weapon (Figure G-29).

(a) Loosen the clamping bars all the way on the MWTS mounting brackets by turning the thumb wheels.

(b) Loosen the locking nuts on the front of the MWTS mounting bracket (Figure G-30, page G-31).

(c) Open the feed tray cover of the M60 and remove the M60 hinge pin and hinge pin latch (Figure G-31, page G-31).

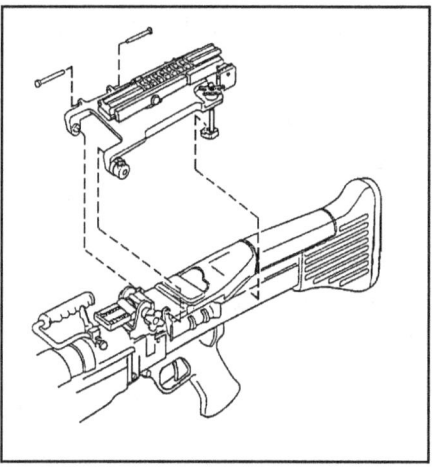

Figure G-29. Mounting the MWTS on the M60.

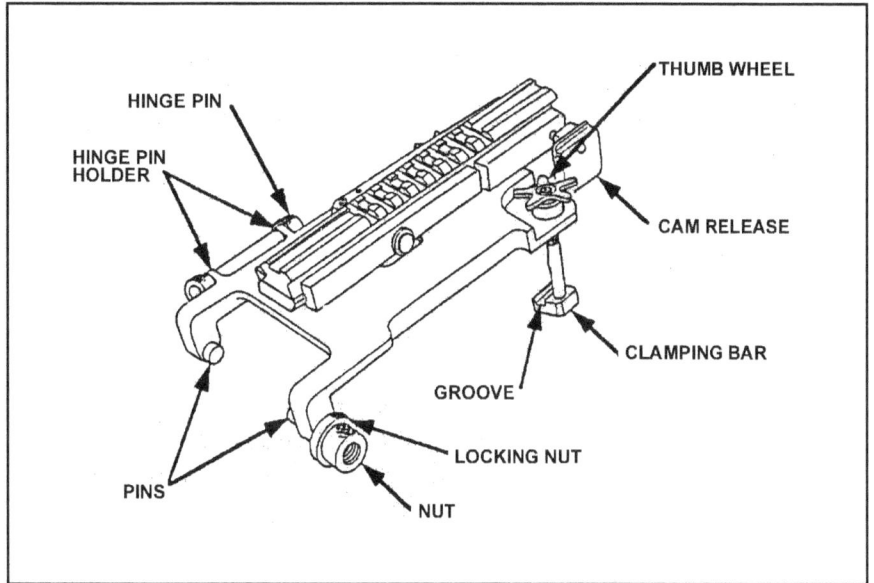

Figure G-30. M60 bracket.

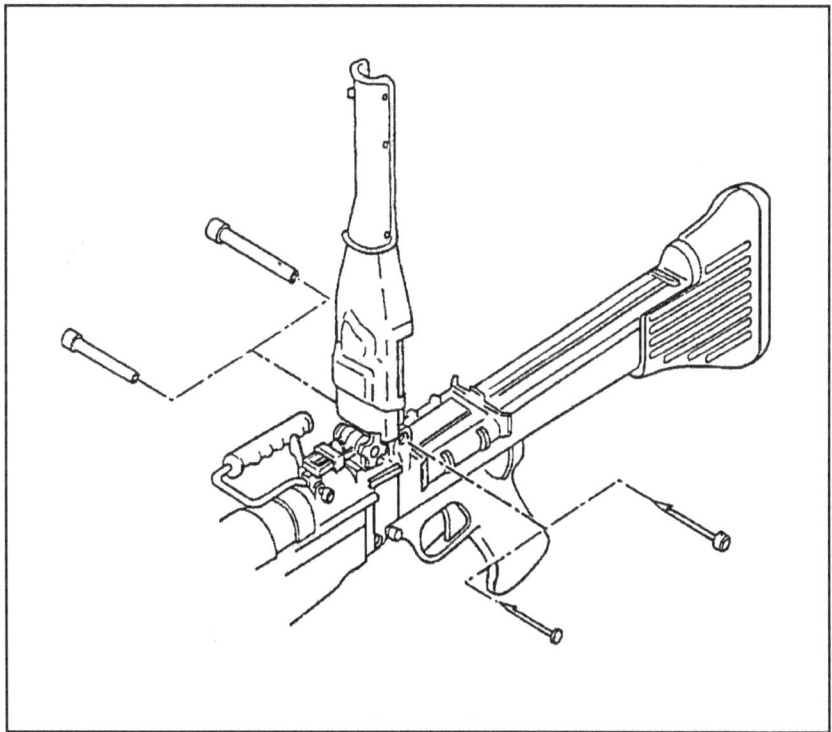

Figure G-31. M60 hinge pin replacement.

(d) Remove the MWTS hinge pin and hinge pin latch from the M60 mounting bracket.

(e) Place the MWTS hinge pin and hinge pin latch through the holes in the feed tray and feed tray cover to secure them to the M60.

(f) Insert the hinge pin (the larger pin) from the left side of the gun. Insert the hinge pin latch (the smaller pin) from the right.

(g) Place the M60 hinge pin and hinge pin latch into the hinge pin holder on the MWTS mounting bracket.

(h) Place the pins on the inside front of the MWTS mounting bracket over the holes in the hinge pin and hinge pin latch.

(i) Place the clamping bars so that the grooves in them fit under the lip of the feed tray cover.

(j) Tighten the locking nuts by hand and tighten the clamping bars by rotating the thumb wheels.

(k) Select a slot on the rail of the bracket and place the bar of the MWTS mount in the slot.

(l) Hand tighten the knob on the MWTS mount until it clicks at least twice.

(2) *Dismounting Procedures.*

(a) Loosen the mounting knob located on the left side of the MWTS mount until it is free of the rail and remove the MWTS.

(b) Unscrew the thumb wheels and locking nuts and remove the mounting bracket from the weapon.

(c) Open the cover of the weapon and remove the MWTS hinge pin.

(d) Remove the M60 hinge pin from the mounting bracket and replace it with the MWTS hinge pin. Secure it with the retaining clip.

(e) Place the cover of the M60 on top of the weapon, aligning the holes in the cover with the slot in the receiver.

(f) Replace and secure the M60 hinge pin to the weapon.

CAUTION

When raising or lowering the cover with the MWTS installed, avoid slamming the MWTS into the heat shield or slamming the cover closed.

---

f. **M240B Machine Gun.**

(1) *Mounting Procedures.* Before zeroing and qualifying with the AN/PAS-13, the gunner must mount the sight on the weapon. The M240B machine gun has a rail mount already attached to the cover assembly.

(a) Install the sight on the M240B rail mount by loosening the mounting knob located on the left side.

(b) Position the sight on the rail mount by placing the bar of the mount in a slot on the rail and hand tighten the knob on the mount until two clicks are heard. Any slot can be used as long as the mount does not hang over the edge of the rail (Figure G-32).

WARNING

Do not store the AN/PAS-13 with batteries installed.

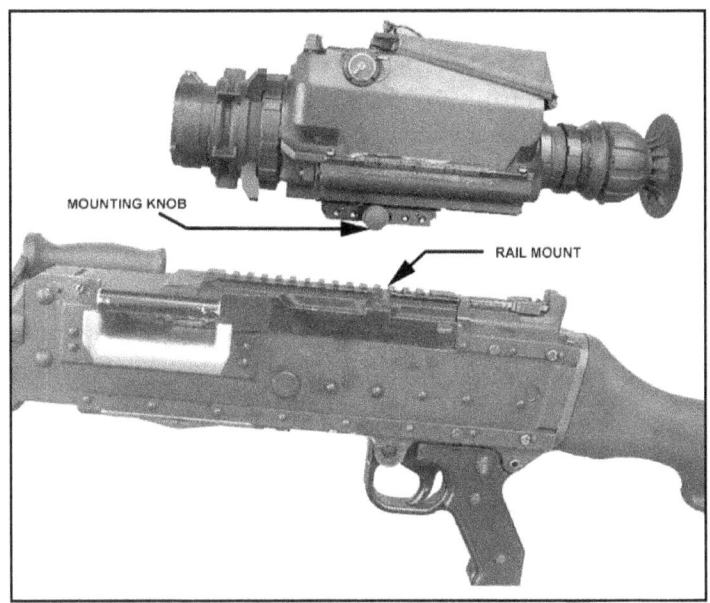

Figure G-32. Mounting the ANPAS-13 to the M240B.

(2) *Dismounting Procedures*.

(a) Unscrew the mounting knob on the left side.

(b) Lift up on the sight to remove it from the M240B machine gun.

g. **Boresighting Procedures**. Follow the instructions to boresight the weapon as outlined in TC 23-AIMSS. Choose the correct reticle for the weapon by pressing the reticle select switch for 2 seconds. Then scroll through the reticles until the correct one is found. Follow the instructions for boresighting the MWTS on the boresight target offset. Adjust the aiming point until the red dot is centered on the cross hair on the offset. You must boresight in both the narrow FOV and wide FOV.

h. **Zeroing Procedures**. Refer to TM 11-5855-309-12&P for zeroing procedures for the M249, M60, and M240B machine guns.

G-16. TRAINING STRATEGIES

The training strategies for the 5.56-mm and 7.62-mm caliber weapons with the MWTS are the same as with the AN/PVS-4 (as outlined in paragraph G-8) for both the night initial and night sustainment training strategies.

Section V. M145 STRAIGHT TELESCOPE (MGO)

The M145 telescope is a fixed 3.4-power, 28-mm optical sight that has been designed to accurately engage targets out to 1,200 meters. The optical sight weighs 24 ounces (681 grams) and is extremely rugged for rough field conditions. The sight has an 8.2-mm diameter exit pupil, which provides excellent vision in low light levels; for example, dawn and dusk, and also for rapid target acquisition.

G-17. DESCRIPTION

The M145 straight telescope is a telescopic sight. The telescope magnifies targets by three and a half times or it appears to bring the shooter three and a half times closer to the target. The telescope shows more clearly the strike of the round and allows more accurate shooting. In low-light conditions, removal of the laser filter enhances target detection far better than that visible to the naked eye (Figure G-33). The lens cover protects the lens when the sight is being transport or stored. The lens cover should always be kept closed when the sight is not in use. The battery has an O-ring that keeps out moisture. With practice you may be able to keep both eyes open. With both eyes open, the gunner is more aware of the surroundings and feels less strain on his eyes. The M145 straight telescope must remain matched with the same weapon, attached at the same slot in the rail system, or if not, it must be rezeroed.

G-18. DATA

The following is the equipment's data.

Weight:	24.0 ounces (681 grams)
Length:	7 inches (175mm)
Battery Life:	175 hours average (fresh battery)
	Sight is packed with a new battery.
Optics:	Antireflective coated lens system, (28mm) clear objective, x3.4 magnification.

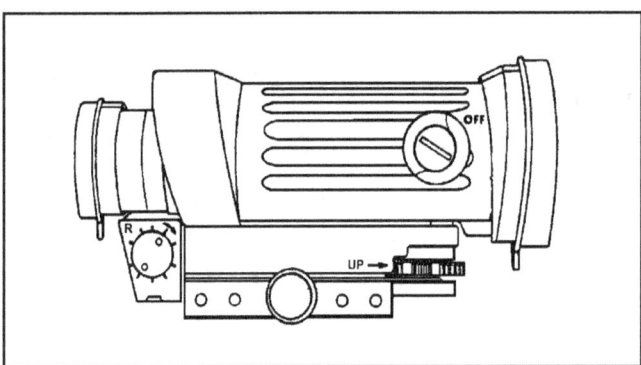

Figure G-33. M145 Telescope (MGO).

G-19. CONTROLS

The following is a brief description of the operation controls and its indicators.

a. **Elevation Adjustment Dial**. The elevation adjustment dial is used for zeroing the telescope to the weapon. The dial can only be rotated when the silver lock (1) is moved to the UP position. Turning the elevation adjustment dial (2) counterclockwise in the direction of the arrows one click moves the point of impact up 2.5 mm at 10 meters. Turning the elevation adjustment dial (2) clockwise (opposite direction to the arrow) one click moves the point of impact down 2.5 mm at 10 meters. Ensure that the silver lock (1) is moved down to prevent any further movement of the elevation adjustment dial (Figure G-34).

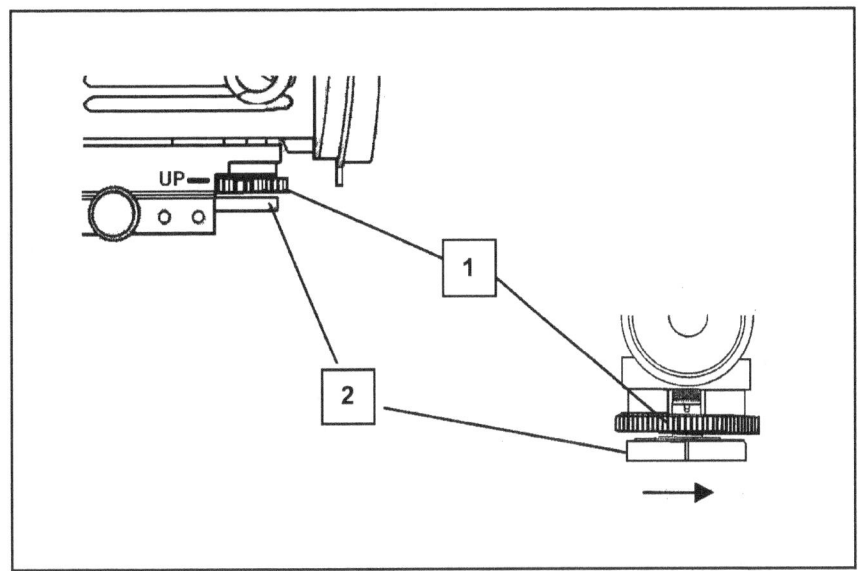

Figure G-34. Rotation of the elevation adjustment dial.

b. **Windage Adjustment Screw.** The windage adjustment screw is used when zeroing the weapon. Turning the windage adjustment screw (3) clockwise one click moves the point of impact left 2.5 mm at 10 meters. Turning the windage adjustment screw (3) counterclockwise, one click moves the point of impact right 2.5 mm at 10 meters (Figure G-35).

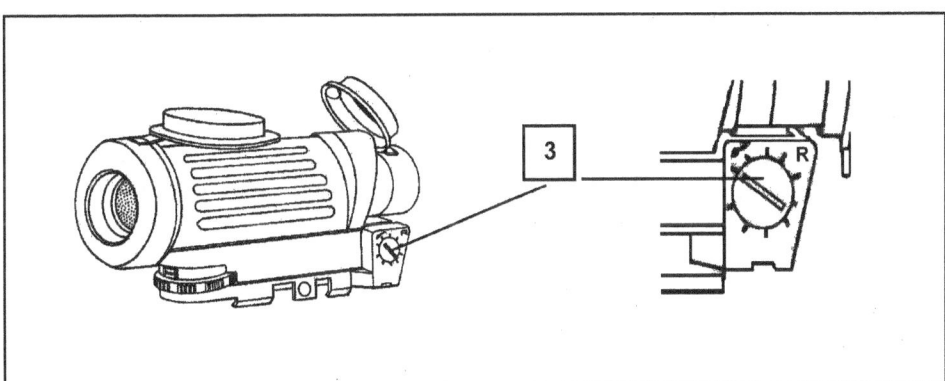

Figure G-35. Rotation of the windage adjustment screw.

G-20. BATTERY
This paragraph explains how to install and check the battery.

a. Remove battery cap (1) by turning it counterclockwise and holding the rotary reticle illumination switch (3) stationary.

CAUTION

Before installing the battery cap, inspect the threads on the battery housing and the battery cap to ensure that they are free of moisture and dirt. Ensure the O-ring (4) in the battery cap (1) is present. Failure to do so could result in loss of electrical power and shorten battery life.

---

    b. Insert battery (2) with positive (+) end to cap (Figure G-36).

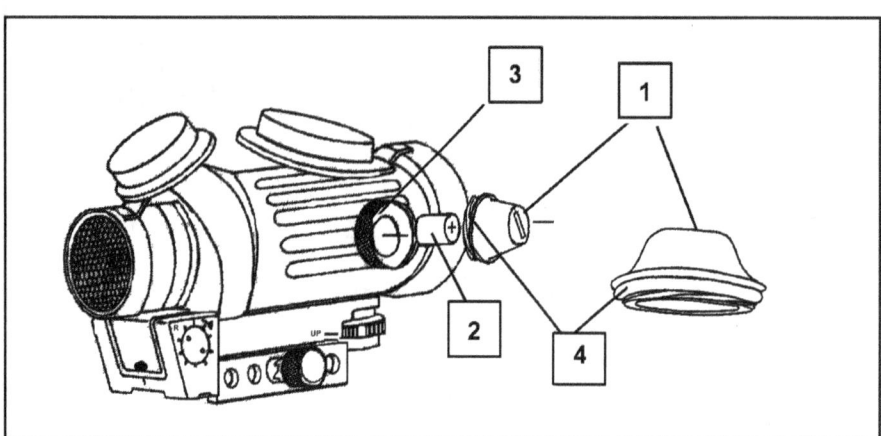

Figure G-36. Installing and checking batteries.

CAUTION

Before installing the battery cap, inspect the threads on battery housing and battery cap to ensure that they are free of moisture and dirt. Ensure the O-ring in the battery cap is present. Failure to do so could result in loss of electrical power and shorten battery life. Tighten the battery cap by hand. Using tools to tighten the battery cap could damage the equipment.

---

    c. Reinstall the battery cap (1) by holding the rotary reticle illumination switch (3) stationary turning clockwise until snug. Tighten by hand only.

    d. Open the rear lens cover (4). Turn the rotary reticle illumination switch (3) and look through rear lens. Verify that the reticle is illuminated. If not, replace the battery. When finished, turn the rotary switch to the OFF position, and then replace the rear lens cover (Figure G-37).

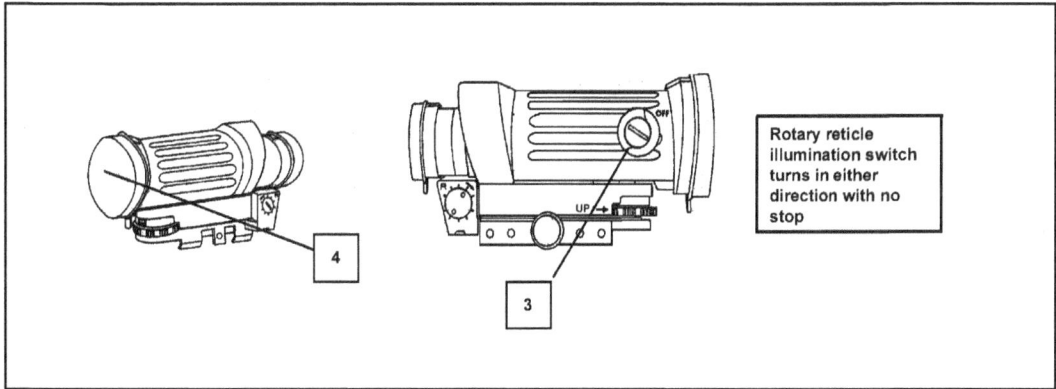

Rotary reticle
illumination switch
turns in either
direction with no
stop

Figure G-37. Rotary reticle illumination switch.

G-21. INSTALLTION

The M145 straight telescope mounts directly to the mounting rail on the M249, and M240B machine guns. It is necessary that you adjust the position of the M145 telescope either backwards or forward on the rail in order to achieve the correct eye relief (distance of the eye from the back of the telescope). If the same sight is installed in the same position slot on the rail on the same weapon, rezeroing is not required.

┌───┐
│   **CAUTION**   │
│ **By hand, tighten the torque limiting knob until you** │
│ **hear two clicks. Using tools to tighten the mounting** │
│ **hardware could damage equipment.**   │
└───┘

a. Back off on the torque limiting knob just enough for the rail grabber to go over the rail. Do not force the torque limiting knob past its intended stop. Mount the M145 straight telescope firmly over the rail. Ensure that the mount is seated squarely over the rail. Tighten the torque limiting knob (clockwise) until it rotates with two clicks. Ensure that the mount is securely fastened before commencing eye relief adjustment. The sight is now mounted to the weapon about 3 inches (70 mm) in front of the firing eye (Figure G-38 [M249] and Figure G-39 [M240B], page G-38). Assume a comfortable firing position and achieve a good stockweld (at trigger pull length) with both eyes closed. Open the sighting eye and compare the view through the scope with the following figures:

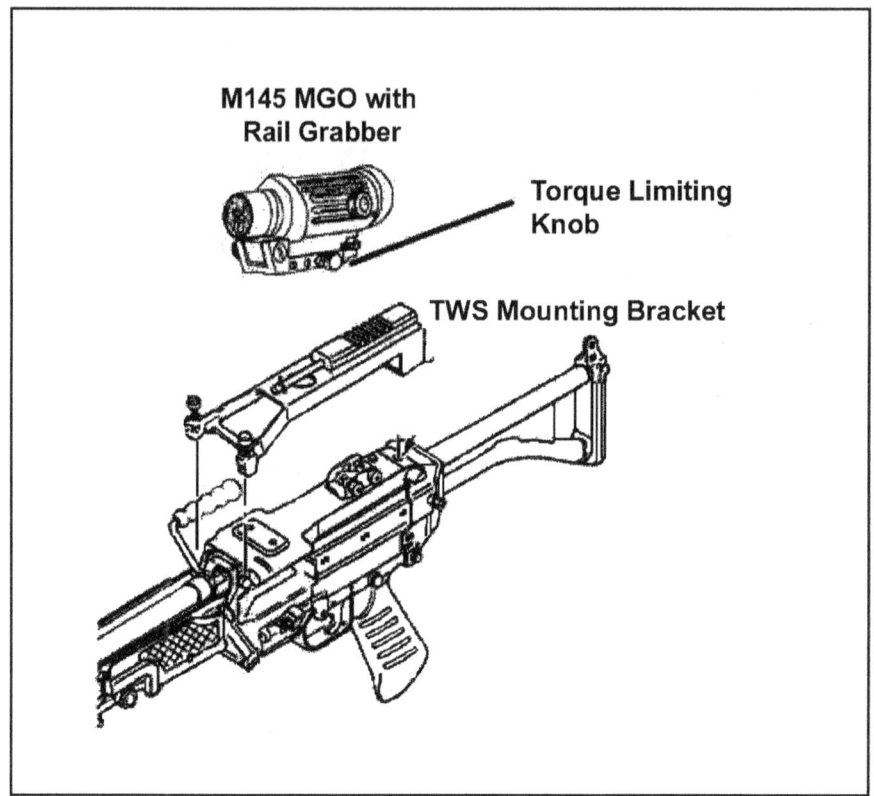

Figure G-38. Mounting the MGO to the M249.

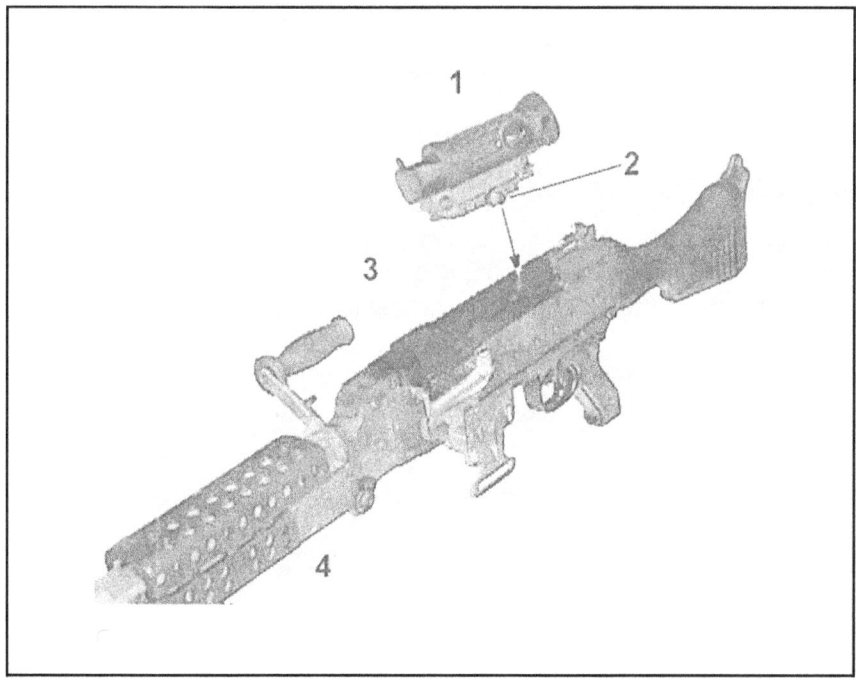

Figure G-39. Mounting the MGO the M240B.

(1) If the target scene fills the scope to provide the maximum field of view, the correct eye relief has been attained (Figure G-40). No further repositioning of the M145 on the mounting rail is required.

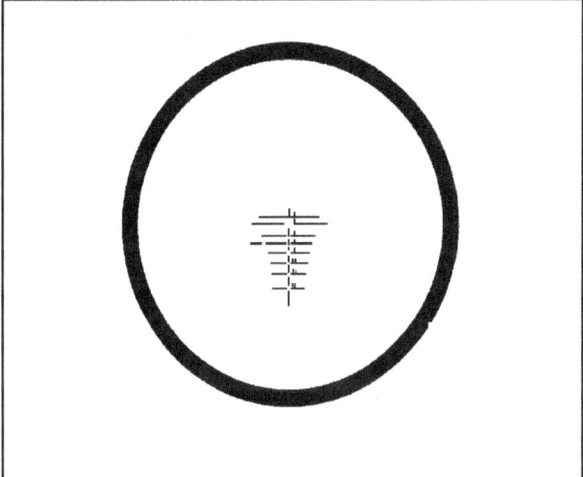

Figure G-40. Correct eye relief.

(2) If the target scene does not fill the sight's field of view, the optical sight must be repositioned on the rail either forwards or backwards (Figure G-41).

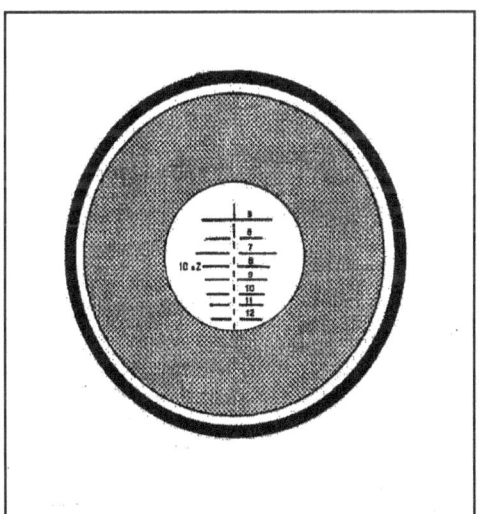

Figure G-41. Incorrect eye relief.

b. The optical sight must be repositioned for correct eye relief. Loosen the torque limiting knob and move the optical sight in the appropriate direction (forward or backward), which provides the full field of view.

c. Repeat a until the correct sight picture is obtained as shown in Figure G-41.

G-22. MOUNTING PROCEDURES (M60 ONLY)

Refer to Figures G-42a and G-42b when mounting MWTS on M60 machine gun.

a. Press on the end of the MWTS hinge pin latch (1) and remove the MWTS hinge pin latch and the MWTS hinge pin (2) from the M60 bracket (3).

b. Install the MWTS hinge pin (2) and the MWTS hinge pin latch (1) on the M60 machine gun (4).

c. Press on the right side end of the M60 hinge pin latch (5) with a pointed object and remove the M60 hinge pin latch.

d. Release the feed tray cover latch (6) and fully raise the feed tray cover (7).

e. Remove the M60 hinge pin (8). Keep the cover held in place.

f. Install the MWTS hinge pin (2) in right side of the hole (9).

g. Insert the MWTS hinge pin latch (1) through the left side of the MWTS hinge pin (2) until interlocked.

h. Lower the feed tray cover (7) and connect the feed tray cover latch (6).

i. Insert the M60 hinge pin (8) through the holes (10) of the bracket (3) and insert the M60 hinge pin latch (5) through the M60 hinge pin until interlocked.

j. Close the objective lens cover.

k. Push in the cam release and slide the rail back until the rail locks in place.

l. Open the M60 machine gun feed tray cover.

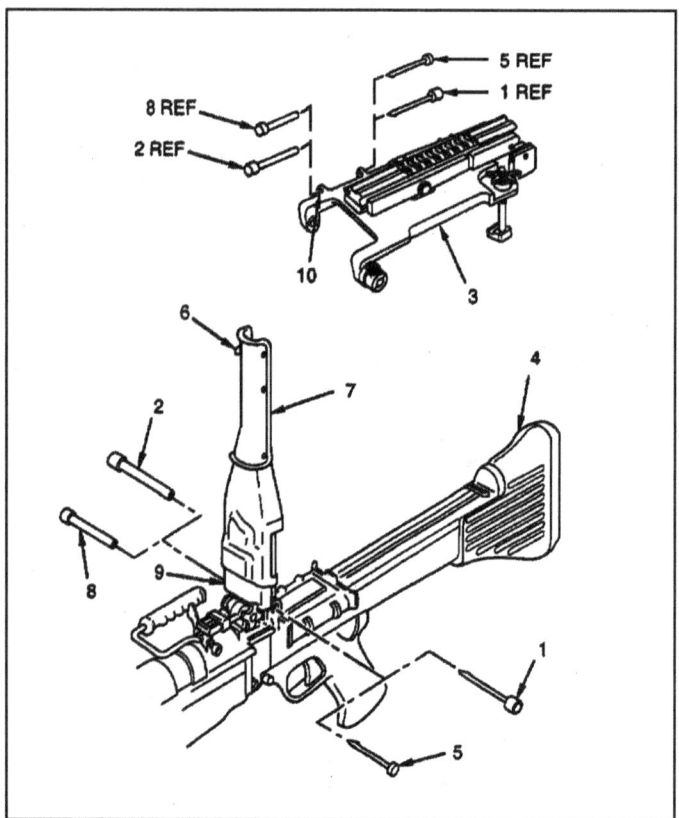

Figure G-42a. Mounting the MGO to the M60 machine gun.

m. Install the bracket (3) on the M60 machine gun (4). Fold the rear sight (11) forward. Place the pins (12) of the bracket (3) in the cups (13) of the MWTS hinge pin (2) and the MWTS hinge pin latch (1) and tighten the nut (14) by hand. Tighten the locking nut (15) by hand. Place the groove (16) of the two clamping bars (17) on the edge of the feed tray cover (4) and tighten the two thumbwheels (18).

n. Install the MGO on the rail. Loosen the clamping knob on the mount. Select the slot on the rail for mounting. Any slot may be used as long as the mount does not hang over edge of rail. Place the bar of the mount in the slot of the rail and tighten the knob on the mount by hand until two clicks are heard.

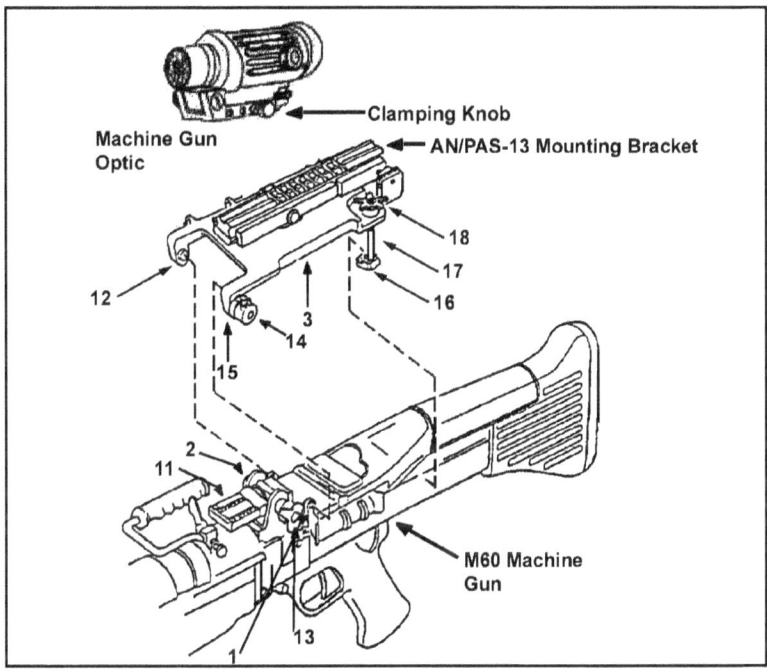

Figure G-42b. Mounting the MGO to the M60 (continued).

G-23. ZEROE PROCEDURES

The following paragraphs explain the different ways to zero the M145 straight telescope on the M240B, M60, and M249 machine guns.

a. **Zeroing to Weapon.** Zeroing the M145 straight telescope aligns the sight to the barrel of the machine gun so that the point of aim equals the point of impact. Adjustment of the M145 straight telescope is centered at the factory.

(1) Open the front (1) and the rear (2) lens covers.

(2) Turn each cover inside out to stow the lens covers while the sight is being used (Figure G-43).

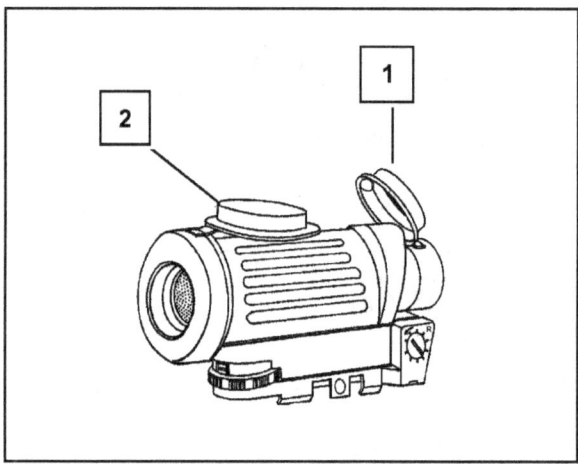

Figure G-43. Stowing the lens covers.

b. **10-Meter Zeroing, Setting to Mechanical Zero.**

(1) Adjust the straight telescope so that the weapon's barrel and the optical sighting axis are in alignment. The sighting axis is about 2 to 3 inches above the machine gun barrel, and therefore the strike of the bullet at a 10-meter range is also about 2 to 3 inches low without further zeroing adjustment (Figure G-44). To bring the strike of the bullet up, lift the silver lock and rotate the elevation adjustment dial counterclockwise (to the right) about one full turn.

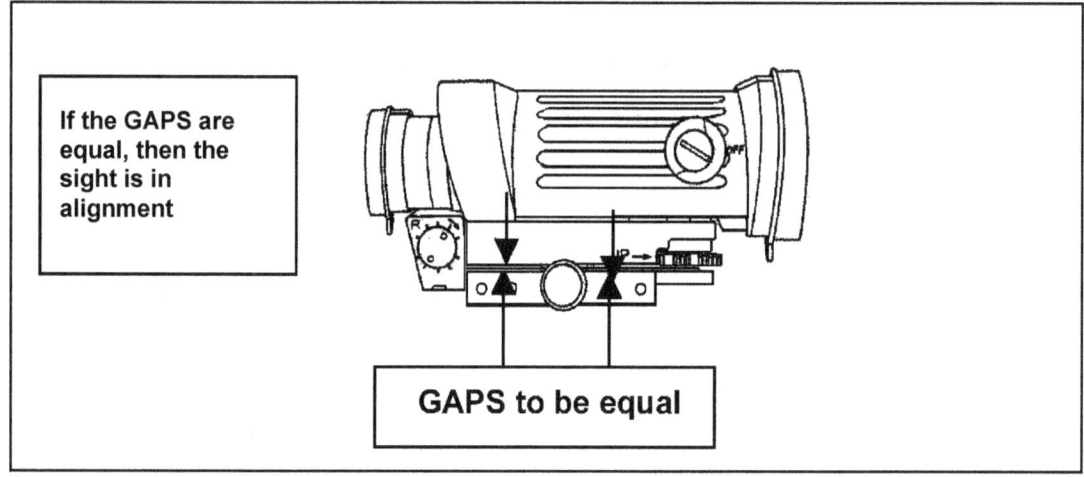

Figure G-44. GAPS to be equal.

(2) Adjust the windage dial to center the markings on the front of the sight. This adjustment brings the bullet's point of impact to the middle of the point of aim

(Figure G-45). Each click of zeroing adjustments makes a 2.5 mm movement of the point of impact at 10 meters.

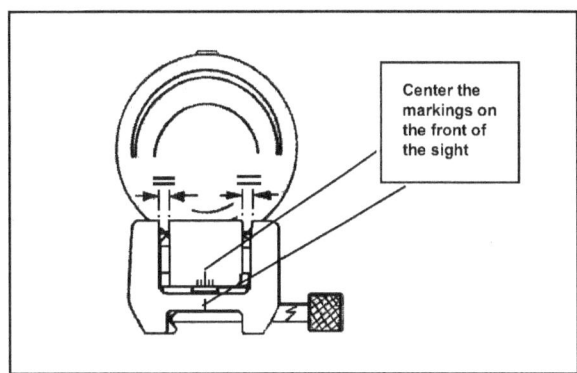

Figure G-45. Centering the markings.

(3) To move the point of impact to the right, turn the windage adjustment screw (2) counterclockwise with the arrow marked on the dial.

(4) To move the point of impact to the left, turn the windage adjustment screw (2) clockwise opposite to the arrow.

(5) To move point of impact up, turn the elevation adjustment screw (1) counterclockwise (right) with the direction of the arrow marked and "UP."

(6) To move the point of impact down, turn the elevation adjustment screw (1) clockwise (left) opposite to the arrow (Figure G-46).

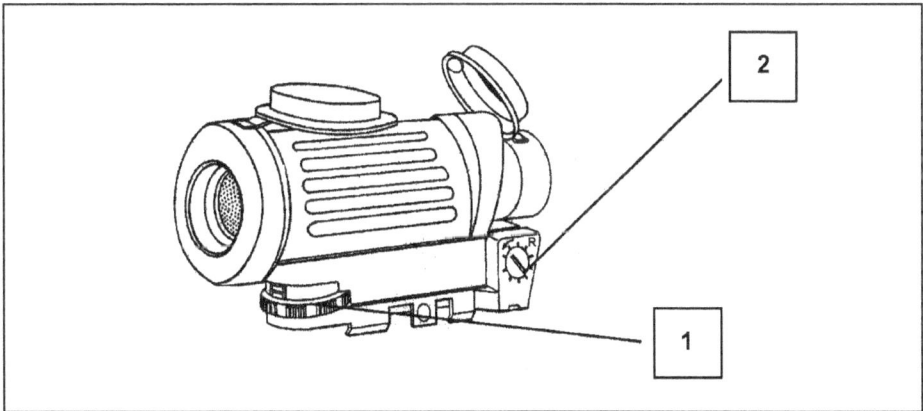

Figure G-46. Adjusting point of impact.

c. **10-Meter Range Zeroing.** In the zeroing process, groups of three-single shot rounds are fired at a target. After each three rounds, the center of the group has to be determined.

(1) Look through the telescope and align the reticle's 10-meter zeroing mark on the center base of the aiming points on the basic machine gun marksmanship target (Figure G-47, page G-44).

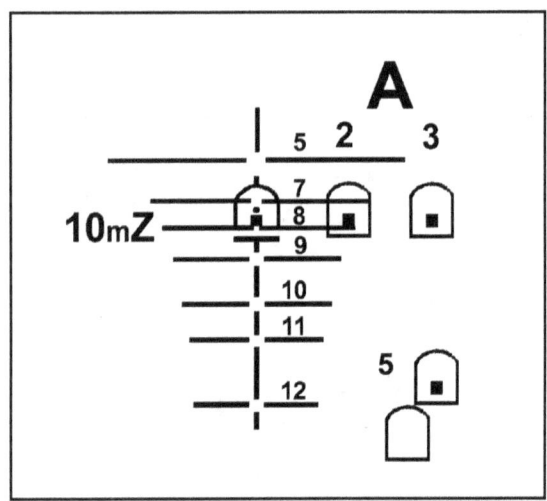

Figure G-47. 10-meter reticle aiming point.

(2) Fire three-single rounds loaded individually without making any sight adjustments.

(3) The three-round shot group should be within a 4-cm circle to establish the center of the shot group in relation to the center base of the aiming paster.

(4) Measure the amount of movement that is required left or right (windage) and either up or down (elevation) to move the three-round shot group onto the center of the aiming paster.

(5) Upon completion, return to the firing line to make corrections to the weapon and refire a three-round shot group to confirm zero (Figure G-48).

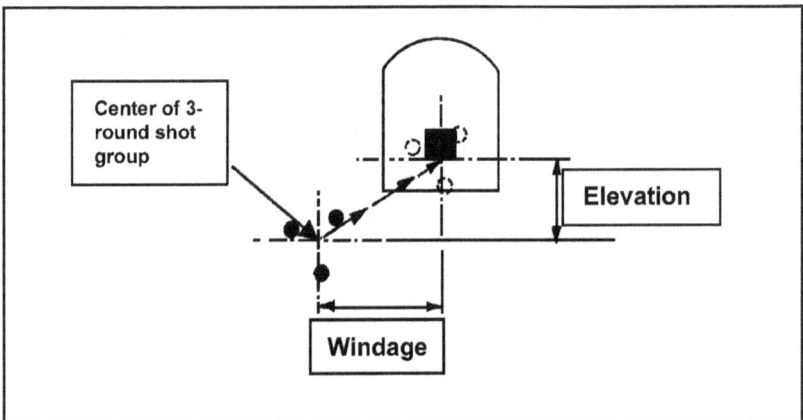

Figure G-48. Three-round shot group with adjustments.

(6) Repeat the above steps until the strike of the round is coincident with the center of the target. Close the silver lock down to prevent any further movement of the elevation zeroing adjustment dial.

d. **Field Zeroing at 500-Meter Range**. Look through the telescope and align the reticle's 500-meter mark on the center of mass of the double "E" silhouette target (Figure G-49):

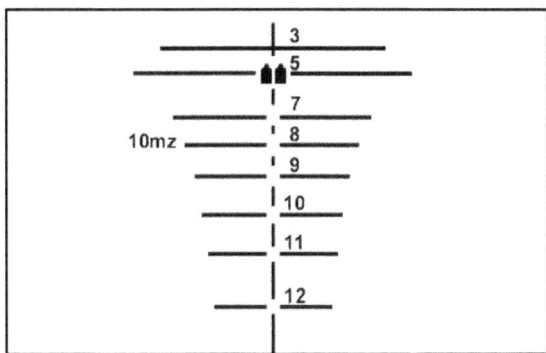

Figure G-49. 500-meter reticle aiming point.

(1) M240B, M60, and M249 machine guns: Fire a 5- to 7-round burst.

(2) Observe the impact of the rounds.

(3) Determine the direction of impact to be moved (up or down, left or right).

(4) Estimate or measure the amount of movement required to move the strike of the round to the center of the target (at 500 meters; 5 inches equals one click of adjustment in both windage and elevations). Repeat these steps until the strike of the round coincides with the center of the target.

NOTE: Close the silver lock down to prevent any further movement of the elevation zeroing adjustment dial. The M145 straight telescope is now zeroed and ready for operational shooting.

e. **Using Reticle to Estimate Range**. The vertical gap in the stadia lines is for estimating ranges. The height of gaps in the stadia lines represents a 60-inch high target at the range noted; for example, 5, 7, 8, 9, 10, 11, or 1,200 meters (Figure G-50).

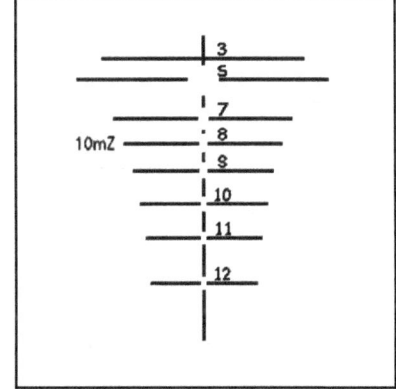

Figure G-50. Reticle stadia lines.

f. **Illuminating the Reticle.** For low light operations, the reticle can be illuminated to show the 300-, 500-, 700-, and 800-meter aiming marks (Figure G-51). The sight is equipped with variable intensity LED illumination of the reticle. It has 10 positions: one OFF position and 9 positions for different reticle intensity settings.

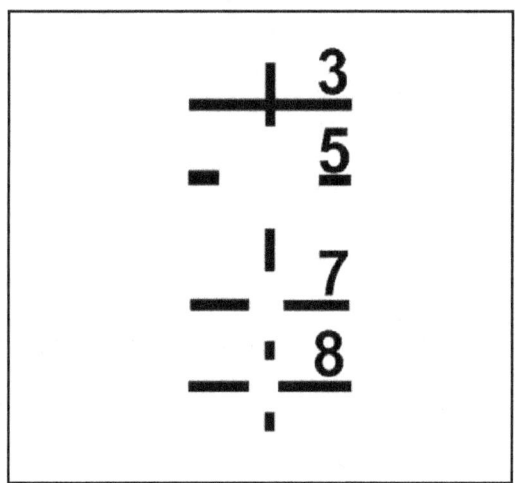

Figure G-51. Illuminated reticle.

(1) To make reticle illumination adjustments, turn the rotary switch (1) clockwise. The intensity of the illumination increases the further the switch is turned (Figure G-52).

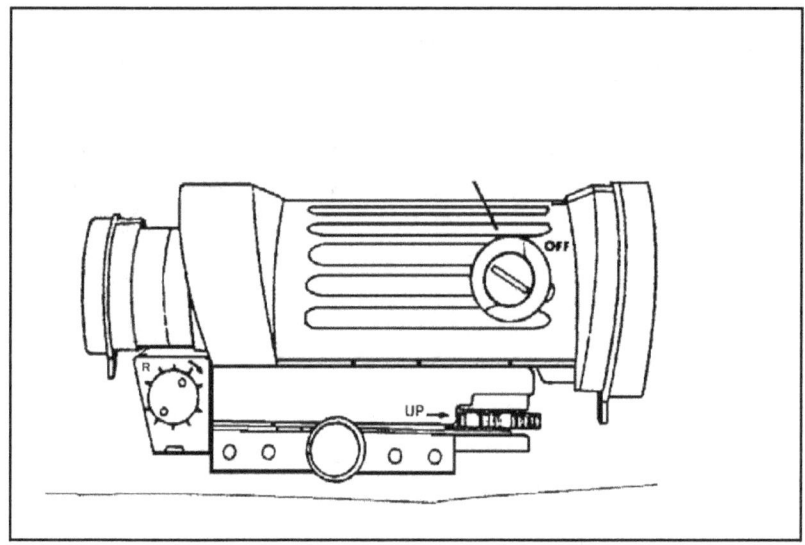

Figure G-52. Illuminated reticle adjustments.

(2) Turn the rotary switch to the OFF position when the telescope is being used during normal daylight or when illumination is not required (Figure G-53). Ensure the reticle illumination switch is turned to the OFF position when not required.

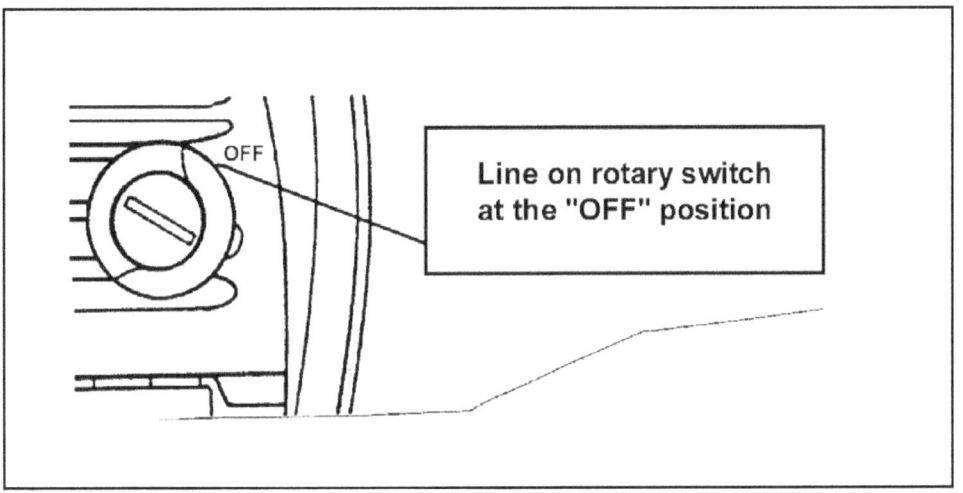

Figure G-53. OFF switch.

G-21. MOUNTING AND ZEROING THE AN/PVS-4

Zeroing aligns the AN/PVS-4 to the M249. The sight may be zeroed during daylight or darkness. (See TM 11-5855-213-10.) If done during daylight, the daylight cover must be used. To obtain a precise zero, it is best done at 300 meters and at night. Once an AN/PVS-4 has been zeroed on an M249 machine gun, any soldier who knows how to use the reticle should fire the weapon effectively. However, there may be some changes in zero when the objective focus is adjusted to engage targets at various ranges and when the diopter focus is adjusted for the vision of different firers. A metal target is excellent for zeroing purposes, because the strike of the round can be easily observed with an AN/PVS-4. The procedures to zero are as follows.

a. **Mounting the Bracket and Device.** Before zeroing and qualifying with the AN/PVS-4, the gunner must mount the bracket and sight onto his weapon.

> CAUTION
> When mounting an AN/PVS-4 to the mounting bracket, make sure that the hole for the screw in the AN/PVS-4 is aligned and flush against the bracket screw. If not, the screw will strip the threads in the screw hole of the AN/PVS-4 and prevent use with the M249 machine gun.

(1) Place the mounting bracket on top of the feed cover mechanism assembly so that the two forked ends are secured around the headless pins.

(2) Remove the screw cover behind the rear sight assembly, and screw the bracket knob in until it is tight.

(3) Position the AN/PVS-4 on top of the bracket so that the mount of the AN/PVS-4 is aligned with the mounting knob of the bracket.

(4) Turn the mounting knob clockwise until the AN/PVS-4 is tight (Figure G-54).

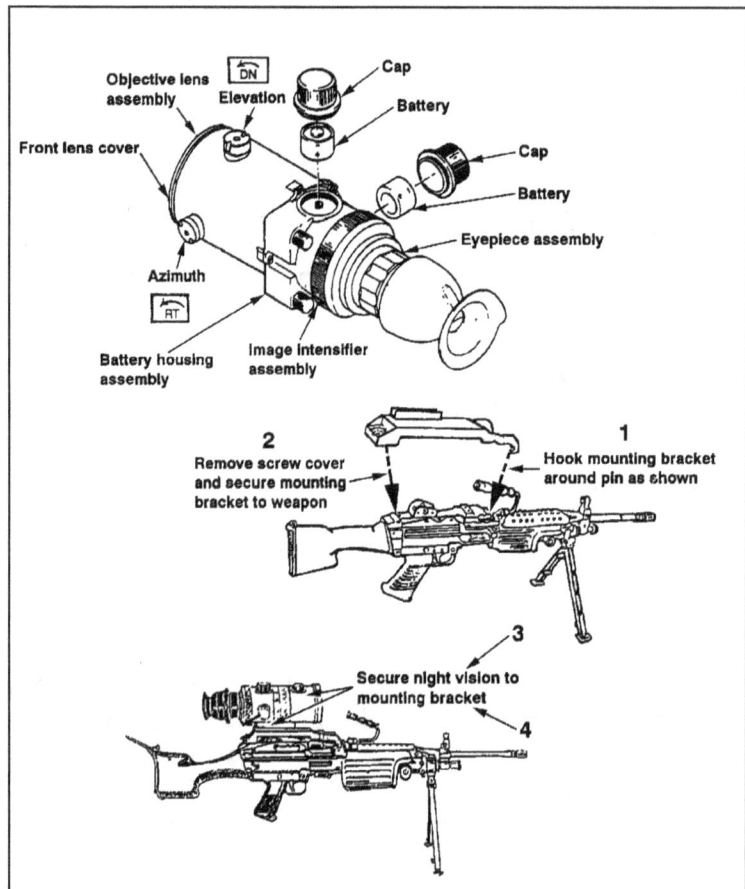

Figure G-54. Mounting the AN/PVS-4 to the M249 light machine gun.

b. **Seating the Device**. Once the device is mounted, the gunner fires a 3-round burst to seat the device, checks and tightens the mounting knob, and then fires another 3-round burst. He checks the device to ensure it is settled and securely fastened and tightens the mounting knob if necessary. He does not fire at the boresight target during this procedure.

c. **Centering the Reticle in the Field of View**. The gunner turns the device on and centers the reticle pattern in the field of view by using the azimuth and elevation actuators. To be accurate, he does this by rotating the elevation and azimuth actuators from one side to the other and from top to bottom, while counting the number of clicks. The elevation actuator has the down direction marked DN with an arrow. This moves strike of the round. The azimuth actuator has the right direction marked with RT with an arrow. This also moves the strike of the round. He divides the number of clicks for each by two and moves the elevation and azimuth actuators that number of clicks. This manually centers the reticle in the field of view horizontally and vertically. This enables the gunner to reach an accurate boresight between the point of aim (reticle) and the center of the bore (Figure G-55).

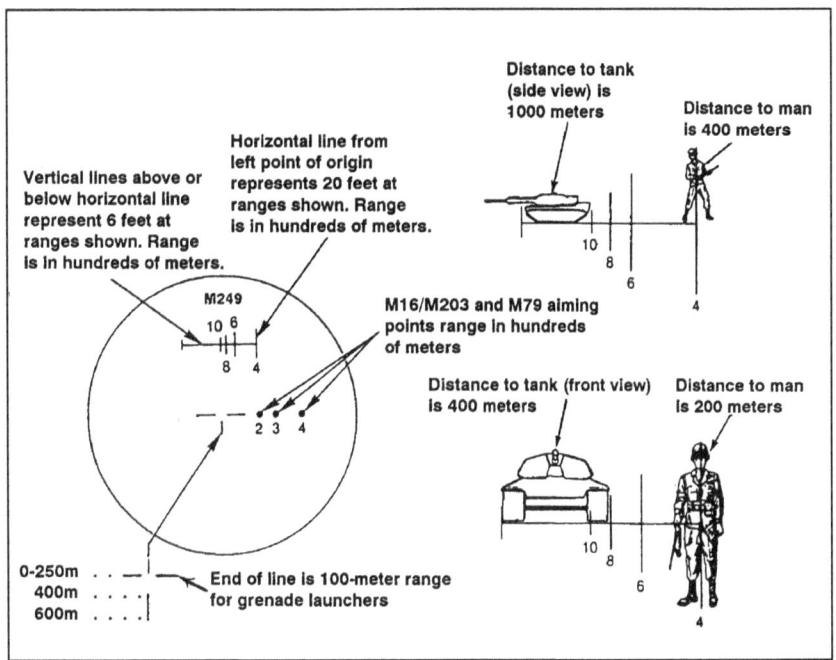

Figure G-55. Centered reticle pattern.

d. **Confirming the Boresight**. To do this, the gunner centers and affixes a 25-meter (M16A2) zero target to the back of a basic machine gun paster target. This provides a large, clear surface for identifying the strike of the round. Then, he emplaces the target 10 meters from the firing position. The gunner places the reticle aiming point on the 25-meter zero target aiming point (Figure G-56, page G-50) and fires a single round. If the round impacts anywhere near the aiming point, he fires two more rounds to establish his group.

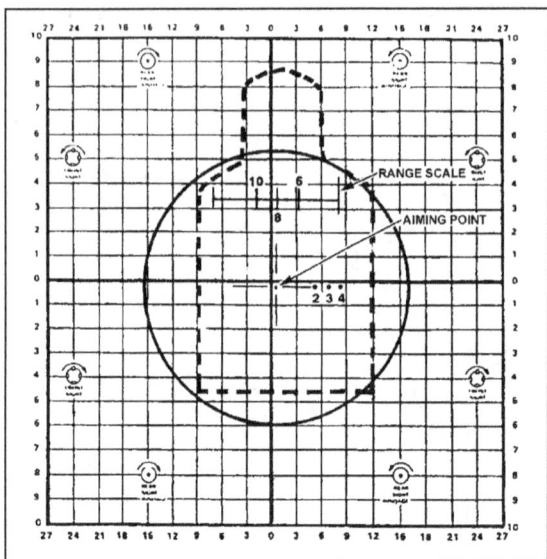

Figure G-56. Reticle aiming point, target aiming point and shot group.

e. **25-Meter Zeroing**. After a boresight has been established, the gunner moves back to a 25-meter firing position. He affixes another 25-meter zero target to the back of a 10-meter machine gun target and fires three rounds.

(1) Locate and triangulate the center of the shot group. From the center of the shot group, adjust the reticle to move the center of the shot group to a point 8 cm below and 2 cm right of the target aiming point (Figure G-57). This location on the 25-meter zero target is 9 squares below (8 cm divided by .9) and 2 squares right (2 cm divided by .9) of the target aiming point. Make the adjustment using the AN/PVS-4 azimuth and elevation adjustment actuators. Each square on the 25-meter zero target is .9 cm. Each click of the actuators moves the strike of the round .25 cm (or .1 inch) at 10-meters. Therefore, 4 clicks on either the elevation or azimuth actuator moves the strike of the round one square.

(2) After making the adjustments, assume a stable position, place the reticle aiming point on the target aiming point, and fire three more single rounds. Repeat the process until the rounds impact within the desired location (9 squares below and 2 squares right).

(3) If you miss the 25-meter zero target with the first round but strike the 10-meter machine gun paster target, make a large adjustment with the elevation and azimuth actuators. Continue this process with three-round groups and adjustments until the rounds strike the desired location.

(4) Do not record the zero because when the AN/PVS-4 is dismounted and remounted on the same M249, some changes may occur. It is best to zero each time.

(5) Once the AN/PVS-4 is mounted and boresighted, fire a 3-round burst at the center base of the target and note the strike of the rounds. While maintaining the reticle aiming point on the target, move the reticle aiming point to the strike of the rounds by manipulating the elevation and azimuth actuators.

(6) Acquire a good sight picture on the target with the reticle aiming point once again and fire another 3-round burst. Note the strike of the rounds and repeat the process until the rounds impact on target.

f. **Mounting the AN/PVS-4 on the M60**. Before zeroing and qualifying with the AN/PVS-4, the gunner must mount the bracket and sight onto his weapon. The M60 machine gun requires a mounting bracket.

> **CAUTION**
> When mounting an AN/PVS-4 to the mounting bracket, make sure that the hole for the screw in the AN/PVS-4 is aligned and flush against the bracket screw. If not, the screw strips the threads in the screw hole of the AN/PVS-4 and prevents its use with the machine gun.

(1) The gunner removes the M60 hinge pin latch and hinge pin from the over assembly by pressing on the latch (open end of pin) with an empty cartridge case, and separates the latch and pin. He places the pin and latch in the aiming guides on the left side of the mounting bracket and presses together.

(2) The gunner positions the mounting bracket assembly on top of the machine gun cover so that the holes in the front of the bracket align with the cover assembly pin holes.

(3) The gunner inserts the longer hinge pin supplied with the bracket through the bracket-and-cover assembly, and secures by inserting the hinge pin latch.

(4) The gunner loosens the wing nuts on both leg clamps and positions the clamps under the cover assembly. He secures the mounting bracket by tightening the wing nuts firmly (Figure G-57).

(5) The split washer is placed next to the wing nut and the flat washer is placed next to the bracket.

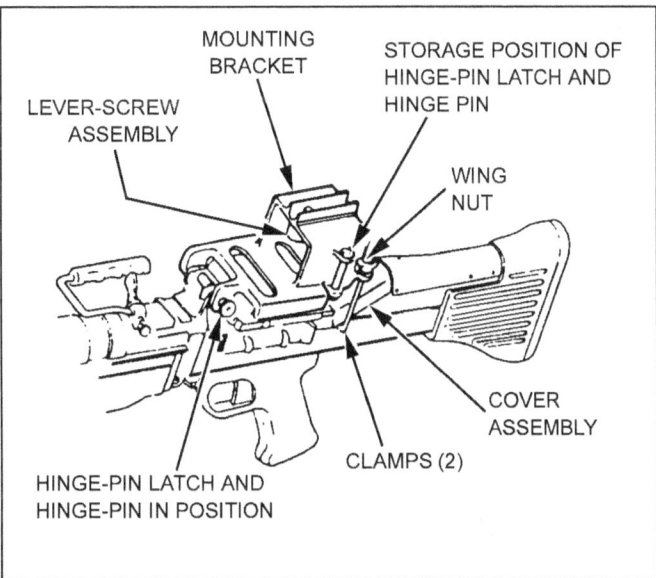

Figure G-57. Installation of mounting bracket.

(5) The gunner installs the sight on the M60 mounting bracket assembly by positioning it in the groove on top of the bracket so that the scribe line on the bracket is aligned with the scribe line on the sight mounting adapter. He tightens the lever screw assembly to secure the sight to the bracket. He uses an empty cartridge case placed over the lever arm to increase leverage as the screw is tightened. (See Figure G-58.)

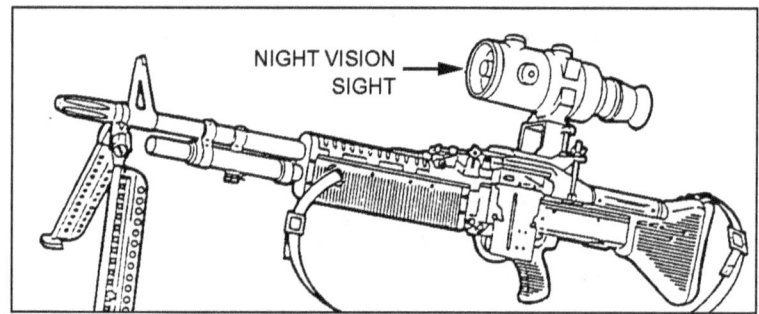

Figure G-58. Mounting the AN/PVS-4.

g. **Mounting the AN/PVS-4 on the M240B.**

Before zeroing and qualifying with the AN/PVS-4, the gunner must mount the sight onto his weapon. The M240B machine gun has a rail mount already attached to the cover assembly (Figure G-59). The gunner installs the sight on the M240B rail mount by loosen the mounting knob located on the left side. Positioning it in a slot on the rail mount. Any slot may be used as long as the mount does not hang over the edge of the rail. By placing the bar of the mount in a slot on the rail and hand tighten knob on mount until clicking noise is heard (2 clicks). As long as the gunner places the sight in the same slot after zeroing the sight will retain its zero to a degree. (See Figure G-60.)

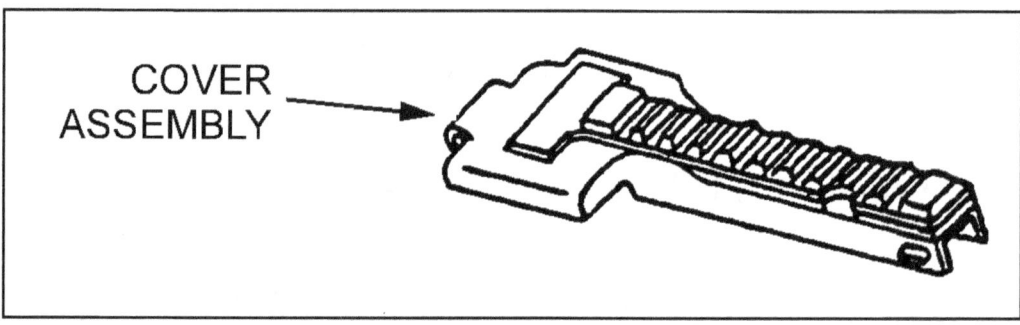

Figure G-59. Rail mount on the M240B.

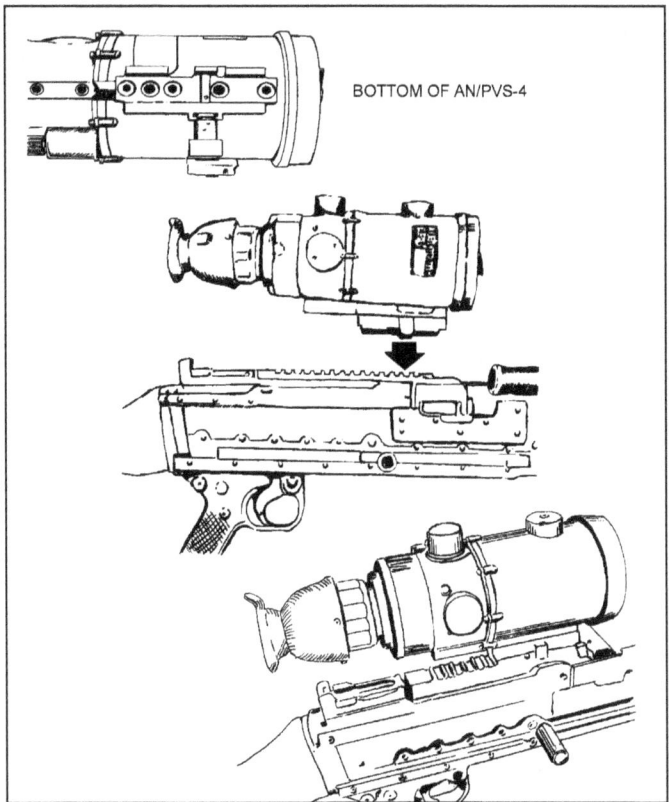

BOTTOM OF AN/PVS-4

Figure G-60. Mounting the AN/PVS-4.

h.   **Zeroing the AN/PVS-4 to the M60/M240B**. Zeroing aligns the AN/PVS-4 to the machine gun. The sight may be zeroed during daylight or darkness. (AN/PVS-4 TM 11-5855-213-10) When zeroing during daylight, the daylight cover must be used. To obtain a precise zero, it is best done at 300 meters and at night. Once the AN/PVS-4 is zeroed on the machine gun, any soldier who knows how to use the reticle should fire the weapon effectively. However, there may be some changes in zero when the objective focus is adjusted to engage targets at various ranges and when the diopter focus is adjusted for the vision of different firers. A metal target is excellent for zeroing purposes, because the strike of the round can be easily observed with an AN/PVS-4. The procedures to zero are as follows:

(1) *Seating the Device*. Once the device is mounted, the gunner fires a seven-round burst to seat the device, checks and tightens the mounting knob, and then fires another three-round burst. He checks the device to ensure it is settled and securely fastened and tightens the mounting knob if necessary. He does not fire at the boresight target during this procedure.

(2) *Centering the Reticle in the Field of View of the AN/PVS-4*. The gunner turns the device on and centers the reticle pattern in the field of view by using the azimuth and elevation actuators. To be accurate, he does this by rotating the elevation and azimuth actuators from one side to the other and from top to bottom, while counting the number of clicks. (The elevation actuator has the down direction marked DN with an arrow.

This moves strike of the round. The azimuth actuator has the right direction marked with RT with an arrow. This also moves the strike of the round.) He divides the number of clicks for each by two and moves the elevation and azimuth actuators that number of clicks. This manually centers the reticle in the field of view horizontally and vertically. This enables the gunner to reach an accurate boresight between the point of aim (reticle) and the center of the bore (Figure G-61).

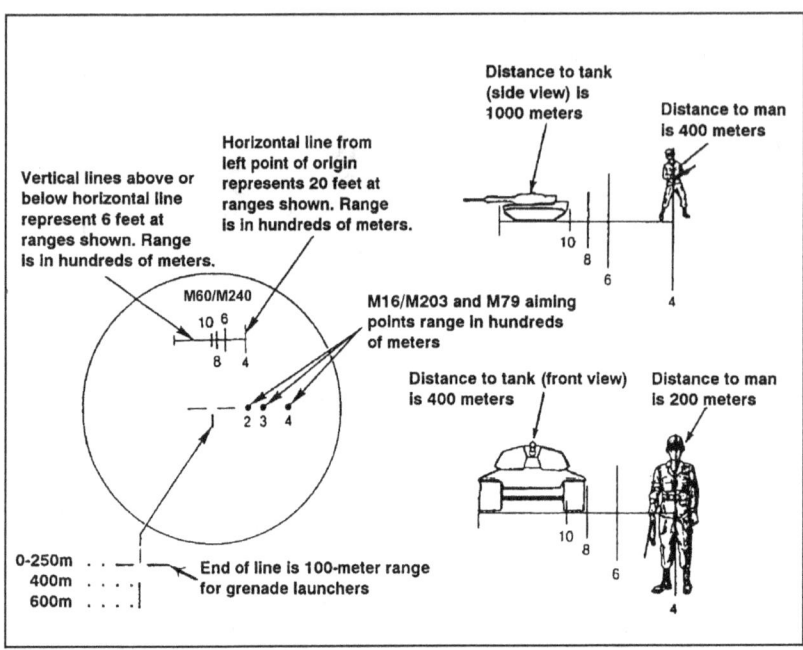

Figure G-61. Centered reticle pattern.

(3) *Confirming the Boresight*. To confirm the boresight, the gunner centers and affixes a 25-meter (M16A2) zero target to the back of a basic machine gun paster target. This provides a large, clear surface for identifying the strike of the round. Then, he emplaces the target 10-meters from the firing position. The gunner places the reticle aiming point on the 25-meter zero target aiming point (Figure G-62) and fires a single round. If the round impacts anywhere near the aiming point, he fires two more rounds to establish his group.

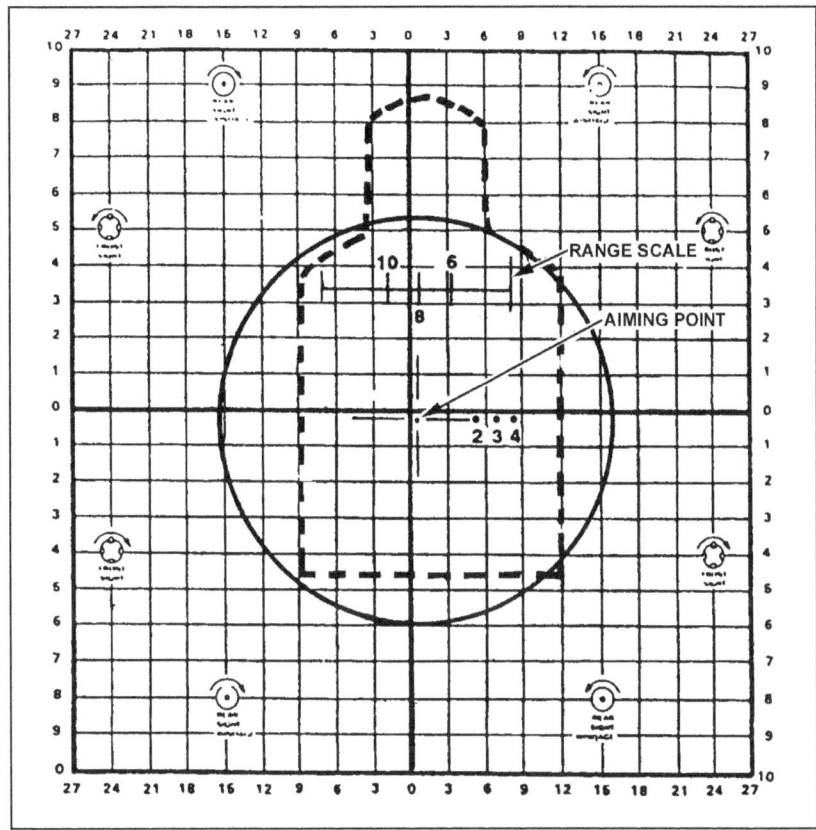

Figure G-62. Reticle aiming point, target aiming point and shot group.

(4) *25-Meter Zeroing AN/PVS-4*. After a boresight has been established, the gunner moves back to a 25-meter firing position. He affixes another 25-meter zero target to the back of a 10-meter machine gun target and fires three rounds.

(a) AN/PVS-4 (M60 and M240B) The gunner locates and triangulates the center of the shot group. From the center of the shot group, he adjusts the reticle to move the center of the shot group to a point 8 cm below and 2 cm right of the target aiming point. This location on the 25-meter zero target is 9 squares below (8 cm divided by .9) and 2 squares right (2 cm divided by .9) of the target aiming point. He makes the adjustment using the AN/PVS-4 azimuth and elevation adjustment actuators. Each square on the 25-meter zero target is .9 cm. Each click of the actuators moves the strike of the round .25 cm (or .1 inch) at 10 meters. Therefore, 4 clicks on either the elevation or azimuth actuator moves the strike of the round one square.

(b) After making the adjustments, the gunner assumes a stable position, places the reticle aiming point on the target aiming point, and fires three more single rounds. He repeats the process until the rounds impact within the desired location (9 squares below and 2 squares right).

(c) If he misses the 25-meter zero target with the first round but strikes the 10-meter machine gun paster target, he makes a large adjustment with the elevation and azimuth actuators. He continues this process with three-round groups and adjustments until the rounds strike the desired location.

(d) He does not record the zero with the old style bracket because when the AN/PVS-4 is dismounted and remounted on the same M60, some changes may occur. It is best to zero each time. The zero is recorded with the new rail bracket because when the AN/PVS-4 is dismounted and remounted on the same machine gun, and as long as the gunner places a mark on the rail slot the sight will have some changes. But the gunner does not need to re-zero his sight to the machine gun.

(e) Once the AN/PVS-4 is mounted and boresighted, the gunner fires a three-round burst at the center base of the target and notes the strike of the rounds. While maintaining the reticle aiming point on the target, he moves the reticle aiming point to the strike of the rounds by manipulating the elevation and azimuth actuators.

(f) The gunner acquires a good sight picture on the target with the reticle aiming point once again and fires another three-round burst. He notes the strike of the rounds and repeats the process until the rounds impact on target.

APPENDIX H
10-METER BORE LIGHT/
25-METER TARGET OFFSETS

This appendix provides all the 10-meter/25-meter target offsets for the M249/M240B weapons mounted with iron sight, optics, MILES, or aiming lasers. A blank reproducible 10-meter target offset is provided along with a table and example of every weapon configuration. The M16A2 300-meter zero target is used for 25-meter zeroing with all weapon configurations.

H-1. 10-METER TARGET OFFSET
To mark the proper 10-meter target offset, the gunner must do the following:
   a. Find the correct template for your weapon configuration.
   b. Count the number of squares starting from center of the bore light circle on the offset to the desired point of aim. Each template also provides you with a number formula for the proper offset. Example (L2.0, U2.4): Starting from the center of the bore light circle (0.0, 0.0) move LEFT 2 squares and UP 2.4 squares.
   c. Place the appropriate symbol or mark (Figure H-1).

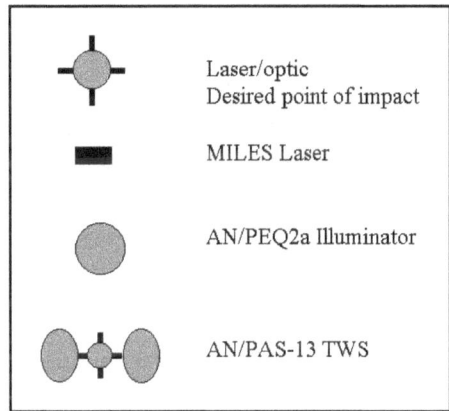

Figure H-1. 10-meter target offset symbols.

H-2. 25-METER TARGET OFFSET
To mark the proper 25-meter target offset do the following:
   a. Use only M16A2 300-meter zero targets.
   b. Find the correct target template for your weapon configuration.
   c. Count the number of squares starting from the center of the 300-meter zeroing silhouette.
   d. Mark the designated strike point by drawing a small circle at the appropriate number of squares from the center of the 300-meter zeroing silhouette.
   e. Draw a 4-centimeter by 4-centimeter square keeping the designated strike point center mass of the 4-centimeter by 4-centimeter square.

H-3. REPRODUCE

Figure H-2 is an example completed 10-meter offset target. Reproduce onto 8 1/2" x 11" paper the blank target located in the back of this manual The quick reference card (Figure H-3) is located on the back of the target. The blank target can be laminated and used over and over again.

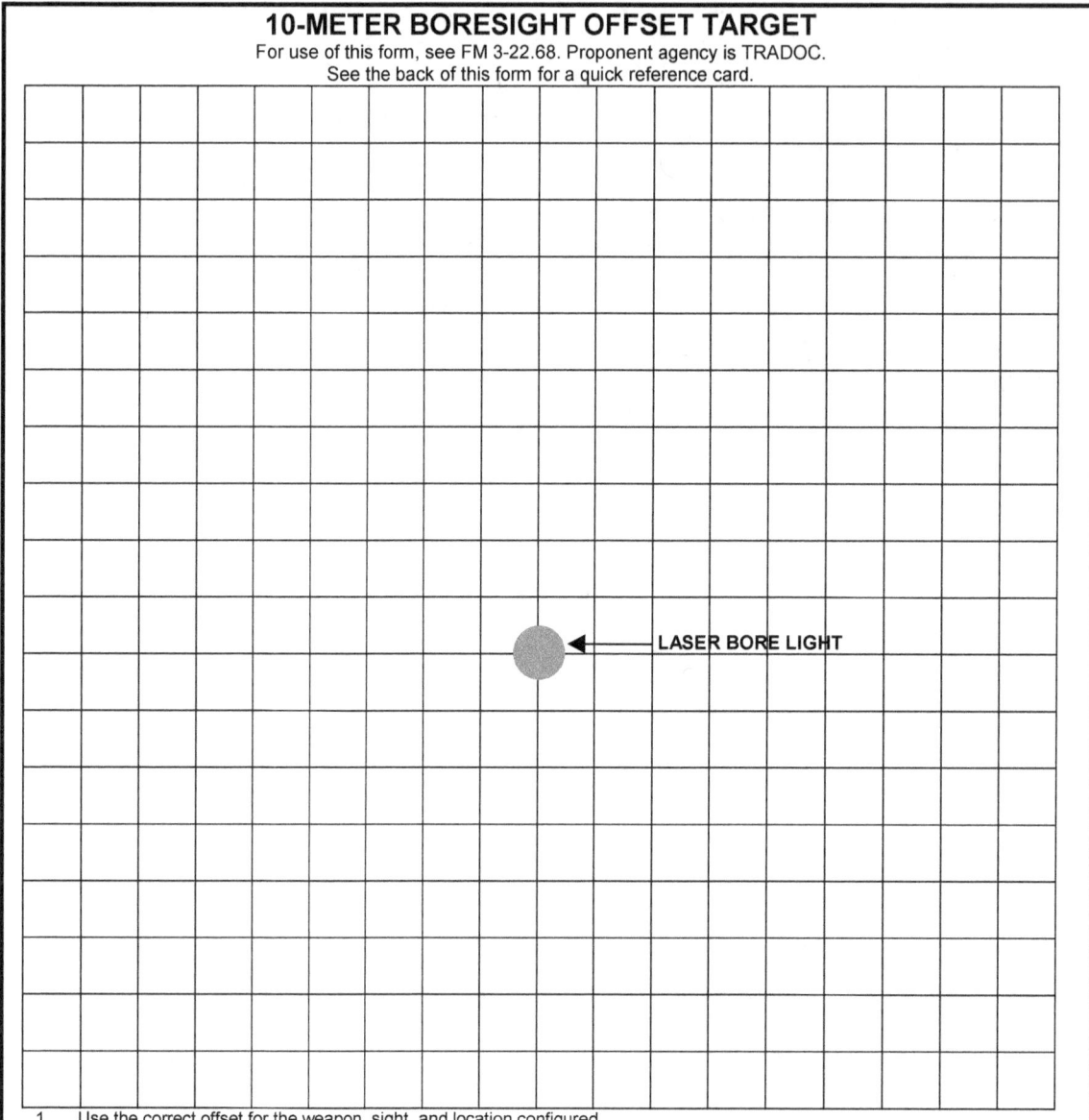

10-METER BORESIGHT OFFSET TARGET

For use of this form, see FM 3-22.68. Proponent agency is TRADOC.
See the back of this form for a quick reference card.

LASER BORE LIGHT

1. Use the correct offset for the weapon, sight, and location configured.
2. Stabilize the weapon and the offset.
3. Zero the bore light while inside the barrel of the weapon.
4. Align the laser of the bore light with the dot on the 10-meter offset.
5. Align the MILES laser with the MILES rectangle on the 10-meter offset (if applicable).
6. Adjust the aiming laser until it is centered on the cross hair.
7. Place the optic aim point centered on the cross hair and make adjustments on the optic until the bore light laser is aligned with the dot on the 10-meter offset.
8. Reconfirm that all devices are still aligned to their aiming mark.

DA FORM 7476-R, OCT 2002   Page 1 of 1

Figure H-2. Example completed DA Form 7476-R.

WPN	ACCESSORY	MOUNT	RANGE ZEROED TO	ZERO TARGET OFFSET	BORESIGHT TARGET OFFSET	MILES OFFSET
M249	IRON SIGHTS	NA	400m	NA	TBD	1.9L/.5U
M249	MGO	IFTC RAIL	400m	TBD	0.0/7.9U	1.9L/.5U
M249	MGO	TWS BRACKET	400m	TBD	0.0/2.15U	1.9L/.6U
M249	AN/PAQ-4C	TWS BRACKET TOP	400m	0.5R/1.5U	1.85L/7.7U	1.9L/.5U
M249	AN/PAQ-4C	AN/PVS4 BRACKET	400m	2.5R/1.5D	4.1L/6.1U	1.9L/.5U
M249	AN/PAQ-4C	INSIGHT RAIL GRABBER WITH IFTC	400m	TBD	1.75L/4.69U	1.9L/.5U
M249	AN/PAQ-4C	PICATINNEY RAILGRABBER WITH IFTC	400m	1.75R/0.0	1.75L/5.39U	1.9L/.5U
M249	AN/PAQ-4C	INSIGHT RAIL GRABBER FORWARD RAILS RIGHT	400m	5.9R/9.6D	5.9R/4.0D	1.9L/.5U
M249	AN/PAQ-4C	INSIGHT RAIL GRABBER FORWARD RAILS LEFT	400m	6.0R/13.3D	6.OR/8.3D	1.9L/.5U
M249	AN/PAQ-4C	PICATINNY RAIL GRABBER WITH AL SPACER FORWARD RAILS RIGHT	400m	7.7R/9.6D	7.7R/4.0D	1.9L/.5U
M249	AN/PAQ4-C	PICATINNY RAIL GRABBER FORWARD RAILS LEFT	400m	7.6R/13.3D	7.6R/8.3D	1.9L/.5U
M249	AN/PEQ-2A	TWS BRACKET TOP	400m	1.8L/2.7D	1.8R/7.95U	1.9L/.5U
M249	AN/PEQ-2A	AN/PVS4 BRACKET WITH SPACER	400m	5.0R/4.0D	.45L/6.5U	1.9L/.5U
M249	AN/PEQ-2A	INSIGHT RAIL GRABBER WITH IFTC	400m	2.0L/1.5U	1.95R/4.79U	1.9L/.5U
M249	AN/PEQ-2A	PICATINNEY RAIL GRABBER WITH IFTC	400m	2.0L/0.5D	1.95R/6.49U	1.9L/.5U
M249	AN/PEQ-2A	INSIGHT RAIL GRABBER FORWARD RAILS RIGHT	400m	6.1R/13.2D	6.1R/7.6D	1.9L/.5U
M249	AN/PEQ-2A	INSIGHT RAIL GRABBER FORWARD RAILS LEFT	400m	6.0R/9.4D	6.0R/4.4D	1.9L/.5U
M249	AN/PEQ-2A	PICATINNY RAIL GRABBER WITH AL SPACER FORWARD RAILS RIGHT	400m	7.8R/13.2D	7.8R/7.6D	1.9L/.5U
M249	AN/PEQ-2A	PICATINNY RAIL GRABBER FORWARD RAILS LEFT	400m	7.6R/9.4D	7.6R/4.4D	1.9L/.5U
M249	AN/PVS-4	IFTC TOP WITH SPACER	400m	0.0/4.3D	0.0/10.00U	1.9L/.5U
M249	AN/PVS-4	AN/PVS-4 BRACKET	400m	2.5R/4.9D	2.25L/11.25U	1.9L/.5U
M249	AN/PAS-13	IFTC TOP	400m	0.0/2.75D	0.0/8.6U	1.9L/.5U
M249	AN/PAS-13	TWS BRACKET	400m	0.0/5.5D	0.0/10.05U	1.9L/.5U
M240B	IRON SIGHTS	NA	500m	TBD	TBD	1.9L/.5U
M240B	MGO	FEEDTRAY COVER RAIL	500m	NA	0.0/0.0	5.0R/4.1D
M240B	AN/PAQ-4C	PICATINNEY RAIL GRABBER TOP	500m	1.75R/2.2D	1.5L/3.5U	5.0R/4.1D
M240B	AN/PEQ-2A	INSIGHT RAIL GRABBER TOP	500m	2.0R/1.5D	1.7R/3.71U	5.0R/4.1D
M240B	AN/PAQ-4C	INSIGHT RAIL GRABBER FORWARD RAILS RIGHT	500m	TBD	TBD	5.0R/4.1D
M240D	AN/PAQ 4C	INSIGHT RAIL GRABBER FORWARD RAILS LEFT	500m	6.2R/16.8D	6.2R/8.1D	5.0R/4.1D
M240B	AN/PAQ-4C	PICATINNY RAIL GRABBER FORWARD RAILS RIGHT	500m	TBD	TBD	5.0R/4.1D
M240B	AN/PAQ-4C	PICATINNY RAIL GRABBER FORWARD RAILS LEFT	500m	7.9R/16.8D	7.9R/8.1D	5.0R/4.1D
M240B	AN/PEQ-2A	INSIGHT RAIL GRABBER FORWARD RAILS RIGHT	500m	TBD	TBD	5.0R/4.1D
M240B	AN/PEQ-2A	INSIGHT RAIL GRABBER FORWARD RAILS LEFT	500m	6.2R/12.8D	6.2R/4.1D	5.0R/4.1D
M240B	AN/PEQ-2A	PICATINNY RAIL GRABBER FORWARD RAILS RIGHT	500m	TBD	TBD	5.0R/4.1D
M240B	AN/PEQ-2A	PICATINNY RAIL GRABBER FORWARD RAILS LEFT	500m	7.9R/12.8D	7.9R/4.1D	5.0R/4.1D
M240B	AN/PVS-4	FEEDTRAY COVER RAIL PICATINNY RAIL GRABBER WITH SPACER	500m	0.0/6.2D	0.0/6.0U	5.0R/4.1D
M240B	AN/PAS-13	FEED TRAY COVER	500m	0.0/2.3U	0.0/8.0U	5.0R/4.1D

DA FORM 7476-R, OCT 2002 Page 1 of 2

Figure H-3. Quick reference card is included on back of DA Form 7476-R.

GLOSSARY

AAR	after-action report
AR	Army regulation
ARTEP	Army Training and Evaluation Program
BFA	blank firing attachment
CLP	cleaner, lubricant, preservative
cm	centimeters
CO	company
DA	Department of the Army
DODAC	Department of Defense Ammunition Code
EST	engagement skills trainer
FM	field manual
FPF	final protective fire
FPL	final protective line
FSN	Federal stock number
FTX	field training exercise
GTA	graphic training aid
HMMWV	high-mobility, multipurpose wheeled vehicle
IAW	in accordance with
IET	initial entry training
IOAC	Infantry officer's advanced course
IOBC	Infantry officer's basic course
instr	instruction
LAW	lubricating oil, arctic weather
LFX	live-fire exercise
LRA	local reproduction authorized
LSA	lubricating oil, semifluid, automatic weapons
LTA	local training area
m	meter
METL	mission-essential task list

MGO	machine gun optic
MILES	multiple-integrated laser engagement system
mm	millimeter
mph	miles per hour
MPRC	multipurpose range complex
MTA	major training area
MTP	mission training plan
MWTS	medium-weapon thermal sight
N/A	not applicable
NATO	North Atlantic Treaty Organization
NBC	nuclear, biological, and chemical
NCO	noncommissioned officer
NCOES	Noncommissioned Officer Education System
NCOIC	noncommissioned officer in charge
NSN	national stock number
NVD	night vision device
OIC	officer in charge
PAM	pamphlet
PDF	principal direction of fire
PLT	platoon
POPP	Pull, Observe, Push, and Press (memory aid for immediate action)
prac	practice
qual	qualification
RD	round
sec	second
SM	soldier's manual
SMCT	soldier's manual of common tasks
SOP	standing operating procedures
sqd	squad
STP	soldier's training publication
STRAC	standards in training commission
STX	situational training exercise
T&E	traversing and elevating
TC	training circular

TM	technical manual
TOE	table of organization and equipment
TPIAL	target pointer/illuminator/aiming light
TRADOC	US Army Training and Doctrine Command
US	United States

REFERENCES

SOURCES USED

These are the sources quoted or paraphrased in this publication.

ARTEP 7-8-MTP   Mission Training Plan for the Infantry Rifle Platoon and Squad. 30 September 1988.

ARTEP 7-8-DRILL   Drills for the Infantry Rifle Platoon and Squad. 3 November 1993.

FM 7-8   Infantry Platoon and Squad. 22 April 1992.

FM 21-26   Map Reading and Land Navigation. 7 May 1993.

DOCUMENTS NEEDED

These documents must be available to the intended uses of this publication.

AR 385-63   Policies and Procedures for Training, Target Practice and Combat. 15 October 1983.

DA Form 2404   Equipment Inspection and Maintenance Worksheet. April 1979.

DA Form 5517-R   Standard Range Card (LRA). February 1986.

DA Form 85-R   Scorecard for M249, M60/M240B Machine Guns. October 2002.

DA Form 7476-R   10-Meter Boresight Offset Target. October 2002.

DA Pam 25-30   Army Electronic Library. 1 July 2002.

DA Pam 350-38   Training Standards for Weapon Training. September 1990.

*FM 3-5   NBC Decontamination. 23 July 1992.

*FM 21-60   Visual Signals. 30 September 1987.

STP 21-24-SMCT   Soldier's Manual of Common Tasks (Skill Levels 2-4). 1 October 2001.

*This source was also used to develop this publication.

*TC 25-8   Training Ranges. 25 February 1992.

TM 9-1005-319-10   Operator's Manual List for Rifle 5.56-mm, M16A2. 1 October 1998.

*TM 9—1005-201-10   Operator's Manual Machine Gun, 5.56-mm, M249 w/Equip. 26 July 1991.

*TM 9-1005-224-10   Operator's Manual for Machine Gun, 7.62-mm, M60, W/E; Mount, Tripod, Machine Gun, 7.62-mm, M122. 2 April 1998.

*TM 9-1005-313-10   Operator's Manual for Machine Gun, 7.62-mm, M240B, W/E; Flex-mount, Tripod, Machine Gun, 7.62-mm, M122A1. 19 July 1996.

*TM 9-1300-200   Ammunition General. 3 October 1969.

*TM 11-5855-213-10   Operator's Manual Night Vision Sight, Individual Served Weapon, AN/PVS-4. 1 February 1993.

INTERNET WEB SITES

U.S. Army Publishing Agency
http://www.usapa.army.mil

Army Doctrine and Training Digital Library
http://www.adtdl.army.mil

*This source was also used to develop this publication.

INDEX

10-METER BORESIGHT OFFSET TARGET

For use of this form, see FM 3-22.68; the proponent agency is TRADOC.

See back of this form for quick reference card.

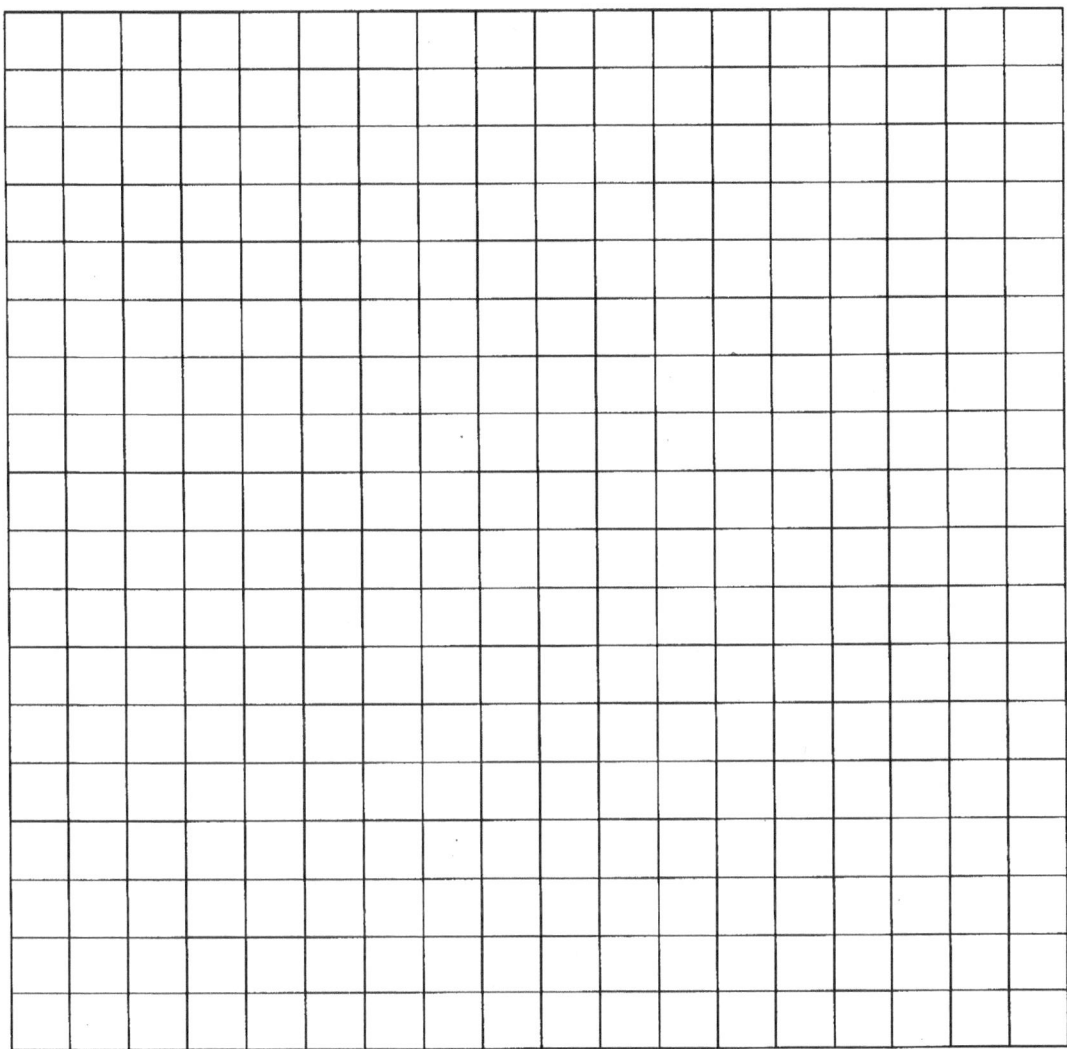

1. Use the correct offset for the weapon, sight, and location configured.
2. Stabilize the weapon and the offset.
3. Zero the bore light while inside the barrel of the weapon.
4. Align the laser of the bore light with the dot on the 10-meter offset.
5. Align the MILES laser with the MILES rectangle on the 10-meter offset (if applicable).
6. Adjust the aiming laser until it is centered on the cross hair.
7. Place the optic aim point centered on the cross hair and make adjustments on the optic until the bore light laser is aligned with the dot on the 10-meter offset.
8. Reconfirm that all devices are still aligned to their aiming mark.

WPN	ACCESSORY	MOUNT	RANGE ZEROED TO	ZERO TARGET OFFSET	BORESIGHT TARGET OFFSET	MILES OFFSET
M249	IRON SIGHTS	NA	400m	NA	TBD	1.9L/.5U
M249	MGO	IFTC RAIL	400m	TBD	0.0/7.9U	1.9L/.5U
M249	MGO	TWS BRACKET	400m	TBD	0.0/2.15U	1.9L/.5U
M249	AN/PAQ-4C	TWS BRACKET TOP	400m	0.5R/1.5U	1.85L/7.7U	1.9L/.5U
M249	AN/PAQ-4C	AN/PVS4 BRACKET	400m	2.5R/1.5D	4.1L/6.1U	1.9L/.5U
M249	AN/PAQ-4C	INSIGHT RAIL GRABBER WITH IFTC	400m	TBD	1.75L/4.69U	1.9L/.5U
M249	AN/PAQ-4C	PICATINNY RAIL GRABBER WITH IFTC	400m	1.75R/0.0	1.75L/5.39U	1.9L/.5U
M249	AN/PAQ-4C	INSIGHT RAIL GRABBER FORWARD RAILS RIGHT	400m	5.9R/9.6D	5.9R/4.0D	1.9L/.5U
M249	AN/PAQ-4C	INSIGHT RAIL GRABBER FORWARD RAILS LEFT	400m	6.0R/13.3D	6.0R/8.3D	1.9L/.5U
M249	AN/PAQ-4C	PICATINNY RAIL GRABBER WITH AL SPACER FORWARD RAILS RIGHT	400m	7.7R/9.6D	7.7R/4.0D	1.9L/.5U
M249	AN/PAQ-4C	PICATINNY RAIL GRABBER FORWARD RAILS LEFT	400m	7.6R/13.3D	7.6R/8.3D	1.9L/.5U
M249	AN/PEQ-2A	TWS BRACKET TOP	400m	1.8L/2.7D	1.8R/7.95U	1.9L/.5U
M249	AN/PEQ-2A	AN/PVS4 BRACKET WITH SPACER	400m	5.0R/4.0D	.45L/6.5U	1.9L/.5U
M249	AN/PEQ-2A	INSIGHT RAIL GRABBER WITH IFTC	400m	2.0L/1.5U	1.95R/4.79U	1.9L/.5U
M249	AN/PEQ-2A	PICATINNY RAIL GRABBER WITH IFTC	400m	2.0L/0.5U	1.95R/6.49U	1.9L/.5U
M249	AN/PEQ-2A	INSIGHT RAIL GRABBER FORWARD RAILS RIGHT	400m	6.1R/13.2D	6.1R/7.6D	1.9L/.5U
M249	AN/PEQ-2A	INSIGHT RAIL GRABBER FORWARD RAILS LEFT	400m	6.0R/9.4D	6.0R/4.4D	1.9L/.5U
M249	AN/PEQ-2A	PICATINNY RAIL GRABBER WITH AL SPACER FORWARD RAILS RIGHT	400m	7.8R/13.2D	7.8R/7.6D	1.9L/.5U
M249	AN/PEQ-2A	PICATINNY RAIL GRABBER FORWARD RAILS LEFT	400m	7.6R/9.4D	7.6R/4.4D	1.9L/.5U
M249	AN/PVS-4	IFTC TOP WITH SPACER	400m	0.0/4.3D	0.0/10.00U	1.9L/.5U
M249	AN/PVS-4	AN/PVS4 BRACKET	400m	2.5R/4.9D	2.25L/11.25U	1.9L/.5U
M249	AN/PVS-4	IFTC TOP	400m	0.0/2.75D	0.0/8.6U	1.9L/.5U
M249	AN/PVS-4	TWS BRACKET	400m	0.0/5.5D	0.010.05U	1.9L/.5U
M240B	IRON SIGHTS	NA	500m	TBD	TBD	1.9L/.5U
M240B	MGO	FEEDTRAY COVER RAIL	500m	NA	0.0/0.0	5.0R/4.1D
M240B	AN/PAQ-4C	PICATINNY RAIL GRABBER TOP	500m	1.75R/2.2D	1.5L/3.5U	5.0R/4.1D
M240B	AN/PEQ-2A	INSIGHT RAIL GRABBER TOP	500m	2.0R/1.5D	1.7R/3.71U	5.0R/4.1D
M240B	AN/PAQ-4C	INSIGHT RAIL GRABBER FORWARD RAILS RIGHT	500m	TBD	TBD	5.0R/4.1D
M240B	AN/PAQ-4C	INSIGHT RAIL GRABBER FORWARD RAILS LEFT	500m	6.2R/16.8D	6.2R/8.1D	5.0R/4.1D
M240B	AN/PAQ-4C	PICATINNY RAIL GRABBER FORWARD RAILS RIGHT	500m	TBD	TBD	5.0R/4.1D
M240B	AN/PAQ-4C	PICATINNY RAIL GRABBER FORWARD RAILS LEFT	500m	7.9R/16.8D	7.9R/8.1D	5.0R/4.1D
M240B	AN/PEQ-2A	INSIGHT RAIL GRABBER FORWARD RAILS RIGHT	500m	TBD	TBD	5.0R/4.1D
M240B	AN/PEQ-2A	INSIGHT RAIL GRABBER FORWARD RAILS LEFT	500m	6.2R/12.8D	6.2R/4.1D	5.0R/4.1D
M240B	AN/PEQ-2A	PICATINNY RAIL GRABBER FORWARD RAILS RIGHT	500m	TBD	TBD	5.0R/4.1D
M240B	AN/PEQ-2A	PICATINNY RAIL GRABBER FORWARD RAILS LEFT	500m	7.9R/12.8D	7.9R/4.1D	5.0R/4.1D
M240B	AN/PVA-4	FEEDTRAY COVER RAIL PICATINNY RAIL GRABBER WITH SPACER	500m	0.0/6.2D	0.0/6.0U	5.0R/4.1D
M240B	AN/PAS-13	FEEDTRAY COVER	500m	0.0/2.3U	0.0/8.0U	5.0R/4.1D

SCORECARD FOR M249, M60/M240B MACHINE GUNS

For use of this form, see FM 3-22.68; the proponent agency is TRADOC.
See back of this form for instructions.

PRIVACY ACT STATEMENT

AUTHORITY: 10 USC 30129(g) Executive Order 9397.

PRINCIPAL PURPOSE: Records individual's performance on record fire range.

ROUTINE USES: Evaluate individual's proficiency and basis for determination of award of proficiency badge; SSN is used for positive identification purposes only.

DISCLOSURE: Voluntary, individuals not providing information cannot be rated/scored on a mass basis.

NAME	SSN	UNIT	DATE (YYYYMMDD)	LANE

TABLE I (10-METERS)

TASK	RANGE (meters)	TIME	HITS
1*	10	N/A	N/A
2*	10	N/A	N/A
3*	10	N/A	N/A
4*	10	N/A	N/A
5*	10	N/A	N/A
6*	10	N/A	N/A
7*	10	N/A	N/A
8*	10	N/A	N/A
9	10	40 SEC	
10	10	50 SEC	
TOTAL HITS (POINTS)			

TABLE II (DAY TRANSITION)

TASK	RANGE (meters)	TIME	*PRACTICE HIT	MISS	**QUALIFY HIT	MISS
1*	500	N/A	N/A	N/A	N/A	N/A
2**	400	10 SEC				
3**	500	15 SEC				
4**	600	20 SEC				
5**	800	30 SEC				
6**	400 / 600	30 SEC				
7**	700 / 800	45 SEC				
8**	400 / 500 / 600	45 SEC				
**TOTAL POINTS						

TABLE III (LIMITED VISIBILITY)

TASK	RANGE (meters)	TIME	*PRACTICE HIT	MISS	**QUALIFY HIT	MISS
1*	10	N/A	N/A	N/A	N/A	N/A
2*	10	N/A	N/A	N/A	N/A	N/A
3*	500	N/A	N/A	N/A	N/A	N/A
4	200	10 SEC				
5	400	15 SEC				
6	100	10 SEC				
7	300	15 SEC				
8	200 / 400	25 SEC				
9	100 / 300	25 SEC				
10	100 / 200 / 400	30 SEC				
TOTAL HITS						

TOTAL SCORE _____

* NONSCORED TASKS
** 10 POINTS PER HIT

CHECK APPROPRIATE WEAPON

EXPERT	FIRST CLASS	SECOND CLASS
☐ M249 182-201	☐ M249 158-181	☐ M249 158-181
☐ M60/M240B 206-227	☐ M60/M240B 180-205	☐ M60/M240B 180-205

OIC SIGNATURE	GRADER	RATING

Use the following procedures to fill out the M249, M60/M241B scorecard:

1. **NAME:** Enter the gunner's last name, first name, middle initial, and rank.

2. **SSN:** Enter the gunner's social security number.

3. **UNIT:** Enter the gunner's unit designation.

4. **DATE:** Enter the date of firing.

5. **LANE:** Enter the lane number for the gunner's firing point.

6. **RECORD:** Tasks used for record and qualification are Firing Table I, tasks 9 through 10; Firing Table II, tasks 2 through 8; and Firing Table III, tasks 4 through 10.

7. **HIT/MISS:** For Table I, tasks 9 through 10, enter the number of rounds impacting within target spaces (maximum of 7 [M249] or 9 [M60/M240B] per space).
   For Table II, tasks 2 through 8, and Table III, tasks 4 through 10, enter an X for hit and an O for a miss (regardless of whether the target is hit on the first or second burst).

8. **TOTAL HITS/ POINTS:** For Table I, tasks 9 through 10, give 1 point for each round impacting within a scoring space.
   For Table II, tasks 2 through 8, give 10 points for each target hit.
   For Table III, tasks 4 through 10, enter the number of targets hit (no points awarded).

9. **TOTAL SCORE:** Add points from Tables IV and V. Use the following qualification levels*:

	M249	**M60/M240B**
EXPERT GUNNER	182-201	206-227
GUNNER 1ST CLASS	158-181	180-205
GUNNER 2D CLASS	133-157	151-179
UNQUALIFIED	0-132	0-150

* The gunner must score 63 points (M249), 81 points (M60/M240B) on Table I, 70 points on Table II, and 6 hits on Table III to meet the minimum score for each

DA FORM 85-R, OCT 2002

By Order of the Secretary of the Army:

ERIC K. SHINSEKI
General, United States Army
Chief of Staff

Official:

Joel B. Hudson

JOEL B. HUDSON
Administrative Assistant to the
Secretary of the Army
0300801

DISTRIBUTION:

Active Army, Army National Guard, and U. S. Army Reserve: To be distributed in accordance with the initial distribution number 115879, requirements for FM 3-22.68.